by

Takako Shigematsu

Volume 5

go!comi

VOLUME:5

CONTENTS

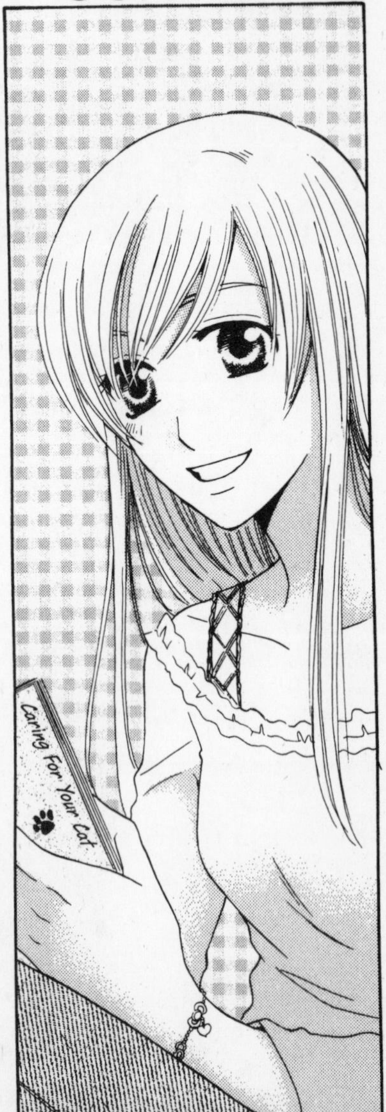

Caring For Your Cat

*** Story so far ***

When Yuzu Yamashita's mother passed away, she thought she was all alone in the world. Then she met Hassaku Kagami - and found out her long-lost grandmother was President of the powerful, multinational Shirayuki Group!

Tapped as her grandmother's potential heir, Yuzu is enrolled in her school's Elite A class. Yuzu develops a crush on her grandmother's personal assistant, Hassaku, only to find out that three potential fiancés have already been lined up for her! Yuzu's first fiancé, Masaya, turns out to be a film director. Her second fiancé, Sudachi-sempai, is an upperclassman Yuzu admired in middle school. The third candidate remains unknown...

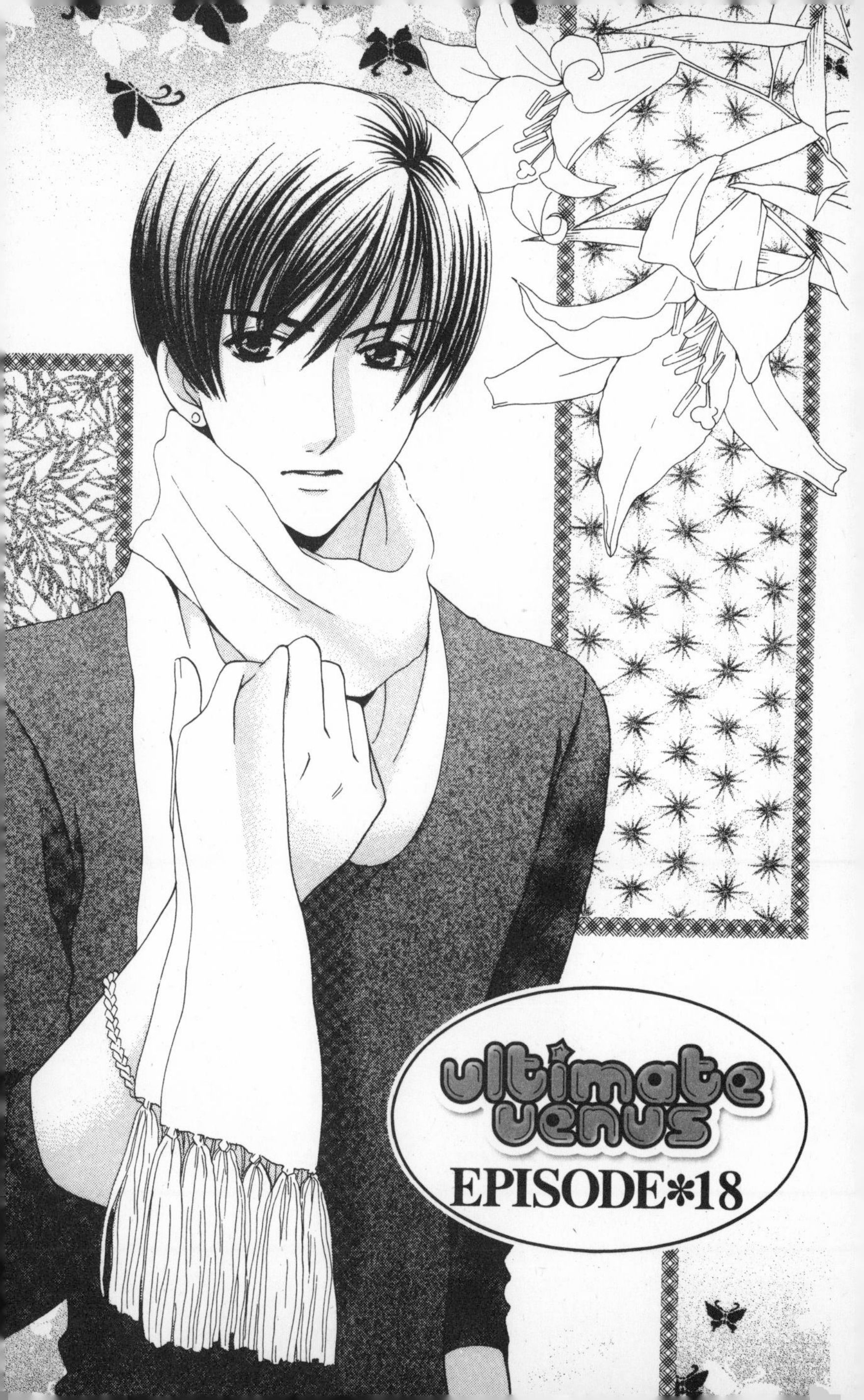
ultimate venus
EPISODE*18

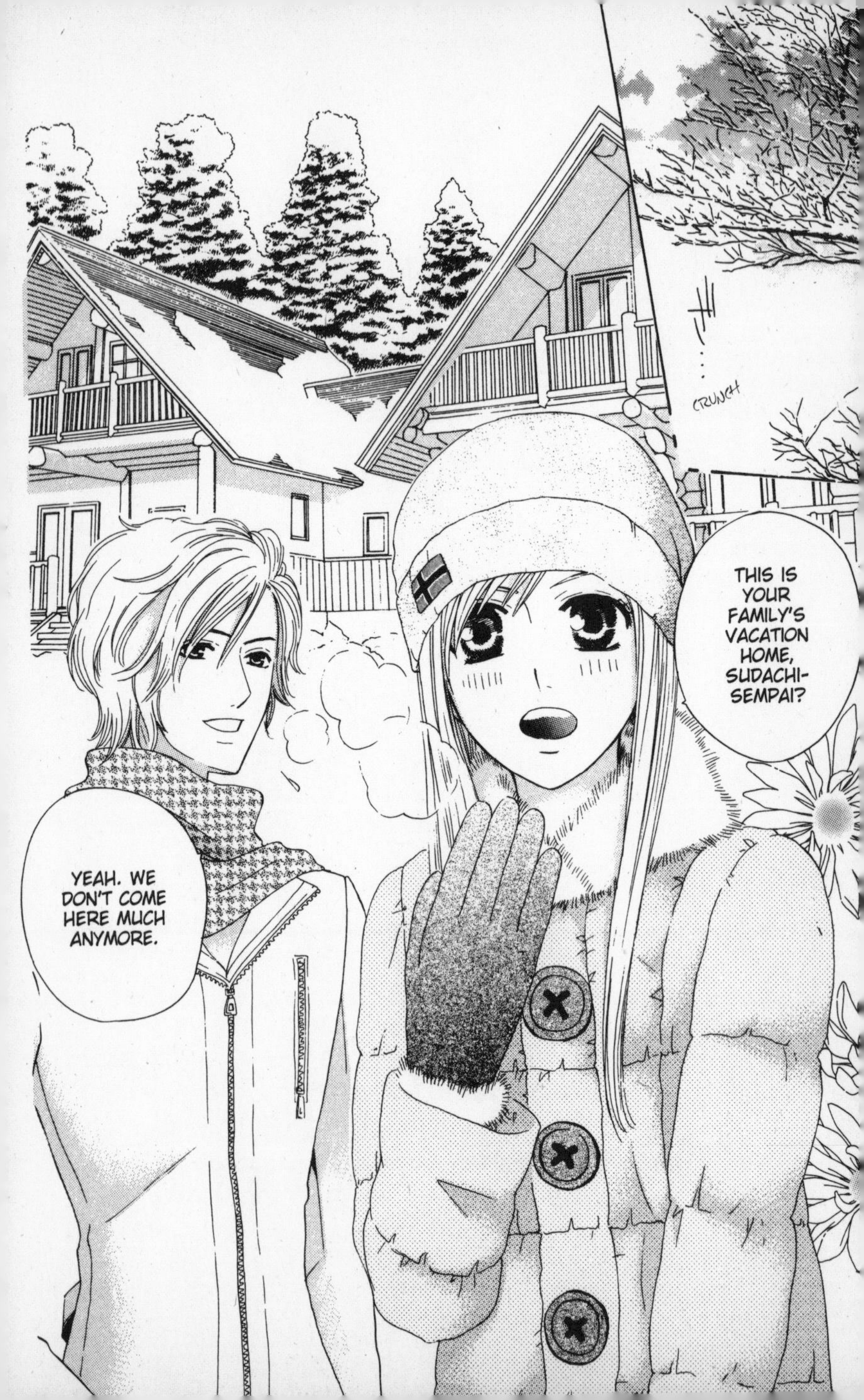
CRUNCH
THIS IS YOUR FAMILY'S VACATION HOME, SUDACHI-SEMPAI?
YEAH. WE DON'T COME HERE MUCH ANYMORE.

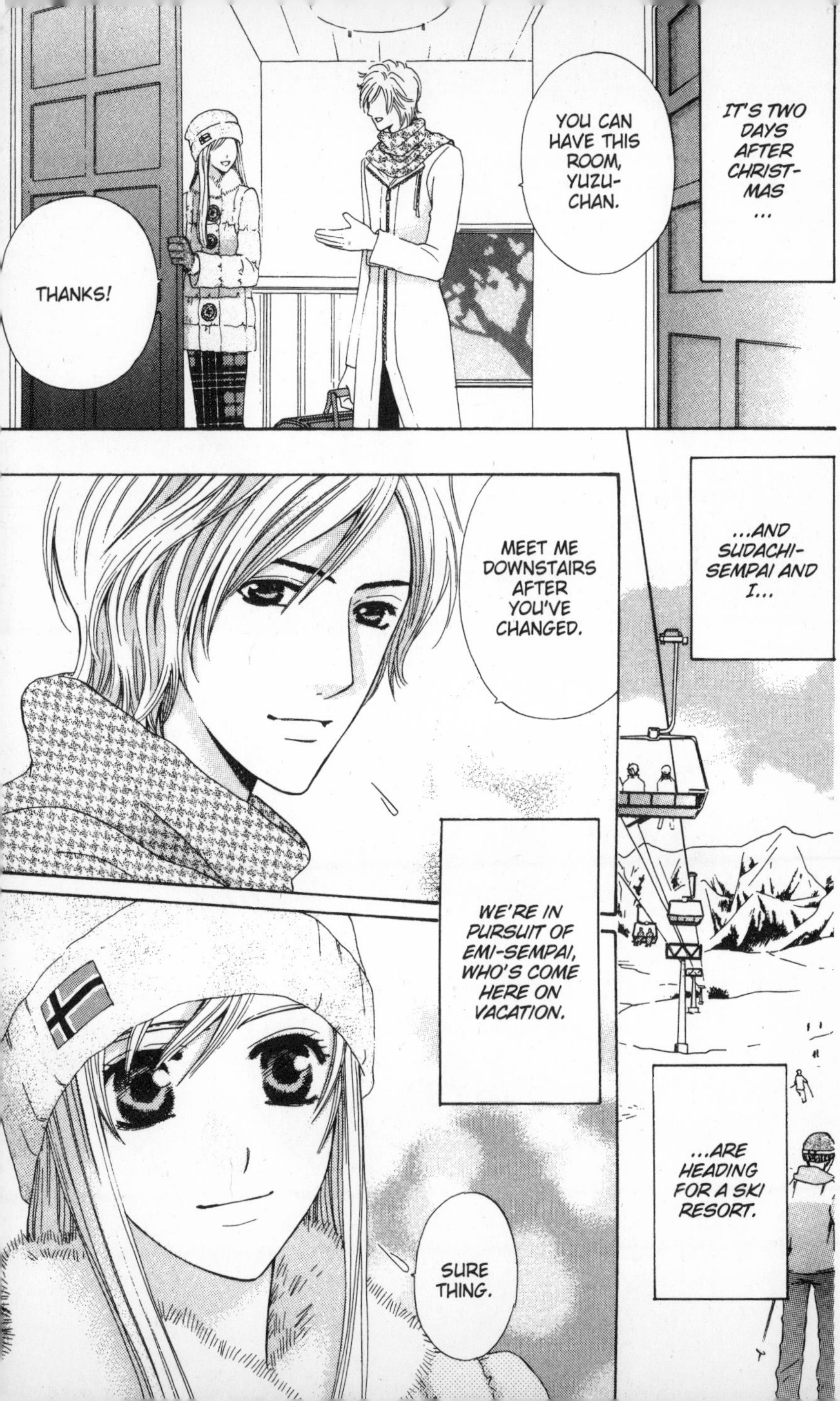
IT'S TWO DAYS AFTER CHRIST-MAS ...
YOU CAN HAVE THIS ROOM, YUZU-CHAN.
THANKS!
...AND SUDACHI-SEMPAI AND I...
MEET ME DOWNSTAIRS AFTER YOU'VE CHANGED.
...ARE HEADING FOR A SKI RESORT.
WE'RE IN PURSUIT OF EMI-SEMPAI, WHO'S COME HERE ON VACATION.
SURE THING.

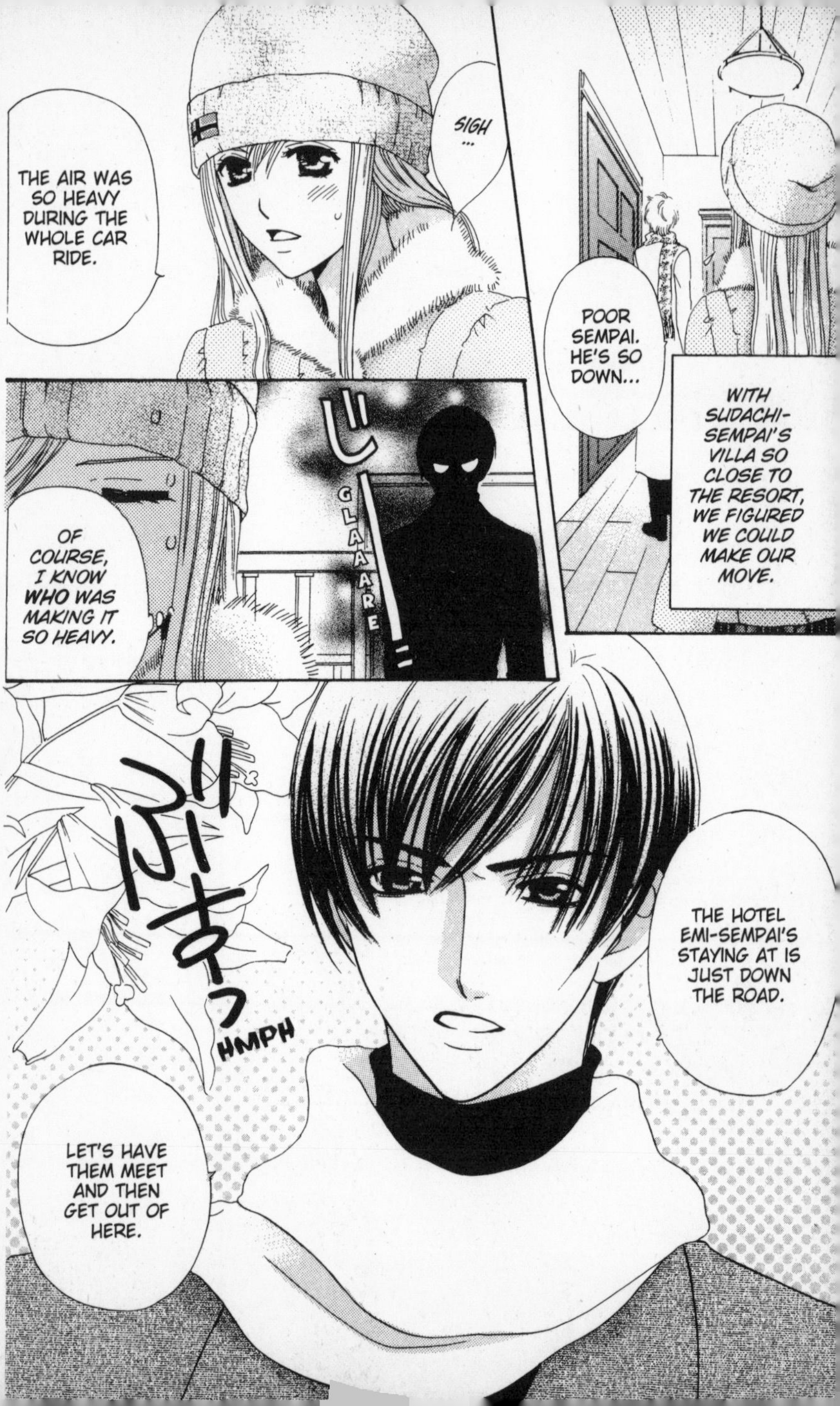
POOR SEMPAI. HE'S SO DOWN...
WITH SUDACHI-SEMPAI'S VILLA SO CLOSE TO THE RESORT, WE FIGURED WE COULD MAKE OUR MOVE.
SIGH...
THE AIR WAS SO HEAVY DURING THE WHOLE CAR RIDE.
じー
GLAAARE
OF COURSE, I KNOW WHO WAS MAKING IT SO HEAVY.
THE HOTEL EMI-SEMPAI'S STAYING AT IS JUST DOWN THE ROAD.
ぷいっ
HMPH
LET'S HAVE THEM MEET AND THEN GET OUT OF HERE.

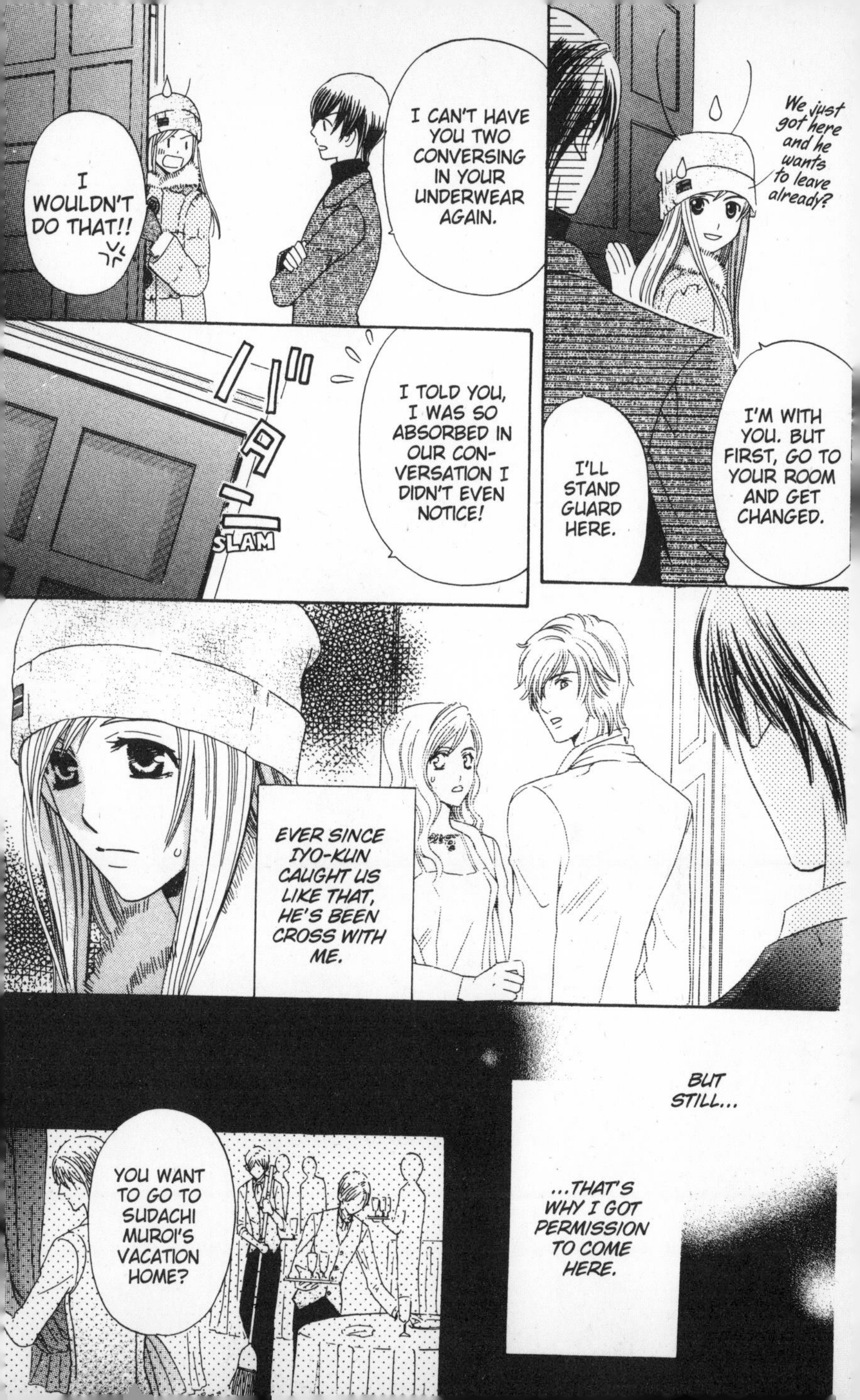
We just got here and he wants to leave already?
I'M WITH YOU. BUT FIRST, GO TO YOUR ROOM AND GET CHANGED.
I'LL STAND GUARD HERE.
I CAN'T HAVE YOU TWO CONVERSING IN YOUR UNDERWEAR AGAIN.
I WOULDN'T DO THAT!!
I TOLD YOU, I WAS SO ABSORBED IN OUR CON-VERSATION I DIDN'T EVEN NOTICE!
SLAM
EVER SINCE IYO-KUN CAUGHT US LIKE THAT, HE'S BEEN CROSS WITH ME.
BUT STILL...
...THAT'S WHY I GOT PERMISSION TO COME HERE.
YOU WANT TO GO TO SUDACHI MUROI'S VACATION HOME?

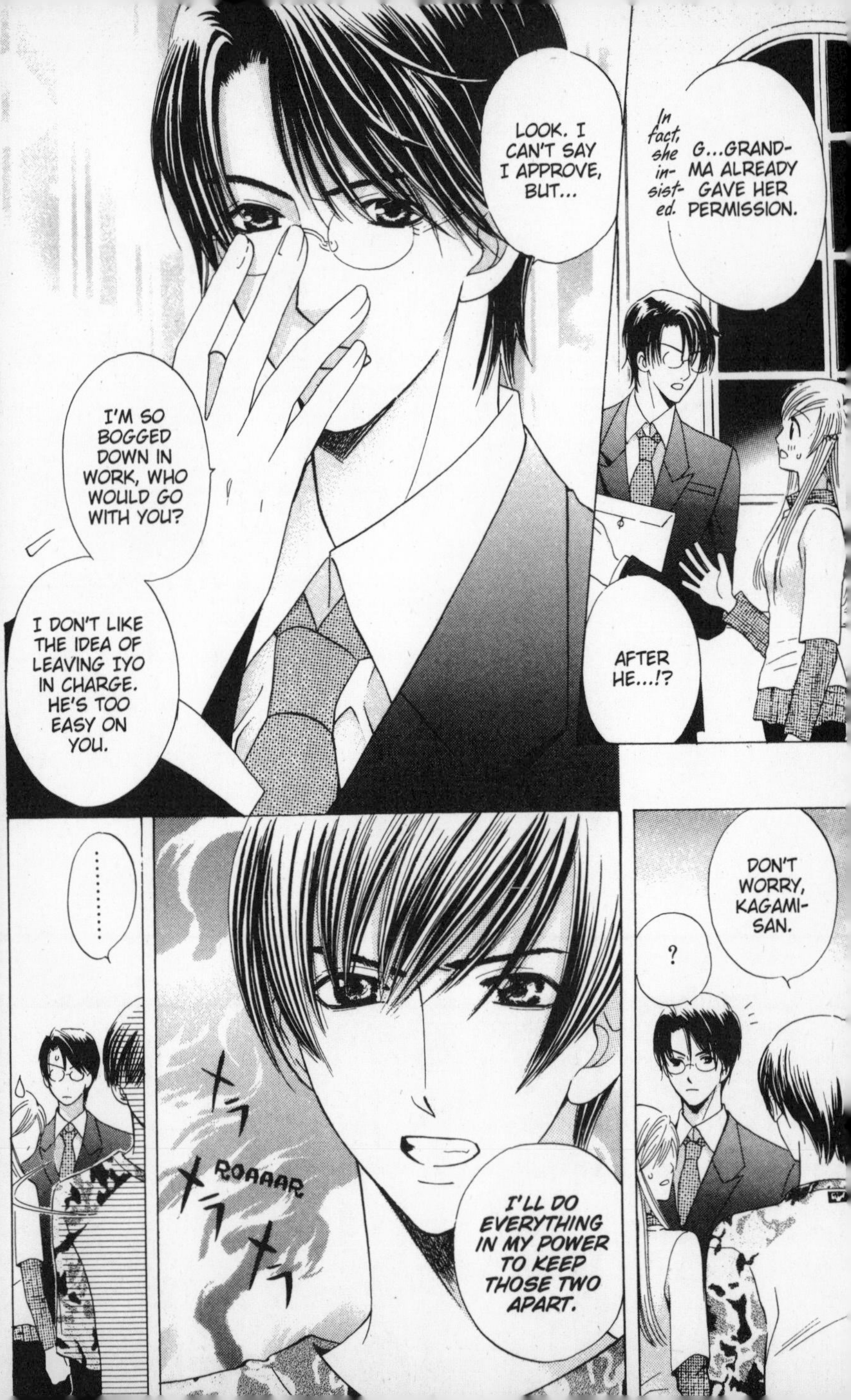
G...GRANDMA ALREADY GAVE HER PERMISSION.
In fact, she insisted.
AFTER HE...!?
LOOK. I CAN'T SAY I APPROVE, BUT...
I'M SO BOGGED DOWN IN WORK, WHO WOULD GO WITH YOU?
I DON'T LIKE THE IDEA OF LEAVING IYO IN CHARGE. HE'S TOO EASY ON YOU.
DON'T WORRY, KAGAMI-SAN.
?
I'LL DO EVERYTHING IN MY POWER TO KEEP THOSE TWO APART.
ROAAAR
....

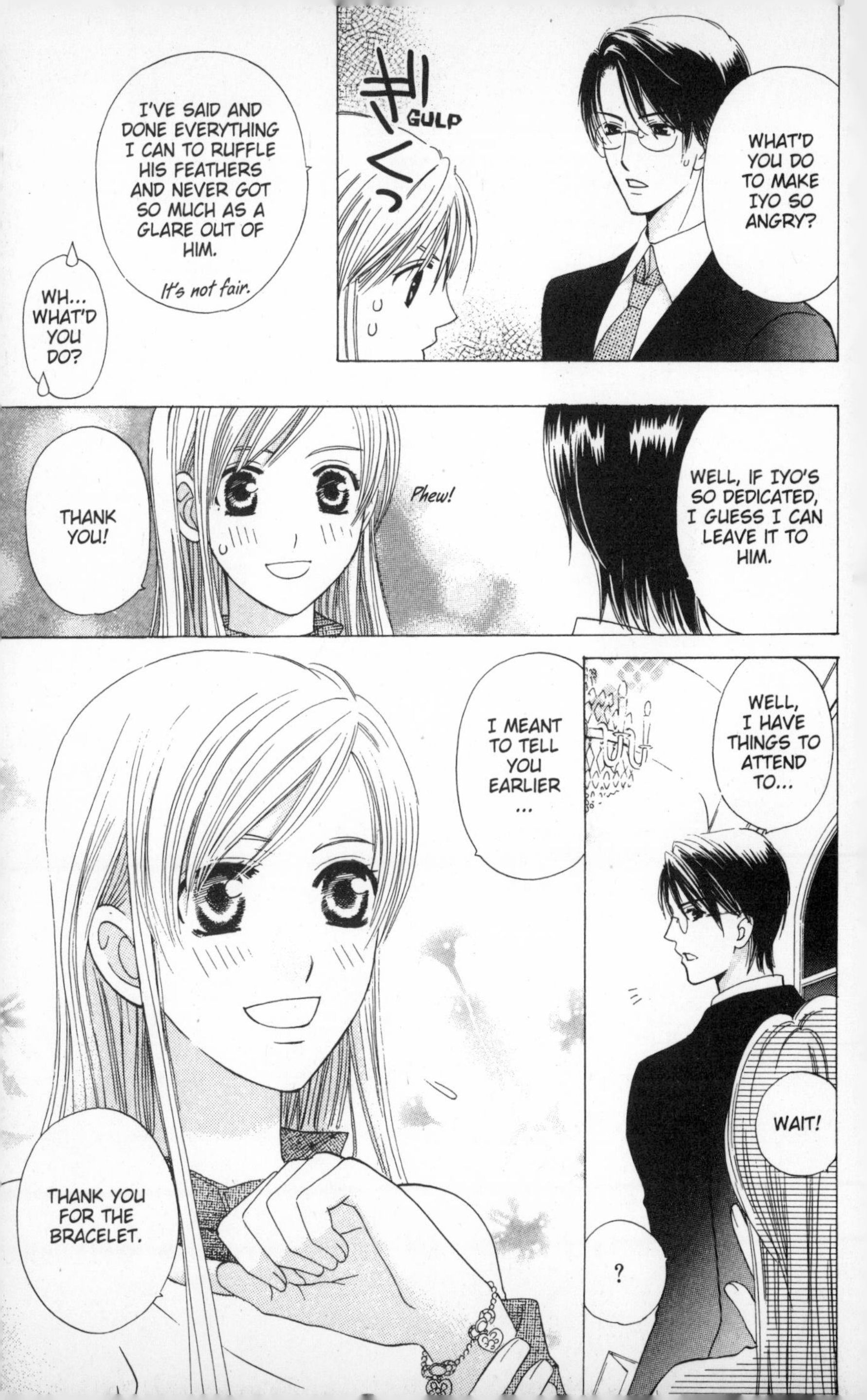
WHAT'D YOU DO TO MAKE IYO SO ANGRY?
GULP
I'VE SAID AND DONE EVERYTHING I CAN TO RUFFLE HIS FEATHERS AND NEVER GOT SO MUCH AS A GLARE OUT OF HIM.
It's not fair.
WH... WHAT'D YOU DO?
WELL, IF IYO'S SO DEDICATED, I GUESS I CAN LEAVE IT TO HIM.
Phew!
THANK YOU!
WELL, I HAVE THINGS TO ATTEND TO...
WAIT!
?
I MEANT TO TELL YOU EARLIER ...
THANK YOU FOR THE BRACELET.

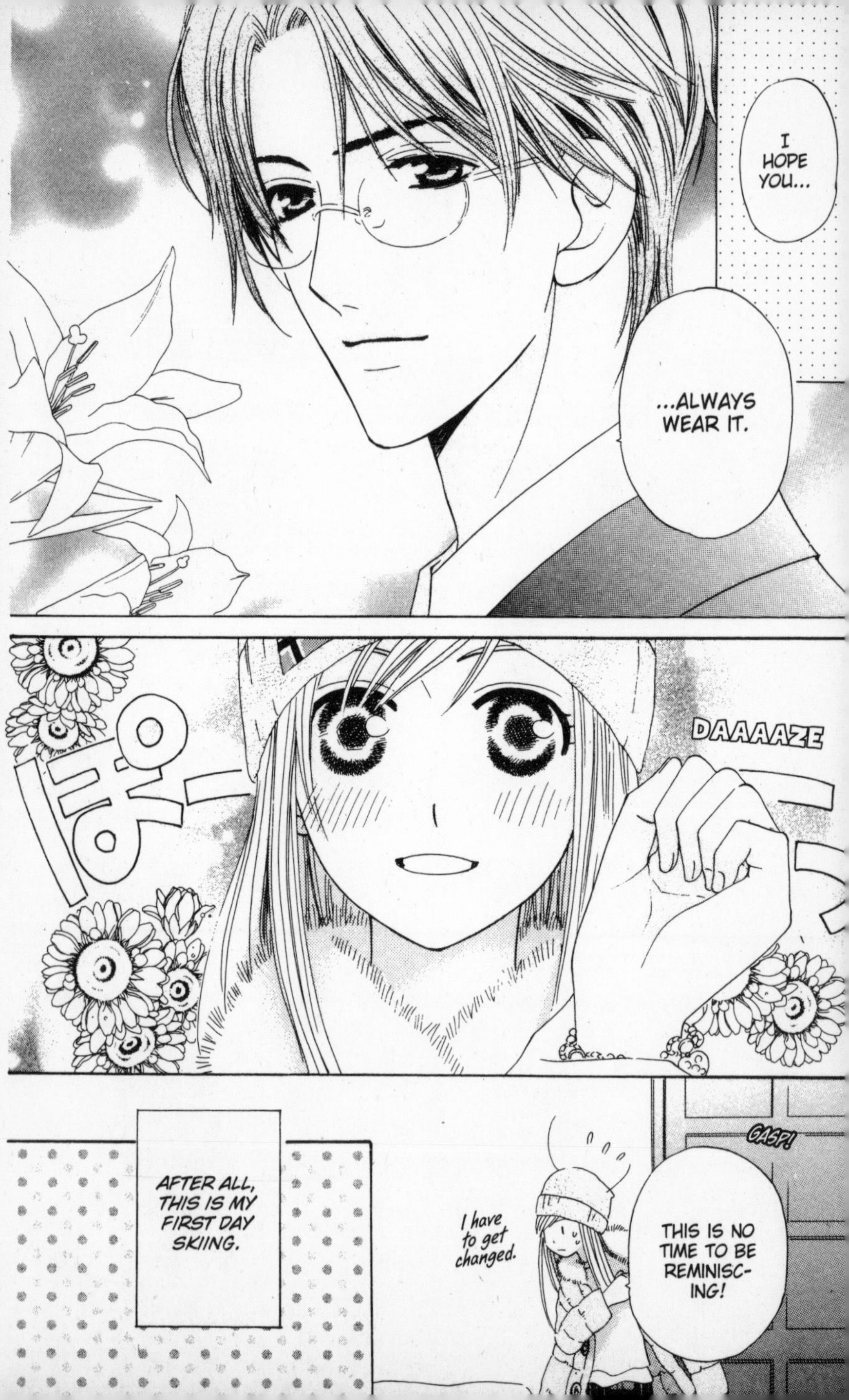
I HOPE YOU...
...ALWAYS WEAR IT.
DAAAAZE
AFTER ALL, THIS IS MY FIRST DAY SKIING.
GASP!
THIS IS NO TIME TO BE REMINISC-ING!
I have to get changed.

GREETINGS

Hello, everyone! To those I'm meeting for the first time, it's my pleasure! Thank you for picking up Volume 5 of Ultimate Venus!
Even though this volume is slated for release in June, it features a winter story. That's because the individual chapters were released in the magazine primarily during winter. ^^ Even though we are entering summer now, re-reading this winter tale has left my internal sense of season a jumble. Ha ha ha! I'm kidding, it's not that jumbled.

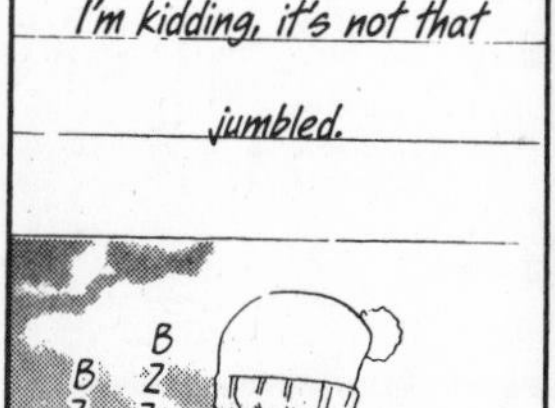
BZZZT
BZZZT

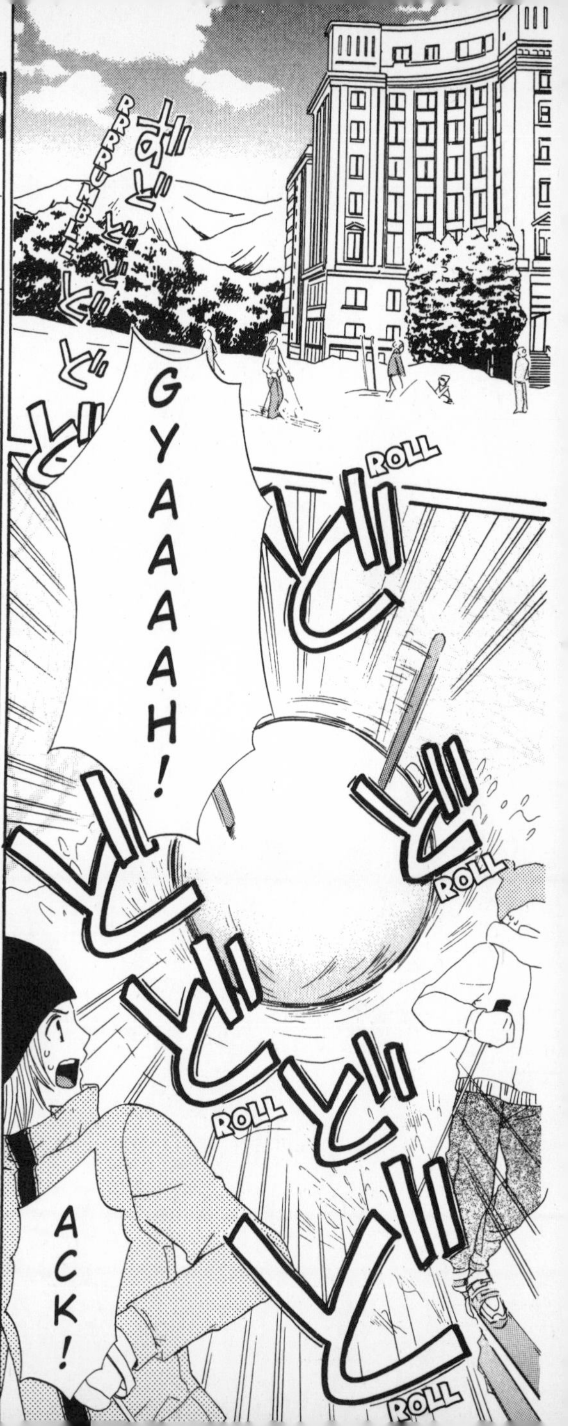
RRRRUMBLE
GYAAAAAH!
ROLL
ROLL
ROLL
ACK!
ROLL

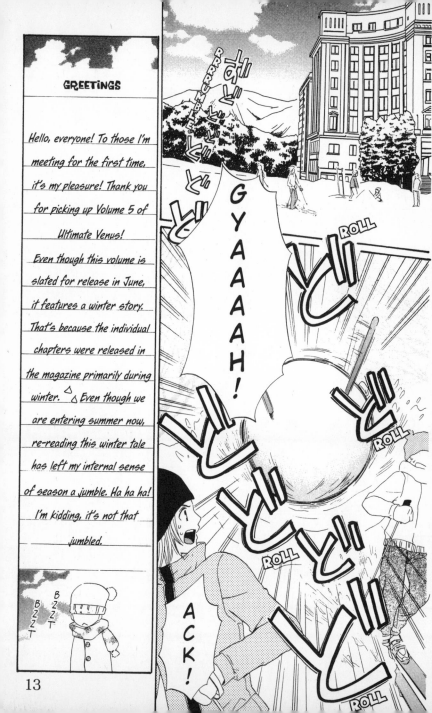

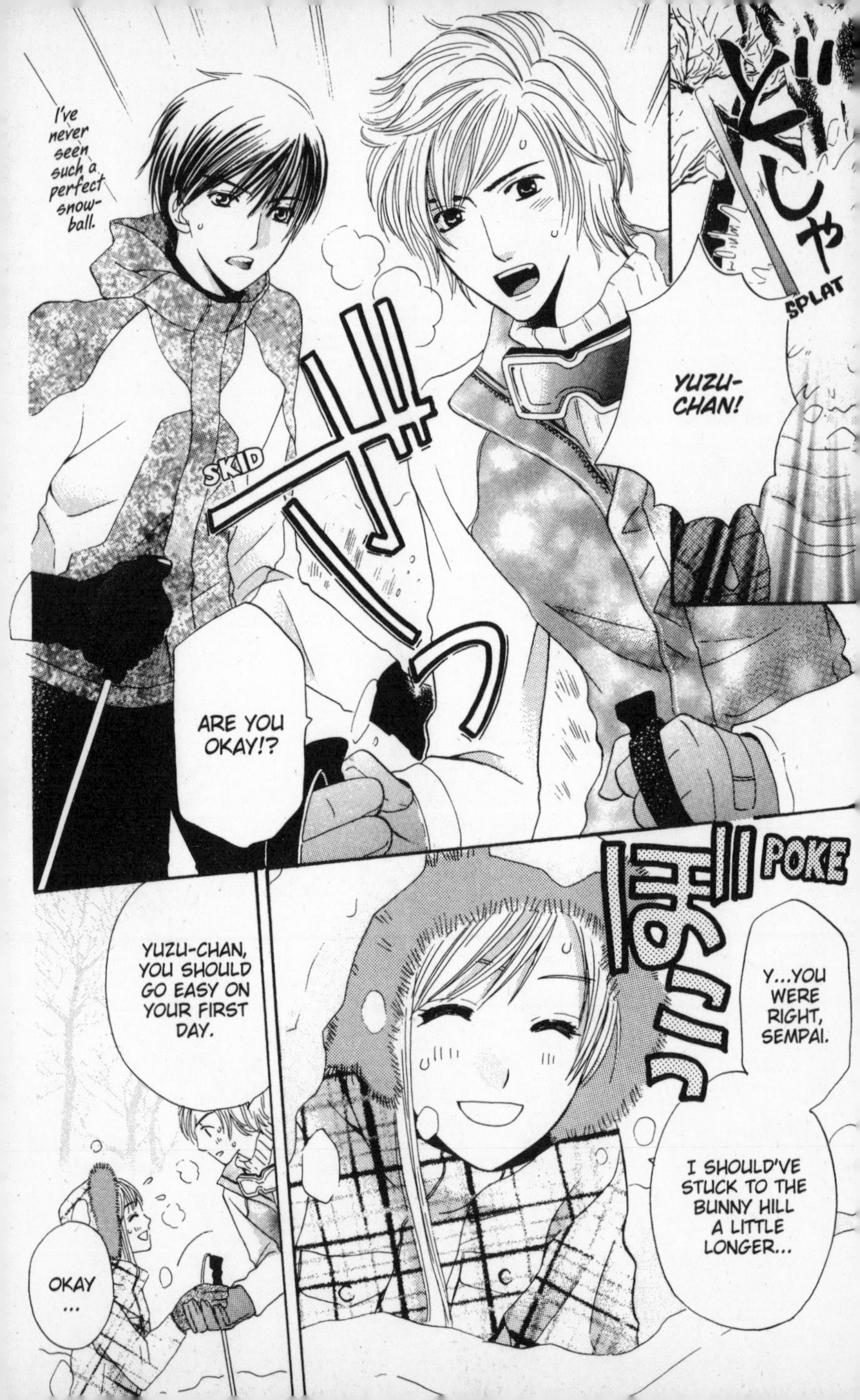
どしゃ
SPLAT
YUZU-CHAN!
I've never seen such a perfect snowball.
SKID
ARE YOU OKAY!?
POKE
Y...YOU WERE RIGHT, SEMPAI.
I SHOULD'VE STUCK TO THE BUNNY HILL A LITTLE LONGER...
YUZU-CHAN, YOU SHOULD GO EASY ON YOUR FIRST DAY.
OKAY ...

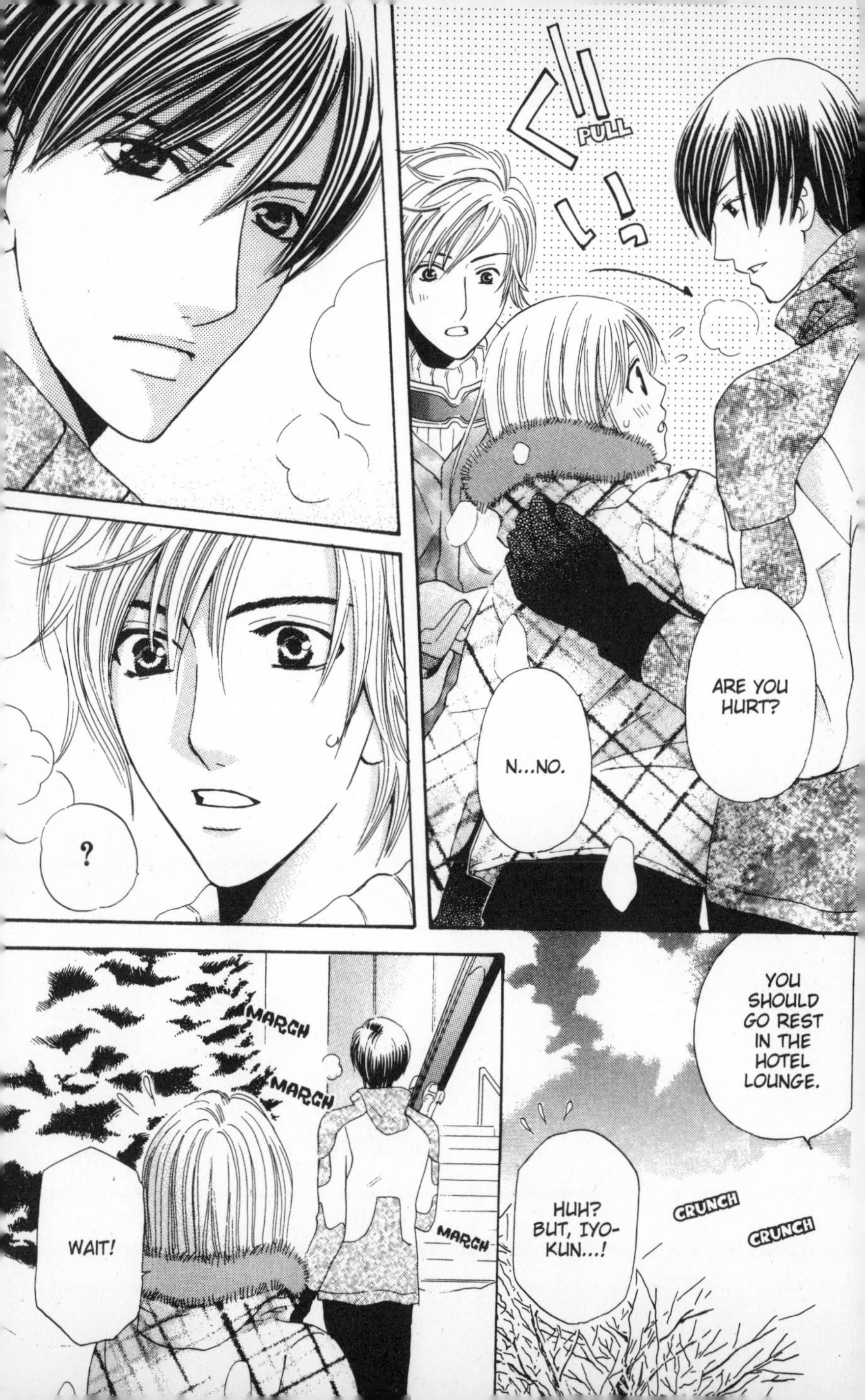
PULL
ARE YOU HURT?
N...NO.
?
YOU SHOULD GO REST IN THE HOTEL LOUNGE.
HUH? BUT, IYO-KUN...!
CRUNCH
CRUNCH
MARCH
MARCH
MARCH
WAIT!

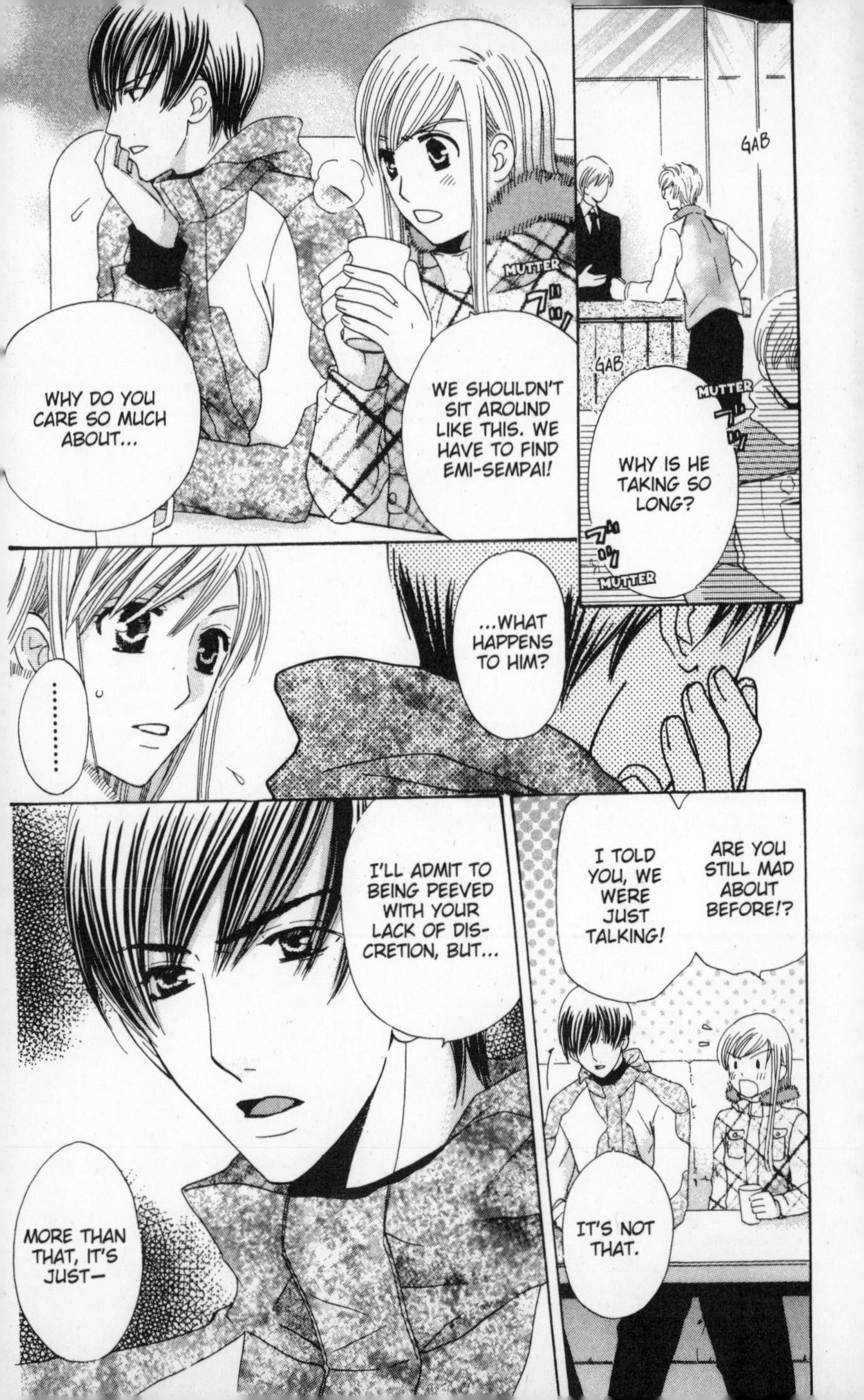
GAB
GAB
MUTTER
MUTTER
WHY IS HE TAKING SO LONG?
MUTTER
MUTTER
WE SHOULDN'T SIT AROUND LIKE THIS. WE HAVE TO FIND EMI-SEMPAI!
WHY DO YOU CARE SO MUCH ABOUT...
...WHAT HAPPENS TO HIM?
......
ARE YOU STILL MAD ABOUT BEFORE!?
I TOLD YOU, WE WERE JUST TALKING!
IT'S NOT THAT.
I'LL ADMIT TO BEING PEEVED WITH YOUR LACK OF DIS-CRETION, BUT...
MORE THAN THAT, IT'S JUST—

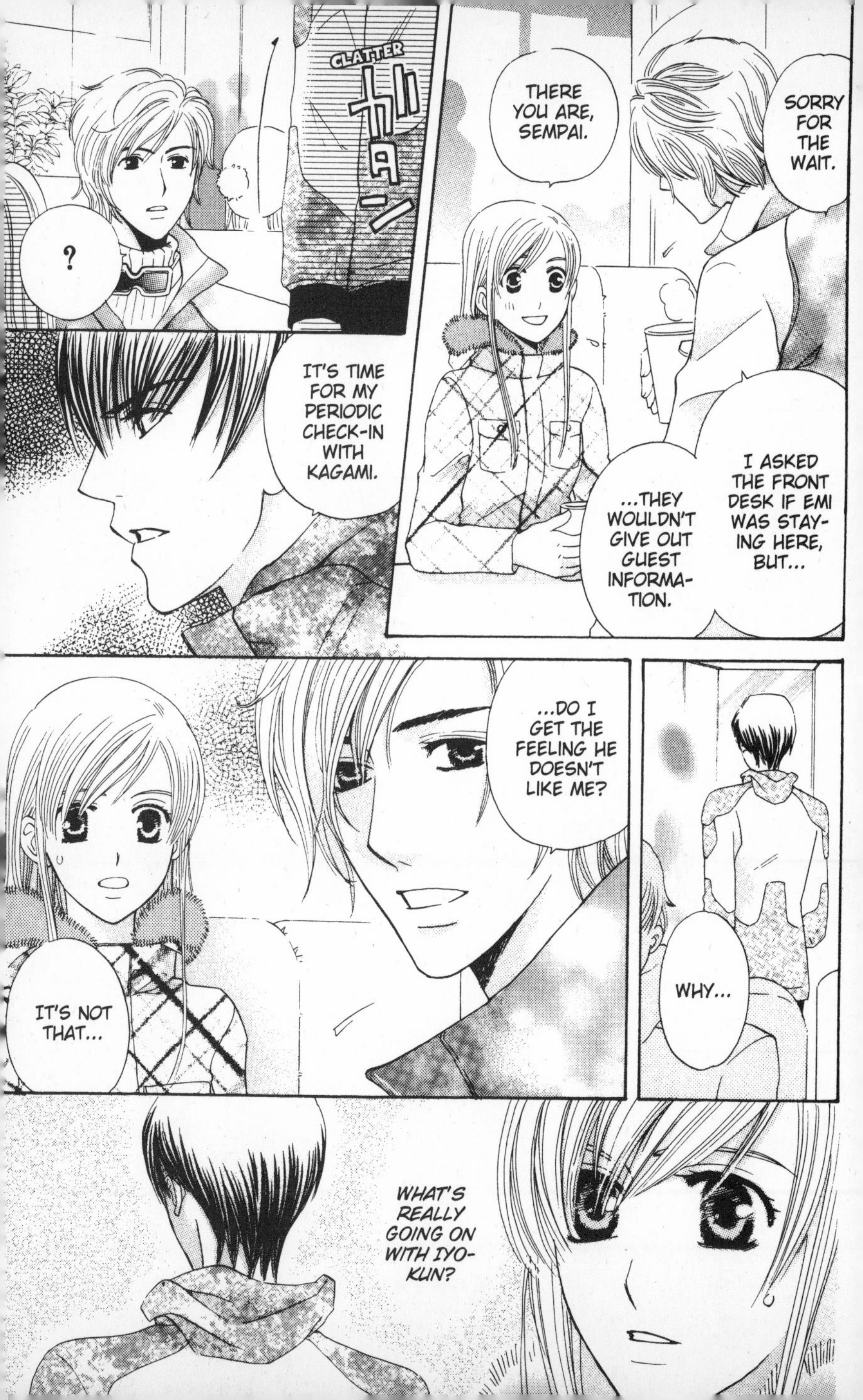
SORRY FOR THE WAIT.
THERE YOU ARE, SEMPAI.
I ASKED THE FRONT DESK IF EMI WAS STAYING HERE, BUT...
...THEY WOULDN'T GIVE OUT GUEST INFORMATION.
CLATTER
?
IT'S TIME FOR MY PERIODIC CHECK-IN WITH KAGAMI.
WHY...
...DO I GET THE FEELING HE DOESN'T LIKE ME?
IT'S NOT THAT...
WHAT'S REALLY GOING ON WITH IYO-KUN?

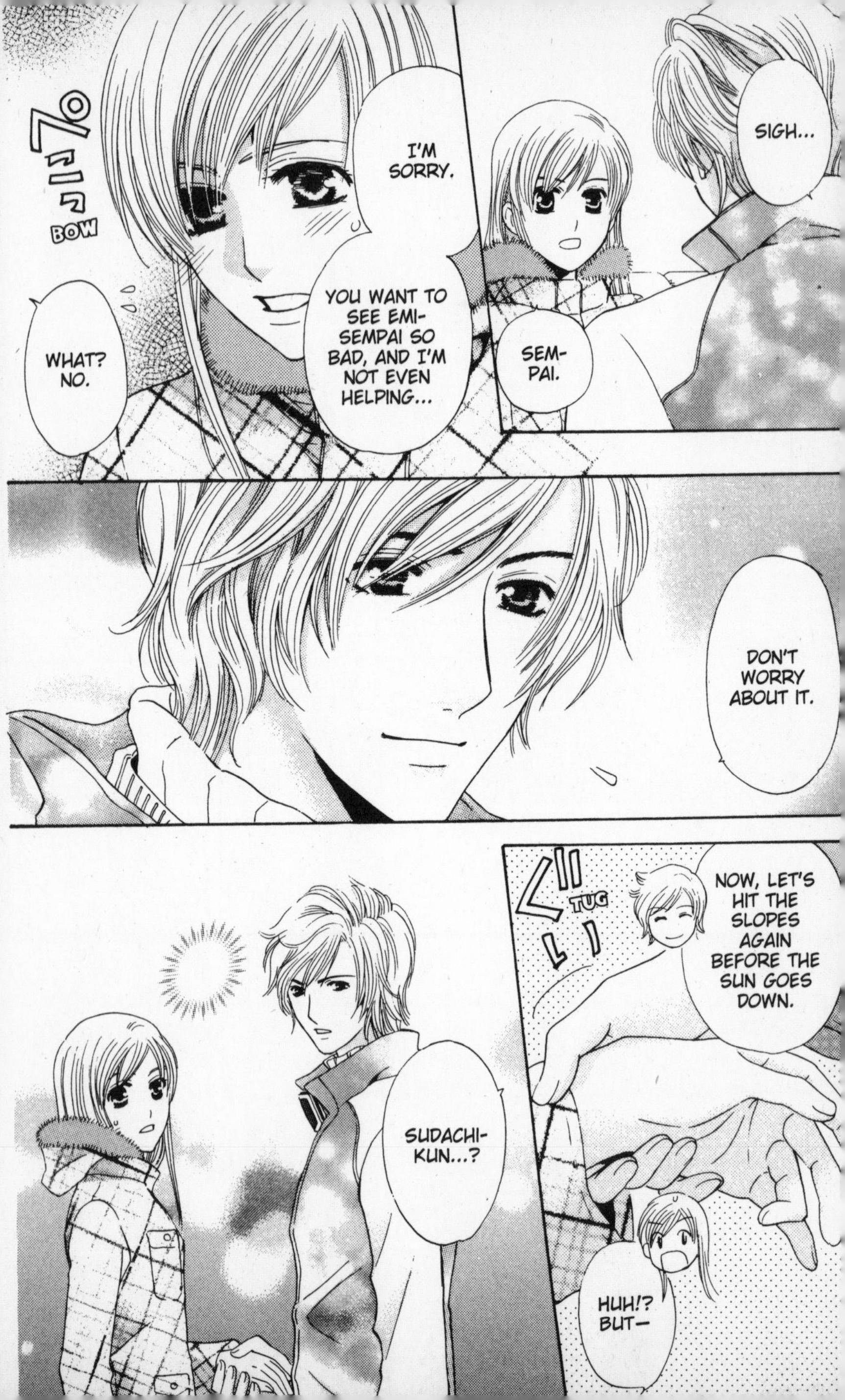
SIGH...
SEMPAI.
I'M SORRY.
YOU WANT TO SEE EMI-SEMPAI SO BAD, AND I'M NOT EVEN HELPING...
BOW
WHAT? NO.
DON'T WORRY ABOUT IT.
TUG
NOW, LET'S HIT THE SLOPES AGAIN BEFORE THE SUN GOES DOWN.
HUH!? BUT—
SUDACHI-KUN...?

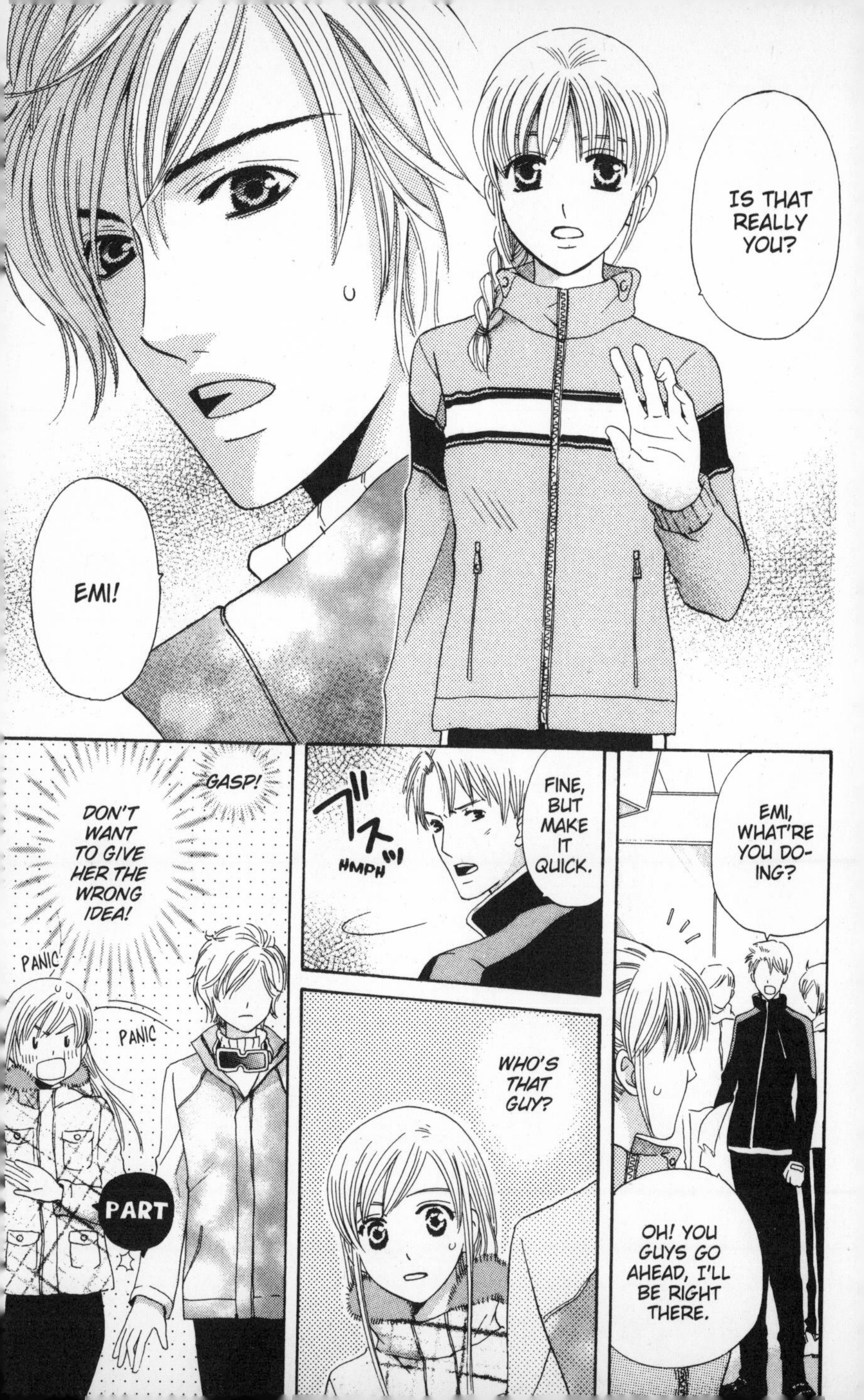
IS THAT REALLY YOU?
EMI!
EMI, WHAT'RE YOU DO-ING?
OH! YOU GUYS GO AHEAD, I'LL BE RIGHT THERE.
FINE, BUT MAKE IT QUICK.
HMPH
WHO'S THAT GUY?
GASP!
DON'T WANT TO GIVE HER THE WRONG IDEA!
PANIC
PANIC
PART

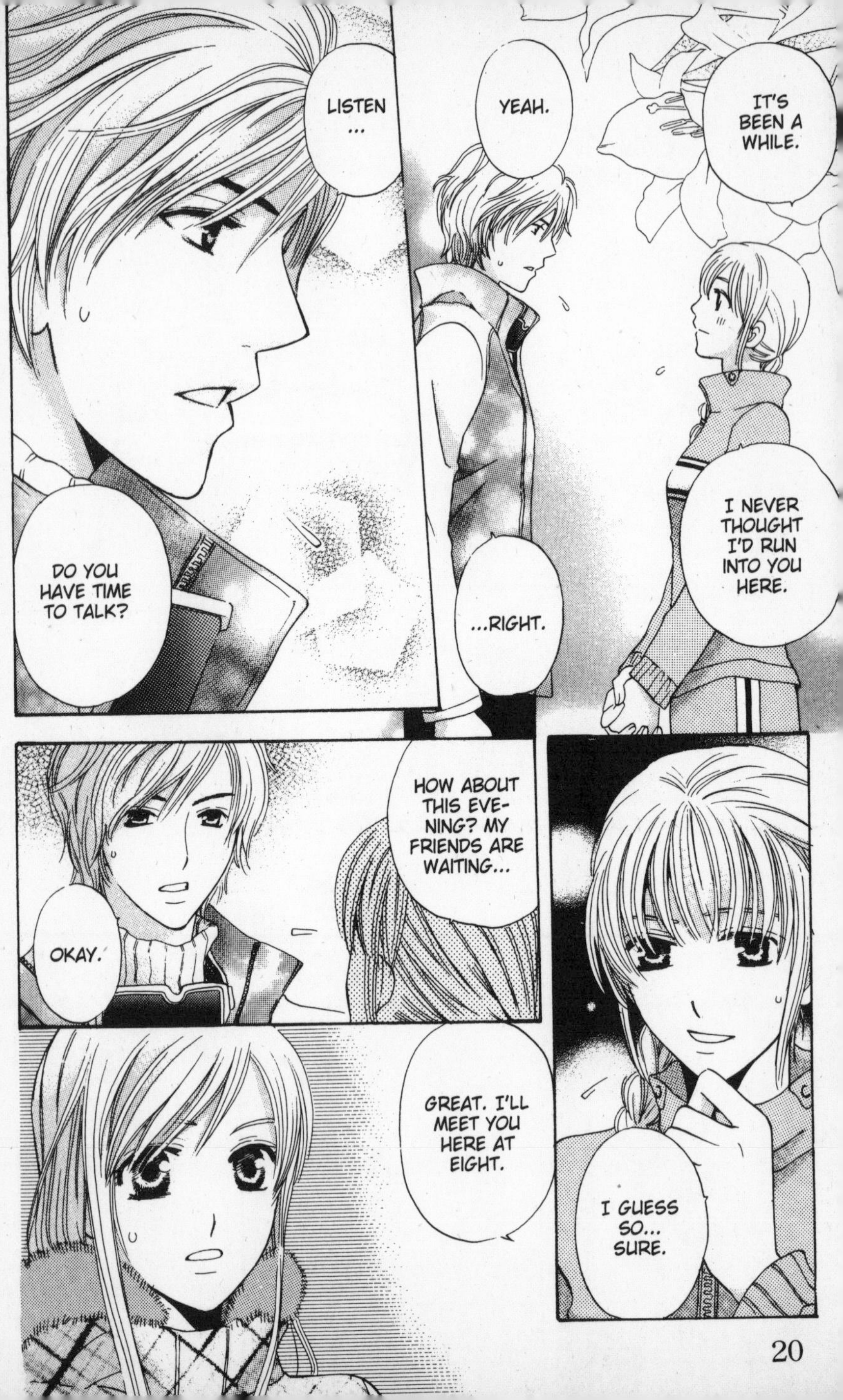
IT'S BEEN A WHILE.
YEAH.
I NEVER THOUGHT I'D RUN INTO YOU HERE.
...RIGHT.
LISTEN ...
DO YOU HAVE TIME TO TALK?
I GUESS SO... SURE.
HOW ABOUT THIS EVE-NING? MY FRIENDS ARE WAITING...
OKAY.
GREAT. I'LL MEET YOU HERE AT EIGHT.

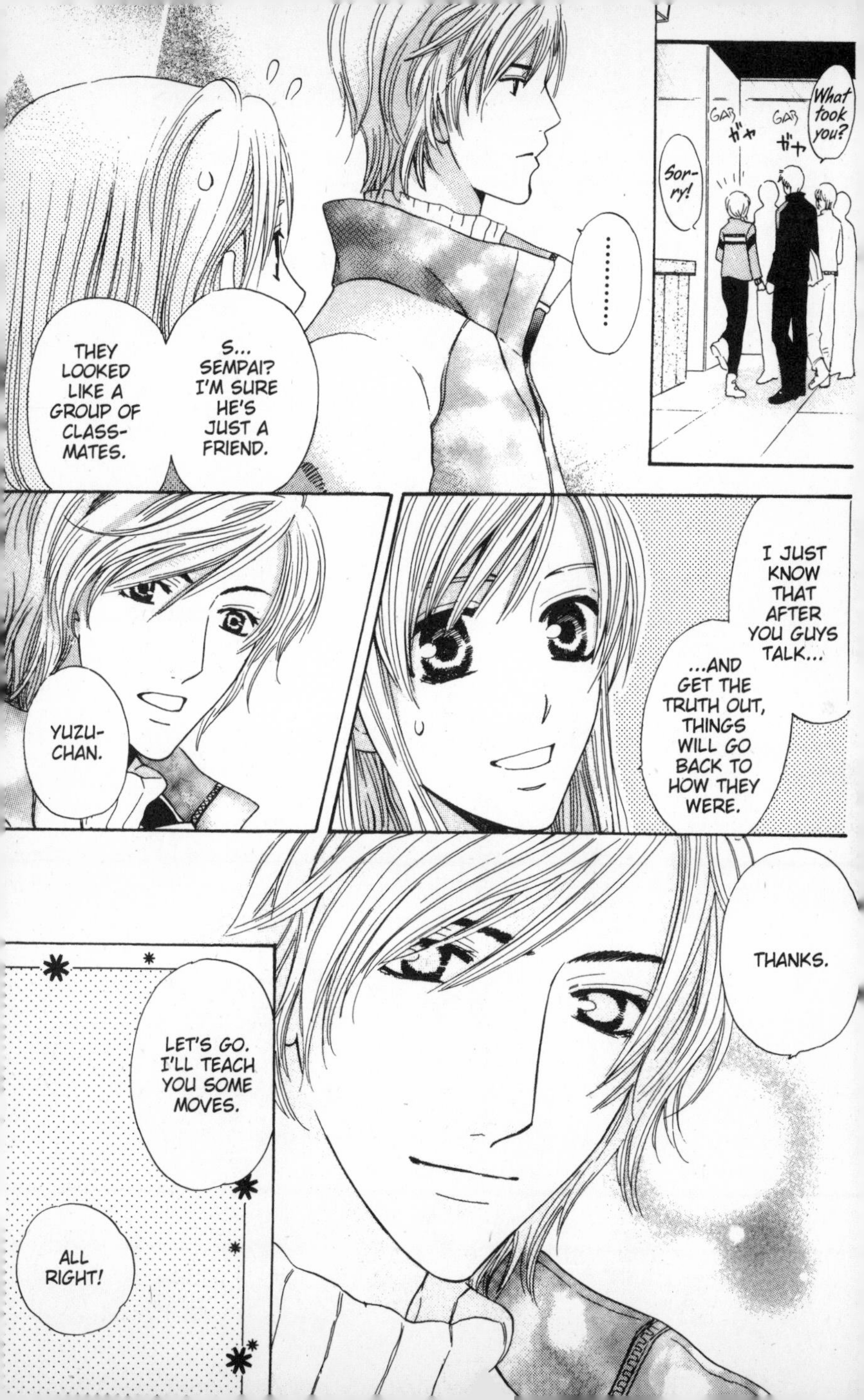
What took you?
GAR ガヤ
GAR ガヤ
Sor-ry!
......
S... SEMPAI? I'M SURE HE'S JUST A FRIEND.
THEY LOOKED LIKE A GROUP OF CLASS-MATES.
I JUST KNOW THAT AFTER YOU GUYS TALK...
...AND GET THE TRUTH OUT, THINGS WILL GO BACK TO HOW THEY WERE.
YUZU-CHAN.
THANKS.
LET'S GO. I'LL TEACH YOU SOME MOVES.
ALL RIGHT!

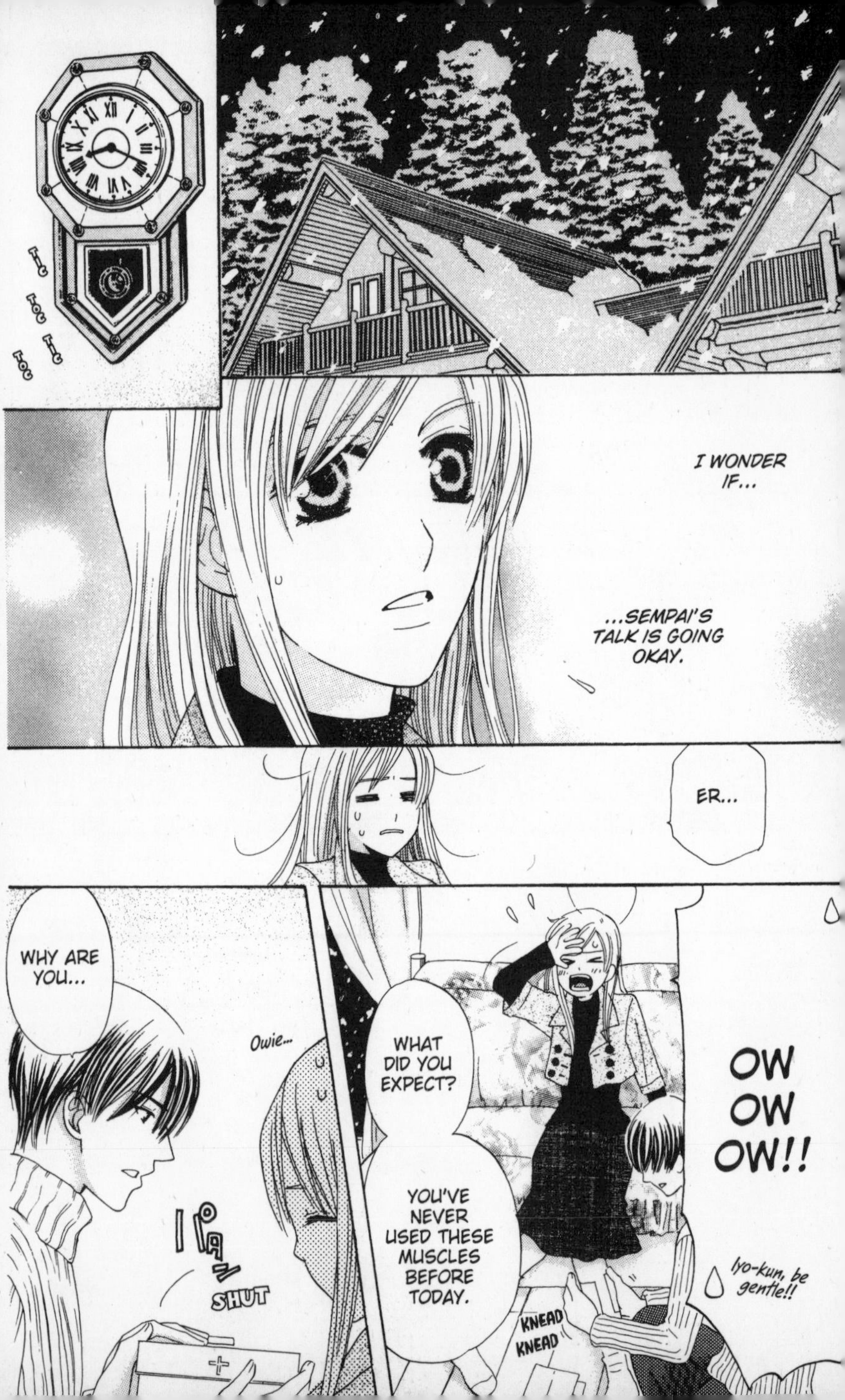
TIC TOC TIC TOC
I WONDER IF...
...SEMPAI'S TALK IS GOING OKAY.
ER...
OW OW OW!!
Iyo-kun, be gentle!!
KNEAD KNEAD
WHAT DID YOU EXPECT?
YOU'VE NEVER USED THESE MUSCLES BEFORE TODAY.
Owie...
WHY ARE YOU...
SHUT

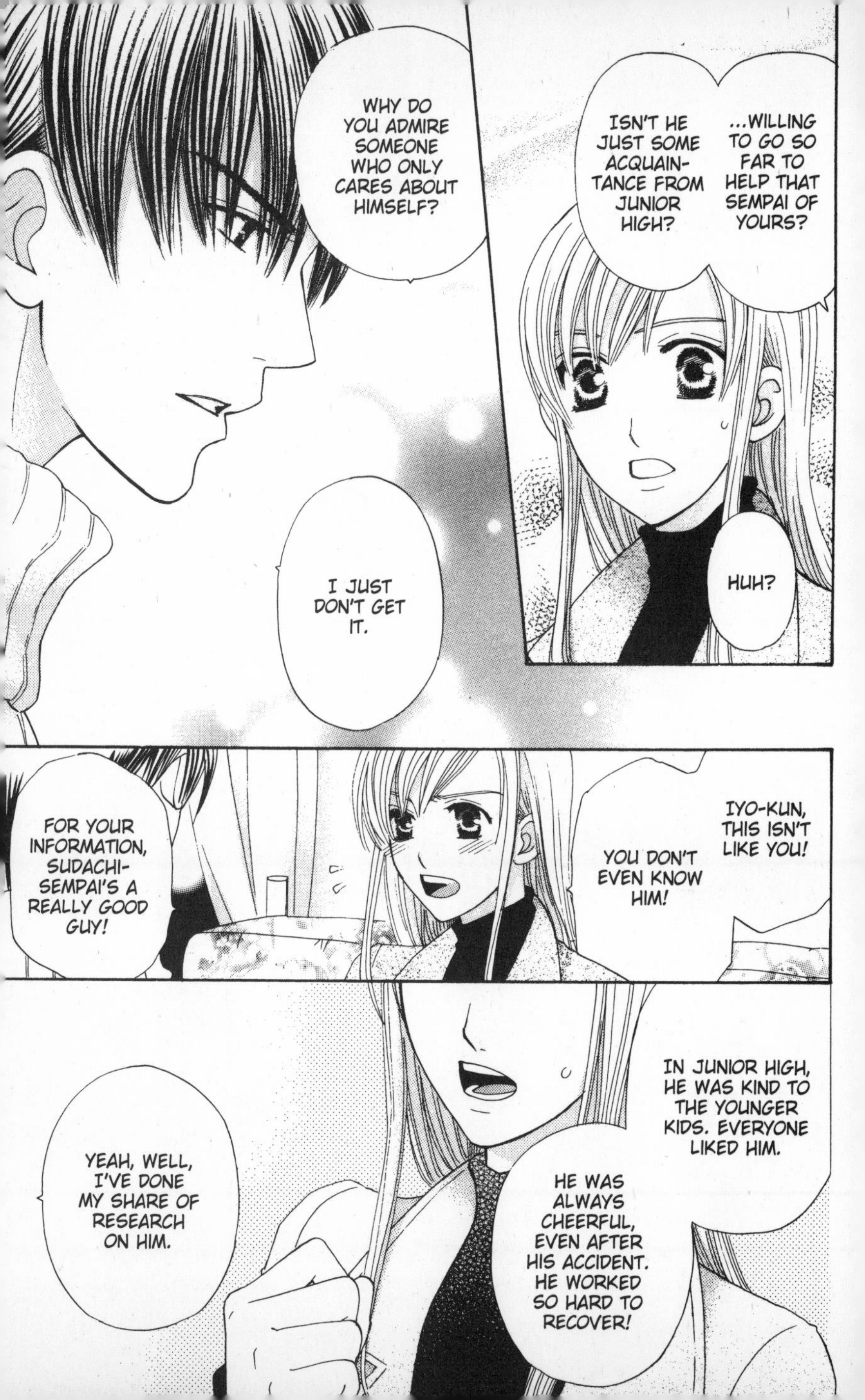
...WILLING TO GO SO FAR TO HELP THAT SEMPAI OF YOURS?
ISN'T HE JUST SOME ACQUAINTANCE FROM JUNIOR HIGH?
HUH?
WHY DO YOU ADMIRE SOMEONE WHO ONLY CARES ABOUT HIMSELF?
I JUST DON'T GET IT.
IYO-KUN, THIS ISN'T LIKE YOU!
YOU DON'T EVEN KNOW HIM!
FOR YOUR INFORMATION, SUDACHI-SEMPAI'S A REALLY GOOD GUY!
IN JUNIOR HIGH, HE WAS KIND TO THE YOUNGER KIDS. EVERYONE LIKED HIM.
HE WAS ALWAYS CHEERFUL, EVEN AFTER HIS ACCIDENT. HE WORKED SO HARD TO RECOVER!
YEAH, WELL, I'VE DONE MY SHARE OF RESEARCH ON HIM.

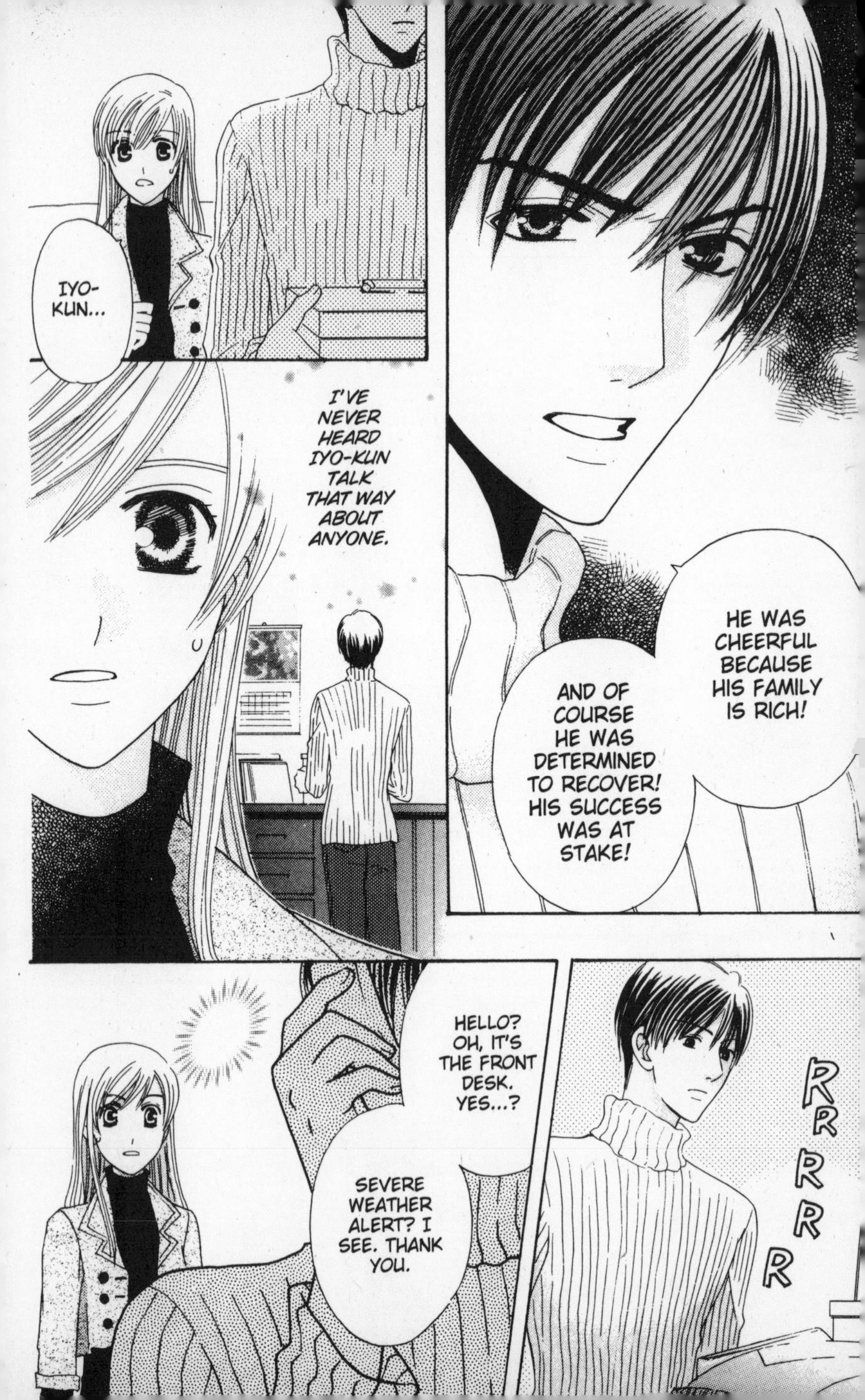
HE WAS CHEERFUL BECAUSE HIS FAMILY IS RICH!
AND OF COURSE HE WAS DETERMINED TO RECOVER! HIS SUCCESS WAS AT STAKE!
IYO-KUN...
I'VE NEVER HEARD IYO-KUN TALK THAT WAY ABOUT ANYONE.
RRRR
HELLO? OH, IT'S THE FRONT DESK. YES...?
SEVERE WEATHER ALERT? I SEE. THANK YOU.

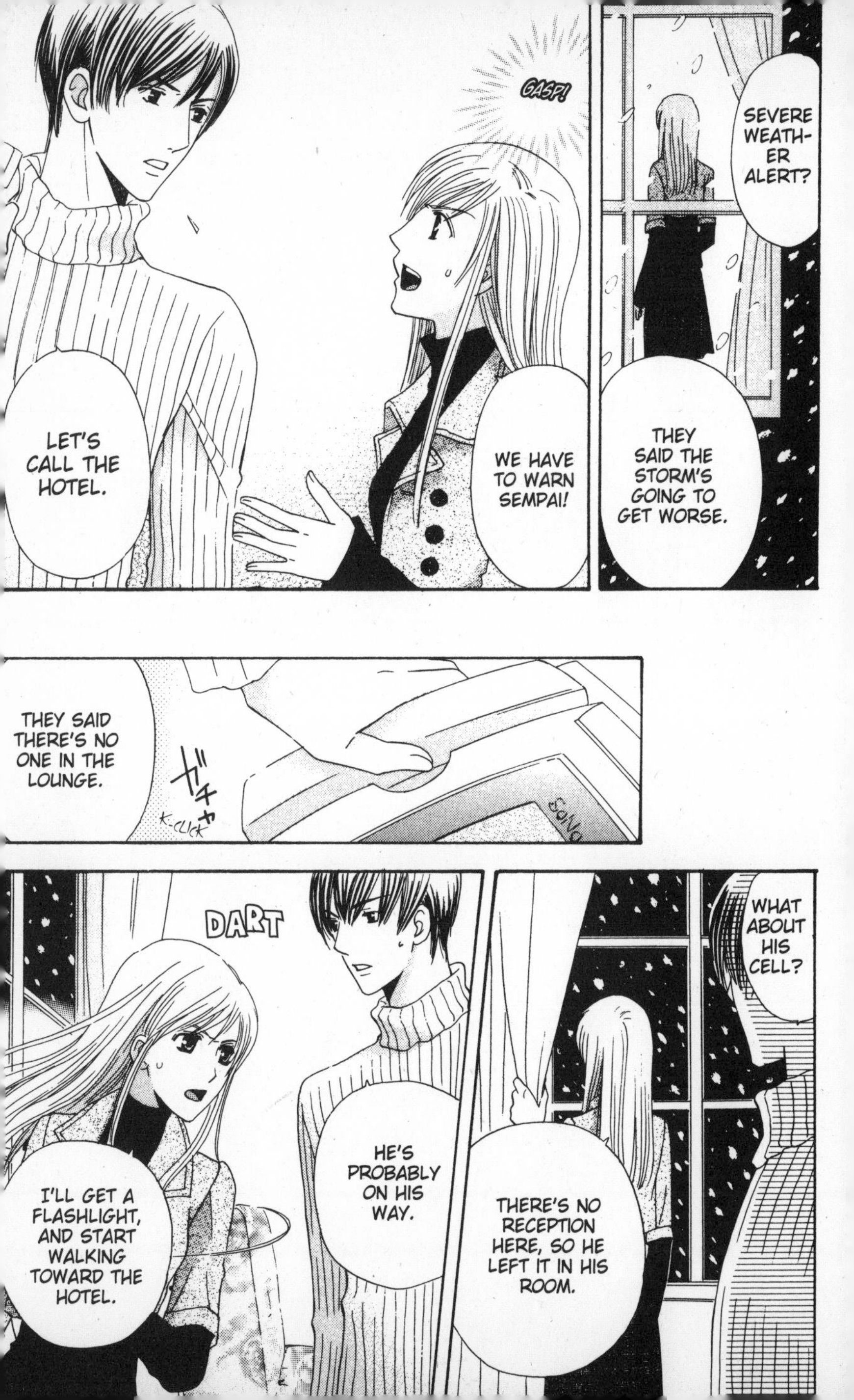
SEVERE WEATHER ALERT?
THEY SAID THE STORM'S GOING TO GET WORSE.
GASP!
WE HAVE TO WARN SEMPAI!
LET'S CALL THE HOTEL.
THEY SAID THERE'S NO ONE IN THE LOUNGE.
K-CLICK
WHAT ABOUT HIS CELL?
THERE'S NO RECEPTION HERE, SO HE LEFT IT IN HIS ROOM.
DART
HE'S PROBABLY ON HIS WAY.
I'LL GET A FLASHLIGHT, AND START WALKING TOWARD THE HOTEL.

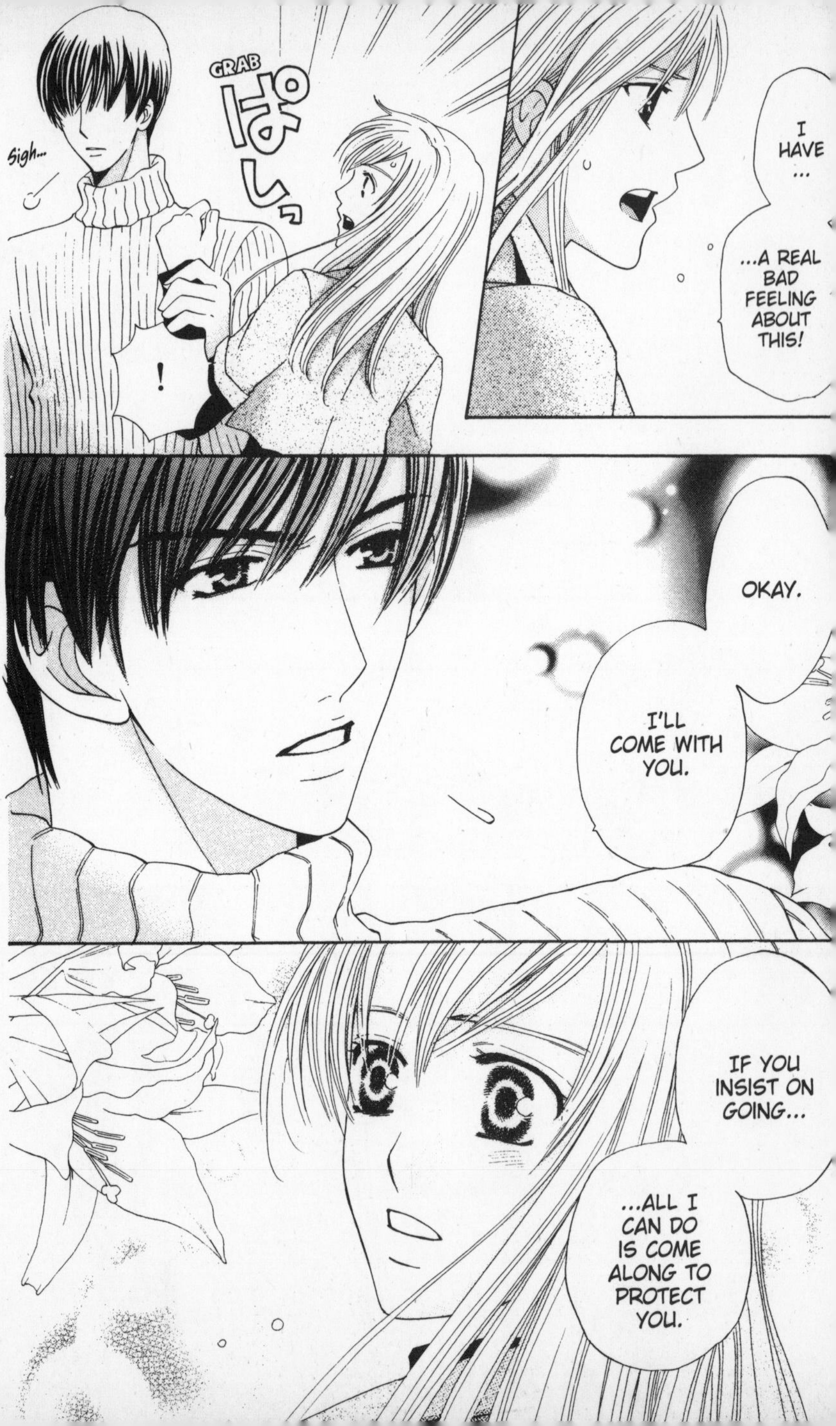
GRAB
ぱしっ
Sigh...
!
I HAVE ...
...A REAL BAD FEELING ABOUT THIS!
OKAY.
I'LL COME WITH YOU.
IF YOU INSIST ON GOING...
...ALL I CAN DO IS COME ALONG TO PROTECT YOU.

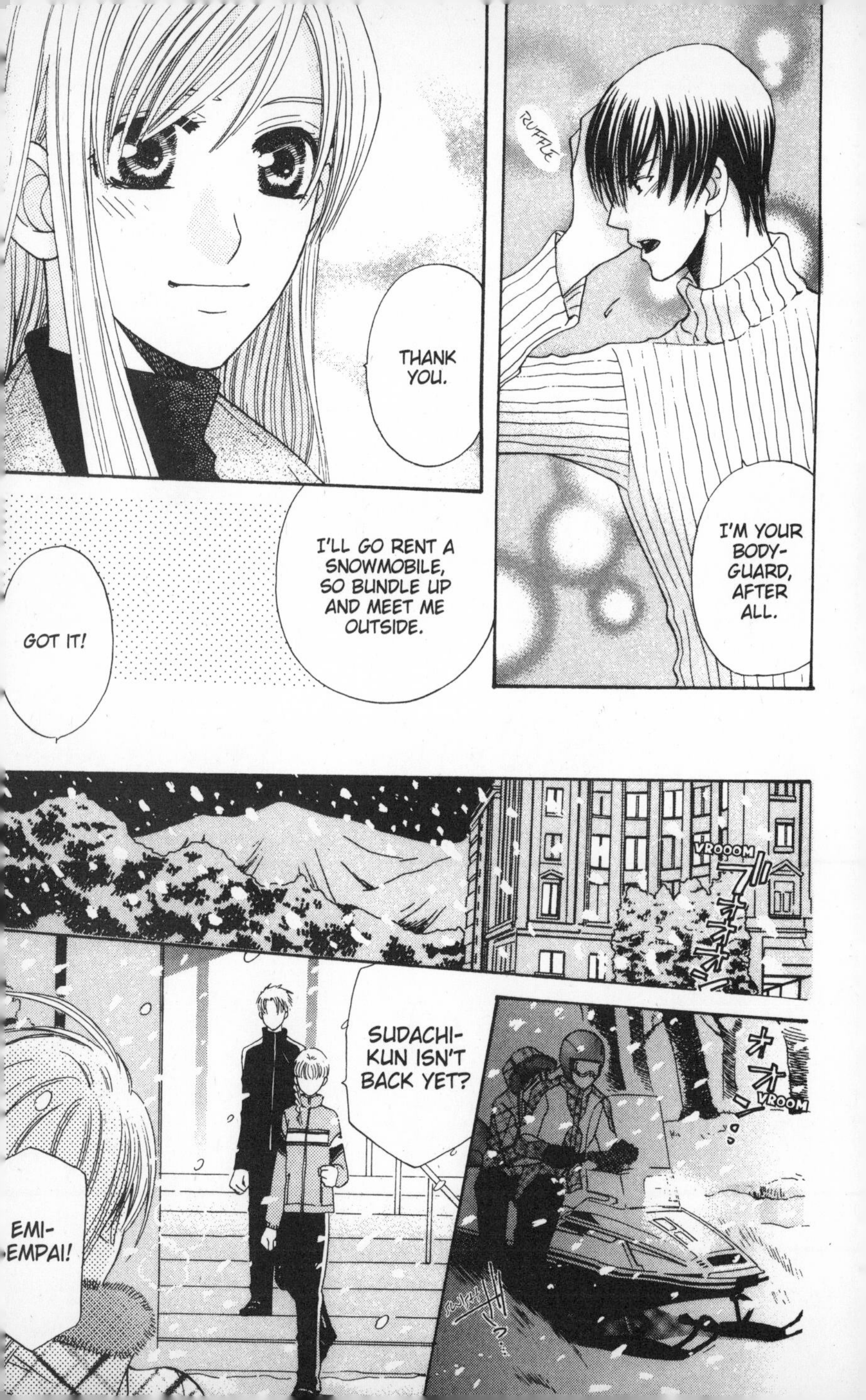
RUFFLE
I'M YOUR BODY-GUARD, AFTER ALL.
THANK YOU.
I'LL GO RENT A SNOWMOBILE, SO BUNDLE UP AND MEET ME OUTSIDE.
GOT IT!
VROOOM
VROOM
SUDACHI-KUN ISN'T BACK YET?
EMI-EMPAI!

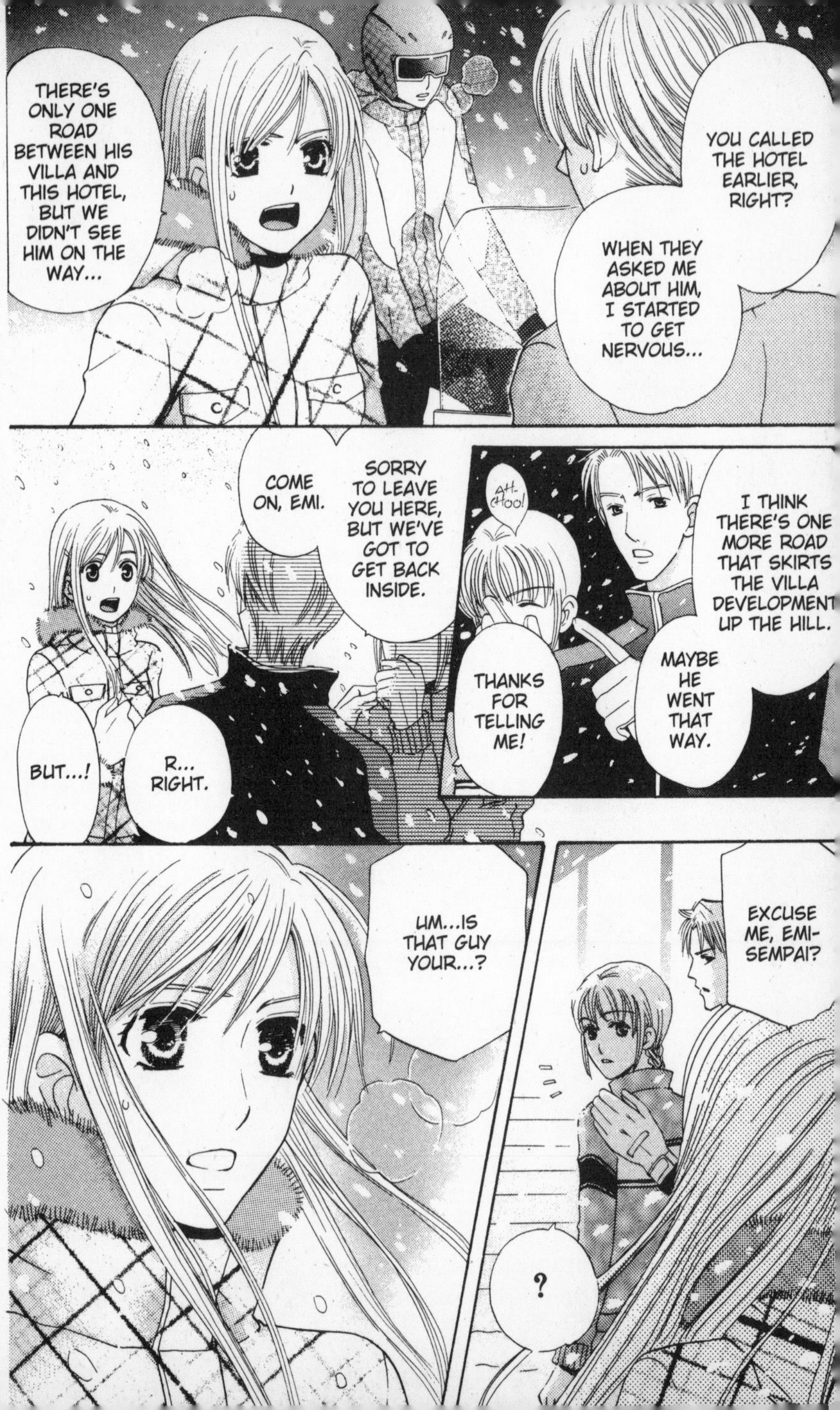
YOU CALLED THE HOTEL EARLIER, RIGHT?
WHEN THEY ASKED ME ABOUT HIM, I STARTED TO GET NERVOUS...
THERE'S ONLY ONE ROAD BETWEEN HIS VILLA AND THIS HOTEL, BUT WE DIDN'T SEE HIM ON THE WAY...
AH-CHOO!
I THINK THERE'S ONE MORE ROAD THAT SKIRTS THE VILLA DEVELOPMENT UP THE HILL.
MAYBE HE WENT THAT WAY.
THANKS FOR TELLING ME!
SORRY TO LEAVE YOU HERE, BUT WE'VE GOT TO GET BACK INSIDE.
COME ON, EMI.
R... RIGHT.
BUT...!
EXCUSE ME, EMI-SEMPAI?
?
UM...IS THAT GUY YOUR...?

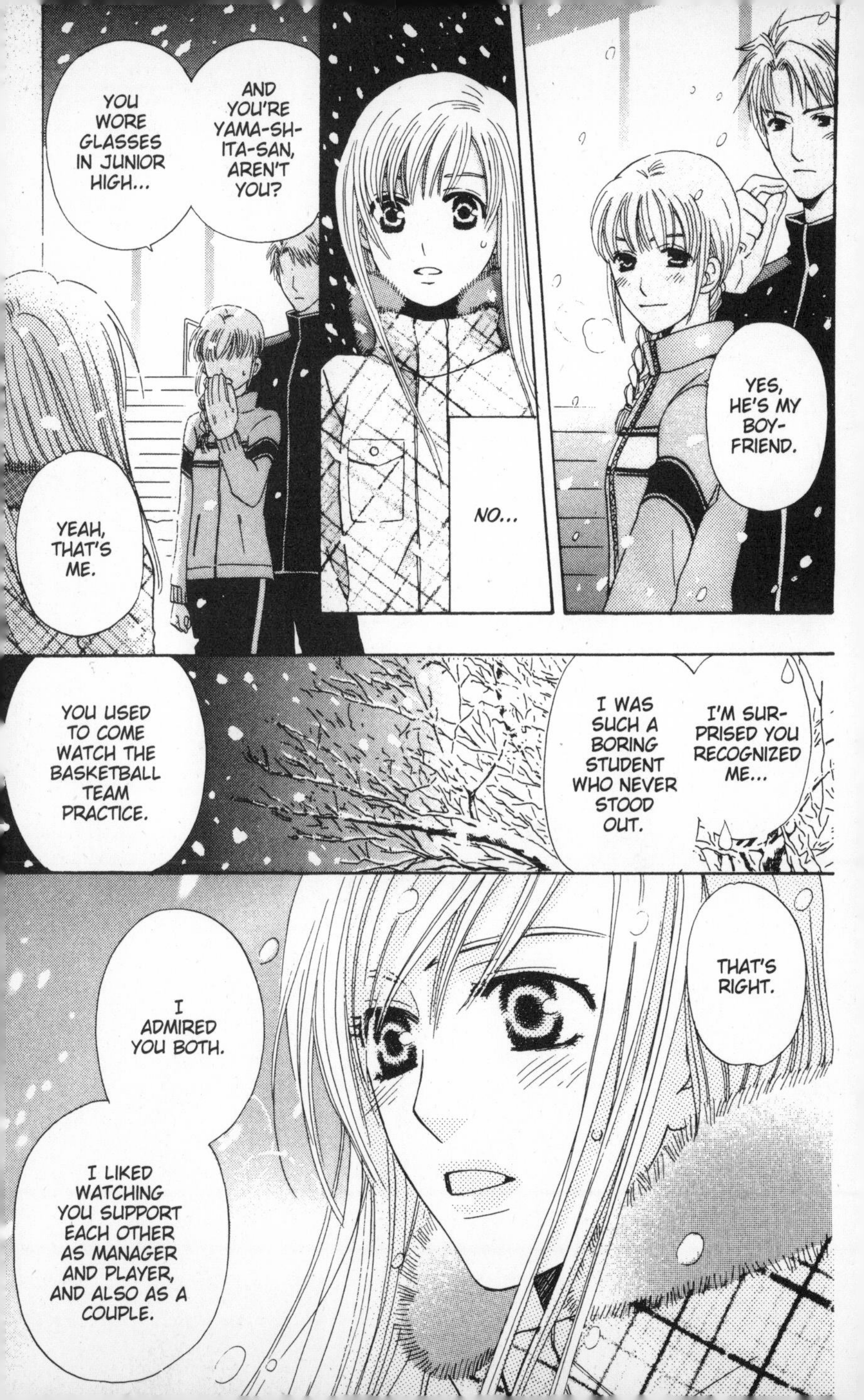
YES, HE'S MY BOY-FRIEND.
NO...
AND YOU'RE YAMA-SHITA-SAN, AREN'T YOU?
YOU WORE GLASSES IN JUNIOR HIGH...
YEAH, THAT'S ME.
I'M SUR-PRISED YOU RECOGNIZED ME...
I WAS SUCH A BORING STUDENT WHO NEVER STOOD OUT.
YOU USED TO COME WATCH THE BASKETBALL TEAM PRACTICE.
THAT'S RIGHT.
I ADMIRED YOU BOTH.
I LIKED WATCHING YOU SUPPORT EACH OTHER AS MANAGER AND PLAYER, AND ALSO AS A COUPLE.

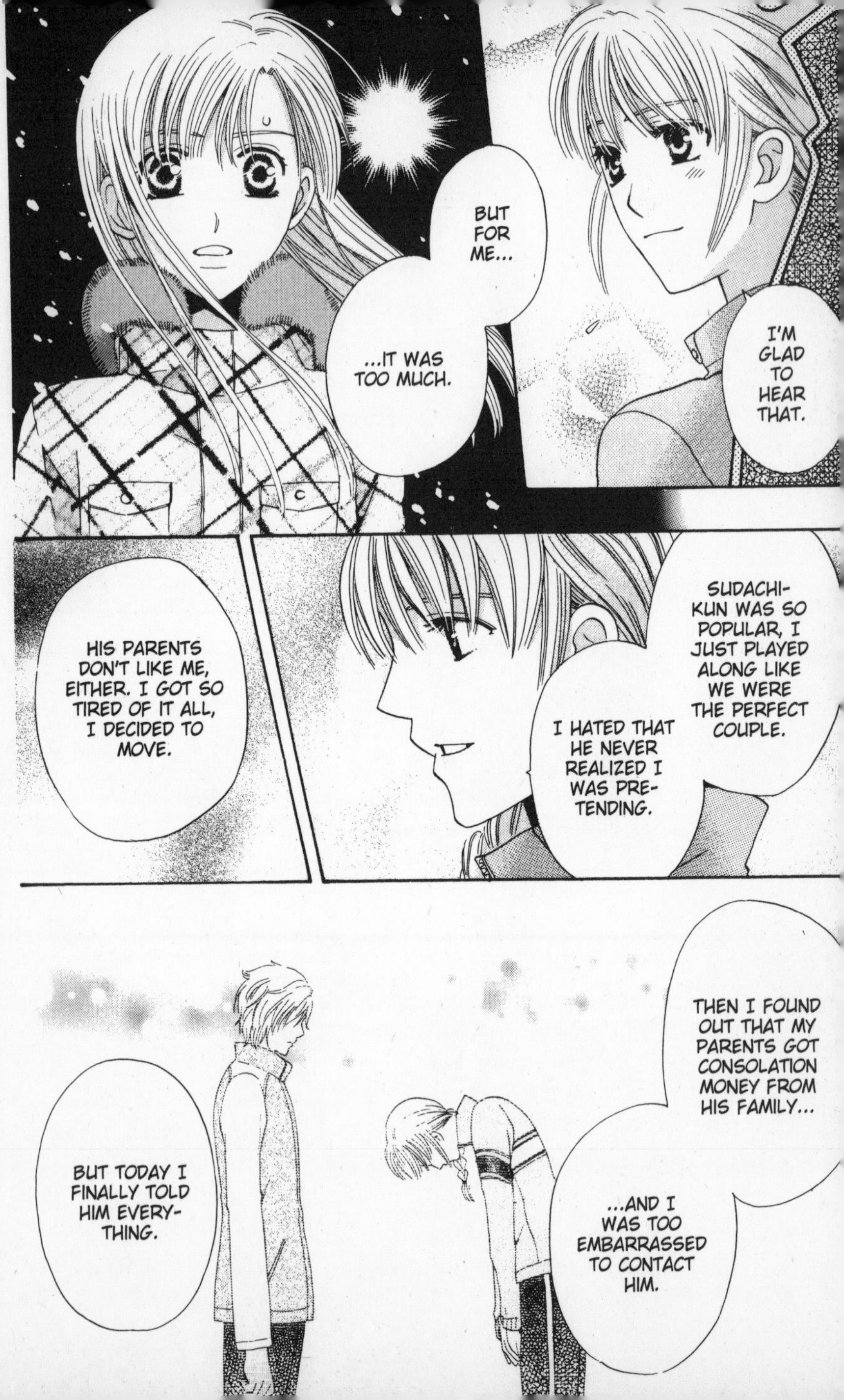
I'M GLAD TO HEAR THAT.
BUT FOR ME...
...IT WAS TOO MUCH.
SUDACHI-KUN WAS SO POPULAR, I JUST PLAYED ALONG LIKE WE WERE THE PERFECT COUPLE.
I HATED THAT HE NEVER REALIZED I WAS PRE-TENDING.
HIS PARENTS DON'T LIKE ME, EITHER. I GOT SO TIRED OF IT ALL, I DECIDED TO MOVE.
THEN I FOUND OUT THAT MY PARENTS GOT CONSOLATION MONEY FROM HIS FAMILY...
...AND I WAS TOO EMBARRASSED TO CONTACT HIM.
BUT TODAY I FINALLY TOLD HIM EVERY-THING.

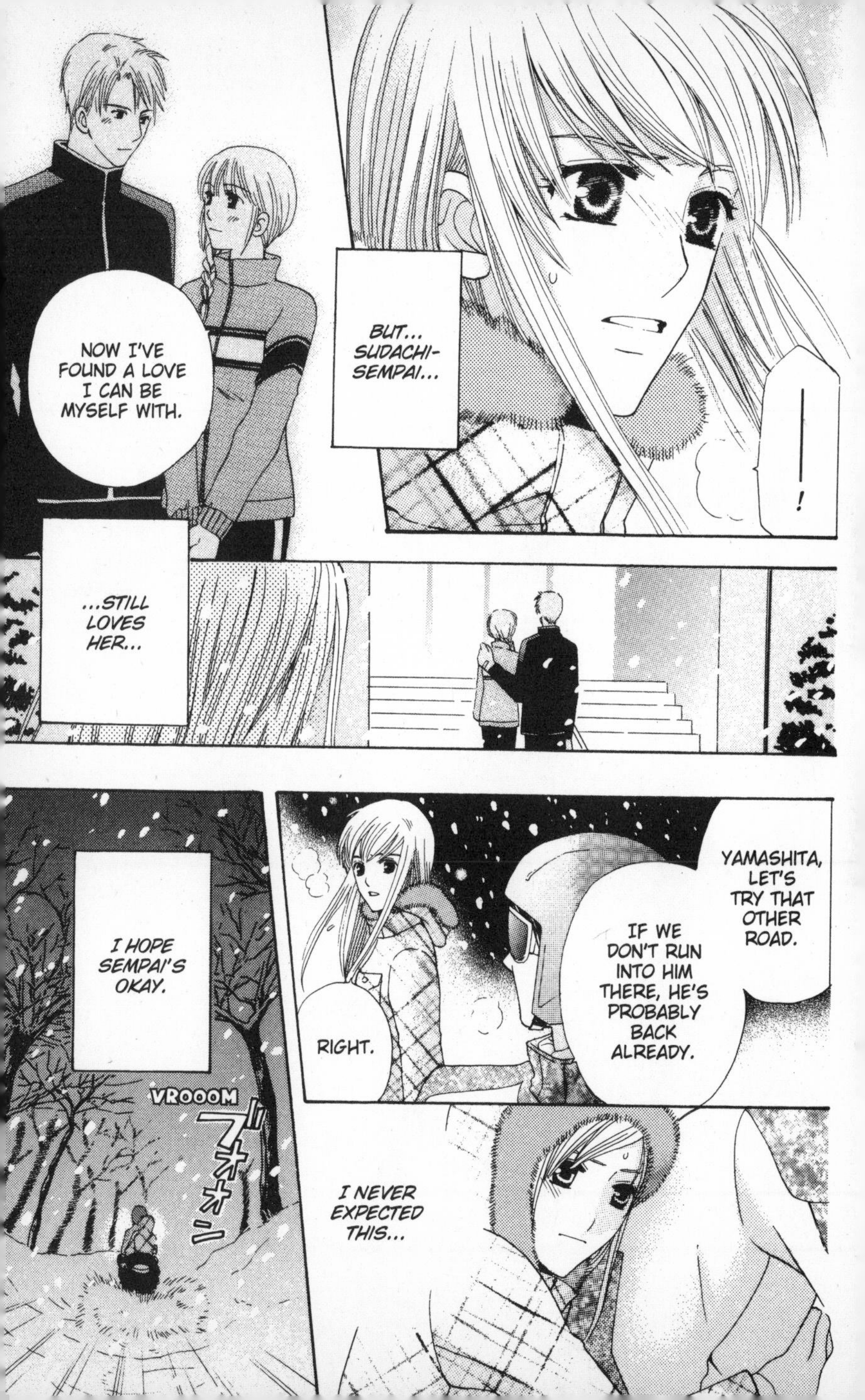
NOW I'VE FOUND A LOVE I CAN BE MYSELF WITH.
—!
BUT... SUDACHI-SEMPAI...
...STILL LOVES HER...
YAMASHITA, LET'S TRY THAT OTHER ROAD.
IF WE DON'T RUN INTO HIM THERE, HE'S PROBABLY BACK ALREADY.
RIGHT.
I NEVER EXPECTED THIS...
I HOPE SEMPAI'S OKAY.
VROOOM

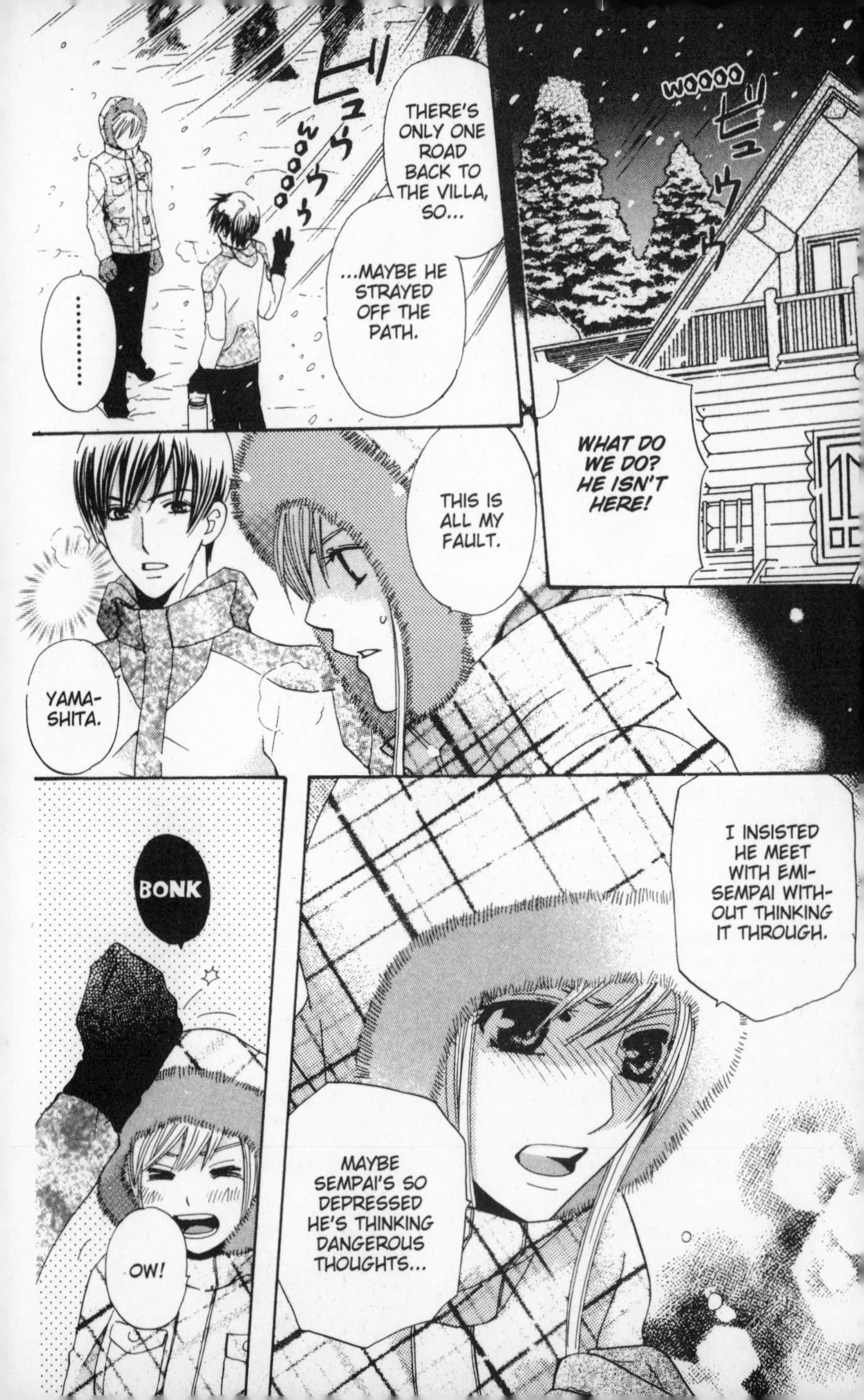
WOOOO
WHAT DO WE DO? HE ISN'T HERE!
THERE'S ONLY ONE ROAD BACK TO THE VILLA, SO...
...MAYBE HE STRAYED OFF THE PATH.
WOOOO
......
THIS IS ALL MY FAULT.
YAMA-SHITA.
I INSISTED HE MEET WITH EMI-SEMPAI WITH-OUT THINKING IT THROUGH.
MAYBE SEMPAI'S SO DEPRESSED HE'S THINKING DANGEROUS THOUGHTS...
BONK
OW!

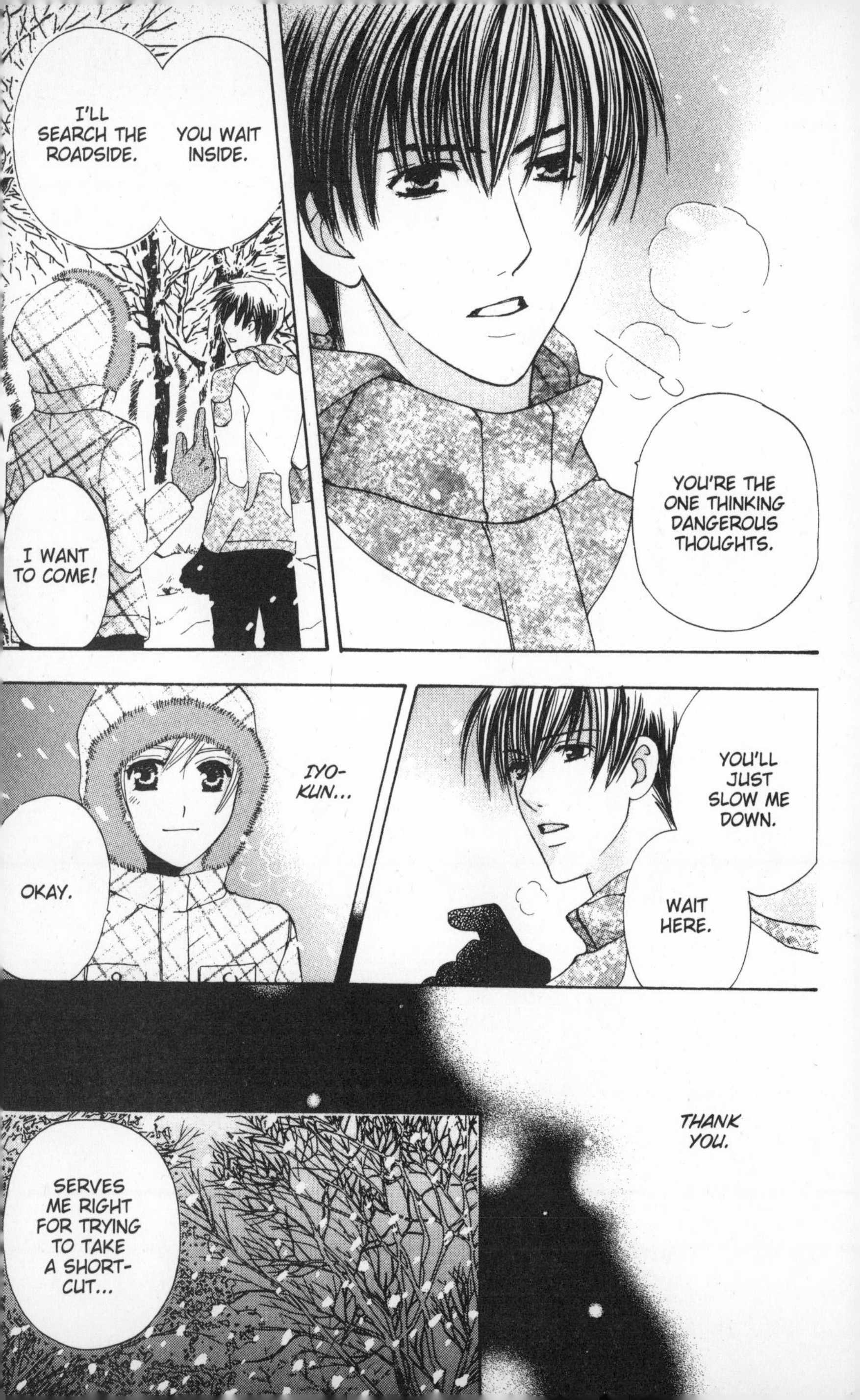
YOU'RE THE ONE THINKING DANGEROUS THOUGHTS.
YOU WAIT INSIDE.
I'LL SEARCH THE ROADSIDE.
I WANT TO COME!
YOU'LL JUST SLOW ME DOWN.
WAIT HERE.
IYO-KUN...
OKAY.
THANK YOU.
SERVES ME RIGHT FOR TRYING TO TAKE A SHORT-CUT...

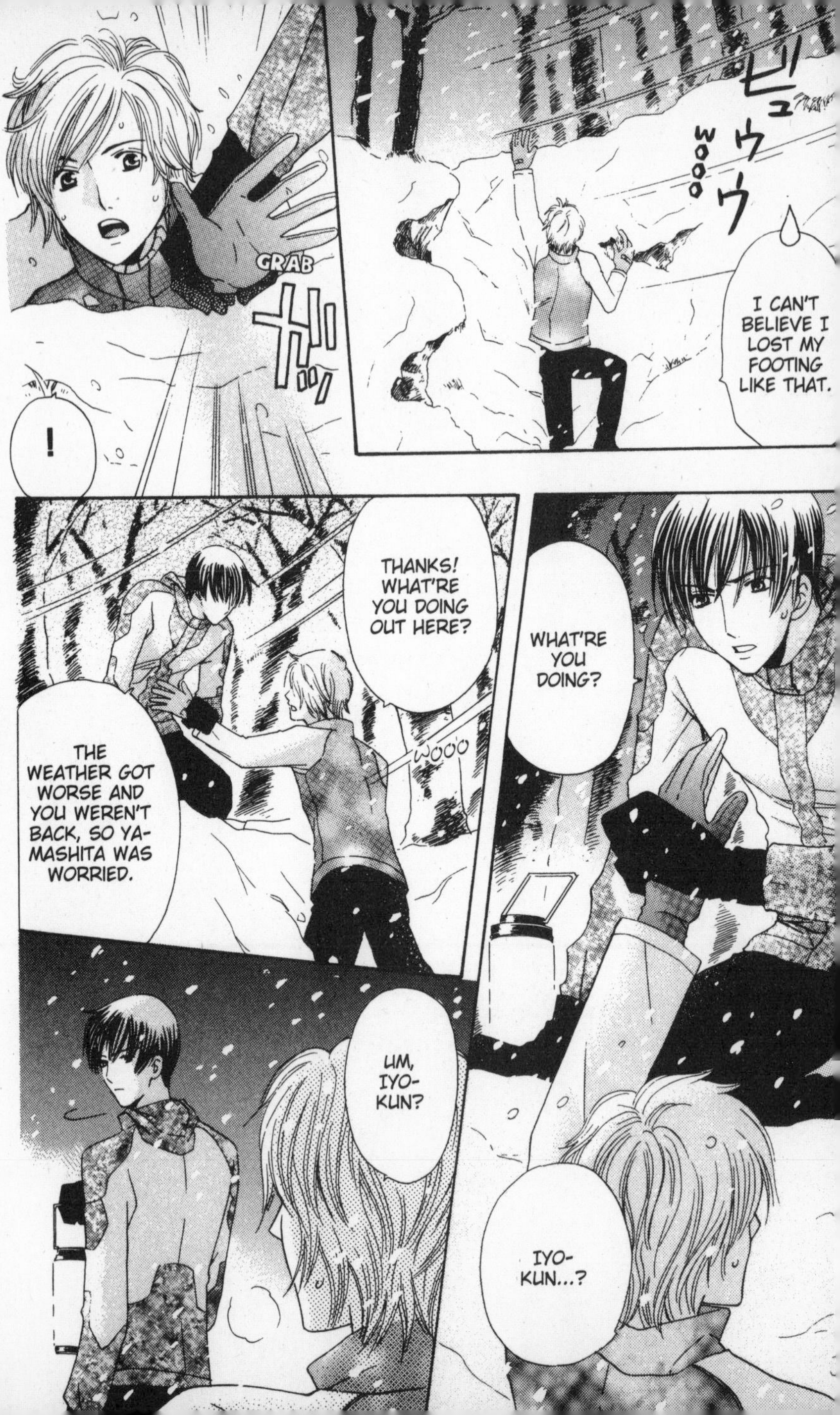
ピュウウ
WOOO
I CAN'T BELIEVE I LOST MY FOOTING LIKE THAT.
GRAB
ガッ
!
WHAT'RE YOU DOING?
THANKS! WHAT'RE YOU DOING OUT HERE?
THE WEATHER GOT WORSE AND YOU WEREN'T BACK, SO YA-MASHITA WAS WORRIED.
WOOO
IYO-KUN...?
UM, IYO-KUN?

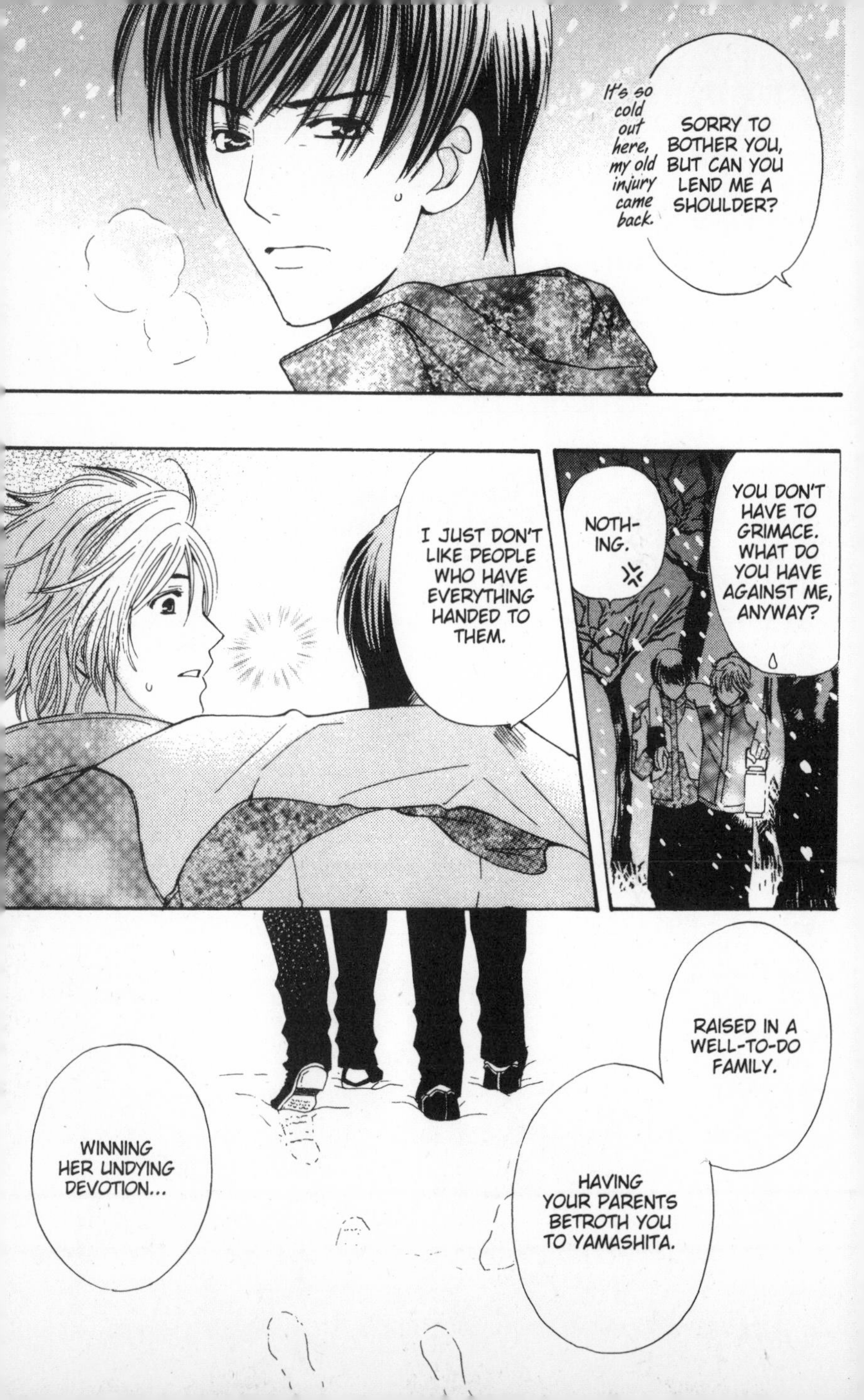
SORRY TO BOTHER YOU, BUT CAN YOU LEND ME A SHOULDER?
It's so cold out here, my old injury came back.
YOU DON'T HAVE TO GRIMACE. WHAT DO YOU HAVE AGAINST ME, ANYWAY?
NOTH-ING.
I JUST DON'T LIKE PEOPLE WHO HAVE EVERYTHING HANDED TO THEM.
RAISED IN A WELL-TO-DO FAMILY.
HAVING YOUR PARENTS BETROTH YOU TO YAMASHITA.
WINNING HER UNDYING DEVOTION...

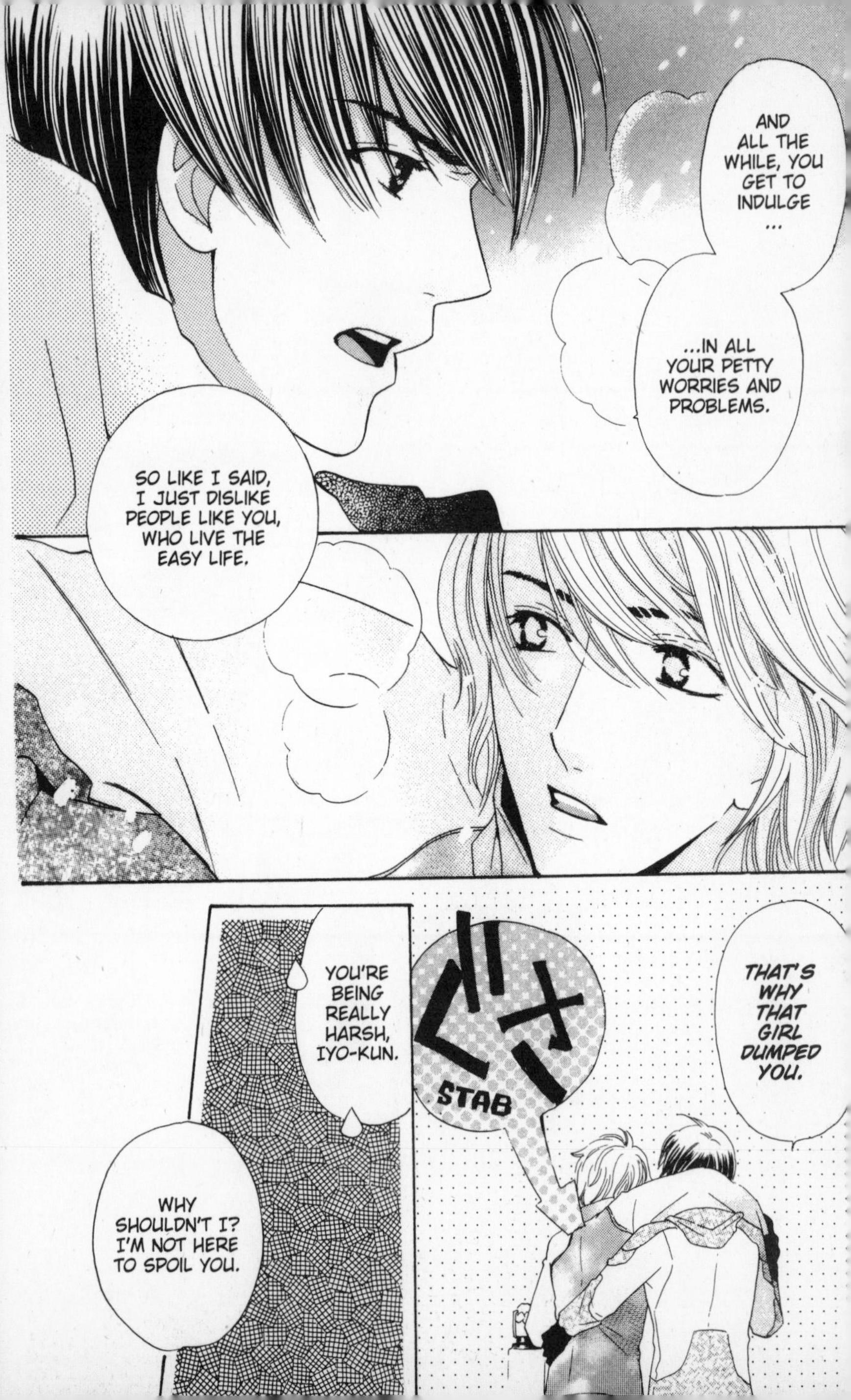
AND ALL THE WHILE, YOU GET TO INDULGE ...
...IN ALL YOUR PETTY WORRIES AND PROBLEMS.
SO LIKE I SAID, I JUST DISLIKE PEOPLE LIKE YOU, WHO LIVE THE EASY LIFE.
THAT'S WHY THAT GIRL DUMPED YOU.
STAB
YOU'RE BEING REALLY HARSH, IYO-KUN.
WHY SHOULDN'T I? I'M NOT HERE TO SPOIL YOU.

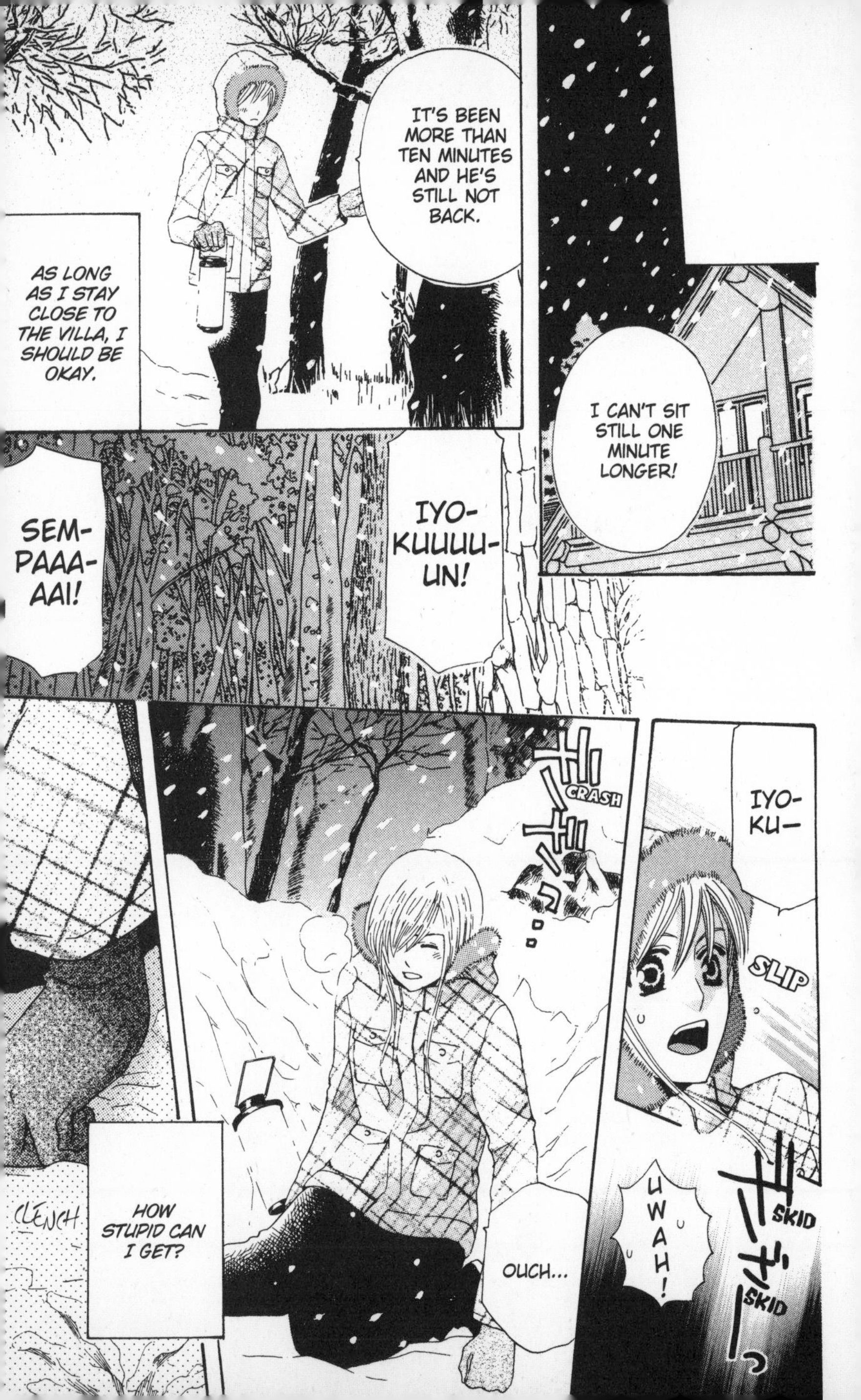
IT'S BEEN MORE THAN TEN MINUTES AND HE'S STILL NOT BACK.
I CAN'T SIT STILL ONE MINUTE LONGER!
AS LONG AS I STAY CLOSE TO THE VILLA, I SHOULD BE OKAY.
IYO-KUUUUUN!
SEM-PAAAA-AAI!
IYO-KU-
SLIP
UWAH!
SKID
SKID
CRASH
OUCH...
HOW STUPID CAN I GET?
CLENCH

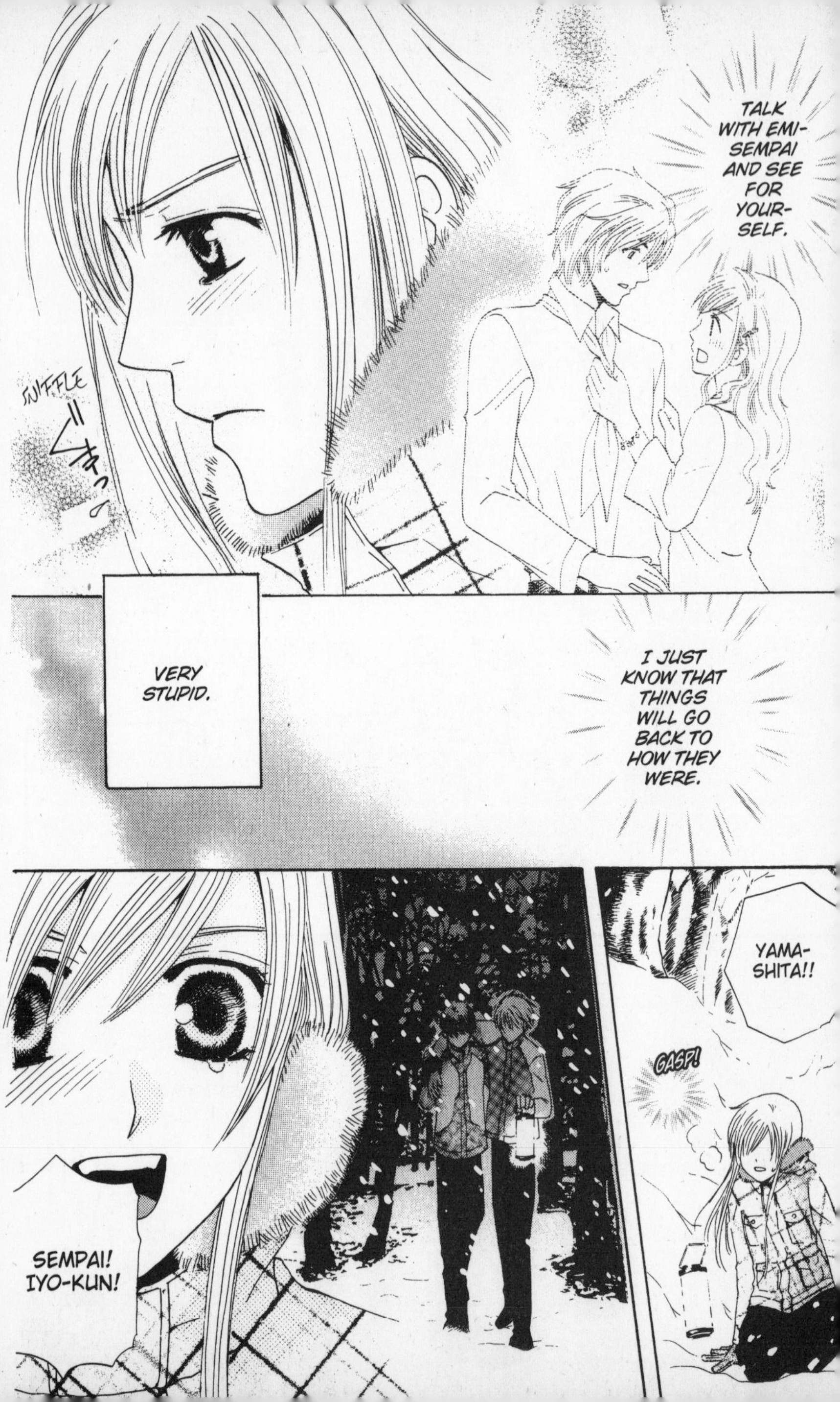
TALK WITH EMI-SEMPAI AND SEE FOR YOURSELF.
SNIFFLE
I JUST KNOW THAT THINGS WILL GO BACK TO HOW THEY WERE.
VERY STUPID.
YAMA-SHITA!!
GASP!
SEMPAI! IYO-KUN!

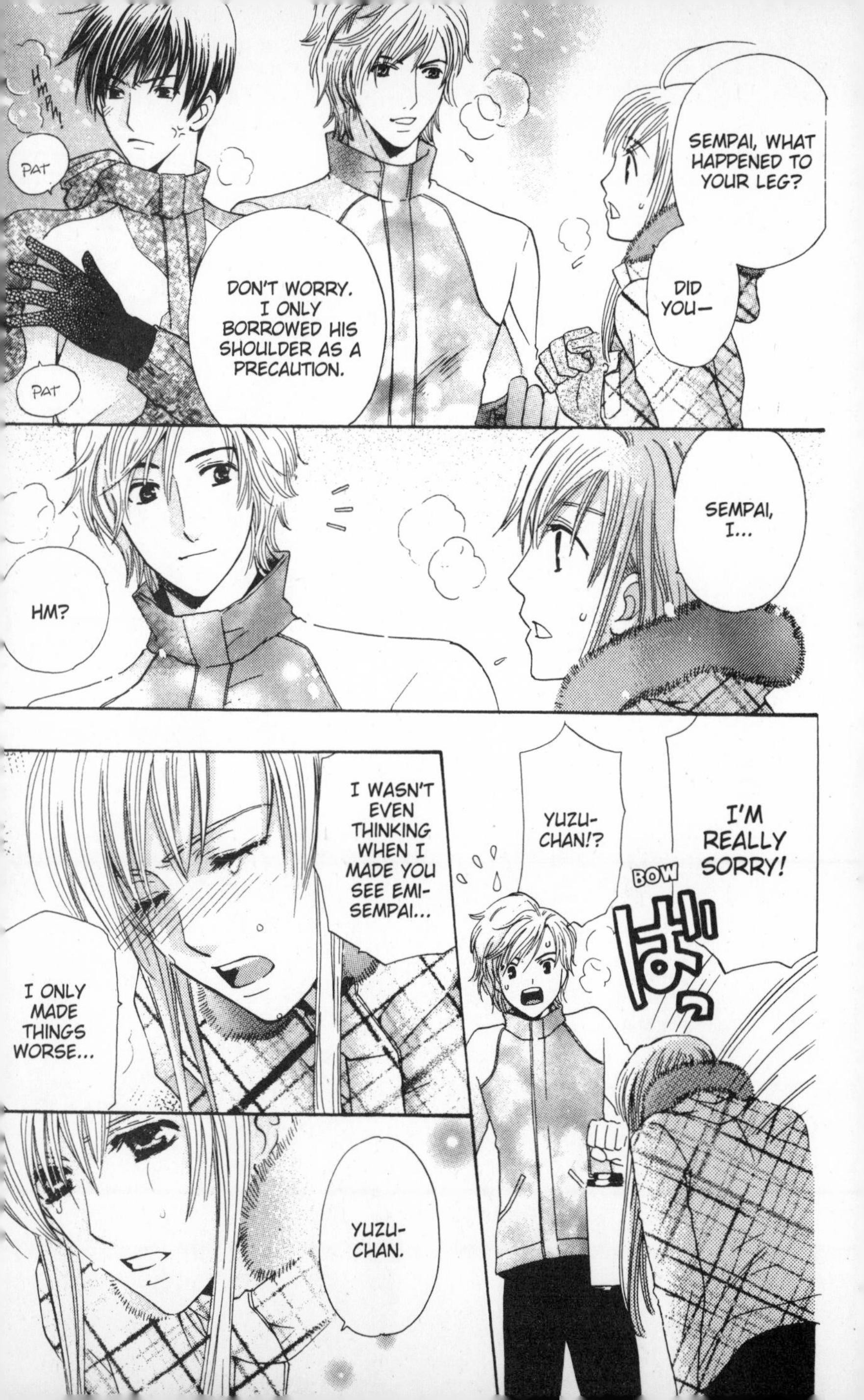

SEMPAI, WHAT HAPPENED TO YOUR LEG?
DID YOU—
HMPH!
PAT
DON'T WORRY. I ONLY BORROWED HIS SHOULDER AS A PRECAUTION.
PAT
SEMPAI, I...
HM?
I'M REALLY SORRY!
BOW
ぱっ
YUZU-CHAN!?
I WASN'T EVEN THINKING WHEN I MADE YOU SEE EMI-SEMPAI...
I ONLY MADE THINGS WORSE...
YUZU-CHAN.

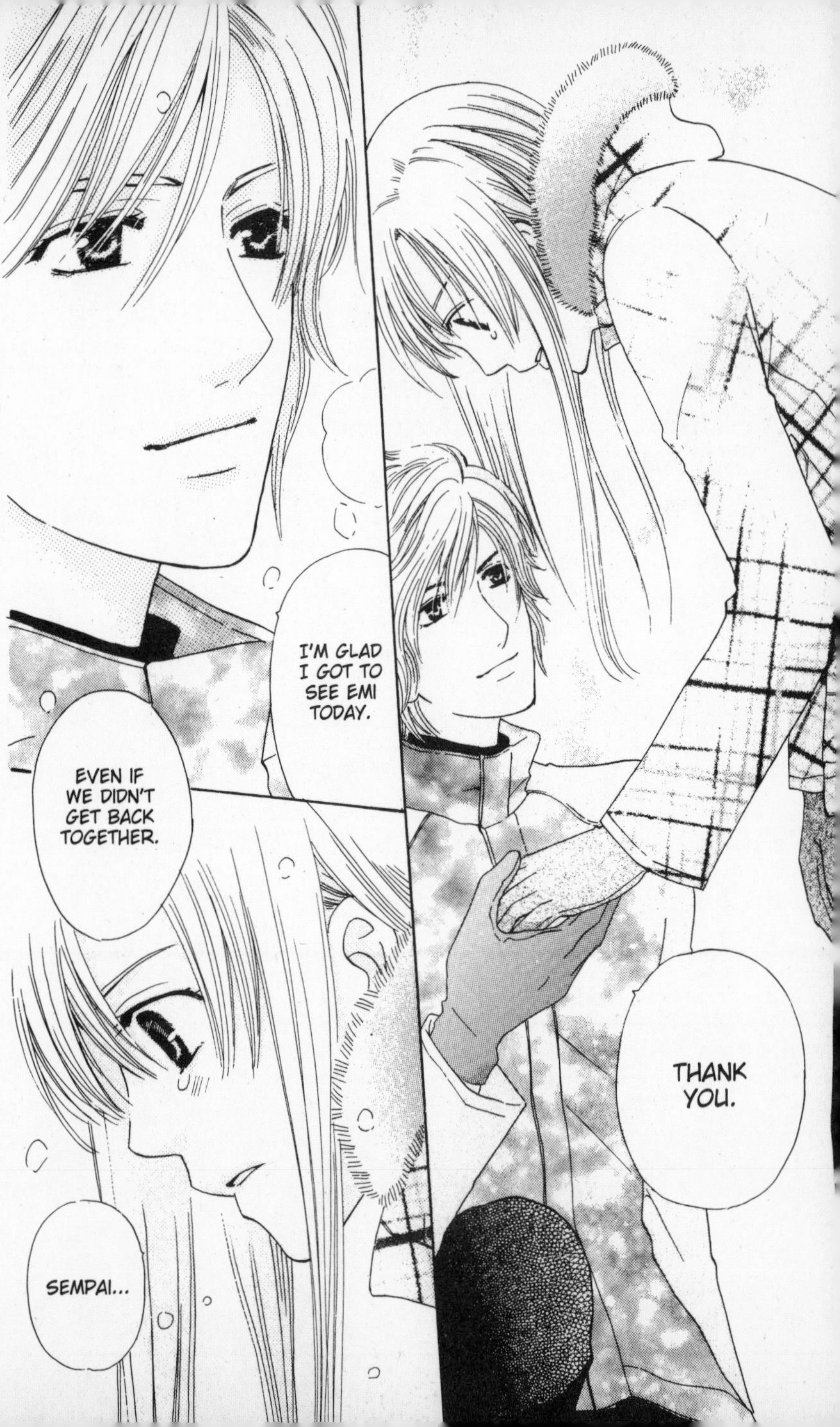
I'M GLAD I GOT TO SEE EMI TODAY.
EVEN IF WE DIDN'T GET BACK TOGETHER.
THANK YOU.
SEMPAI...

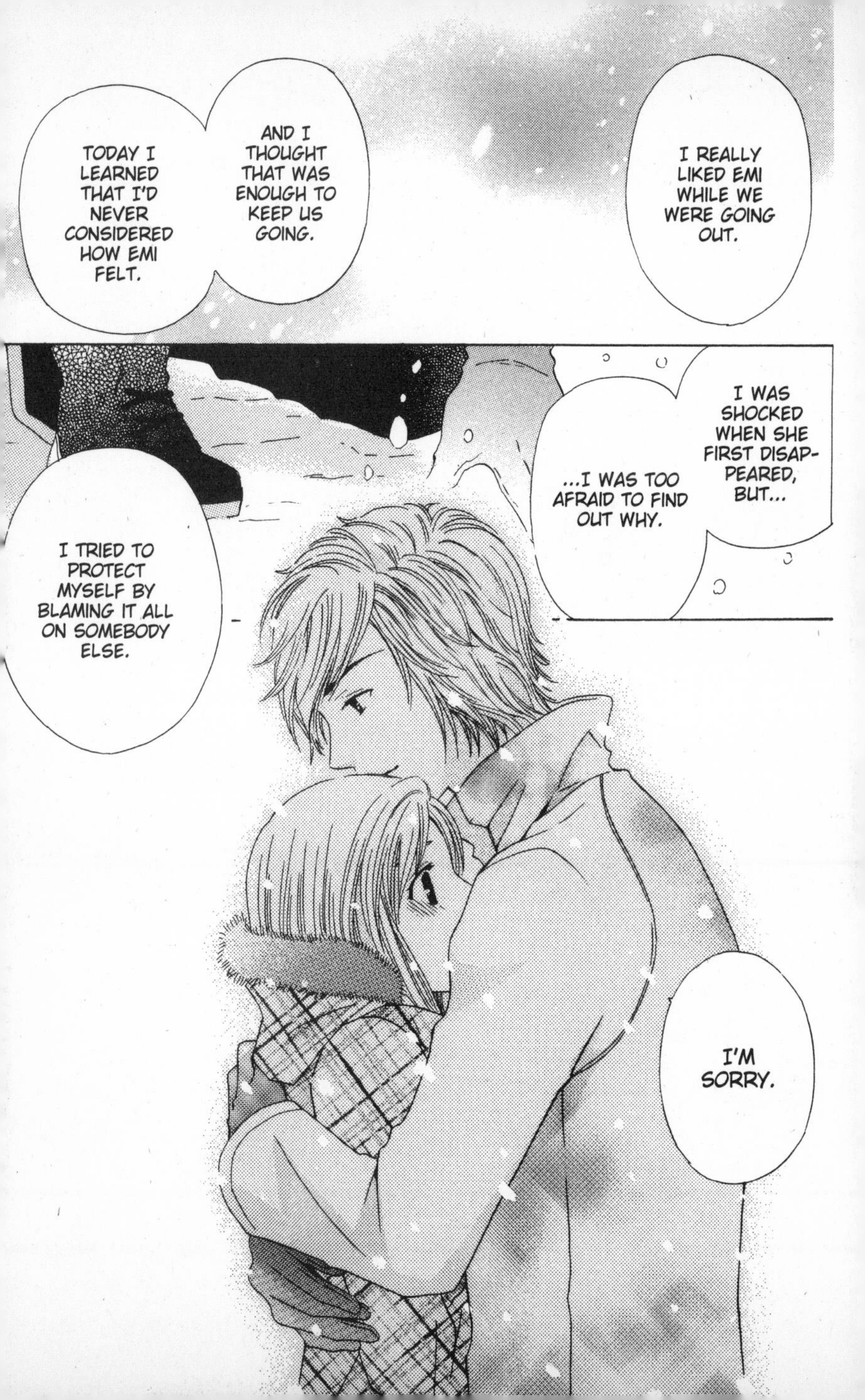
I REALLY LIKED EMI WHILE WE WERE GOING OUT.
AND I THOUGHT THAT WAS ENOUGH TO KEEP US GOING.
TODAY I LEARNED THAT I'D NEVER CONSIDERED HOW EMI FELT.
I WAS SHOCKED WHEN SHE FIRST DISAPPEARED, BUT...
...I WAS TOO AFRAID TO FIND OUT WHY.
I TRIED TO PROTECT MYSELF BY BLAMING IT ALL ON SOMEBODY ELSE.
I'M SORRY.

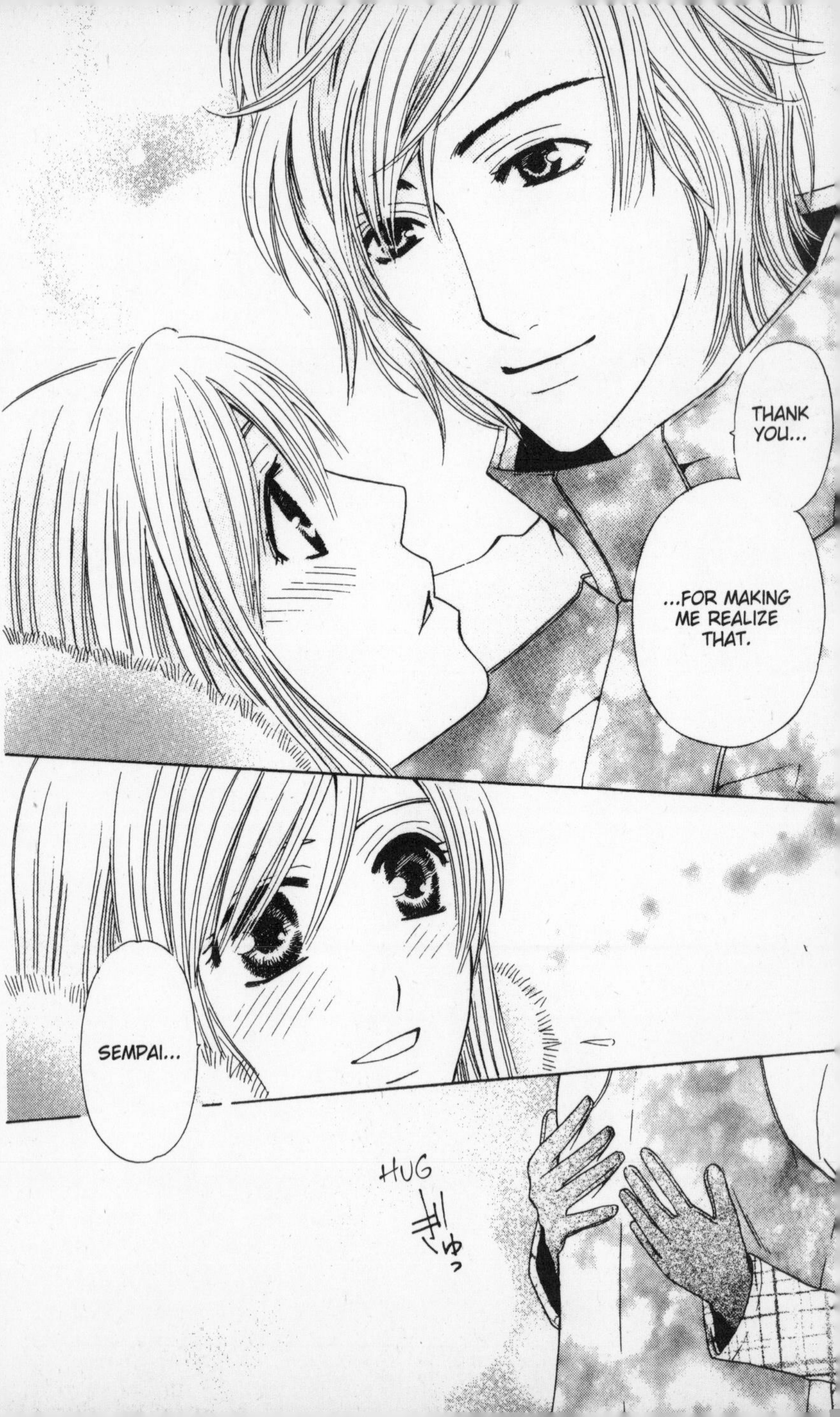
THANK YOU...
...FOR MAKING ME REALIZE THAT.
SEMPAI...
HUG
ぎゅっ

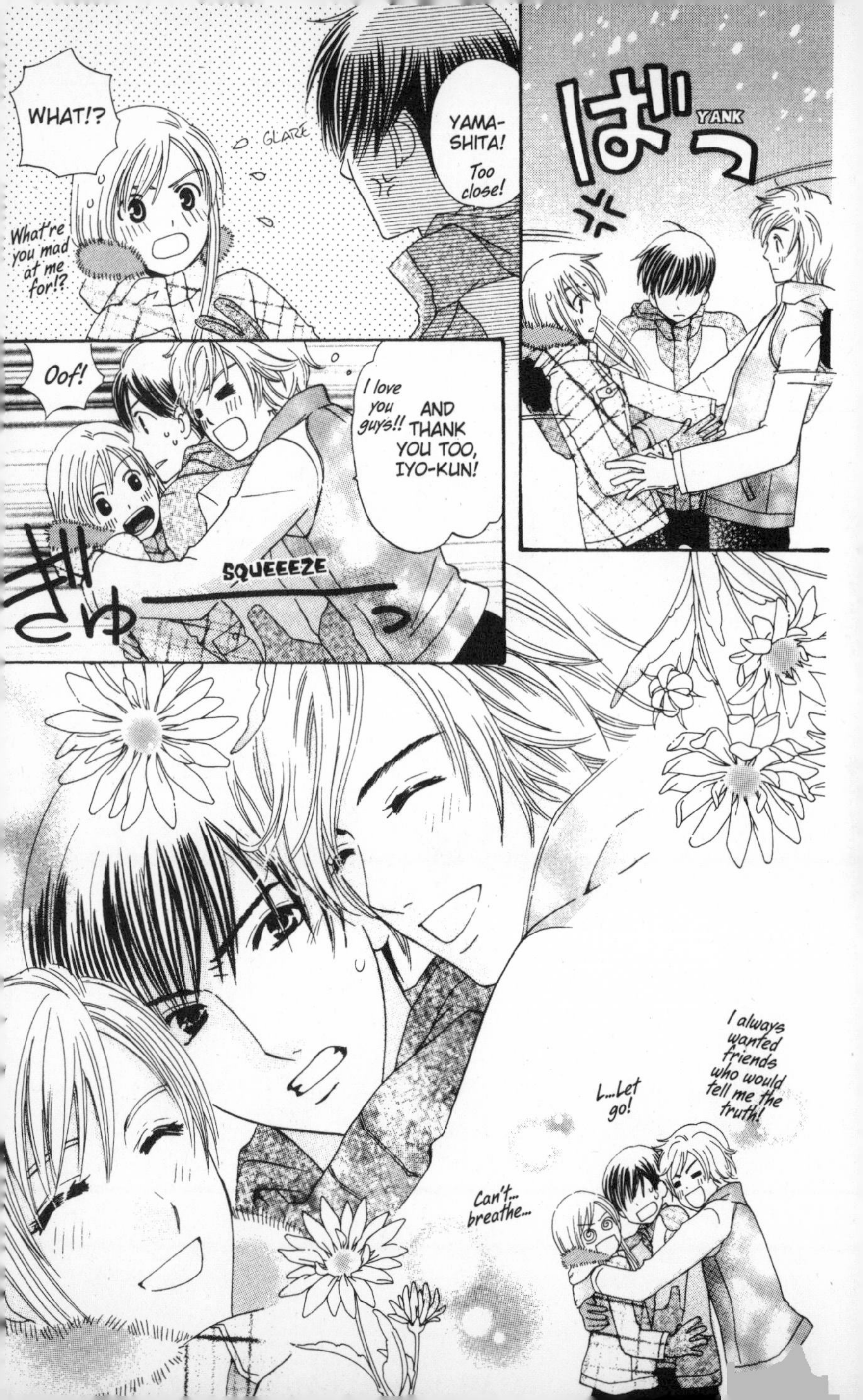
ばっ
YANK
YAMA-SHITA! Too close!
GLARE
WHAT!?
What're you mad at me for!?
I love you guys!!
AND THANK YOU TOO, IYO-KUN!
Oof!
ぎゅーっ
SQUEEEZE
I always wanted friends who would tell me the truth!
L...Let go!
Can't... breathe...

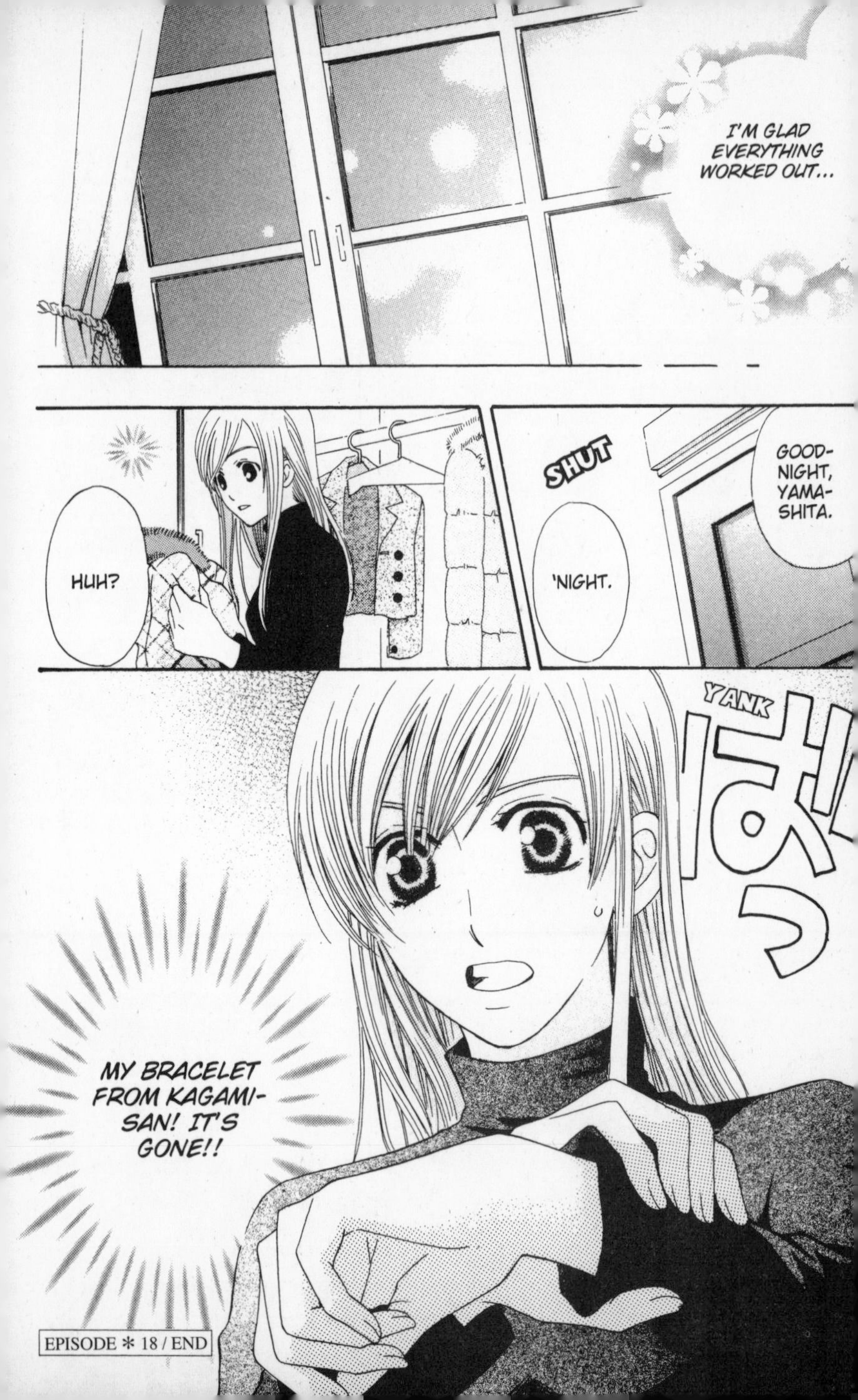
I'M GLAD EVERYTHING WORKED OUT...
GOOD-NIGHT, YAMA-SHITA.
SHUT
'NIGHT.
HUH?
YANK
はっ
MY BRACELET FROM KAGAMI-SAN! IT'S GONE!!
EPISODE * 18 / END

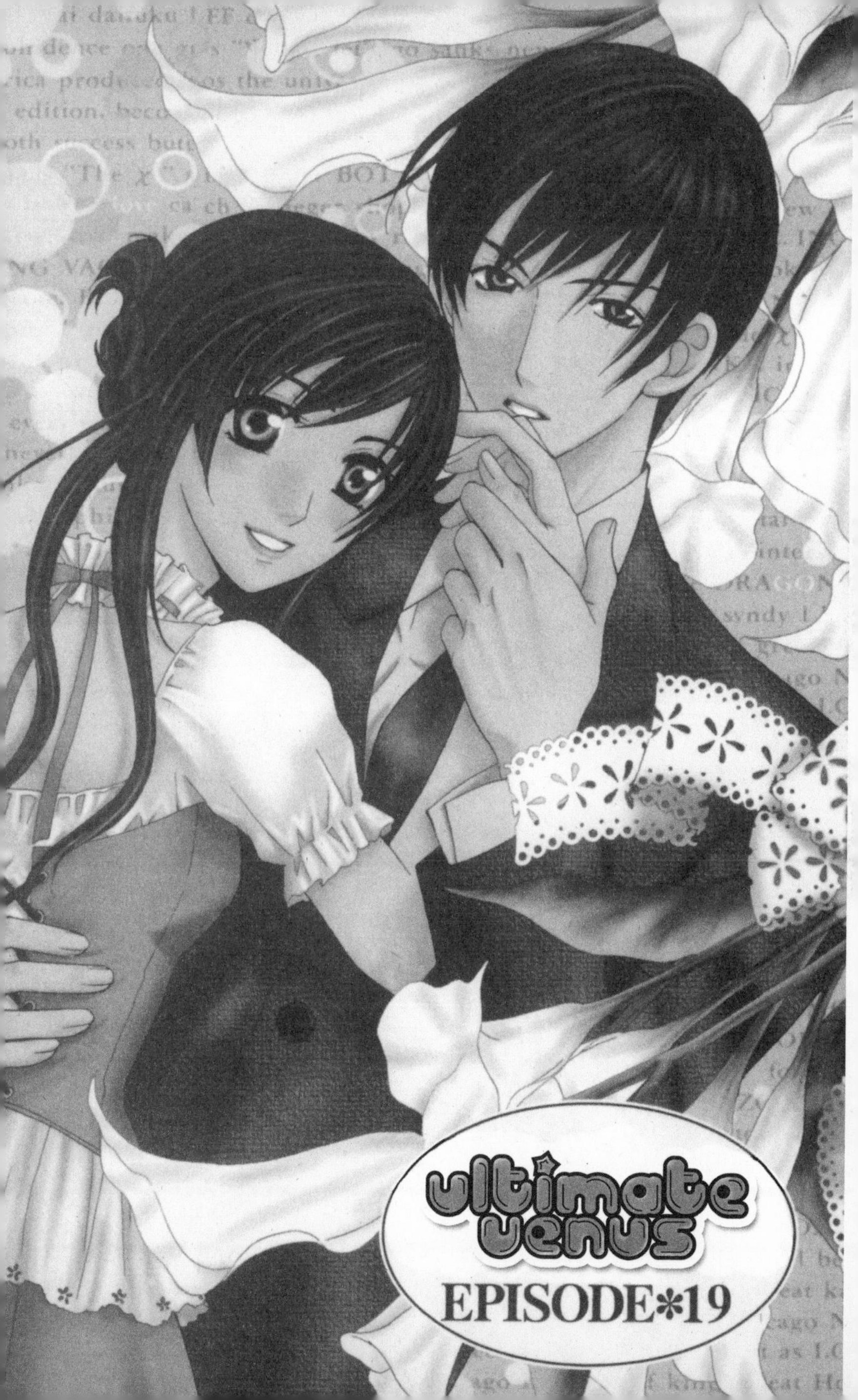
ultimate venus
EPISODE*19

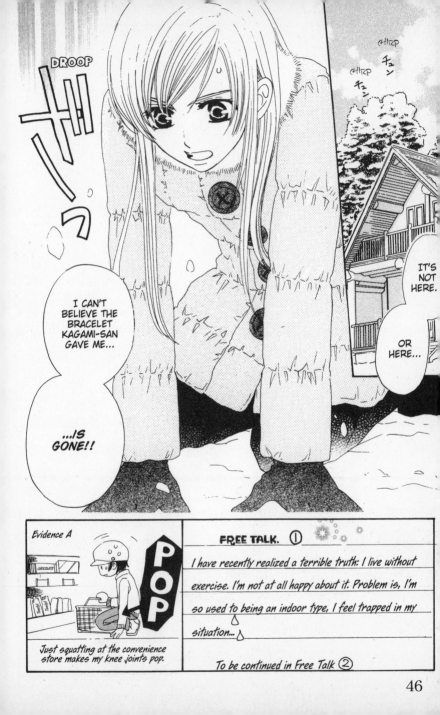

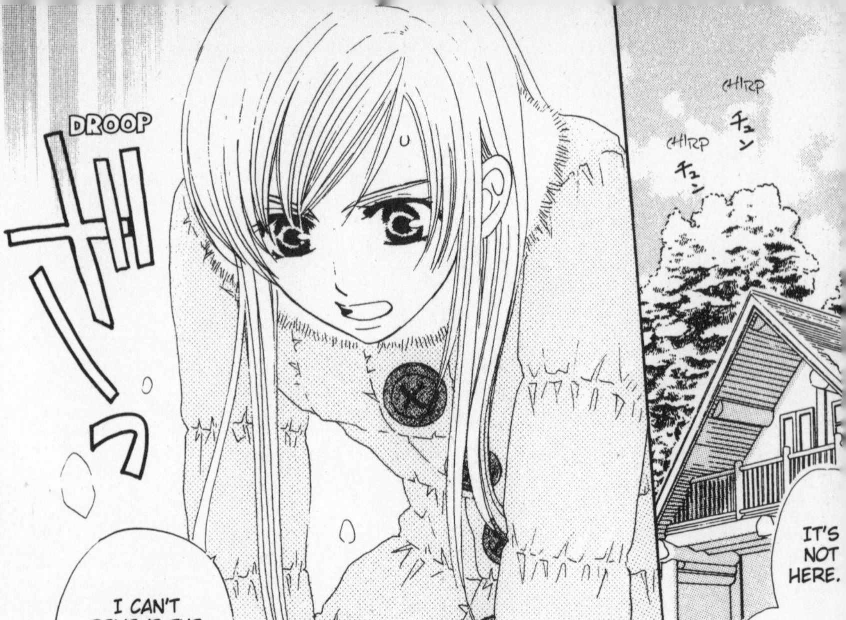
CHIRP
チュン
CHIRP
チュン
IT'S NOT HERE.
OR HERE...
DROOP
I CAN'T BELIEVE THE BRACELET KAGAMI-SAN GAVE ME...
...IS GONE!!

Evidence A

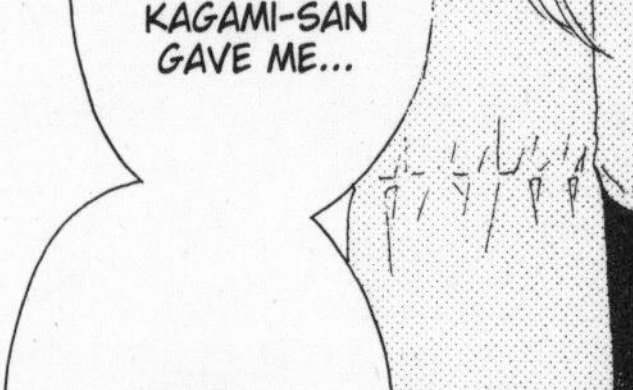
CHOCOLATE
POP

Just squatting at the convenience store makes my knee joints pop.

FREE TALK. ①

I have recently realized a terrible truth: I live without exercise. I'm not at all happy about it. Problem is, I'm so used to being an indoor type, I feel trapped in my situation...

To be continued in Free Talk ②

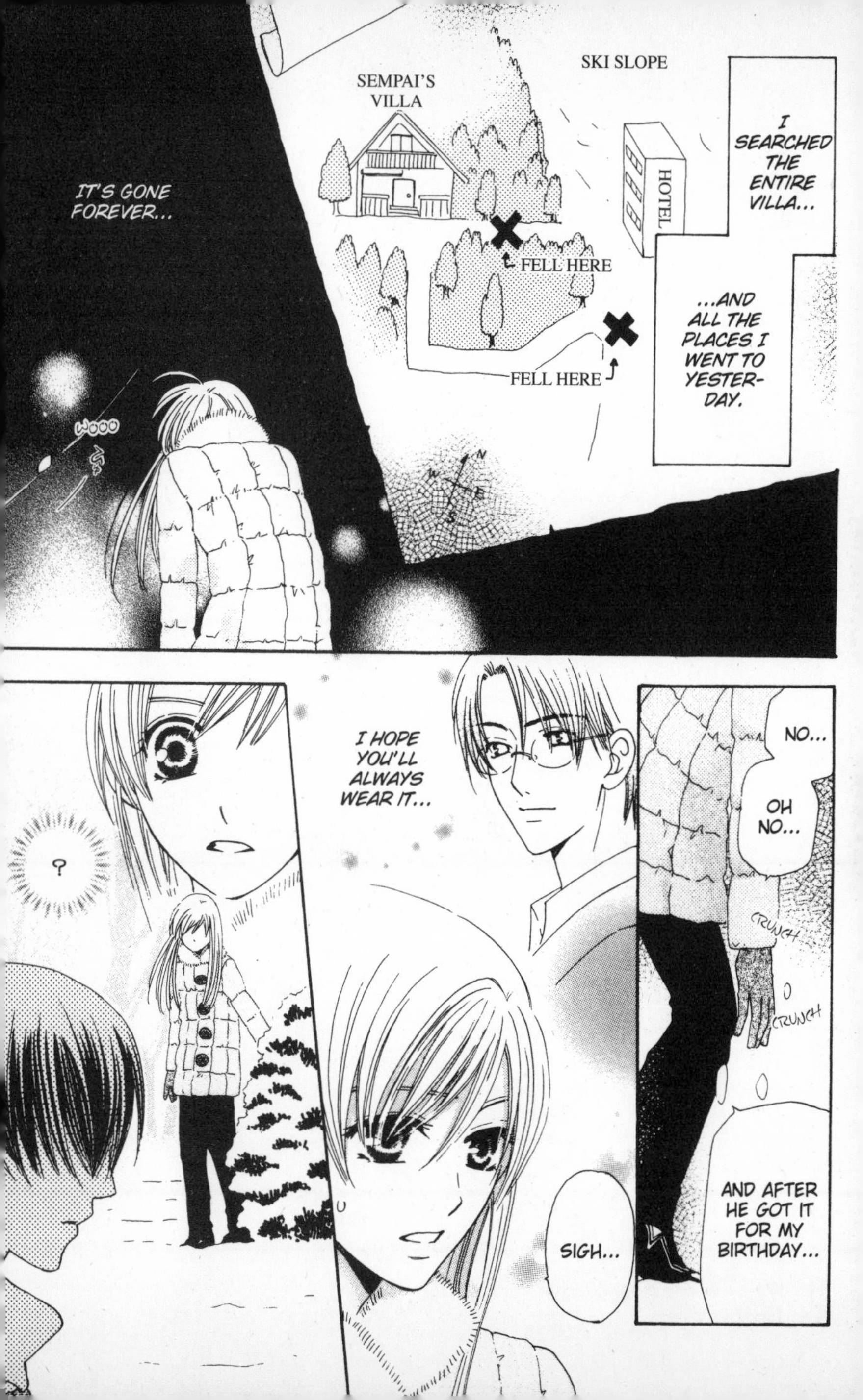
I SEARCHED THE ENTIRE VILLA...
...AND ALL THE PLACES I WENT TO YESTER-DAY.
SKI SLOPE
HOTEL
SEMPAI'S VILLA
FELL HERE
FELL HERE
IT'S GONE FOREVER...
WOOO
NO...
OH NO...
CRUNCH
CRUNCH
AND AFTER HE GOT IT FOR MY BIRTHDAY...
SIGH...
I HOPE YOU'LL ALWAYS WEAR IT...
?

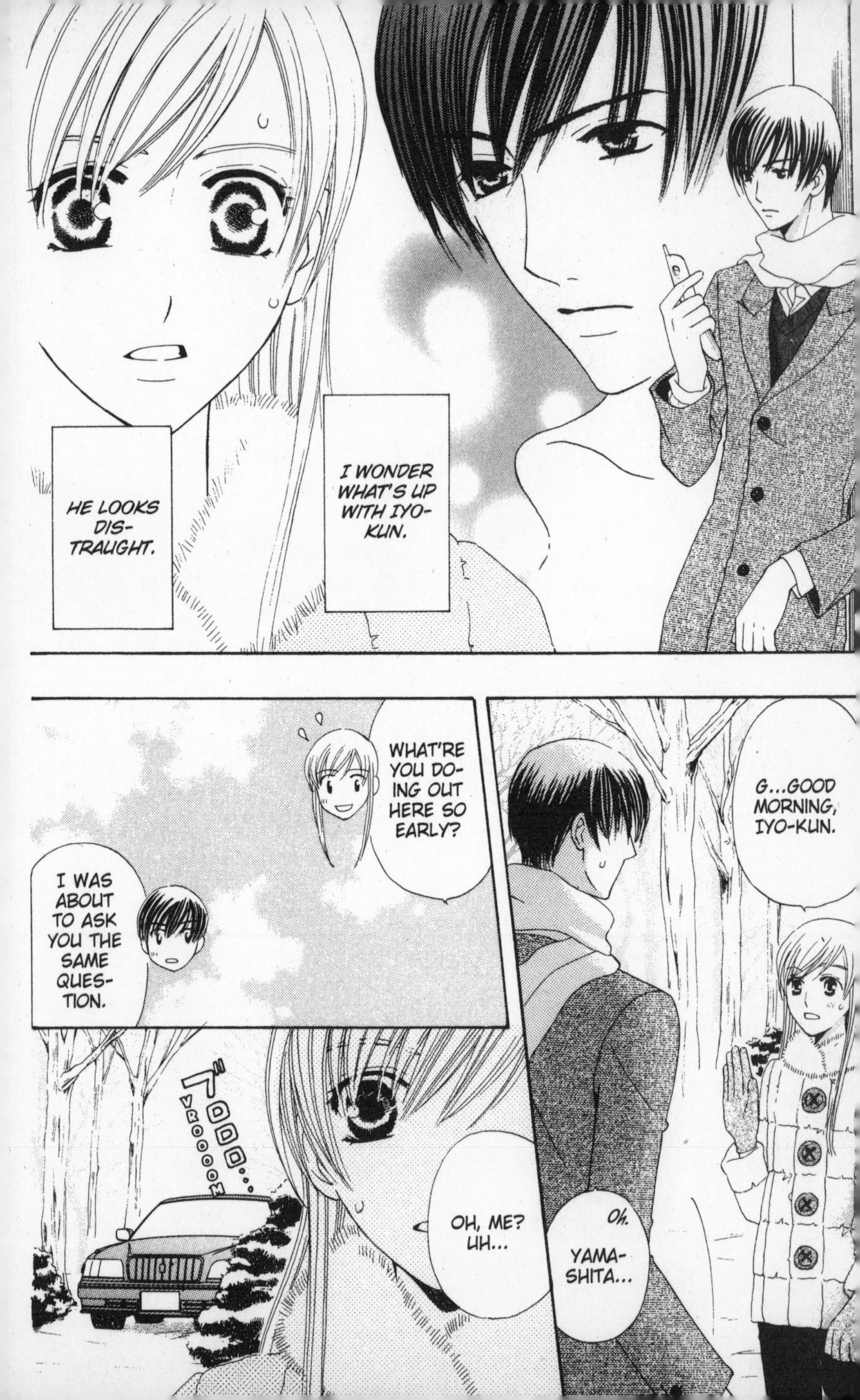
I WONDER WHAT'S UP WITH IYO-KUN.
HE LOOKS DIS-TRAUGHT.
G...GOOD MORNING, IYO-KUN.
WHAT'RE YOU DO-ING OUT HERE SO EARLY?
I WAS ABOUT TO ASK YOU THE SAME QUES-TION.
Oh.
YAMA-SHITA...
OH, ME? UH...
VROOOOOM

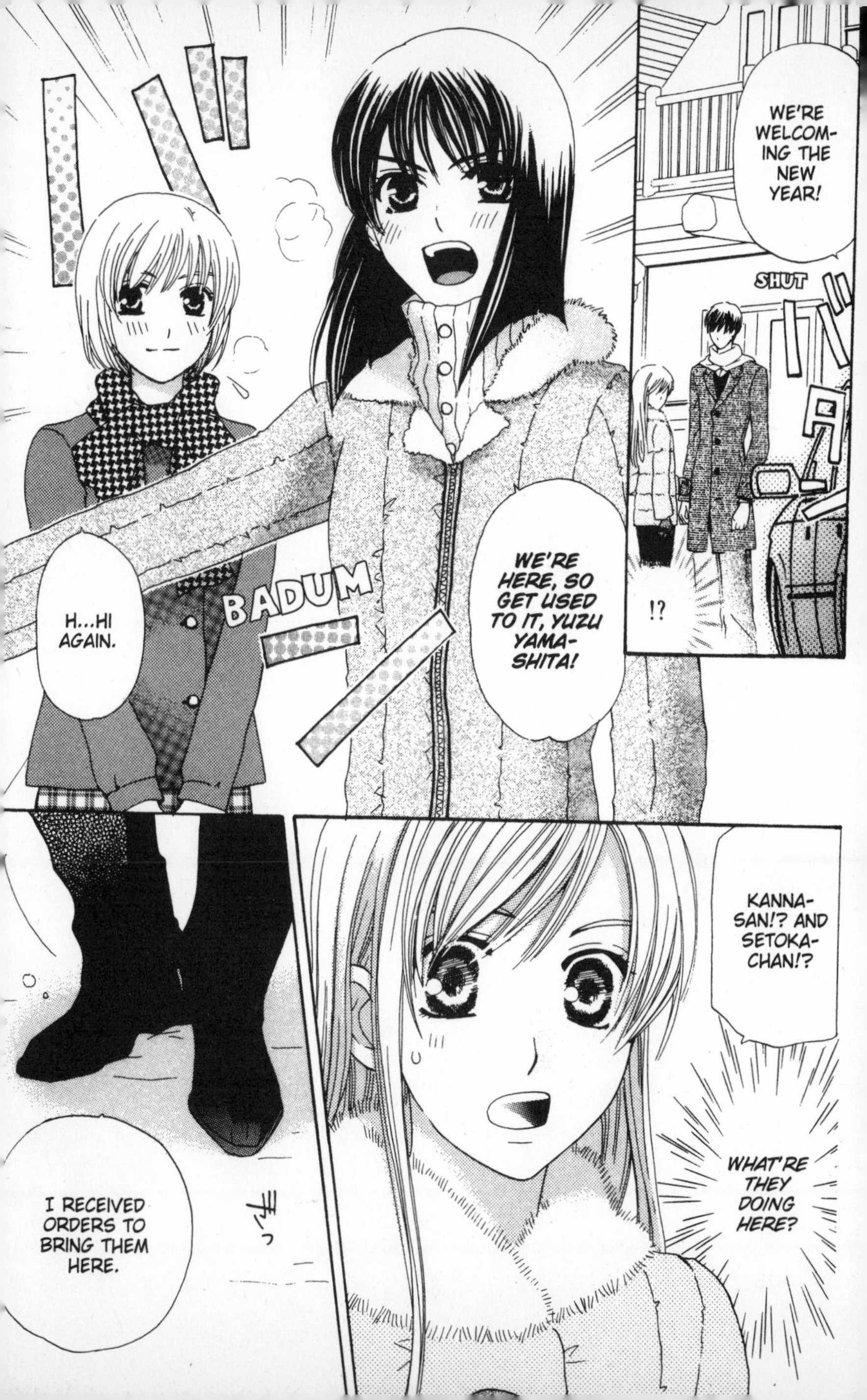
WE'RE WELCOMING THE NEW YEAR!
SHUT
!?
WE'RE HERE, SO GET USED TO IT, YUZU YAMASHITA!
BADUM
H...HI AGAIN.
KANNA-SAN!? AND SETOKA-CHAN!?
WHAT'RE THEY DOING HERE?
I RECEIVED ORDERS TO BRING THEM HERE.

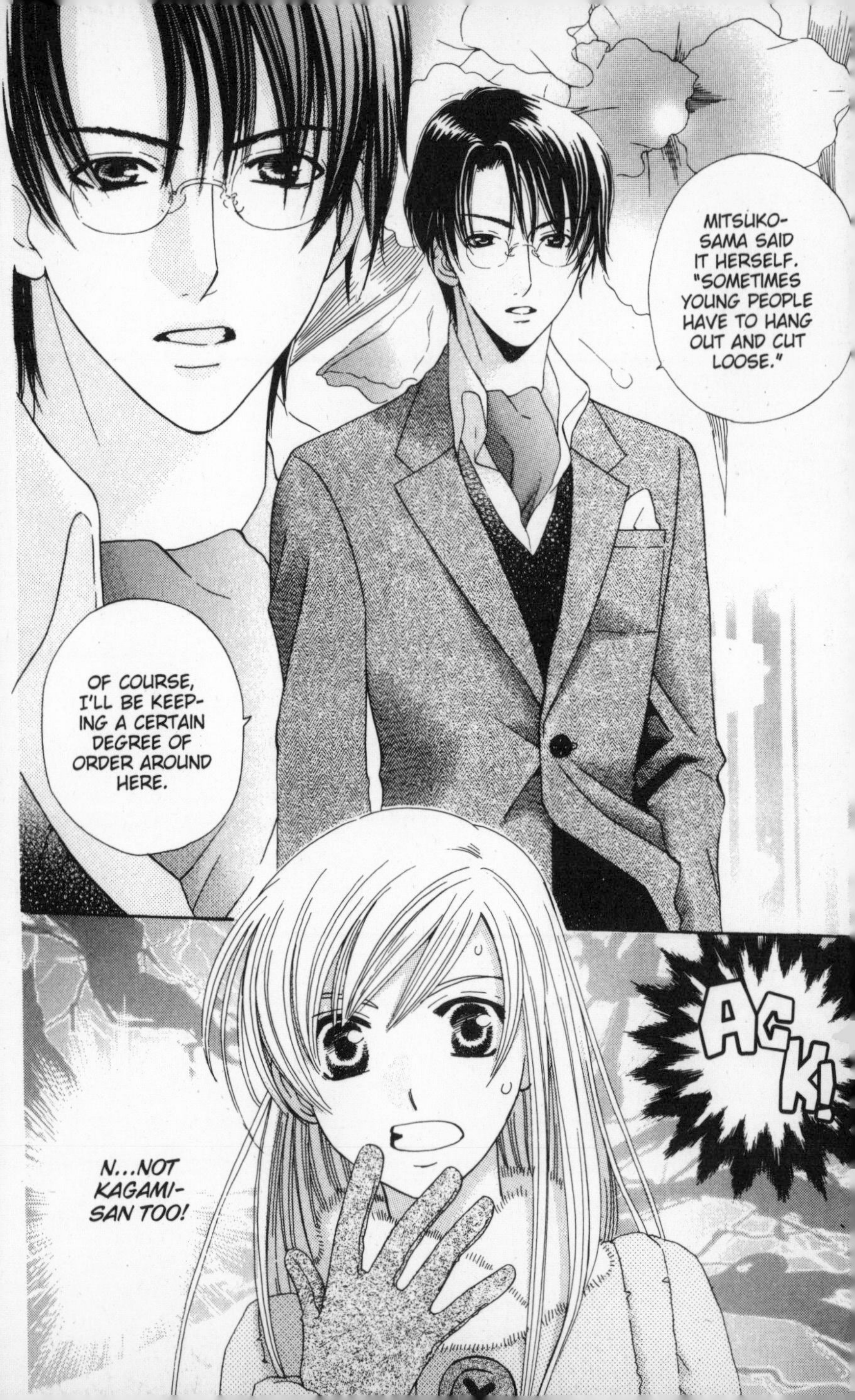
MITSUKO-SAMA SAID IT HERSELF. "SOMETIMES YOUNG PEOPLE HAVE TO HANG OUT AND CUT LOOSE."
OF COURSE, I'LL BE KEEPING A CERTAIN DEGREE OF ORDER AROUND HERE.
ACK!
N...NOT KAGAMI-SAN TOO!

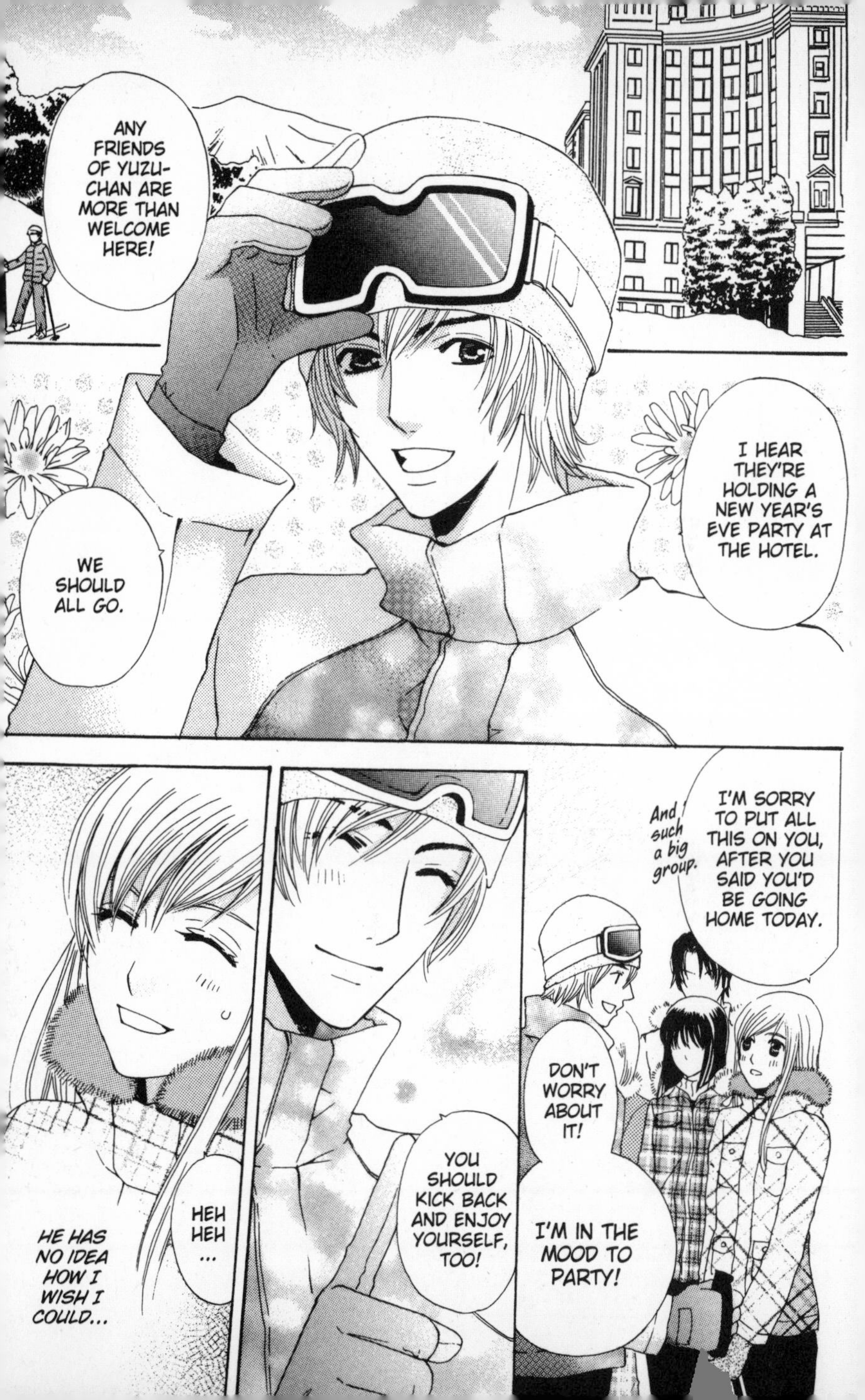
ANY FRIENDS OF YUZU-CHAN ARE MORE THAN WELCOME HERE!
I HEAR THEY'RE HOLDING A NEW YEAR'S EVE PARTY AT THE HOTEL.
WE SHOULD ALL GO.
I'M SORRY TO PUT ALL THIS ON YOU, AFTER YOU SAID YOU'D BE GOING HOME TODAY.
And such a big group.
DON'T WORRY ABOUT IT!
I'M IN THE MOOD TO PARTY!
YOU SHOULD KICK BACK AND ENJOY YOURSELF, TOO!
HEH HEH ...
HE HAS NO IDEA HOW I WISH I COULD...

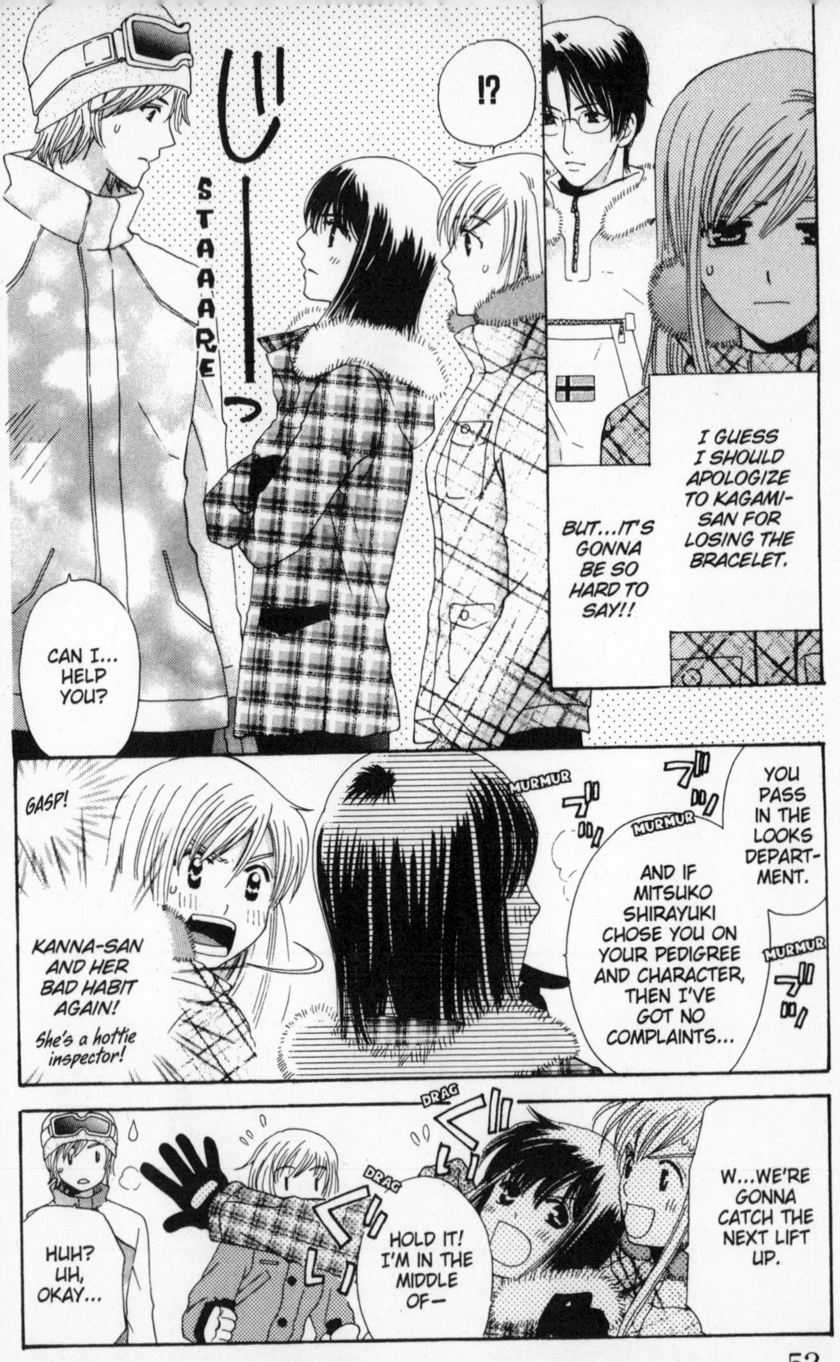
I GUESS I SHOULD APOLOGIZE TO KAGAMI-SAN FOR LOSING THE BRACELET.
BUT...IT'S GONNA BE SO HARD TO SAY!!
!?
STAAARE
CAN I... HELP YOU?
YOU PASS IN THE LOOKS DEPARTMENT.
MURMUR
MURMUR
MURMUR
AND IF MITSUKO SHIRAYUKI CHOSE YOU ON YOUR PEDIGREE AND CHARACTER, THEN I'VE GOT NO COMPLAINTS...
GASP!
KANNA-SAN AND HER BAD HABIT AGAIN!
She's a hottie inspector!
W...WE'RE GONNA CATCH THE NEXT LIFT UP.
DRAG
DRAG
HOLD IT! I'M IN THE MIDDLE OF—
HUH? UH, OKAY...

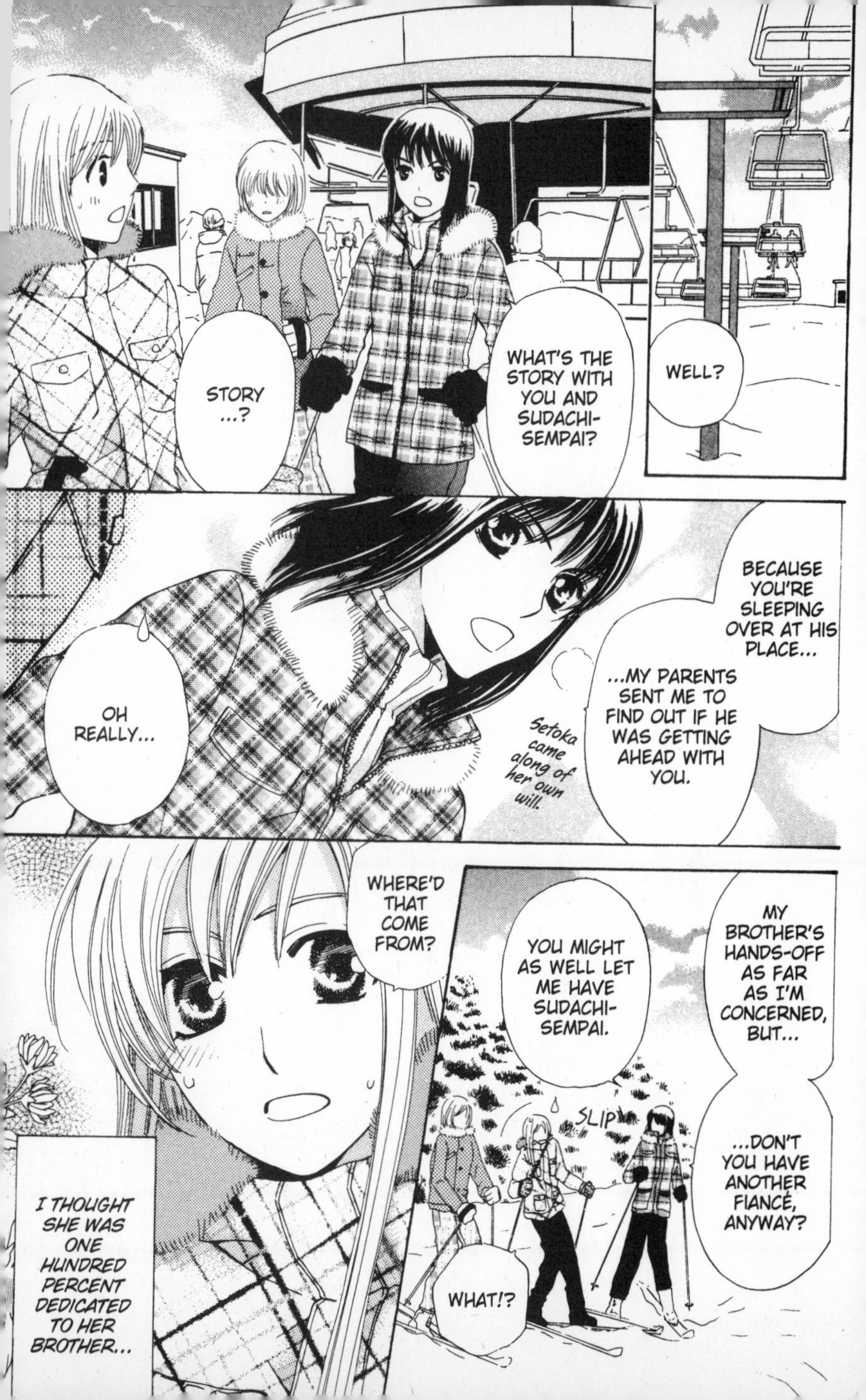
WELL?
WHAT'S THE STORY WITH YOU AND SUDACHI-SEMPAI?
STORY ...?
BECAUSE YOU'RE SLEEPING OVER AT HIS PLACE...
...MY PARENTS SENT ME TO FIND OUT IF HE WAS GETTING AHEAD WITH YOU.
Setoka came along of her own will.
OH REALLY...
MY BROTHER'S HANDS-OFF AS FAR AS I'M CONCERNED, BUT...
...DON'T YOU HAVE ANOTHER FIANCÉ, ANYWAY?
YOU MIGHT AS WELL LET ME HAVE SUDACHI-SEMPAI.
SLIP
WHAT!?
WHERE'D THAT COME FROM?
I THOUGHT SHE WAS ONE HUNDRED PERCENT DEDICATED TO HER BROTHER...

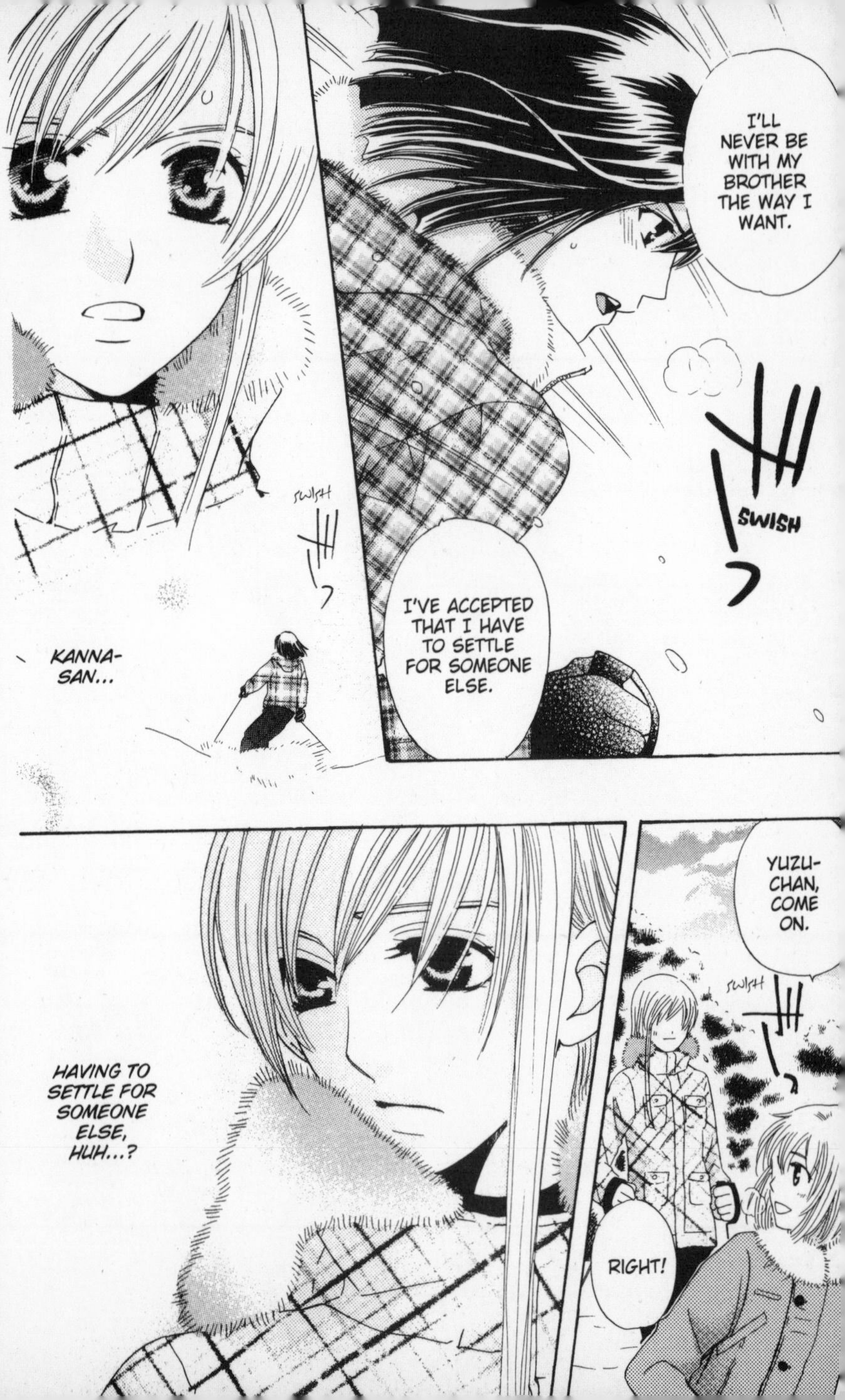
I'LL NEVER BE WITH MY BROTHER THE WAY I WANT.
SWISH
I'VE ACCEPTED THAT I HAVE TO SETTLE FOR SOMEONE ELSE.
SWISH
KANNA-SAN...
YUZU-CHAN, COME ON.
SWISH
RIGHT!
HAVING TO SETTLE FOR SOMEONE ELSE, HUH...?

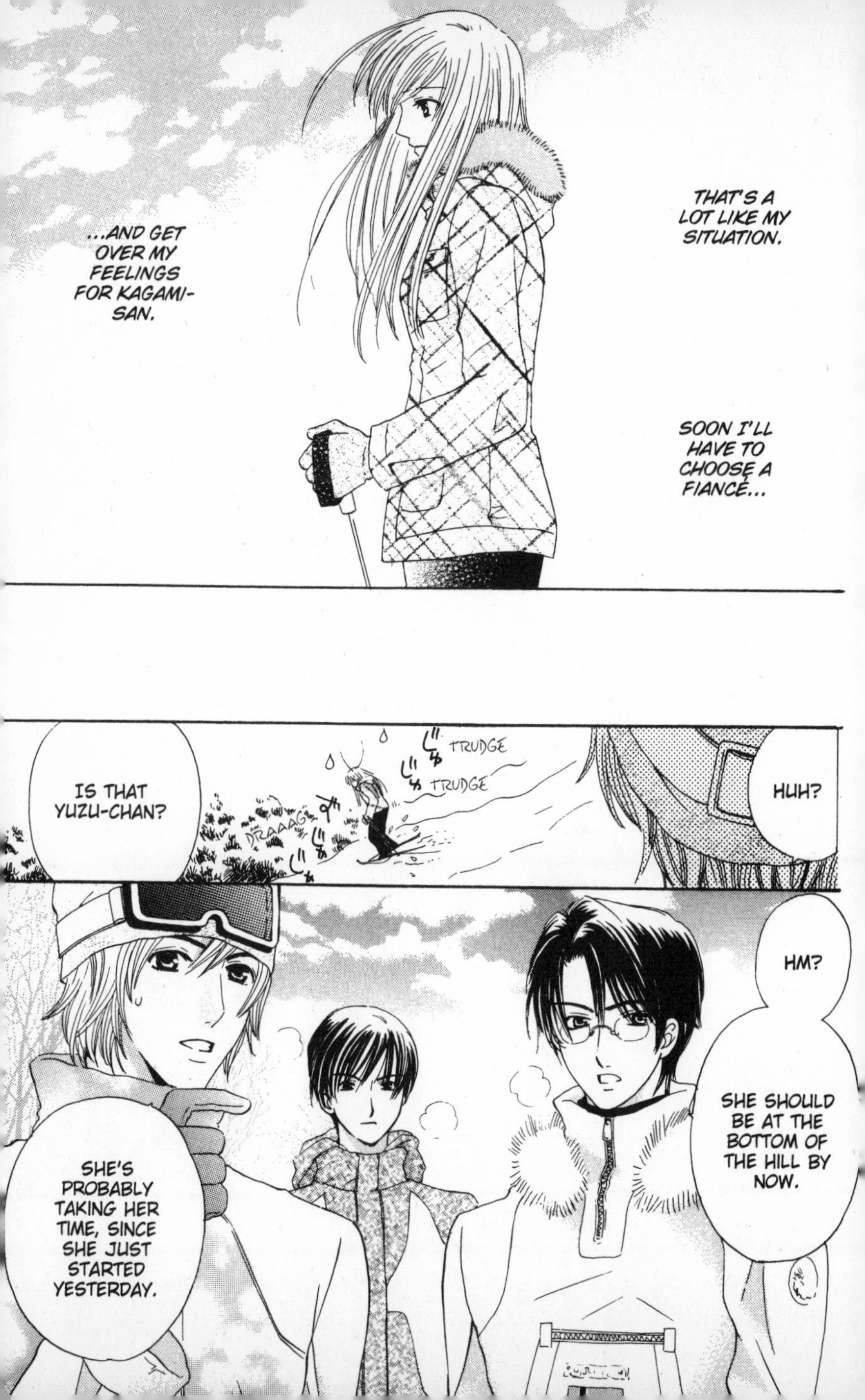
THAT'S A LOT LIKE MY SITUATION.
SOON I'LL HAVE TO CHOOSE A FIANCÉ...
...AND GET OVER MY FEELINGS FOR KAGAMI-SAN.
HUH?
TRUDGE
TRUDGE
DRAAAG
IS THAT YUZU-CHAN?
HM?
SHE SHOULD BE AT THE BOTTOM OF THE HILL BY NOW.
SHE'S PROBABLY TAKING HER TIME, SINCE SHE JUST STARTED YESTERDAY.

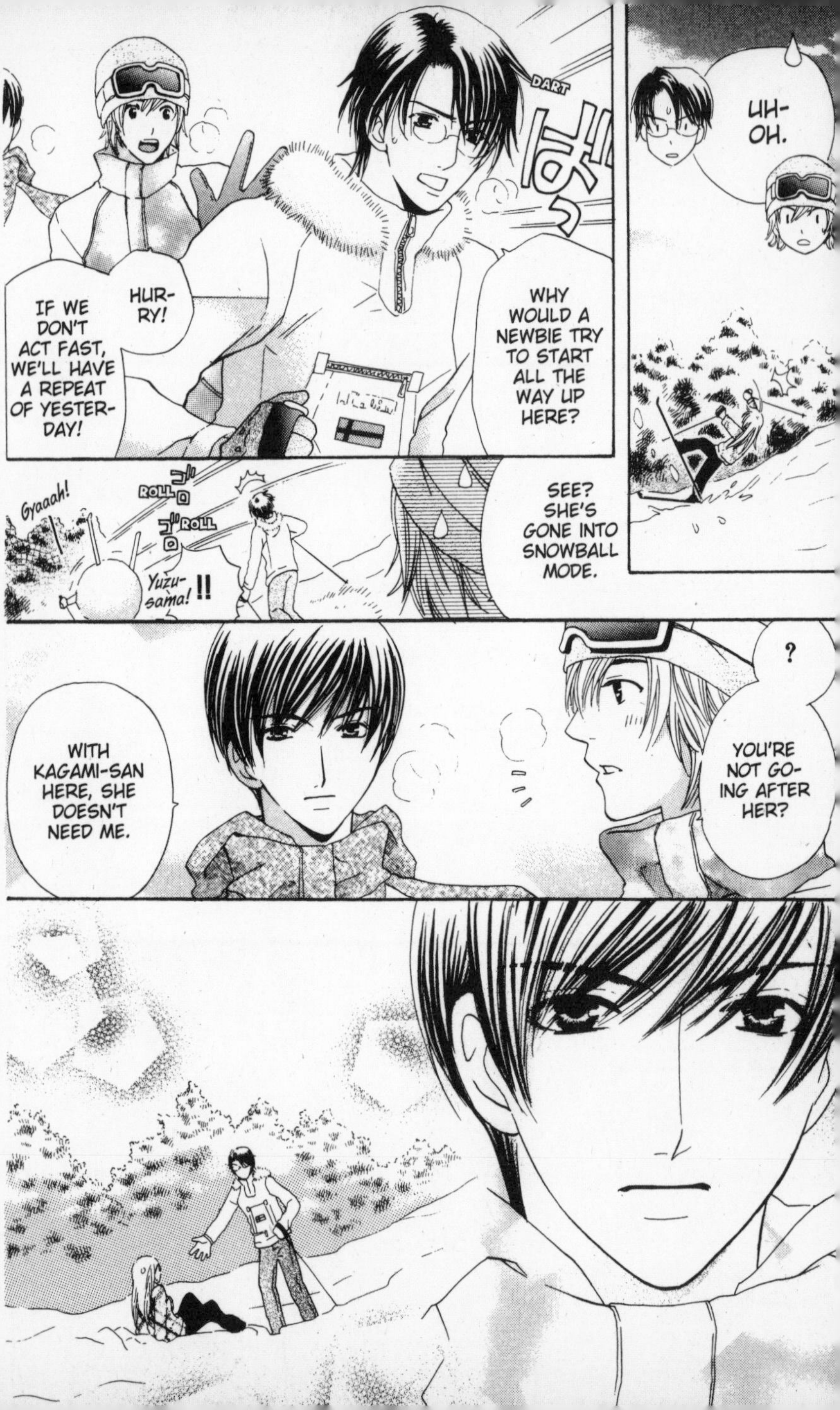

UH-OH.
DART
はっ
WHY WOULD A NEWBIE TRY TO START ALL THE WAY UP HERE?
HURRY!
IF WE DON'T ACT FAST, WE'LL HAVE A REPEAT OF YESTERDAY!
SEE? SHE'S GONE INTO SNOWBALL MODE.
Yuzu-sama! !!
ROLL
ROLL
Gyaaah!
?
YOU'RE NOT GOING AFTER HER?
WITH KAGAMI-SAN HERE, SHE DOESN'T NEED ME.

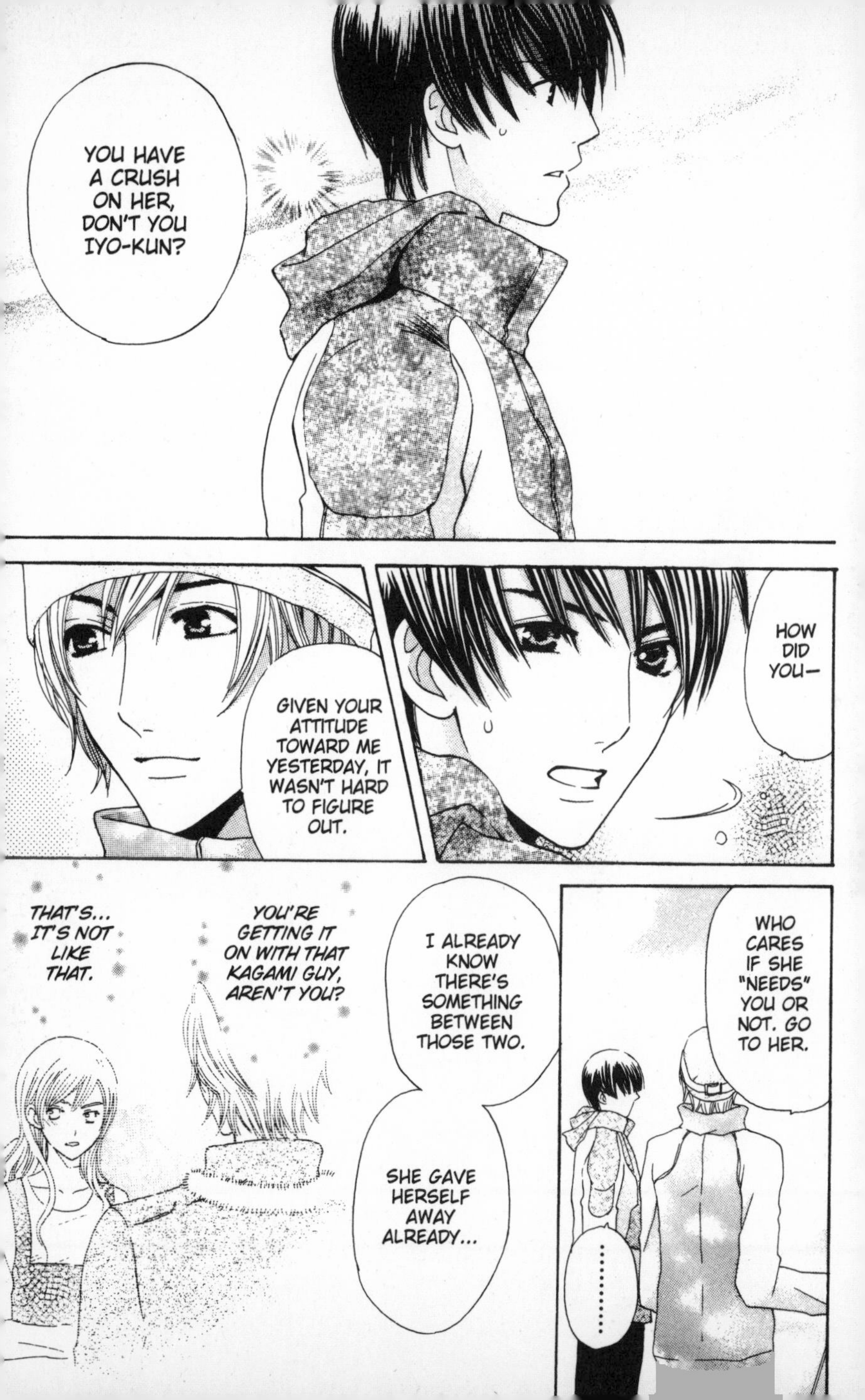
YOU HAVE A CRUSH ON HER, DON'T YOU IYO-KUN?
HOW DID YOU—
GIVEN YOUR ATTITUDE TOWARD ME YESTERDAY, IT WASN'T HARD TO FIGURE OUT.
WHO CARES IF SHE "NEEDS" YOU OR NOT. GO TO HER.
......
I ALREADY KNOW THERE'S SOMETHING BETWEEN THOSE TWO.
SHE GAVE HERSELF AWAY ALREADY...
YOU'RE GETTING IT ON WITH THAT KAGAMI GUY, AREN'T YOU?
THAT'S... IT'S NOT LIKE THAT.

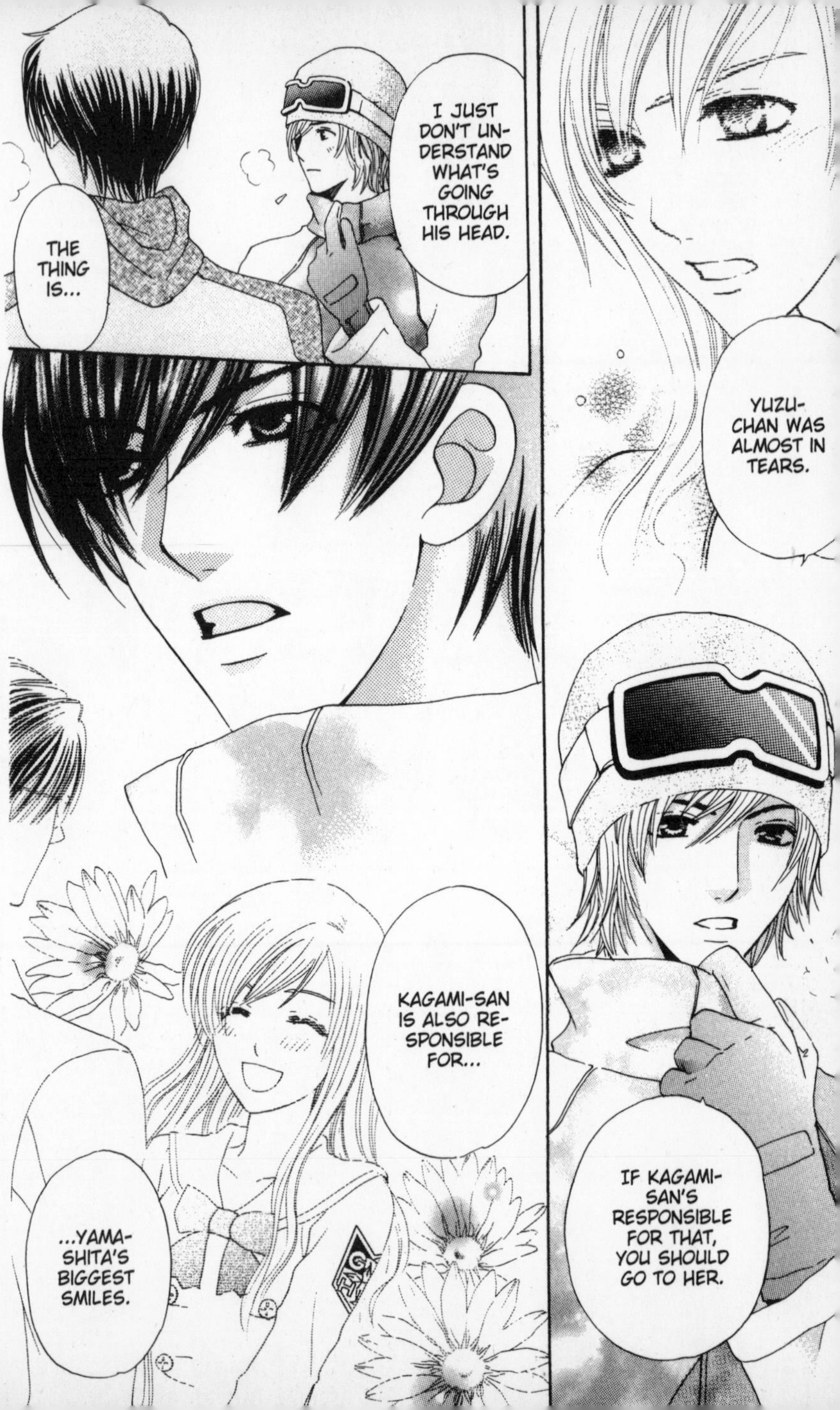
YUZU-CHAN WAS ALMOST IN TEARS.
IF KAGAMI-SAN'S RESPONSIBLE FOR THAT, YOU SHOULD GO TO HER.
I JUST DON'T UNDERSTAND WHAT'S GOING THROUGH HIS HEAD.
THE THING IS...
KAGAMI-SAN IS ALSO RESPONSIBLE FOR...
...YAMASHITA'S BIGGEST SMILES.

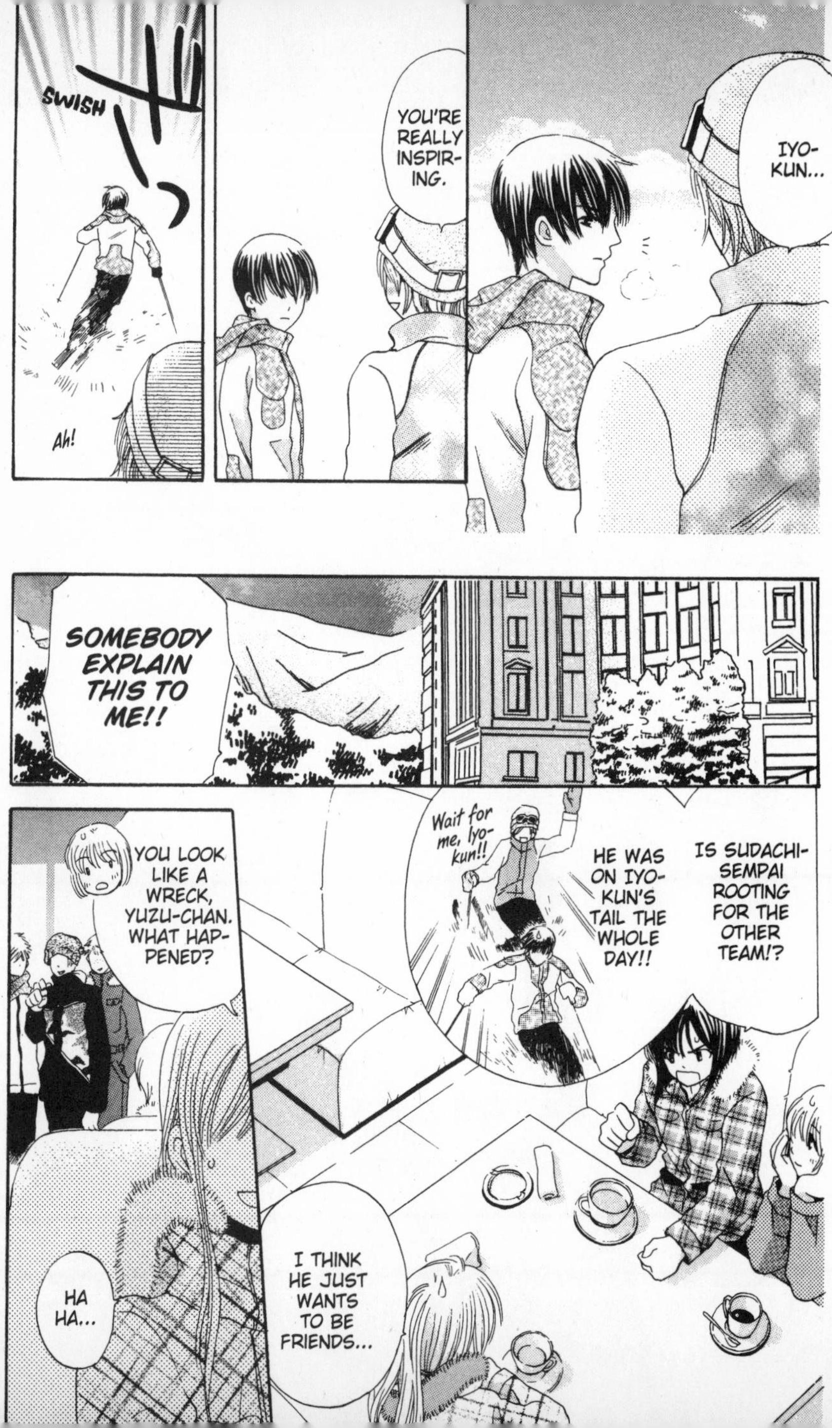
IYO-KUN...
YOU'RE REALLY INSPIRING.
SWISH
Ah!
SOMEBODY EXPLAIN THIS TO ME!!
IS SUDACHI-SEMPAI ROOTING FOR THE OTHER TEAM!?
HE WAS ON IYO-KUN'S TAIL THE WHOLE DAY!!
Wait for me, Iyo-kun!!
YOU LOOK LIKE A WRECK, YUZU-CHAN. WHAT HAPPENED?
I THINK HE JUST WANTS TO BE FRIENDS...
HA HA...

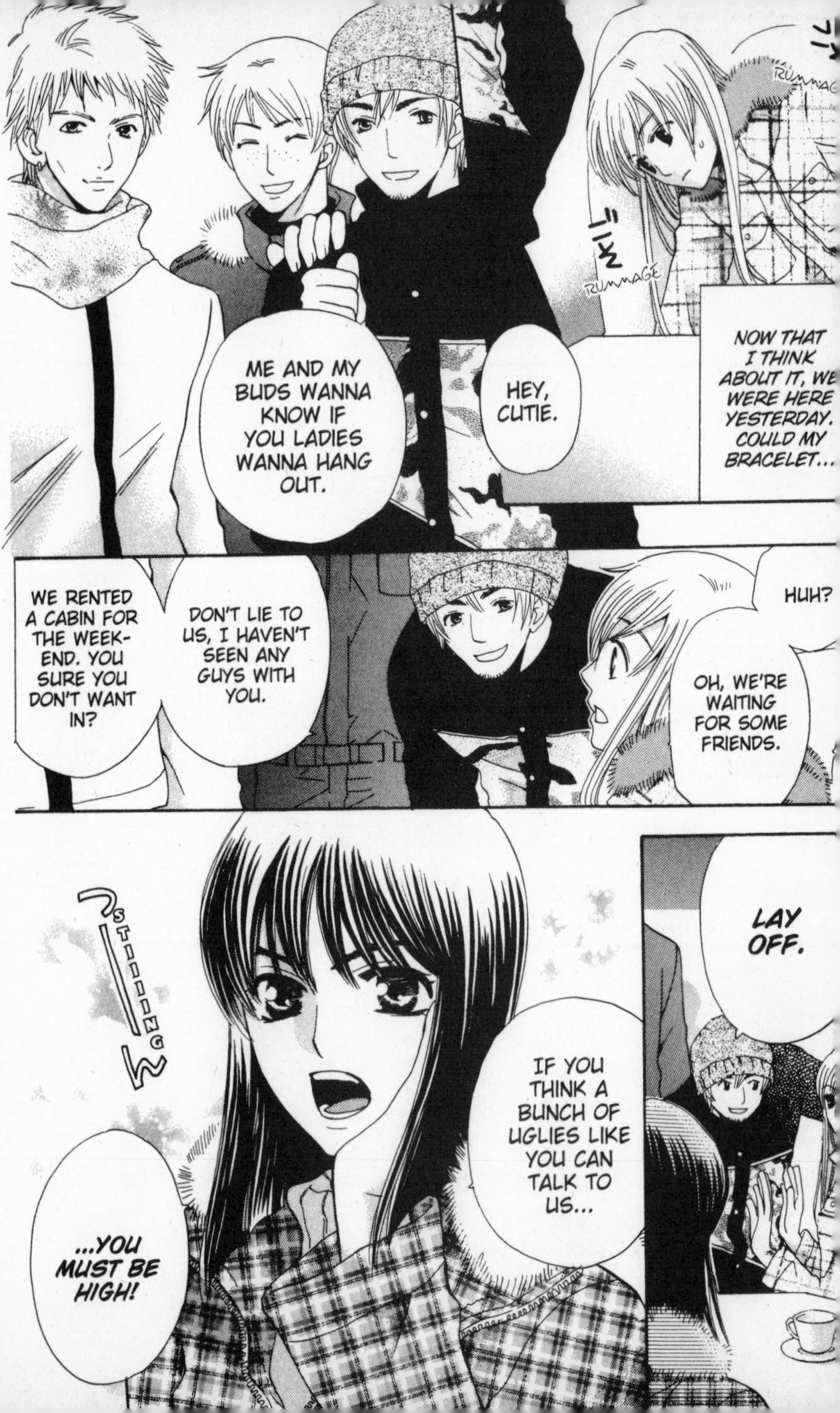
RUMMAGE
RUMMAGE
NOW THAT I THINK ABOUT IT, WE WERE HERE YESTERDAY. COULD MY BRACELET...
HEY, CUTIE.
ME AND MY BUDS WANNA KNOW IF YOU LADIES WANNA HANG OUT.
HUH?
OH, WE'RE WAITING FOR SOME FRIENDS.
DON'T LIE TO US, I HAVEN'T SEEN ANY GUYS WITH YOU.
WE RENTED A CABIN FOR THE WEEK-END. YOU SURE YOU DON'T WANT IN?
LAY OFF.
IF YOU THINK A BUNCH OF UGLIES LIKE YOU CAN TALK TO US...
STIIIING
...YOU MUST BE HIGH!

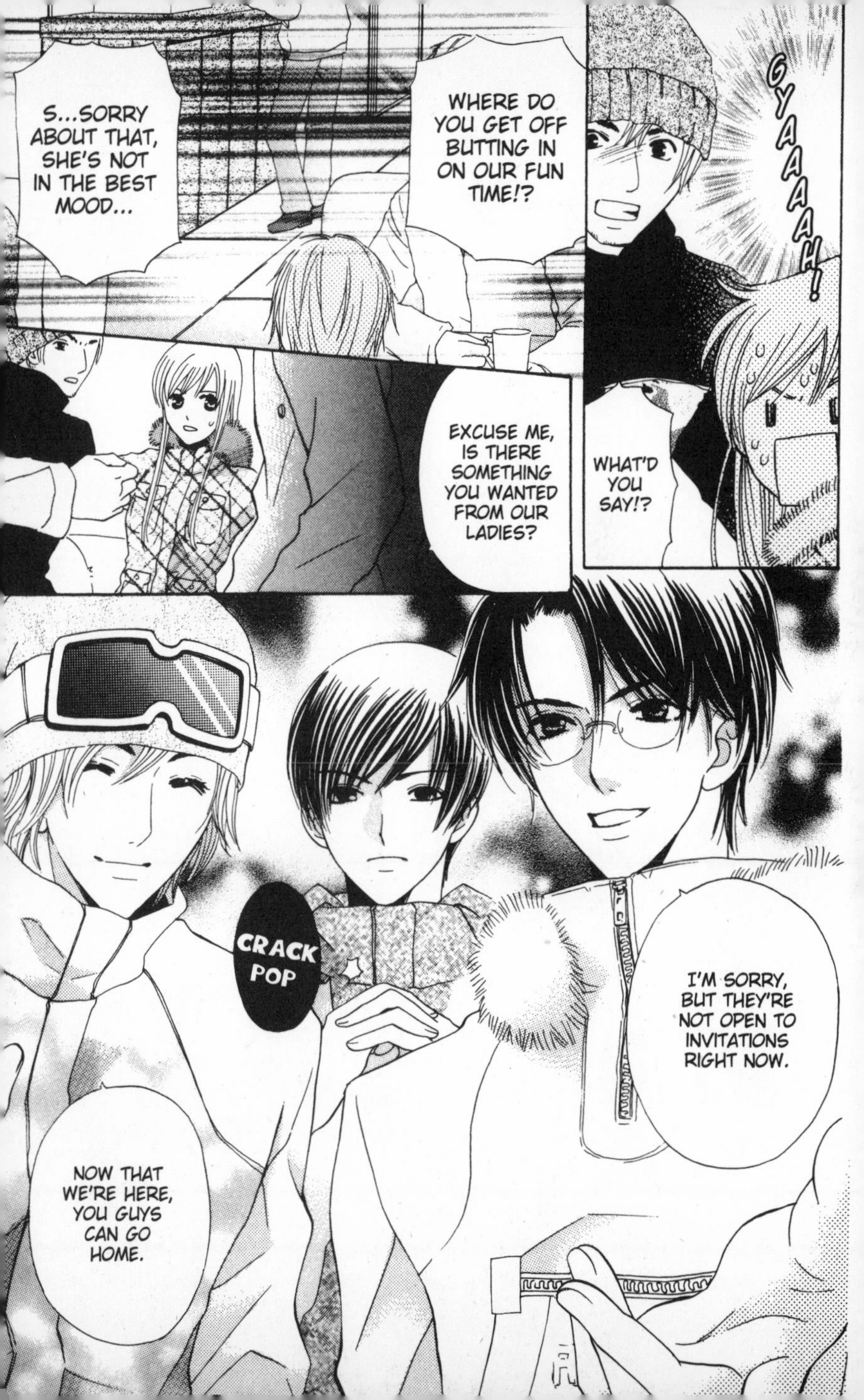
GYAAAAAH!
WHERE DO YOU GET OFF BUTTING IN ON OUR FUN TIME!?
S...SORRY ABOUT THAT, SHE'S NOT IN THE BEST MOOD...
WHAT'D YOU SAY!?
EXCUSE ME, IS THERE SOMETHING YOU WANTED FROM OUR LADIES?
I'M SORRY, BUT THEY'RE NOT OPEN TO INVITATIONS RIGHT NOW.
CRACK POP
NOW THAT WE'RE HERE, YOU GUYS CAN GO HOME.

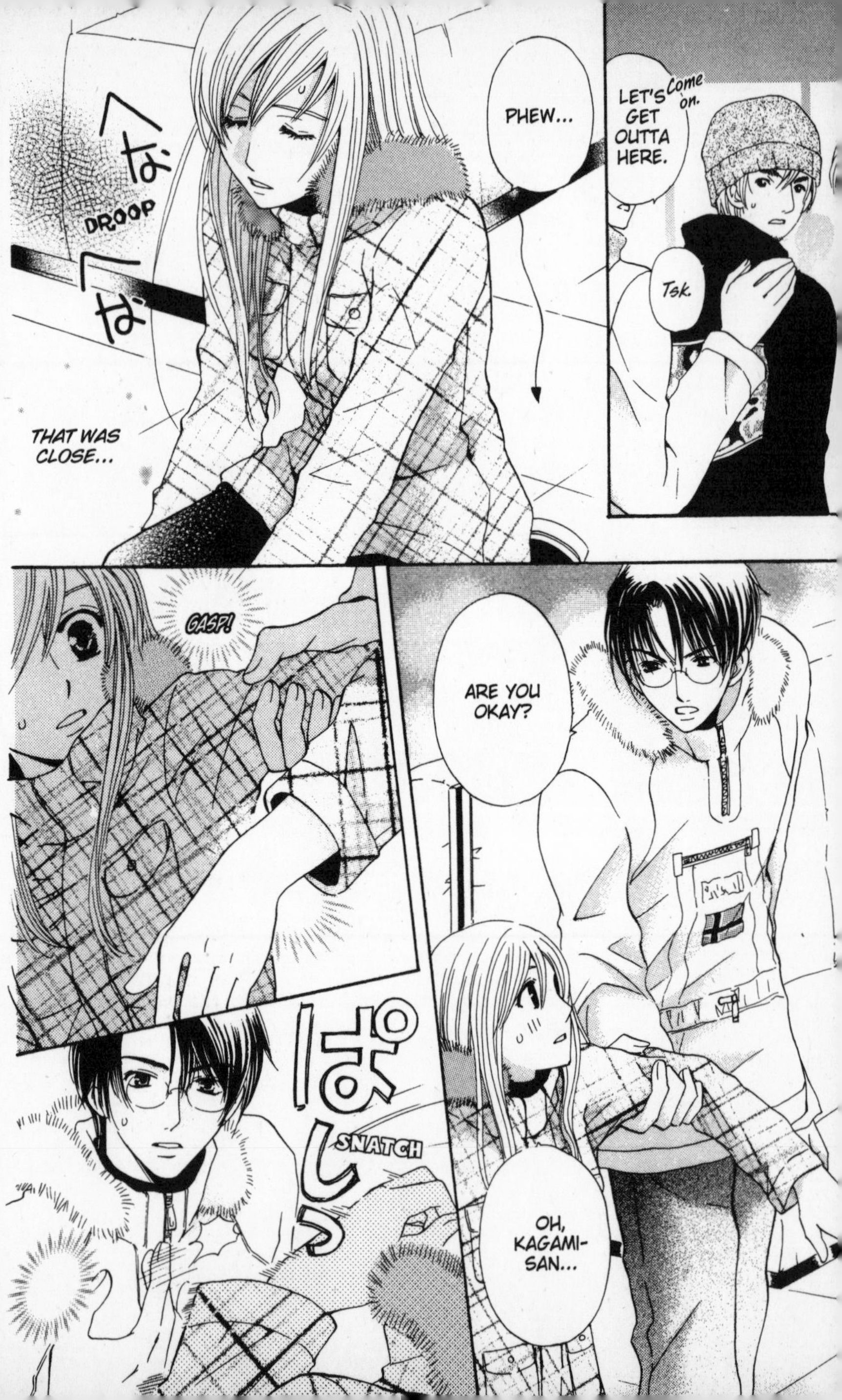
LET'S GET OUTTA HERE.
Come on.
Tsk.
PHEW...
へなへな
DROOP
THAT WAS CLOSE...
ARE YOU OKAY?
OH, KAGAMI-SAN...
GASP!
ぱしっ
SNATCH

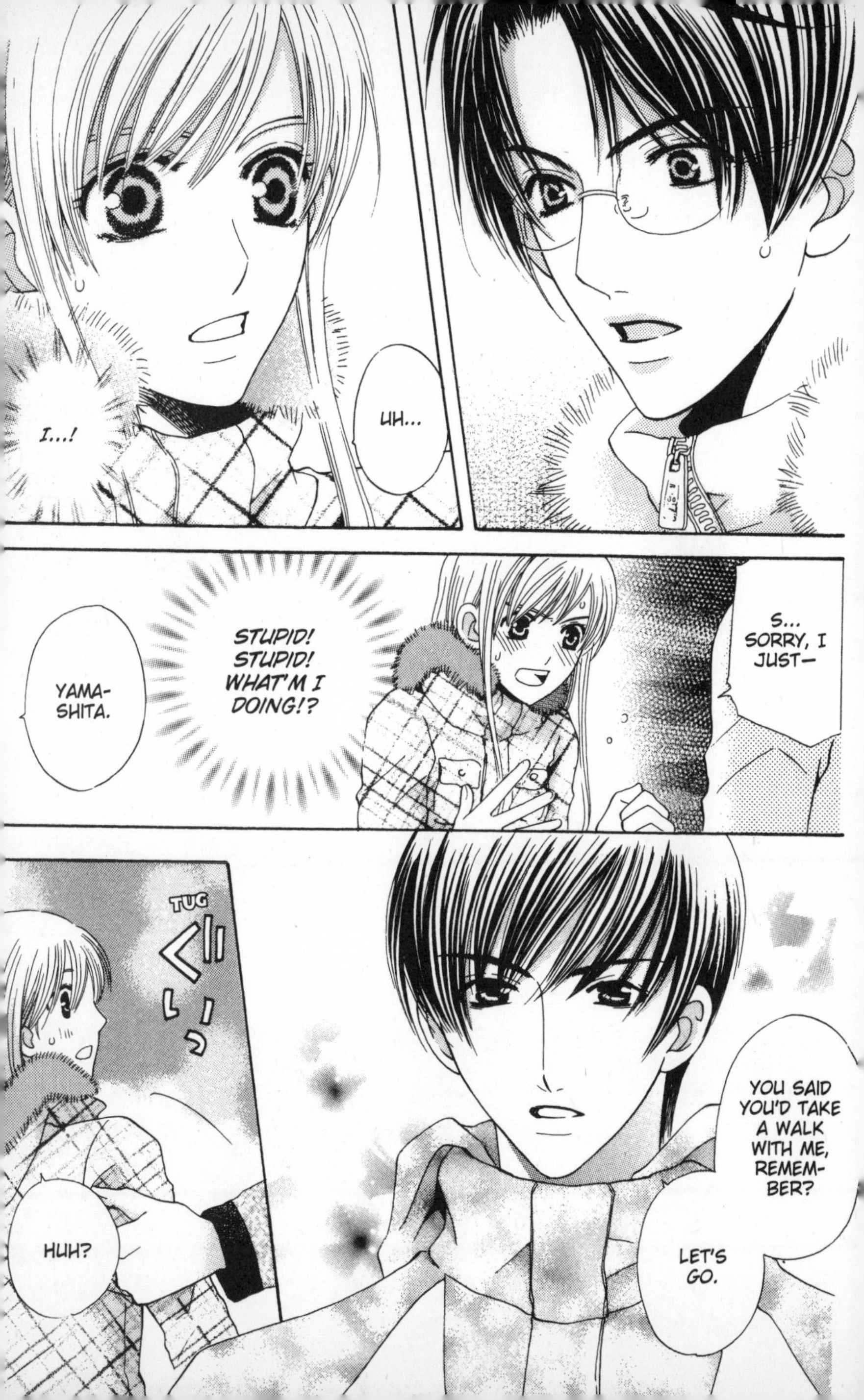
UH...
I...!
S... SORRY, I JUST—
STUPID! STUPID! WHAT'M I DOING!?
YAMA-SHITA.
YOU SAID YOU'D TAKE A WALK WITH ME, REMEMBER?
LET'S GO.
TUG
HUH?

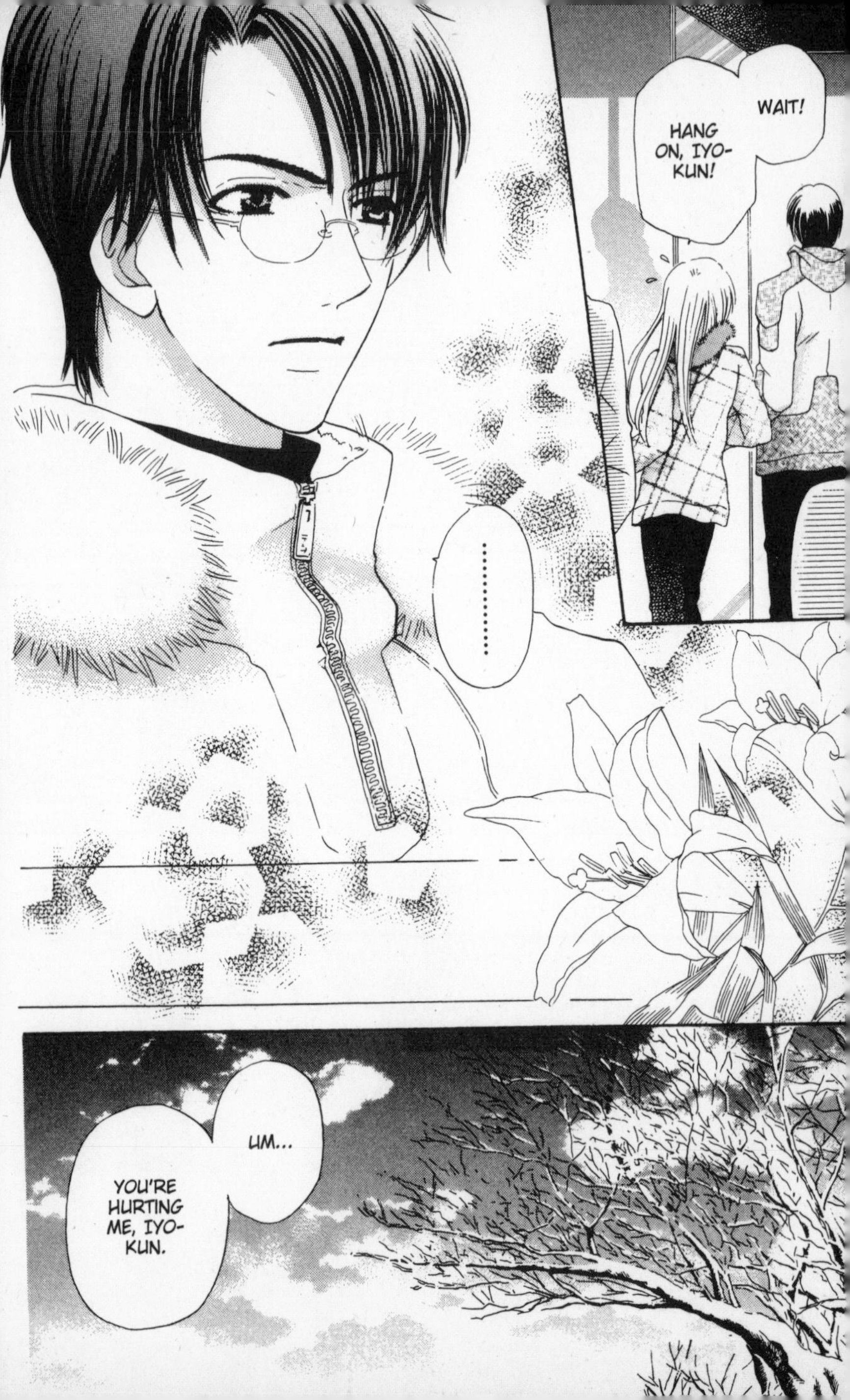
WAIT!
HANG ON, IYO-KUN!
......
UM...
YOU'RE HURTING ME, IYO-KUN.

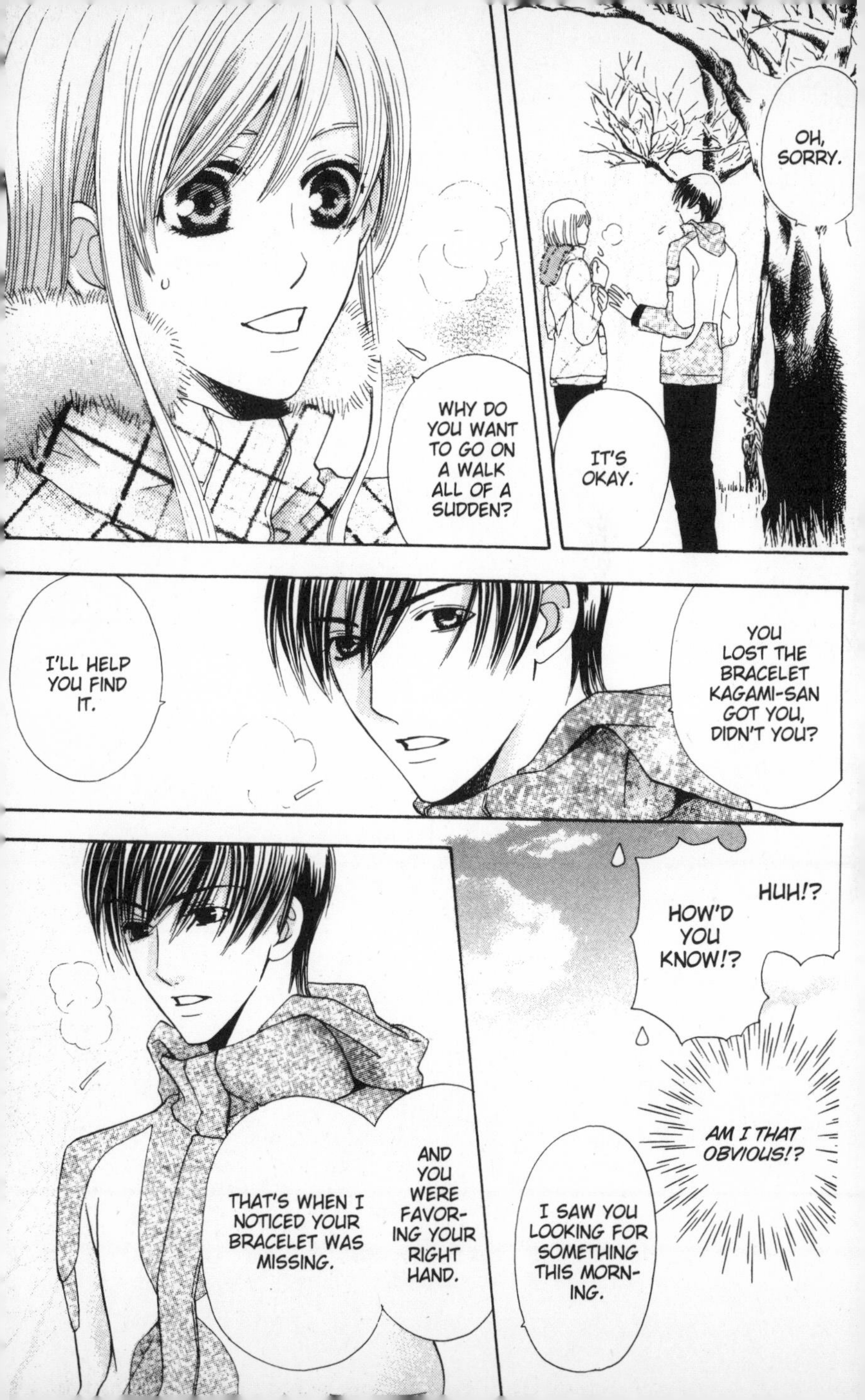
OH, SORRY.
IT'S OKAY.
WHY DO YOU WANT TO GO ON A WALK ALL OF A SUDDEN?
YOU LOST THE BRACELET KAGAMI-SAN GOT YOU, DIDN'T YOU?
I'LL HELP YOU FIND IT.
HUH!? HOW'D YOU KNOW!?
AM I THAT OBVIOUS!?
I SAW YOU LOOKING FOR SOMETHING THIS MORN-ING.
AND YOU WERE FAVOR-ING YOUR RIGHT HAND.
THAT'S WHEN I NOTICED YOUR BRACELET WAS MISSING.

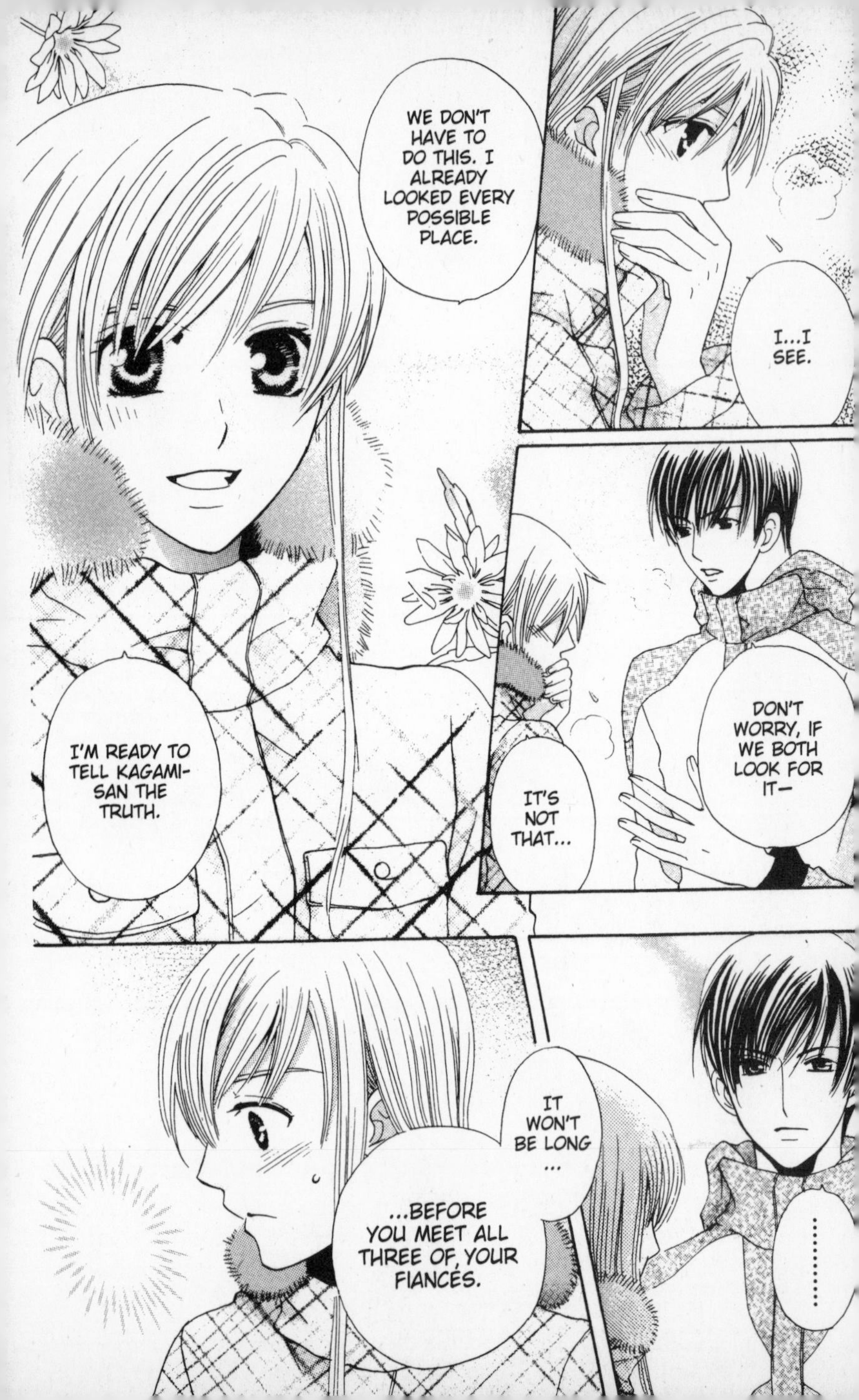

WE DON'T HAVE TO DO THIS. I ALREADY LOOKED EVERY POSSIBLE PLACE.
I...I SEE.
DON'T WORRY, IF WE BOTH LOOK FOR IT—
IT'S NOT THAT...
I'M READY TO TELL KAGAMI-SAN THE TRUTH.
....
IT WON'T BE LONG ...
...BEFORE YOU MEET ALL THREE OF, YOUR FIANCES.

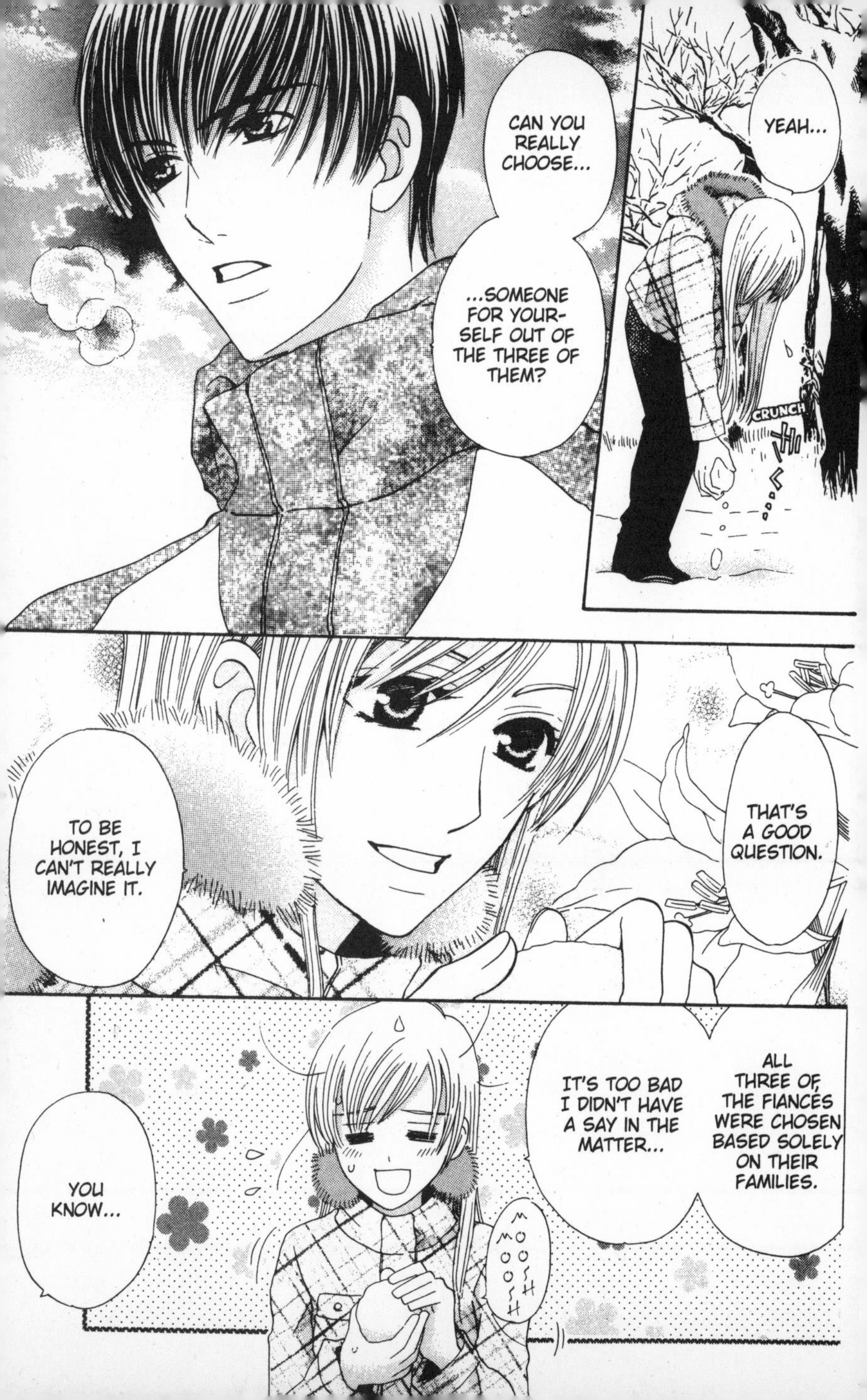
YEAH...
CRUNCH
CAN YOU REALLY CHOOSE...
...SOMEONE FOR YOUR-SELF OUT OF THE THREE OF THEM?
THAT'S A GOOD QUESTION.
TO BE HONEST, I CAN'T REALLY IMAGINE IT.
ALL THREE OF THE FIANCES WERE CHOSEN BASED SOLELY ON THEIR FAMILIES.
IT'S TOO BAD I DIDN'T HAVE A SAY IN THE MATTER...
MOOOOSH
YOU KNOW...

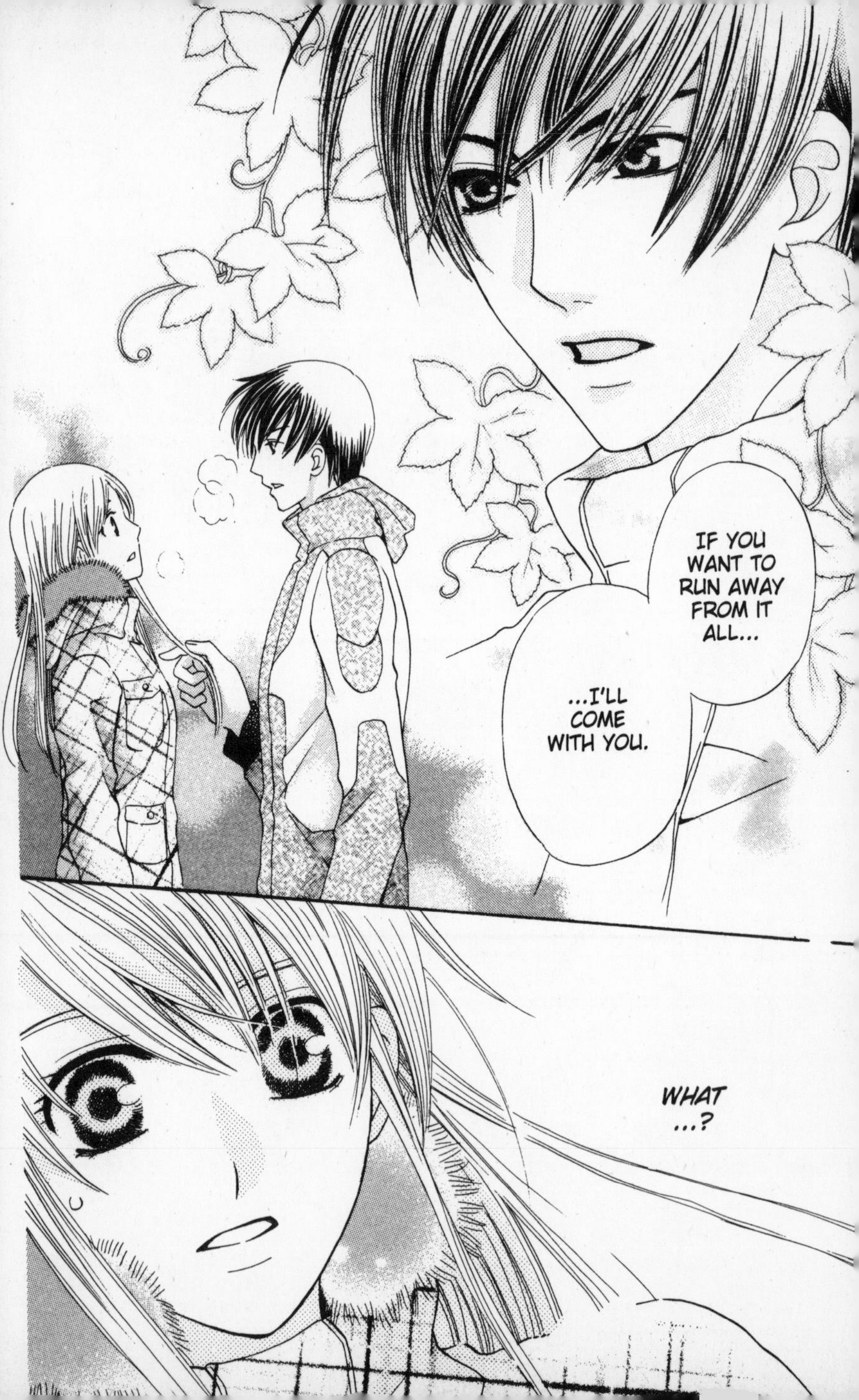
IF YOU WANT TO RUN AWAY FROM IT ALL...
...I'LL COME WITH YOU.
WHAT ...?

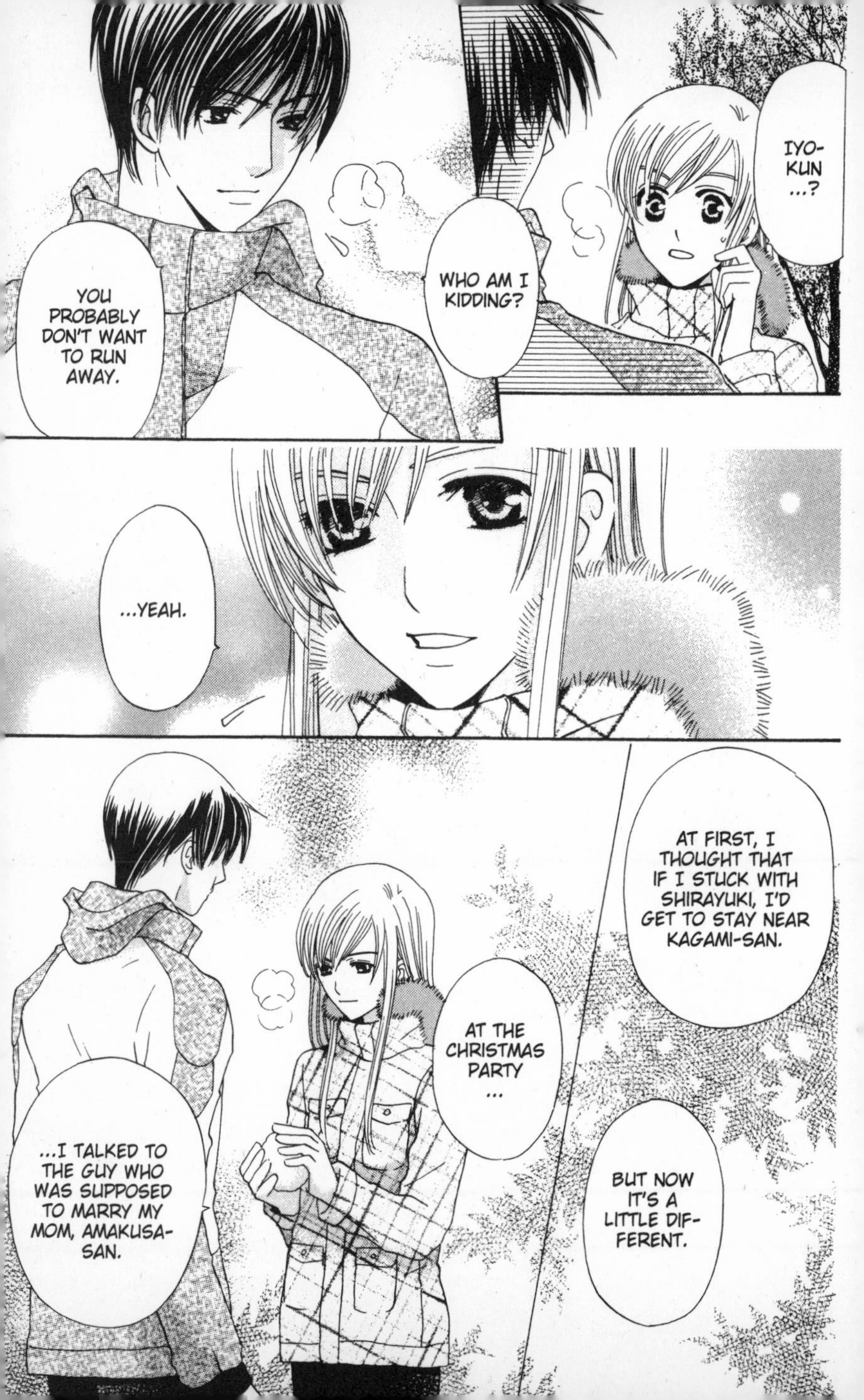
IYO-KUN ...?
WHO AM I KIDDING?
YOU PROBABLY DON'T WANT TO RUN AWAY.
...YEAH.
AT FIRST, I THOUGHT THAT IF I STUCK WITH SHIRAYUKI, I'D GET TO STAY NEAR KAGAMI-SAN.
BUT NOW IT'S A LITTLE DIF-FERENT.
AT THE CHRISTMAS PARTY ...
...I TALKED TO THE GUY WHO WAS SUPPOSED TO MARRY MY MOM, AMAKUSA-SAN.

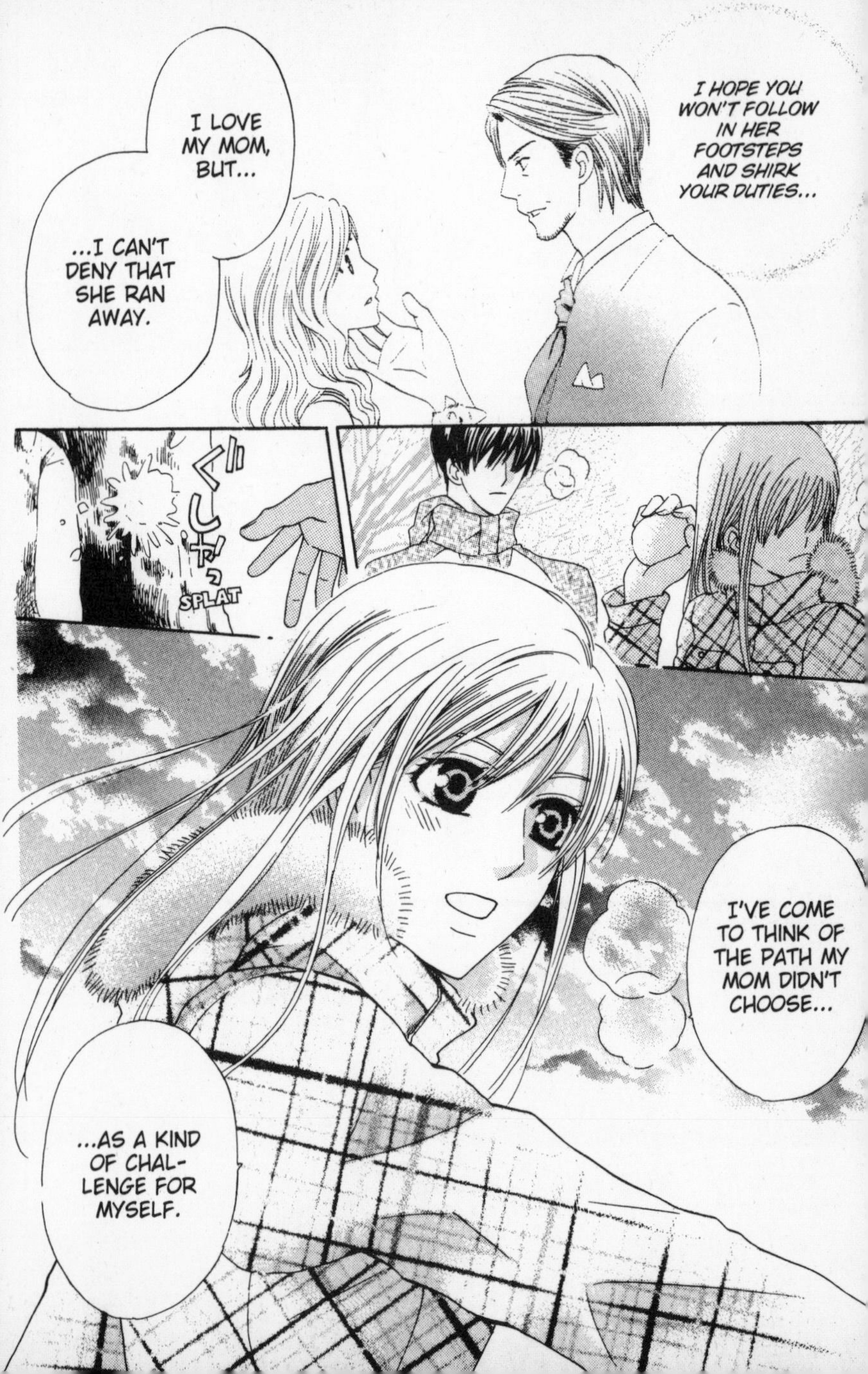
I HOPE YOU WON'T FOLLOW IN HER FOOTSTEPS AND SHIRK YOUR DUTIES...
I LOVE MY MOM, BUT...
...I CAN'T DENY THAT SHE RAN AWAY.
ぐしゃっ
SPLAT
I'VE COME TO THINK OF THE PATH MY MOM DIDN'T CHOOSE...
...AS A KIND OF CHAL-LENGE FOR MYSELF.

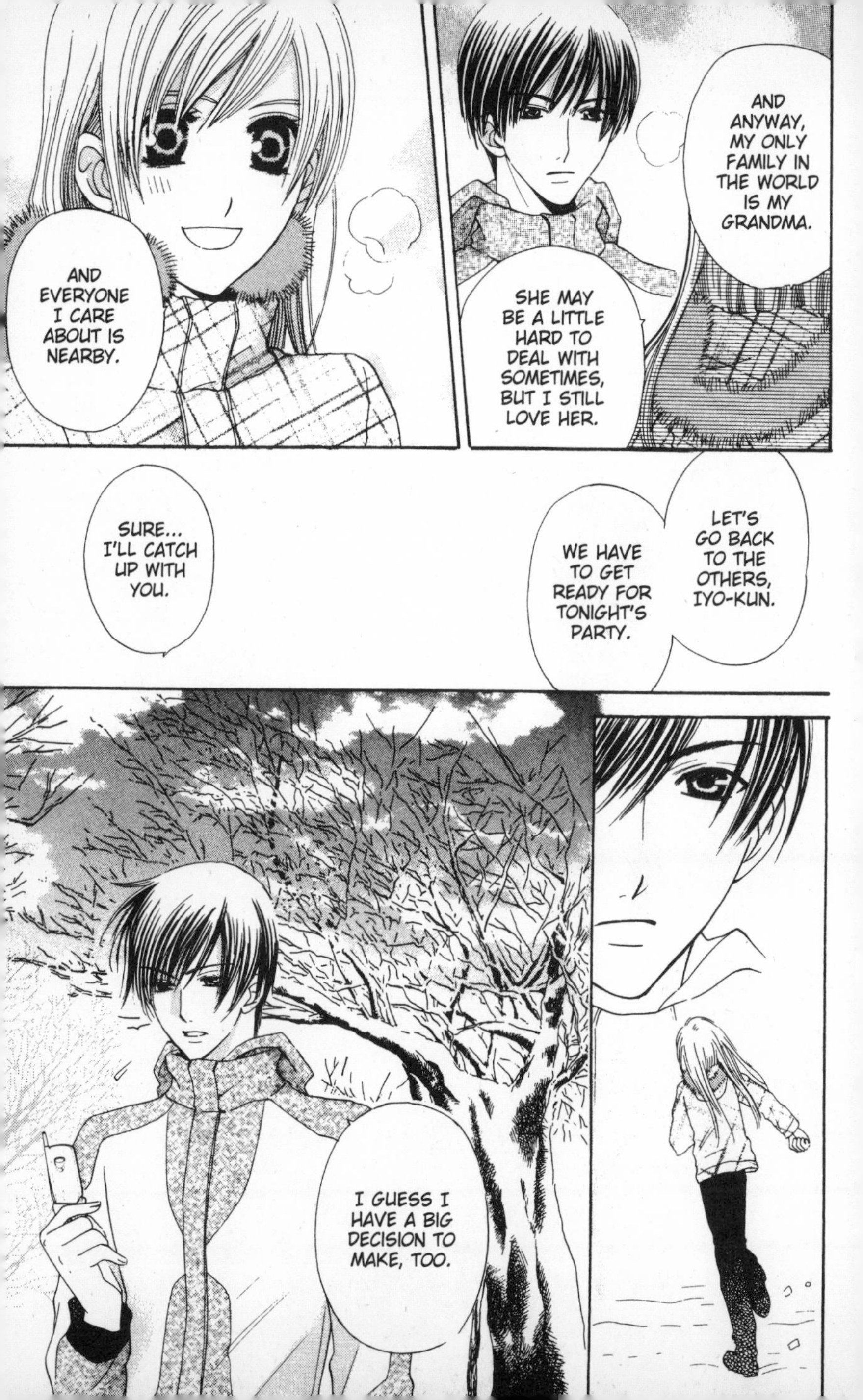
AND ANYWAY, MY ONLY FAMILY IN THE WORLD IS MY GRANDMA.
SHE MAY BE A LITTLE HARD TO DEAL WITH SOMETIMES, BUT I STILL LOVE HER.
AND EVERYONE I CARE ABOUT IS NEARBY.
LET'S GO BACK TO THE OTHERS, IYO-KUN.
WE HAVE TO GET READY FOR TONIGHT'S PARTY.
SURE... I'LL CATCH UP WITH YOU.
I GUESS I HAVE A BIG DECISION TO MAKE, TOO.

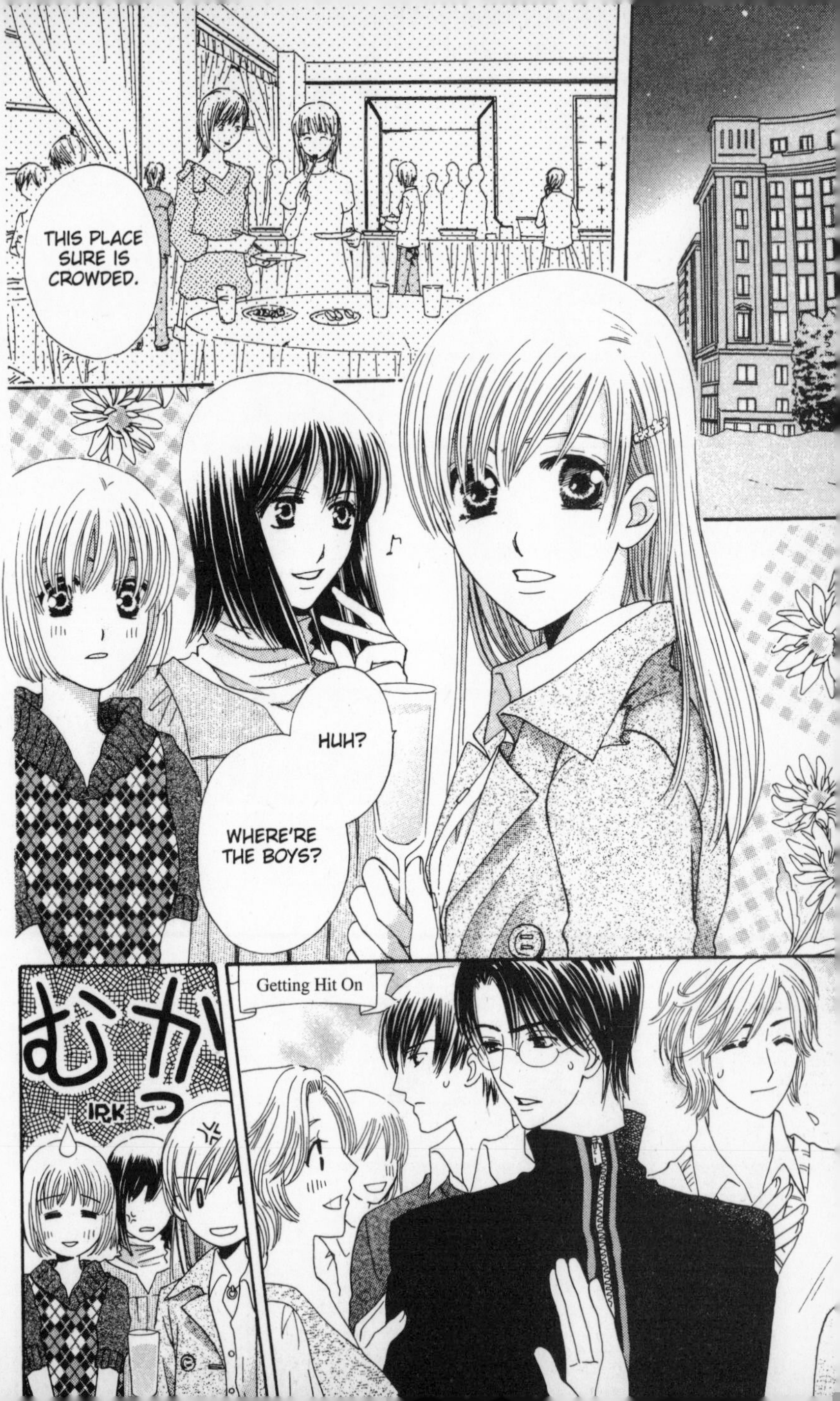
THIS PLACE SURE IS CROWDED.
HUH?
WHERE'RE THE BOYS?
Getting Hit On
むかっ
IRK

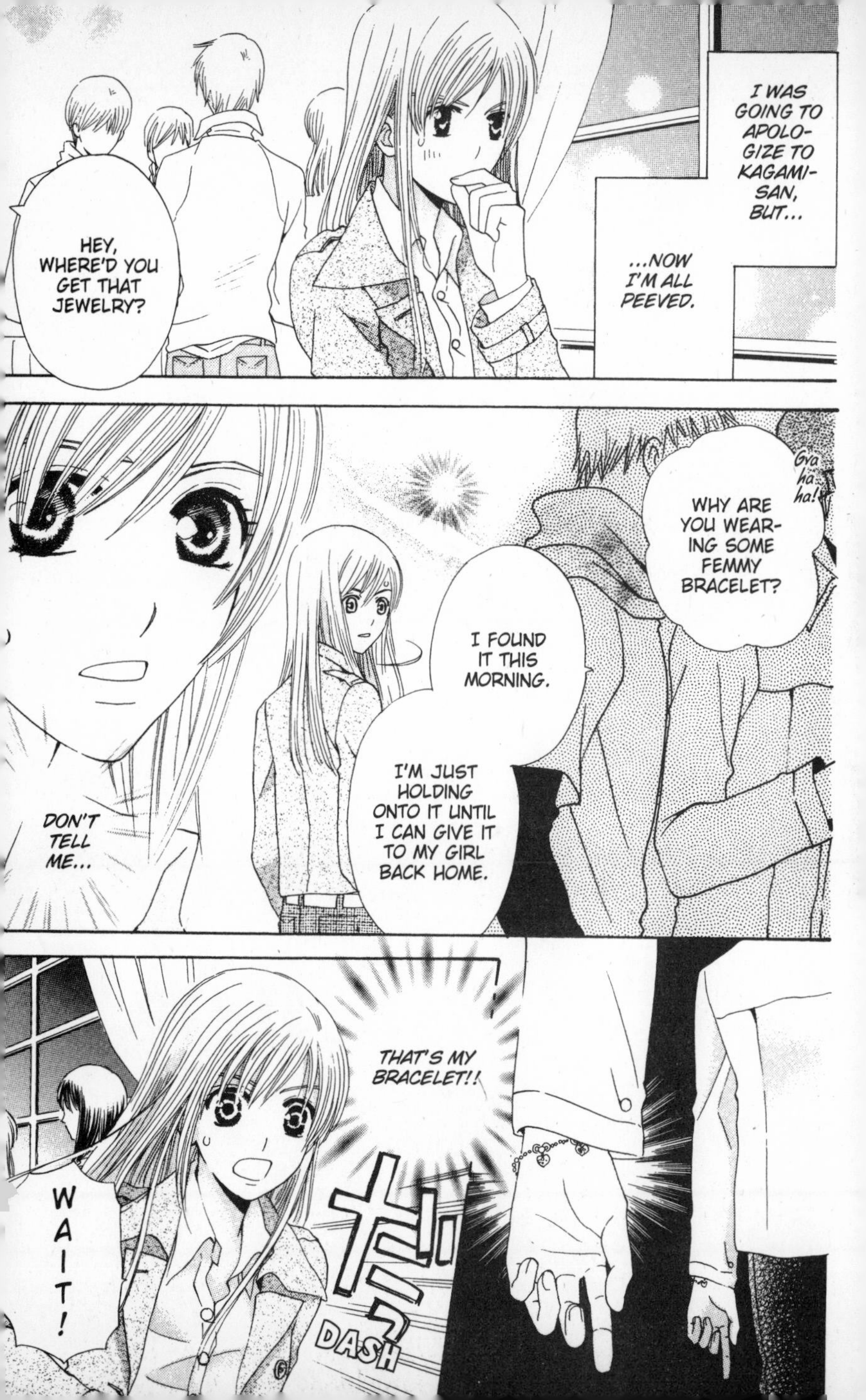
I WAS GOING TO APOLOGIZE TO KAGAMI-SAN, BUT...
...NOW I'M ALL PEEVED.
HEY, WHERE'D YOU GET THAT JEWELRY?
Gva ha ha!
WHY ARE YOU WEARING SOME FEMMY BRACELET?
I FOUND IT THIS MORNING.
I'M JUST HOLDING ONTO IT UNTIL I CAN GIVE IT TO MY GIRL BACK HOME.
DON'T TELL ME...
THAT'S MY BRACELET!!
DASH
WAIT!

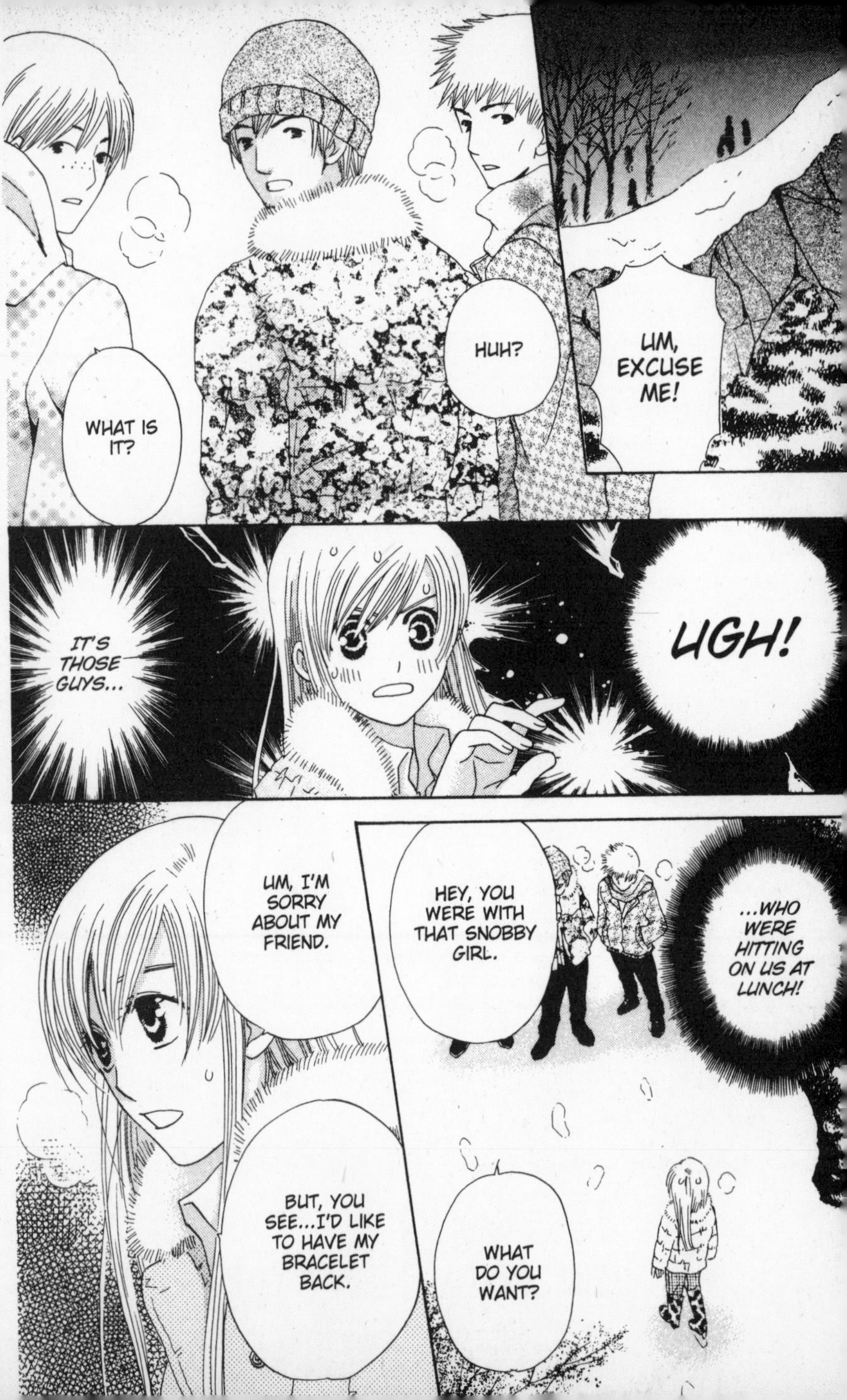
UM, EXCUSE ME!
HUH?
WHAT IS IT?
UGH!
IT'S THOSE GUYS...
...WHO WERE HITTING ON US AT LUNCH!
HEY, YOU WERE WITH THAT SNOBBY GIRL.
WHAT DO YOU WANT?
UM, I'M SORRY ABOUT MY FRIEND.
BUT, YOU SEE...I'D LIKE TO HAVE MY BRACELET BACK.

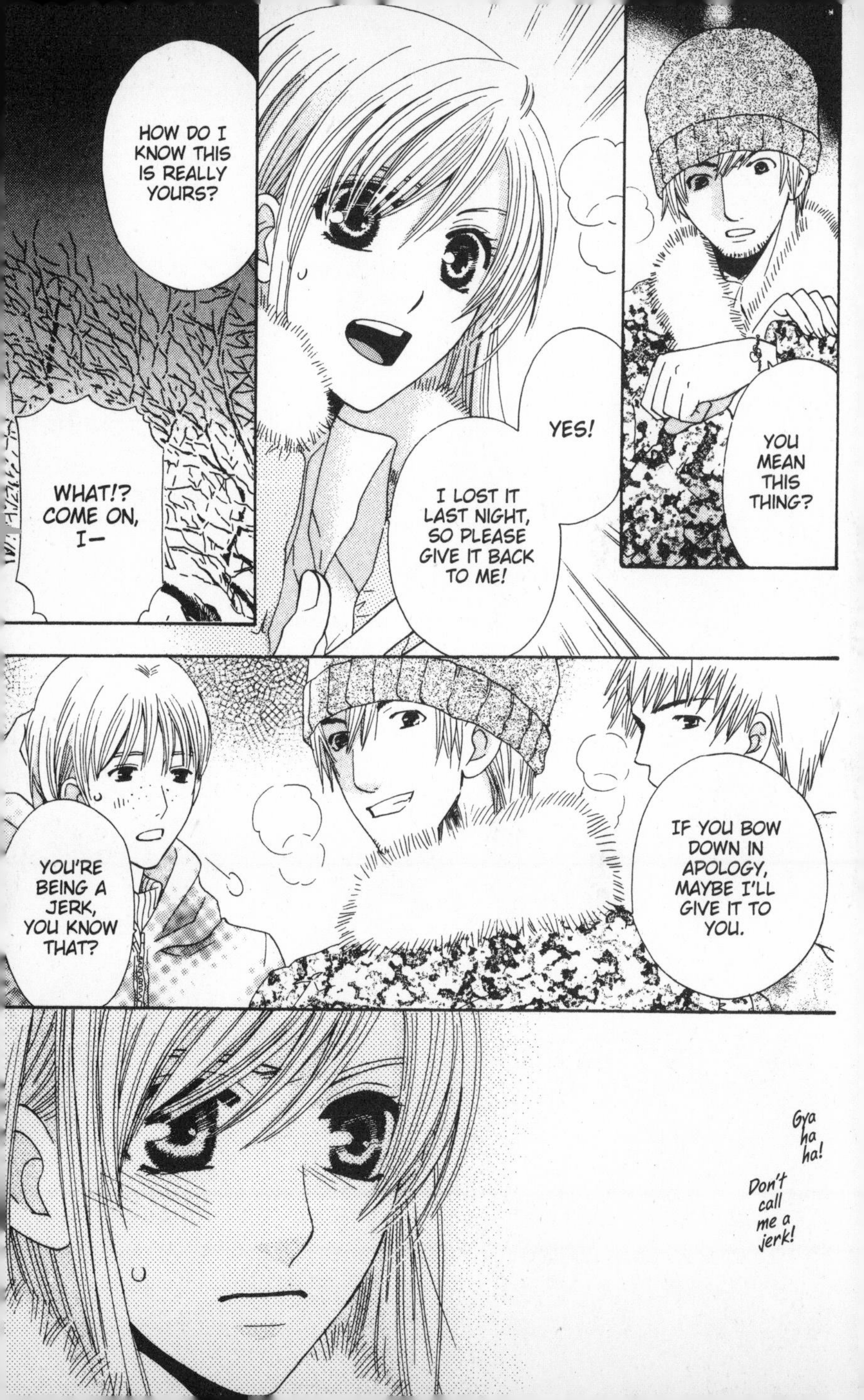
YOU MEAN THIS THING?
YES!
I LOST IT LAST NIGHT, SO PLEASE GIVE IT BACK TO ME!
HOW DO I KNOW THIS IS REALLY YOURS?
WHAT!? COME ON, I—
IF YOU BOW DOWN IN APOLOGY, MAYBE I'LL GIVE IT TO YOU.
YOU'RE BEING A JERK, YOU KNOW THAT?
Gya ha ha!
Don't call me a jerk!

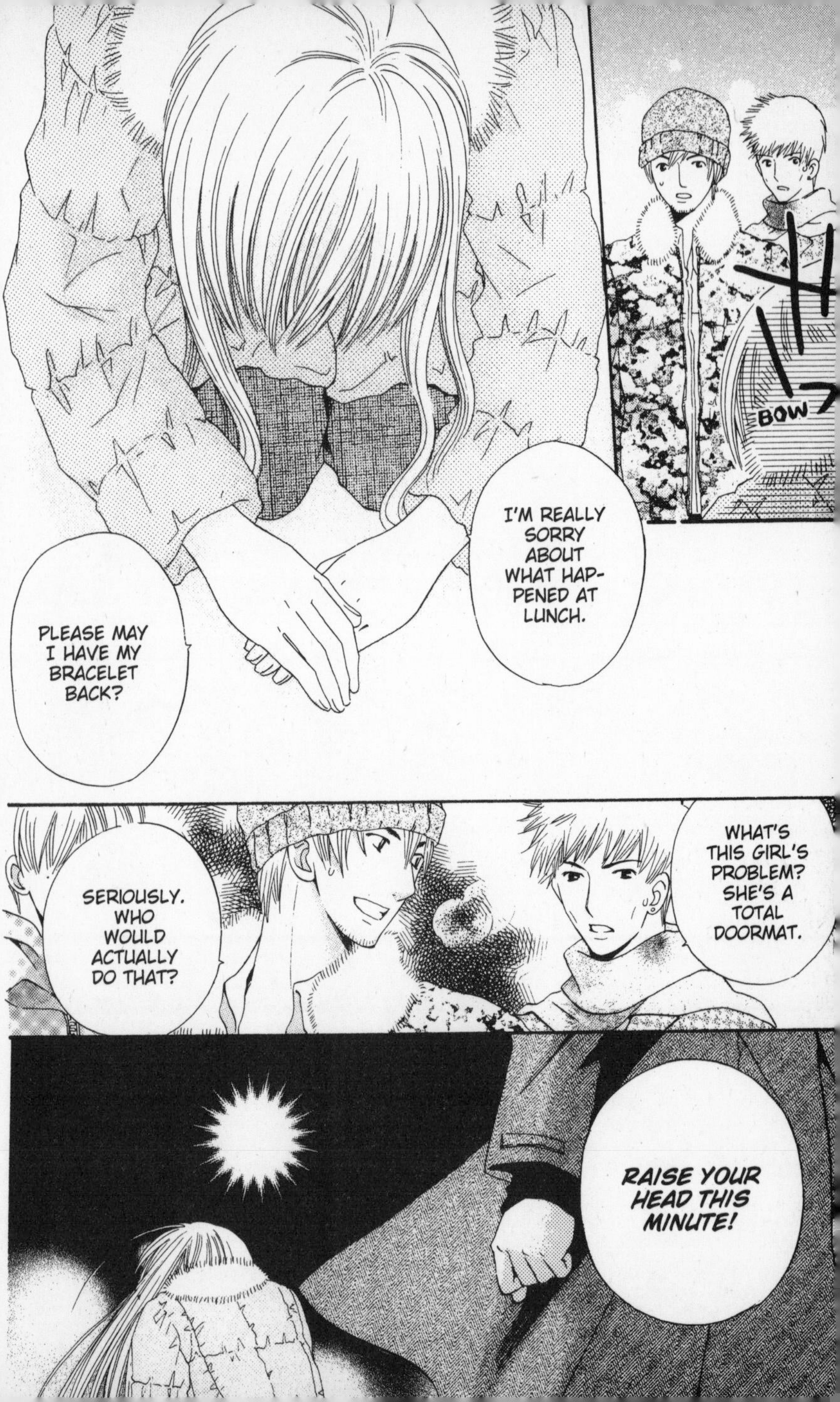
BOW
I'M REALLY SORRY ABOUT WHAT HAP-PENED AT LUNCH.
PLEASE MAY I HAVE MY BRACELET BACK?
WHAT'S THIS GIRL'S PROBLEM? SHE'S A TOTAL DOORMAT.
SERIOUSLY. WHO WOULD ACTUALLY DO THAT?
RAISE YOUR HEAD THIS MINUTE!

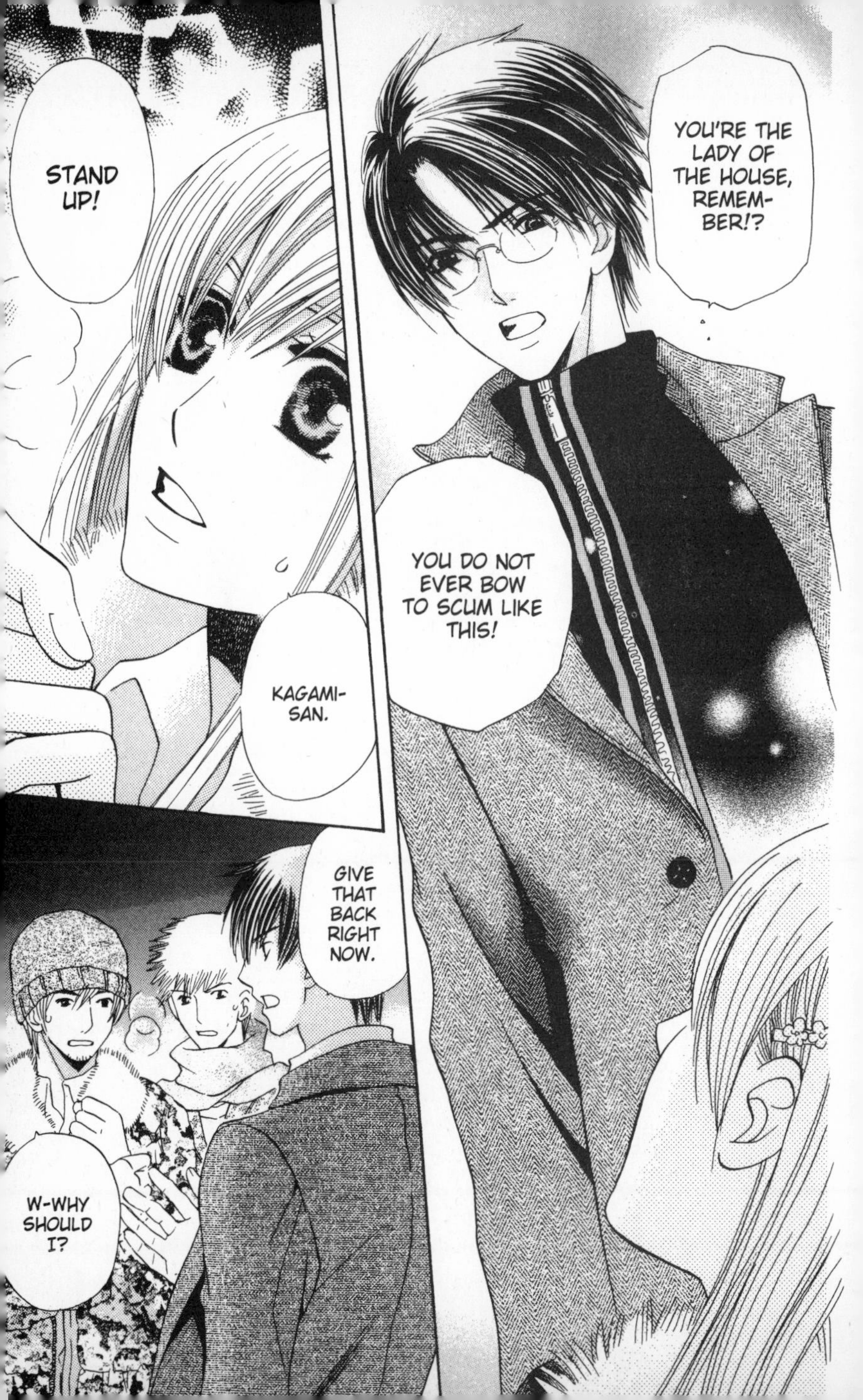
YOU'RE THE LADY OF THE HOUSE, REMEMBER!?
YOU DO NOT EVER BOW TO SCUM LIKE THIS!
STAND UP!
KAGAMI-SAN.
GIVE THAT BACK RIGHT NOW.
W-WHY SHOULD I?

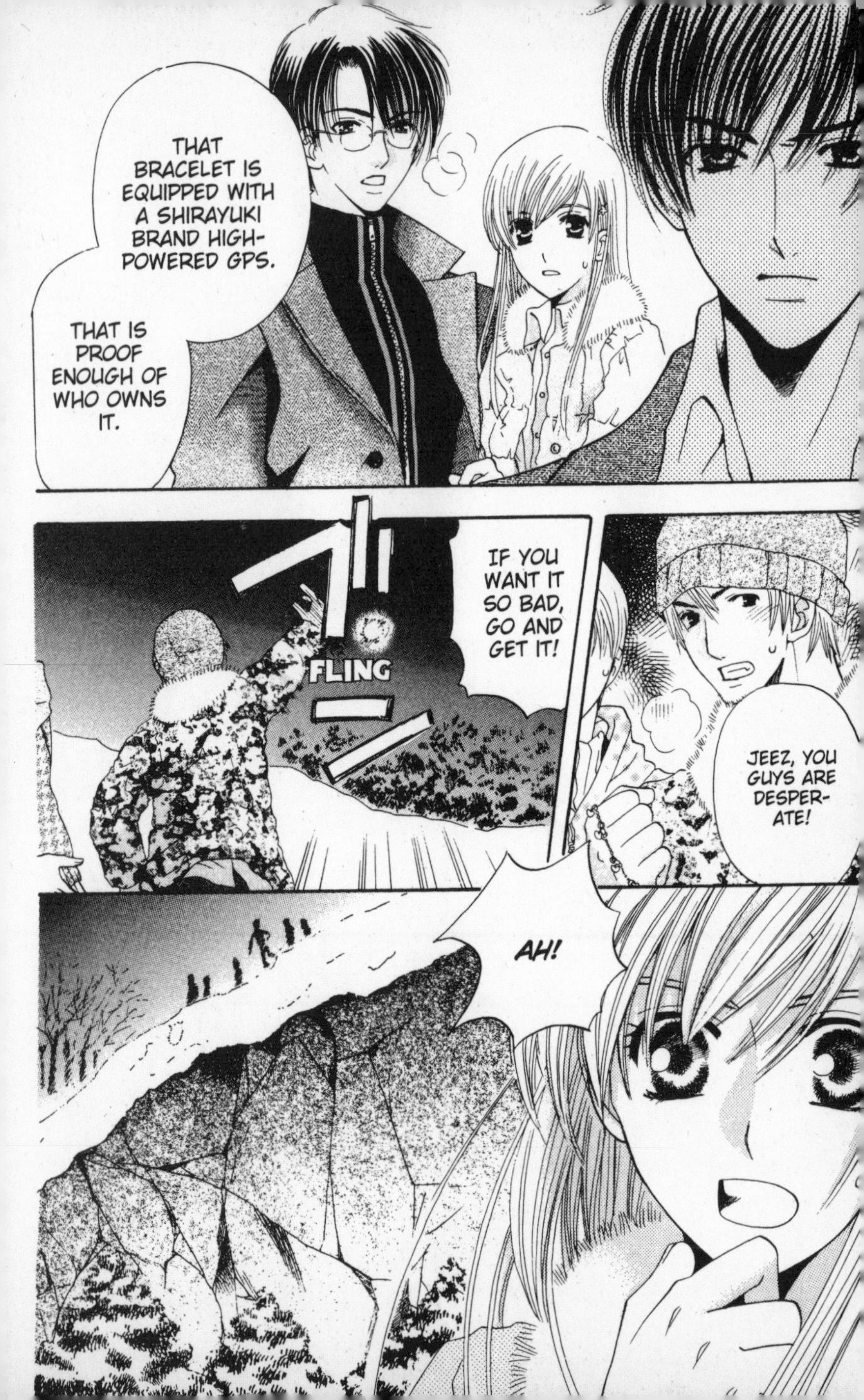
THAT BRACELET IS EQUIPPED WITH A SHIRAYUKI BRAND HIGH-POWERED GPS.
THAT IS PROOF ENOUGH OF WHO OWNS IT.
IF YOU WANT IT SO BAD, GO AND GET IT!
JEEZ, YOU GUYS ARE DESPER-ATE!
FLING
AH!

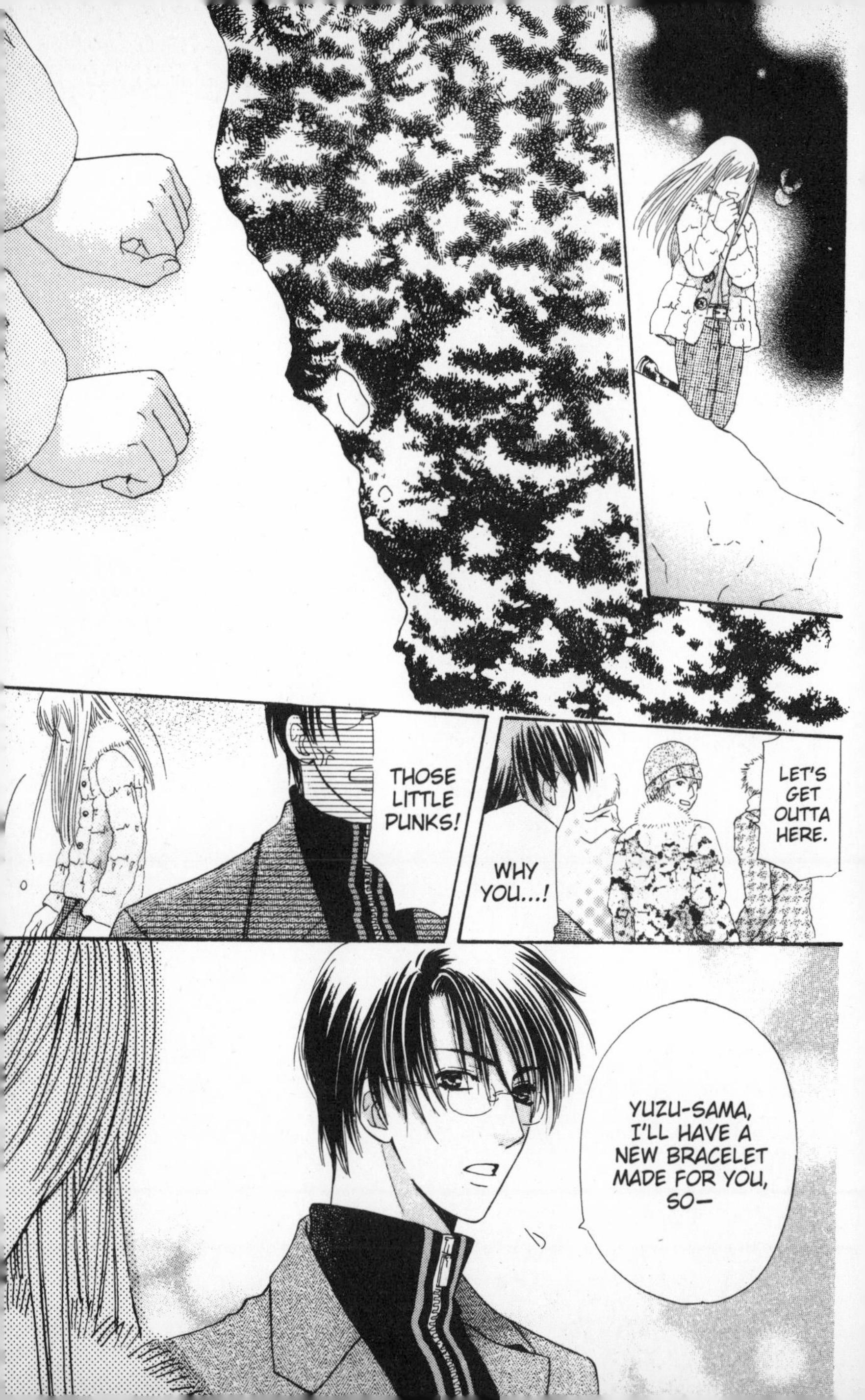
LET'S GET OUTTA HERE.
WHY YOU...!
THOSE LITTLE PUNKS!
YUZU-SAMA, I'LL HAVE A NEW BRACELET MADE FOR YOU, SO—

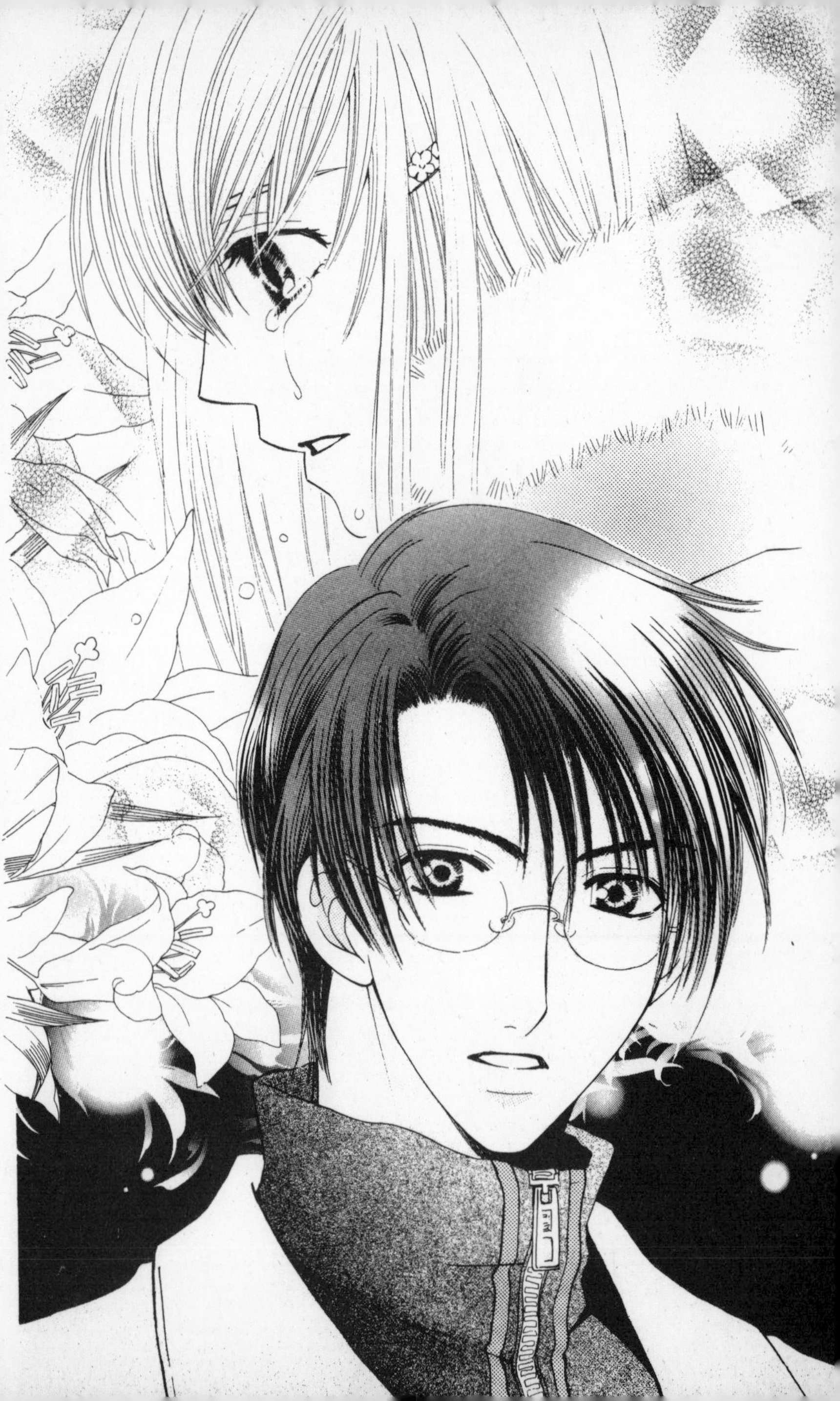

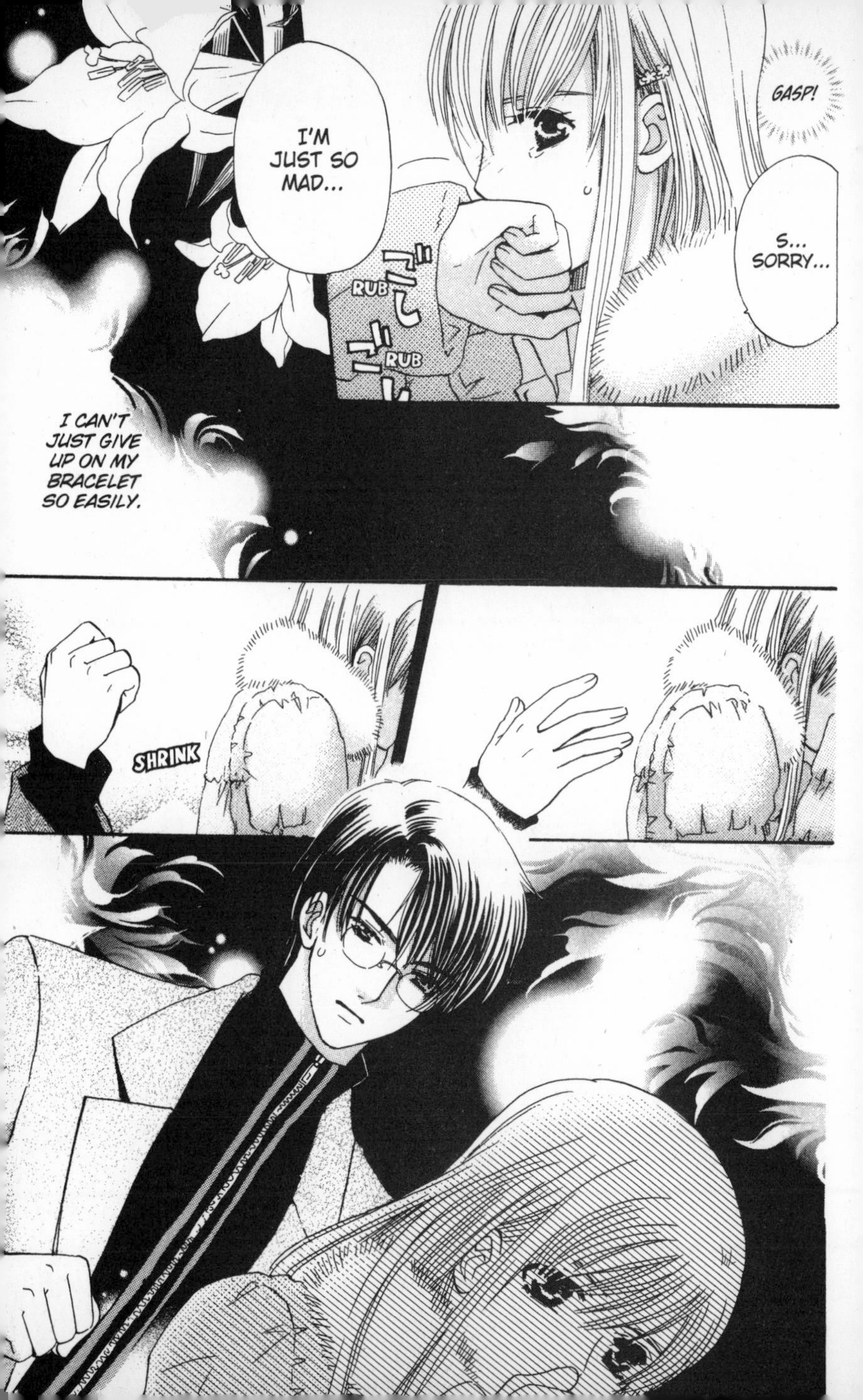
GASP!
S... SORRY...
I'M JUST SO MAD...
RUB
RUB
I CAN'T JUST GIVE UP ON MY BRACELET SO EASILY.
SHRINK

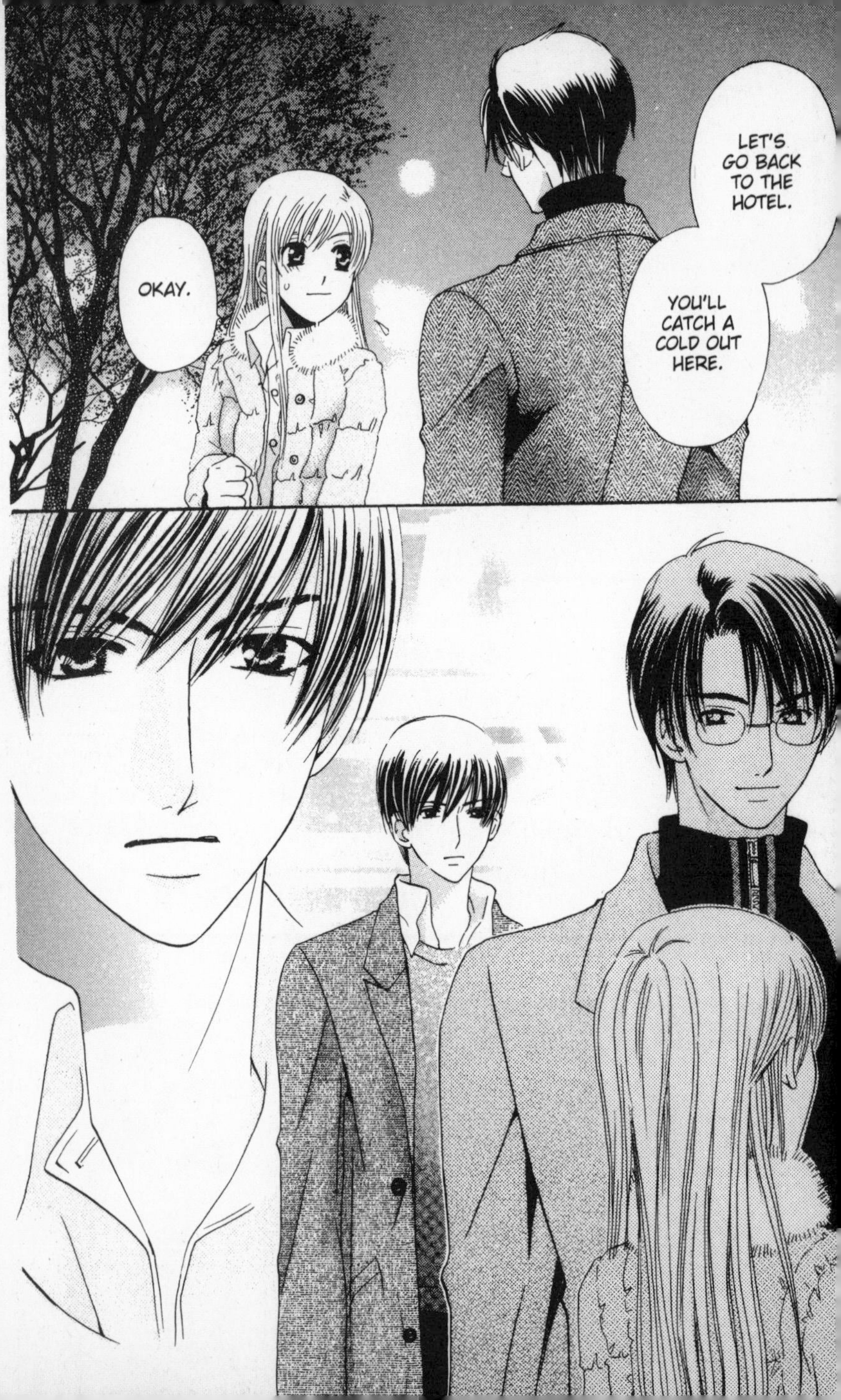
LET'S GO BACK TO THE HOTEL.
YOU'LL CATCH A COLD OUT HERE.
OKAY.

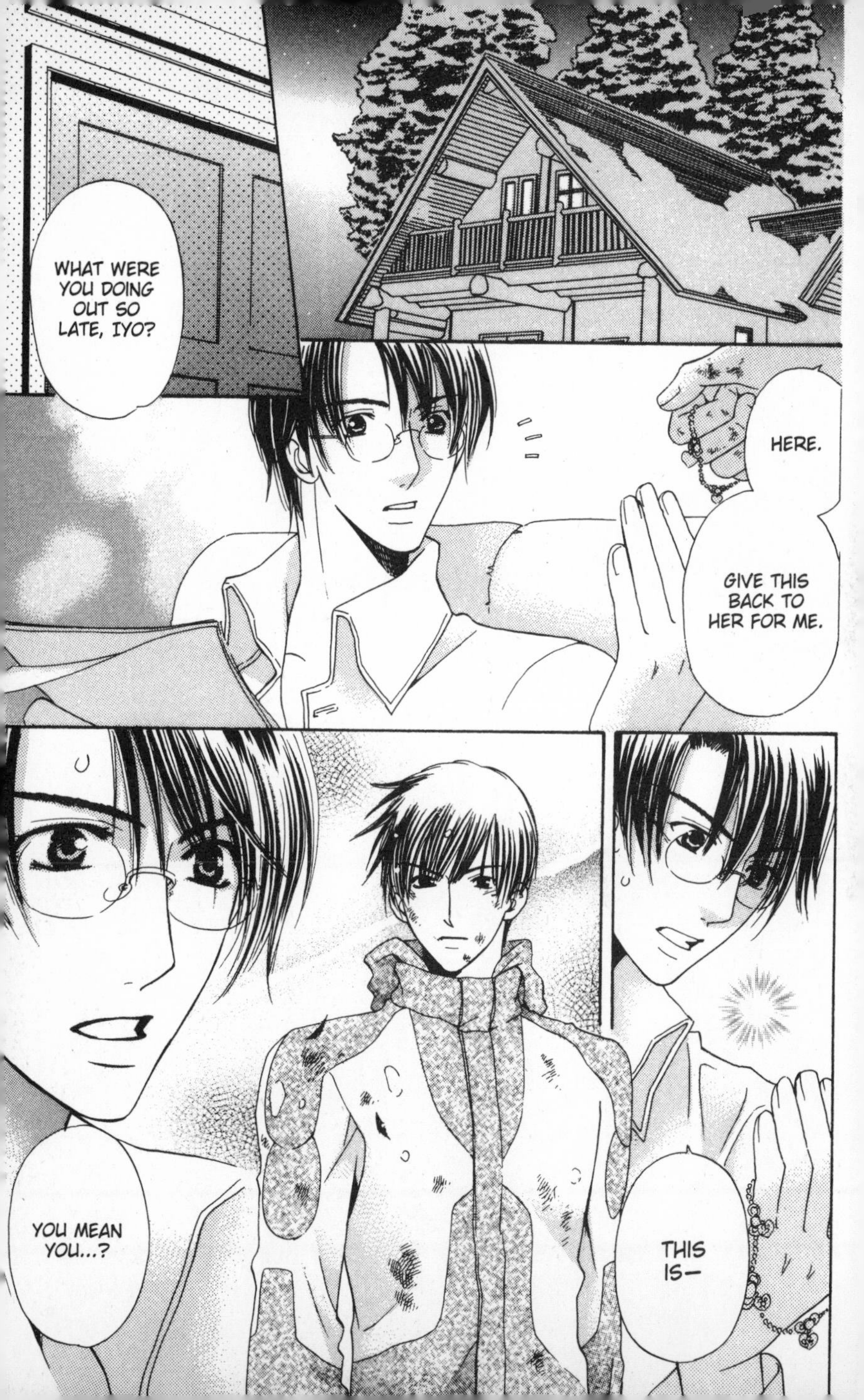

WHAT WERE YOU DOING OUT SO LATE, IYO?
HERE.
GIVE THIS BACK TO HER FOR ME.
THIS IS—
YOU MEAN YOU...?

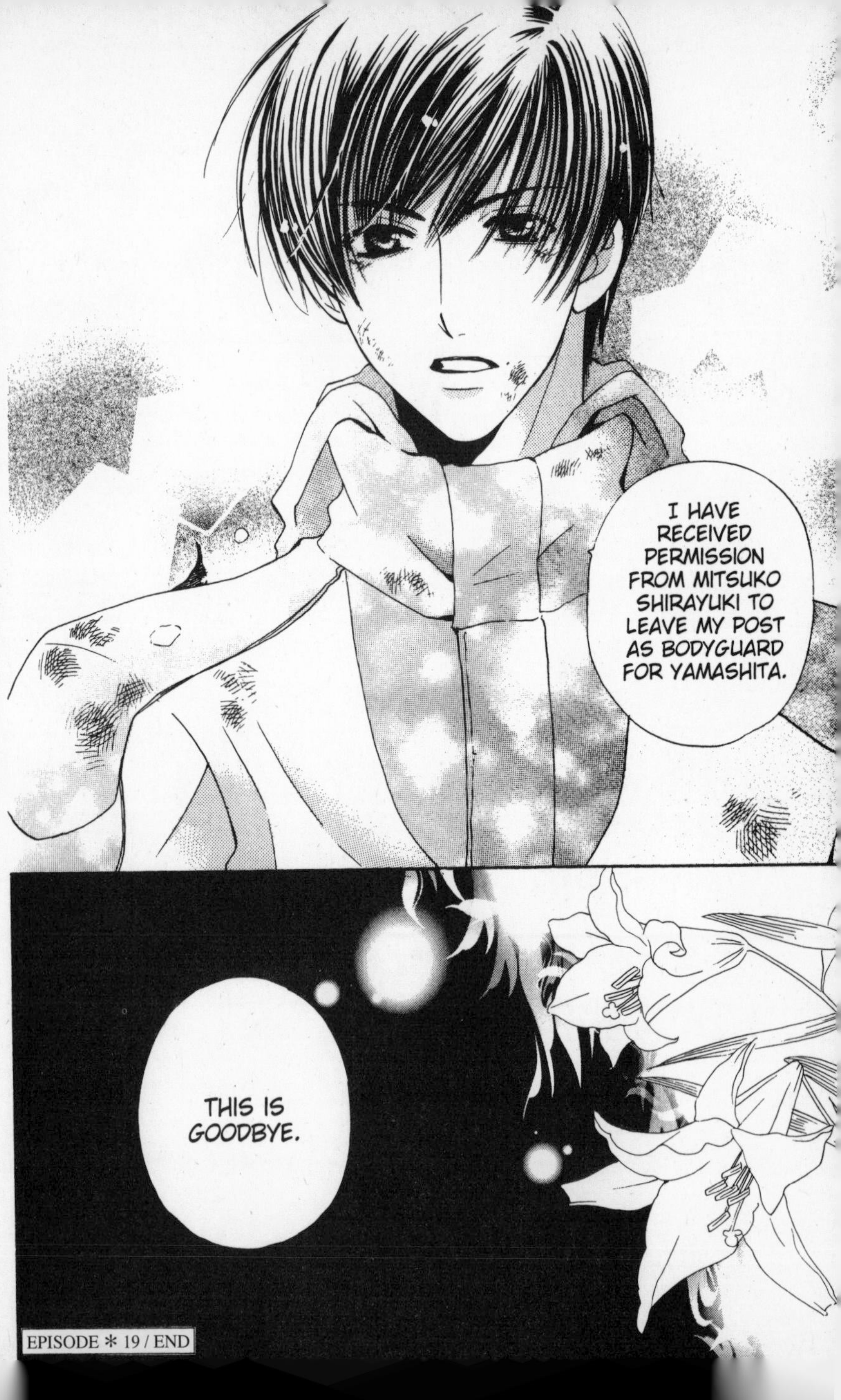
I HAVE RECEIVED PERMISSION FROM MITSUKO SHIRAYUKI TO LEAVE MY POST AS BODYGUARD FOR YAMASHITA.
THIS IS GOODBYE.
EPISODE ＊ 19 / END

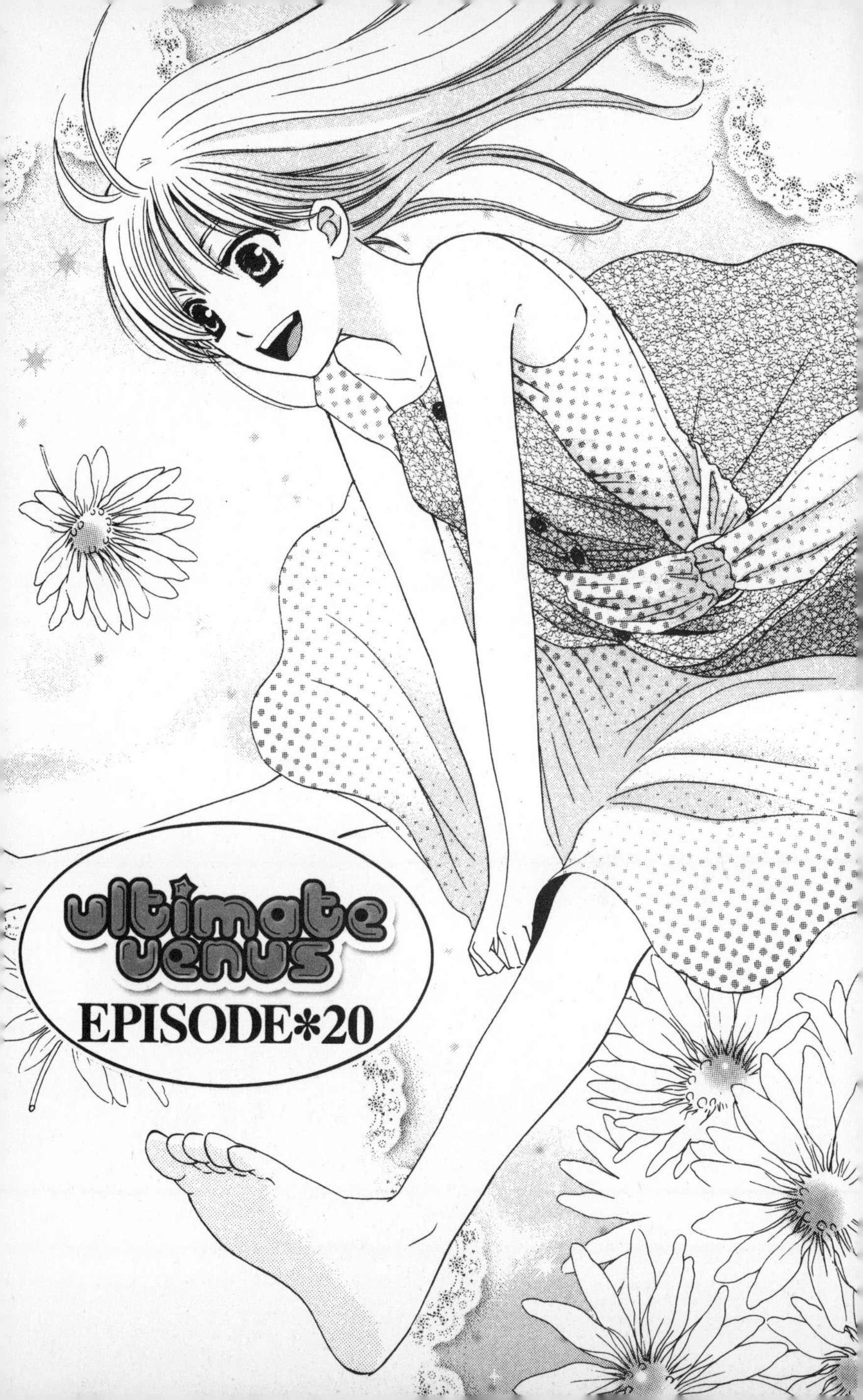
ultimate venus
EPISODE*20

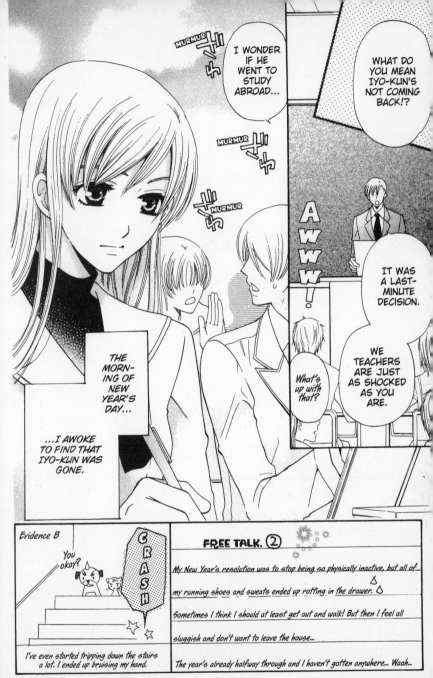

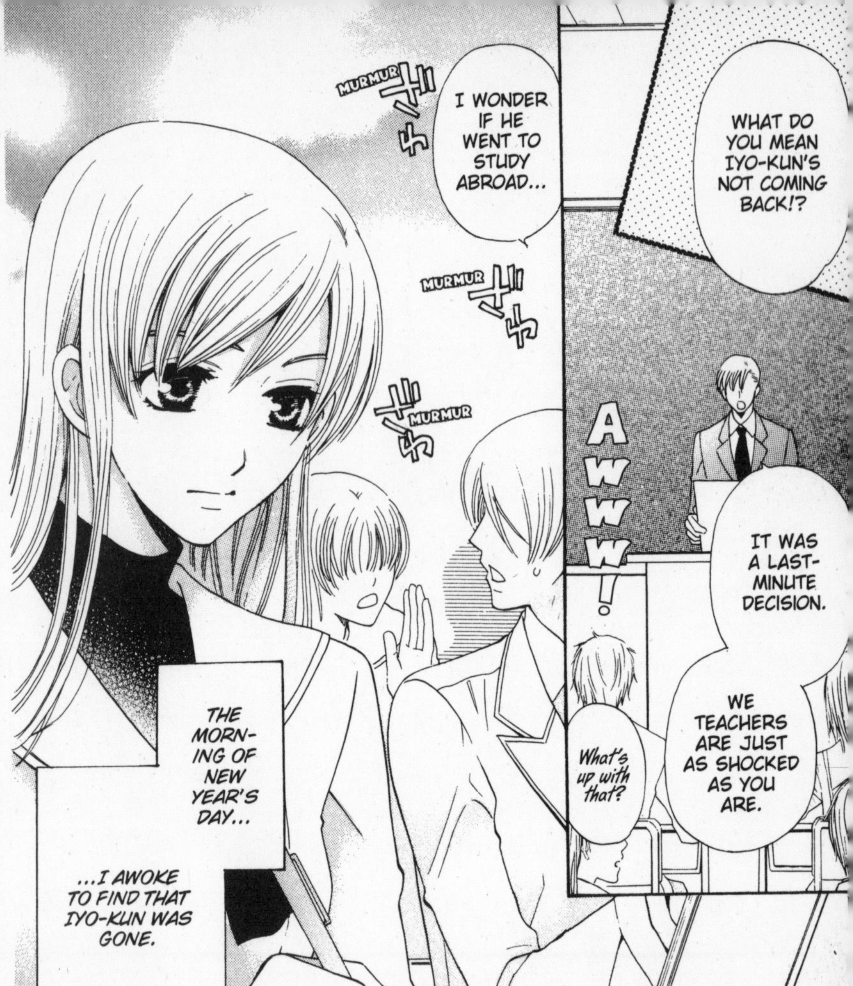
WHAT DO YOU MEAN IYO-KUN'S NOT COMING BACK!?
I WONDER IF HE WENT TO STUDY ABROAD...
MURMUR
MURMUR
MURMUR
AWWW!
IT WAS A LAST-MINUTE DECISION.
WE TEACHERS ARE JUST AS SHOCKED AS YOU ARE.
What's up with that?
THE MORNING OF NEW YEAR'S DAY...
...I AWOKE TO FIND THAT IYO-KUN WAS GONE.

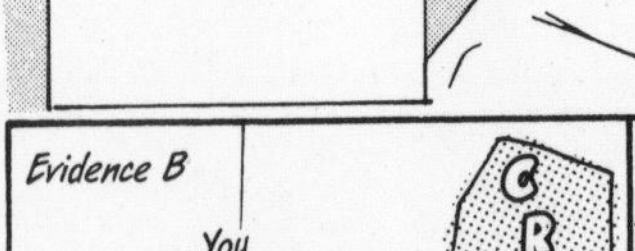
Evidence B
You okay?
CRASH

I've even started tripping down the stairs a lot. I ended up bruising my hand.

FREE TALK. ②

My New Year's resolution was to stop being so physically inactive, but all of my running shoes and sweats ended up rotting in the drawer.

Sometimes I think I should at least get out and walk! But then I feel all sluggish and don't want to leave the house...

The year's already halfway through and I haven't gotten anywhere... Waah...

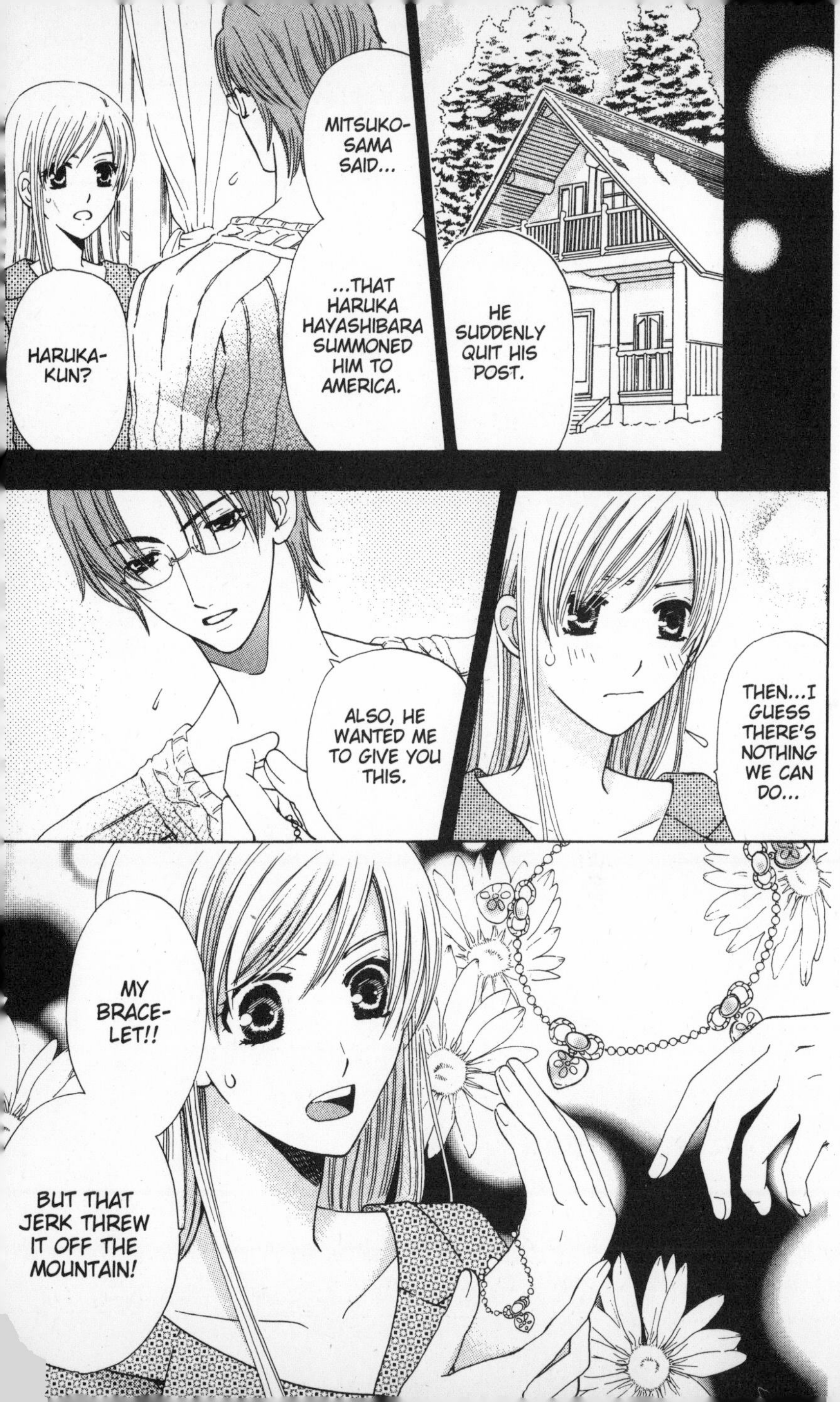
HE SUDDENLY QUIT HIS POST.
MITSUKO-SAMA SAID...
...THAT HARUKA HAYASHIBARA SUMMONED HIM TO AMERICA.
HARUKA-KUN?
THEN...I GUESS THERE'S NOTHING WE CAN DO...
ALSO, HE WANTED ME TO GIVE YOU THIS.
MY BRACE-LET!!
BUT THAT JERK THREW IT OFF THE MOUNTAIN!

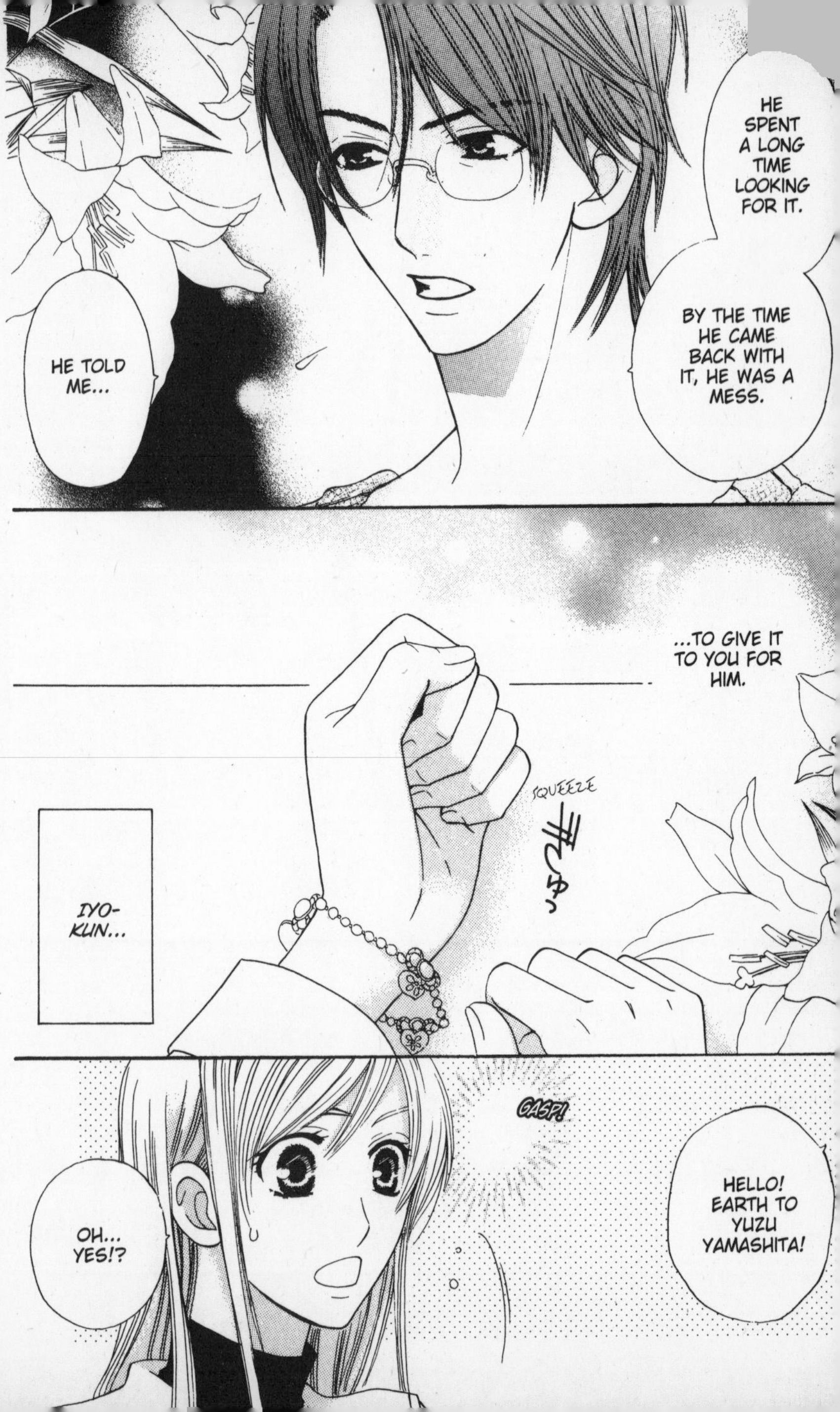
HE SPENT A LONG TIME LOOKING FOR IT.
BY THE TIME HE CAME BACK WITH IT, HE WAS A MESS.
HE TOLD ME...
...TO GIVE IT TO YOU FOR HIM.
SQUEEZE
IYO-KUN...
HELLO! EARTH TO YUZU YAMASHITA!
GASP!
OH... YES!?

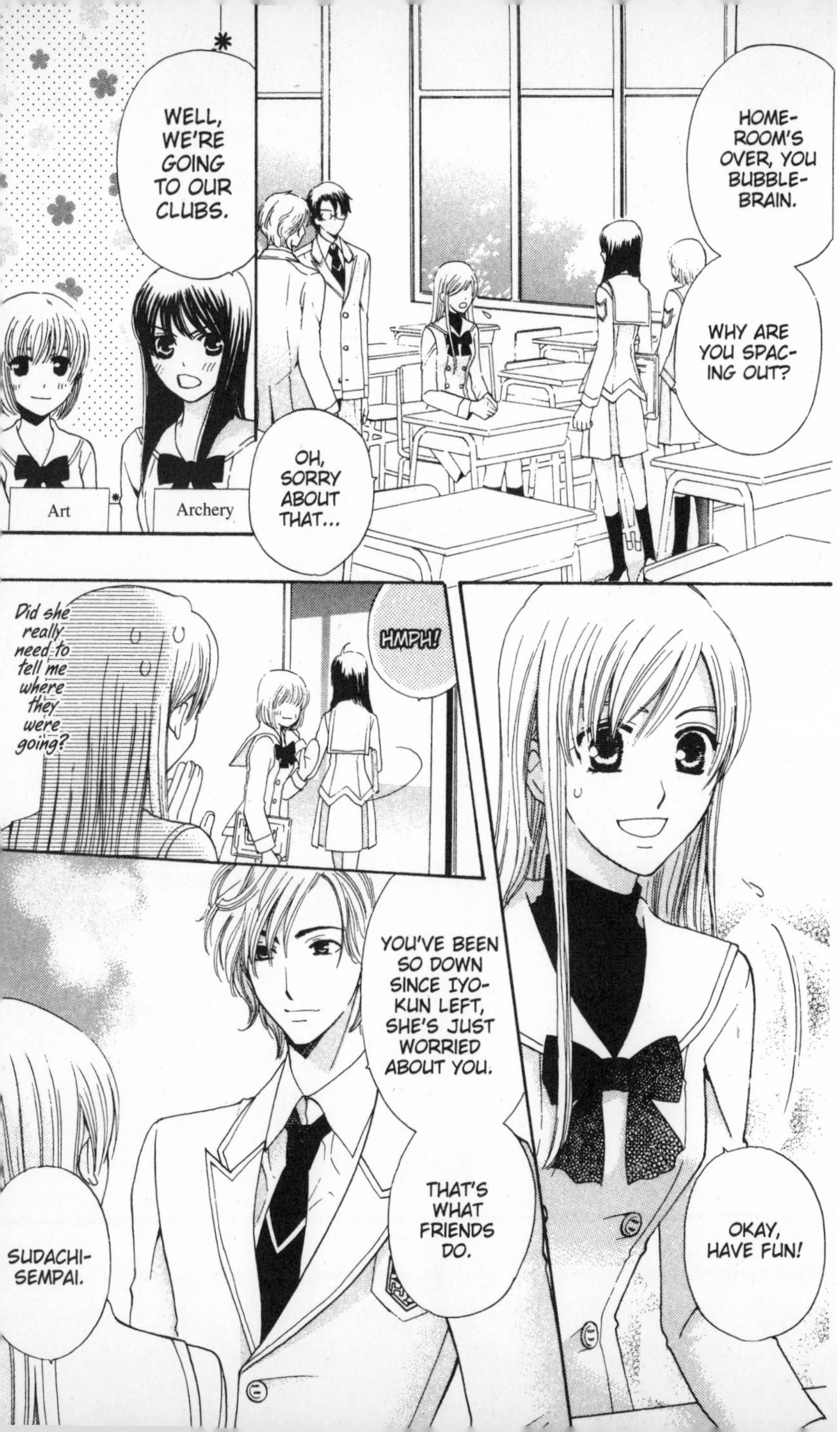

HOME-ROOM'S OVER, YOU BUBBLE-BRAIN.
WHY ARE YOU SPACING OUT?
OH, SORRY ABOUT THAT...
WELL, WE'RE GOING TO OUR CLUBS.
Archery
Art
OKAY, HAVE FUN!
HMPH!
Did she really need to tell me where they were going?
YOU'VE BEEN SO DOWN SINCE IYO-KUN LEFT, SHE'S JUST WORRIED ABOUT YOU.
THAT'S WHAT FRIENDS DO.
SUDACHI-SEMPAI.

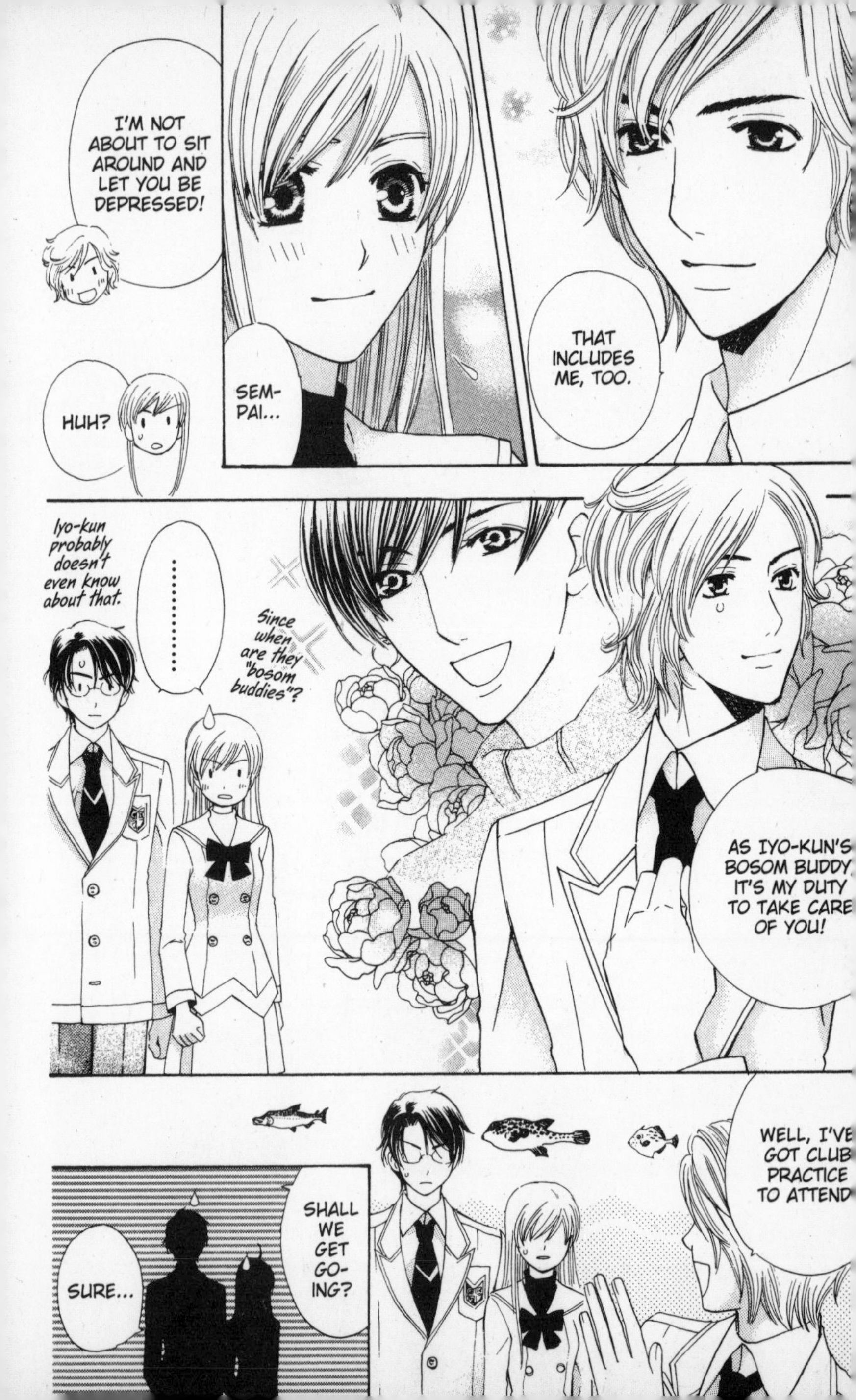
THAT INCLUDES ME, TOO.
SEM-PAI...
I'M NOT ABOUT TO SIT AROUND AND LET YOU BE DEPRESSED!
HUH?
AS IYO-KUN'S BOSOM BUDDY, IT'S MY DUTY TO TAKE CARE OF YOU!
Since when are they "bosom buddies"?
......
Iyo-kun probably doesn't even know about that.
WELL, I'VE GOT CLUB PRACTICE TO ATTEND
SHALL WE GET GO-ING?
SURE...

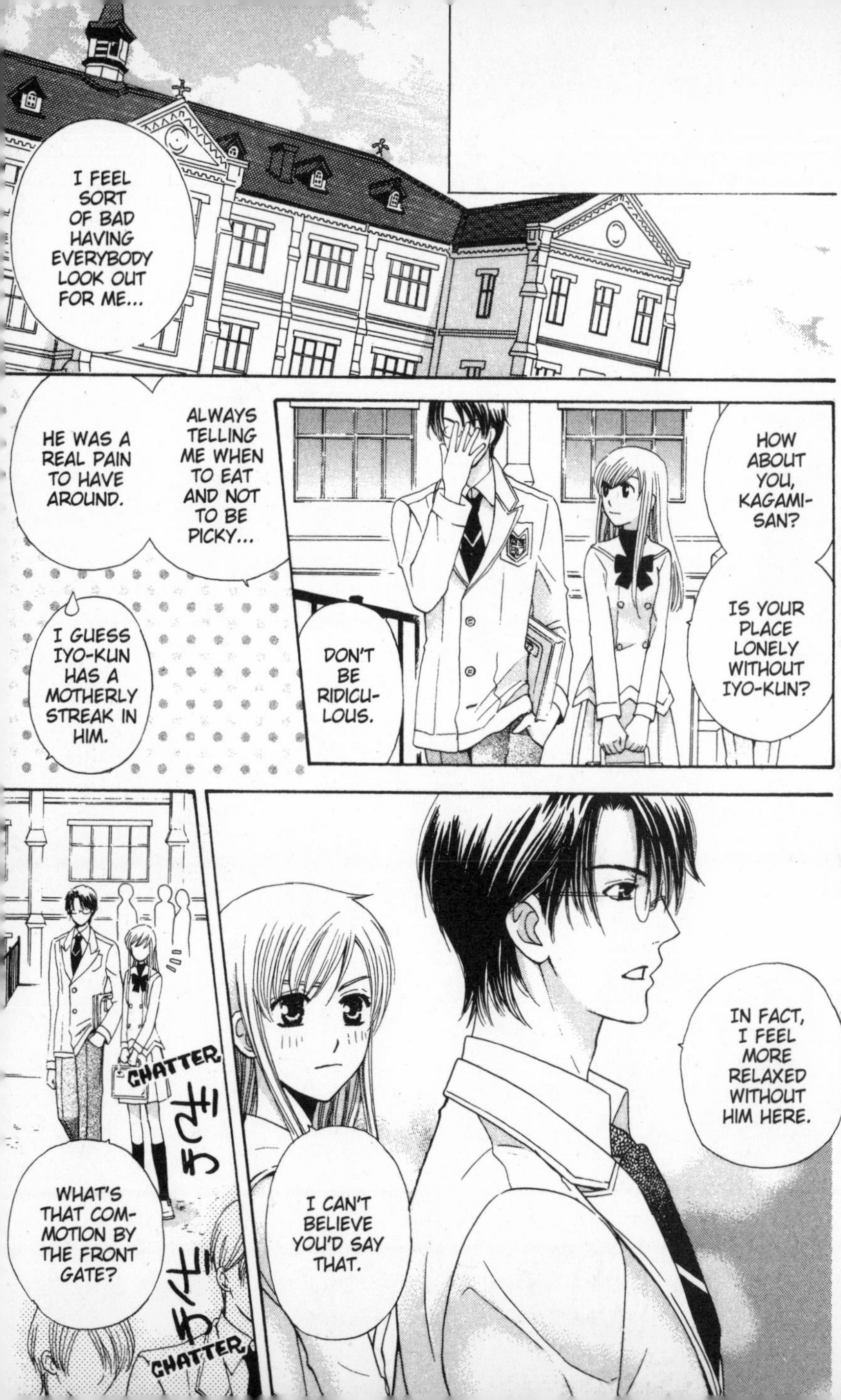
I FEEL SORT OF BAD HAVING EVERYBODY LOOK OUT FOR ME...
HOW ABOUT YOU, KAGAMI-SAN?
IS YOUR PLACE LONELY WITHOUT IYO-KUN?
DON'T BE RIDICULOUS.
ALWAYS TELLING ME WHEN TO EAT AND NOT TO BE PICKY...
HE WAS A REAL PAIN TO HAVE AROUND.
I GUESS IYO-KUN HAS A MOTHERLY STREAK IN HIM.
IN FACT, I FEEL MORE RELAXED WITHOUT HIM HERE.
I CAN'T BELIEVE YOU'D SAY THAT.
CHATTER
CHATTER
WHAT'S THAT COMMOTION BY THE FRONT GATE?

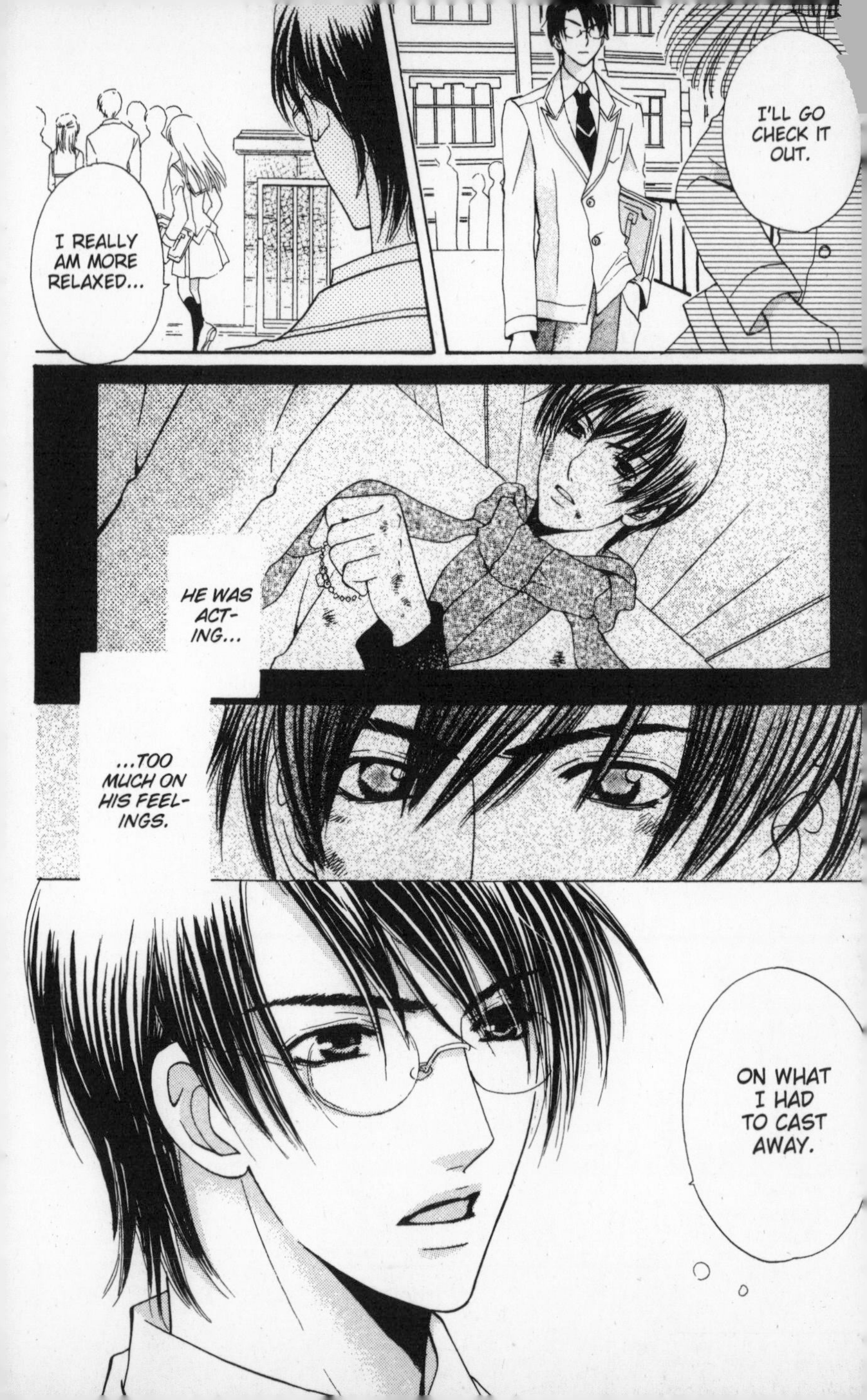
I'LL GO CHECK IT OUT.
I REALLY AM MORE RELAXED...
HE WAS ACT-ING...
...TOO MUCH ON HIS FEEL-INGS.
ON WHAT I HAD TO CAST AWAY.

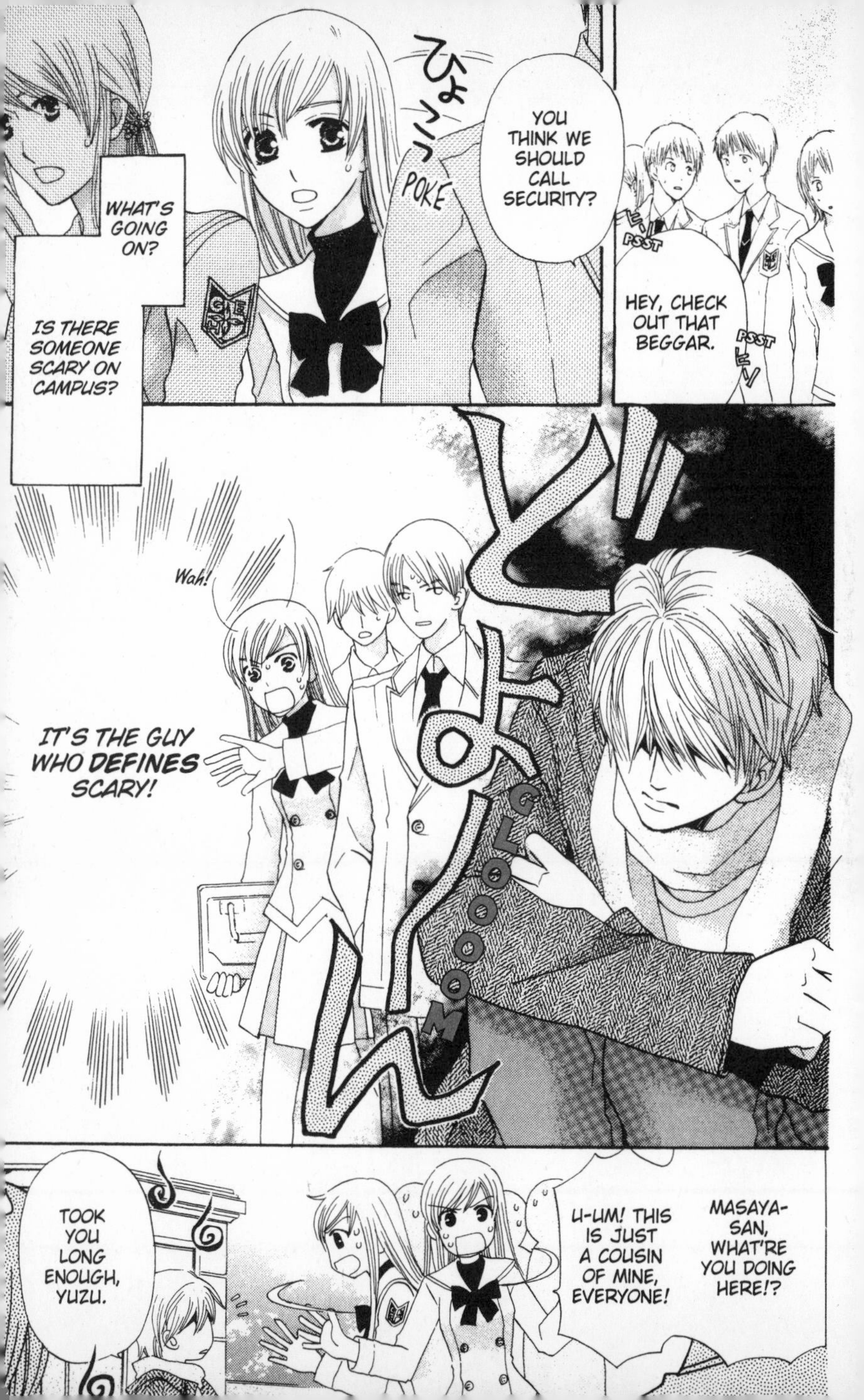
PSST
HEY, CHECK OUT THAT BEGGAR.
PSST
YOU THINK WE SHOULD CALL SECURITY?
POKE
WHAT'S GOING ON?
IS THERE SOMEONE SCARY ON CAMPUS?
Wah!
IT'S THE GUY WHO DEFINES SCARY!
GLOOOOOM
MASAYA-SAN, WHAT'RE YOU DOING HERE!?
U-UM! THIS IS JUST A COUSIN OF MINE, EVERYONE!
TOOK YOU LONG ENOUGH, YUZU.

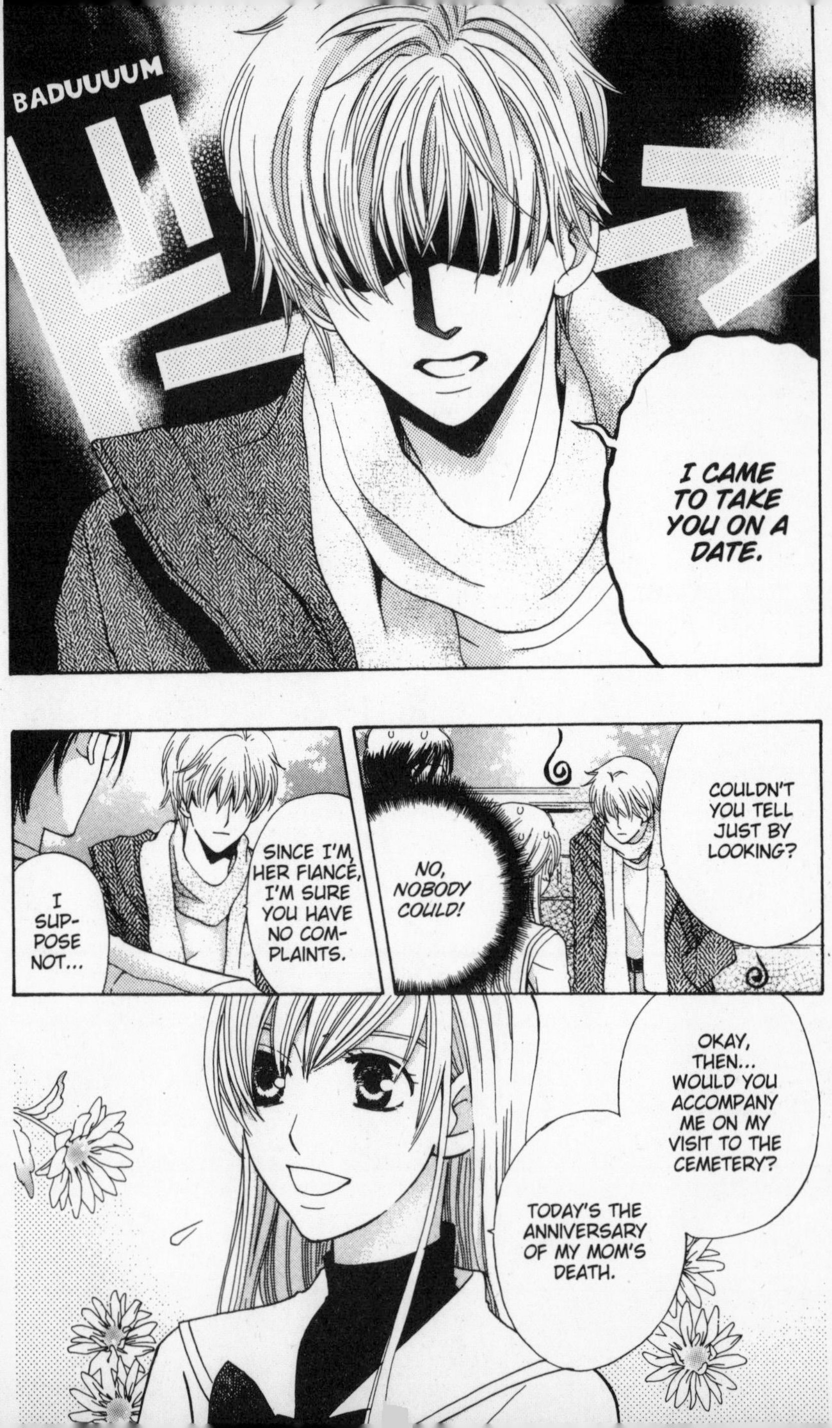
BADUUUUM
I CAME TO TAKE YOU ON A DATE.
COULDN'T YOU TELL JUST BY LOOKING?
NO, NOBODY COULD!
SINCE I'M HER FIANCÉ, I'M SURE YOU HAVE NO COMPLAINTS.
I SUPPOSE NOT...
OKAY, THEN... WOULD YOU ACCOMPANY ME ON MY VISIT TO THE CEMETERY?
TODAY'S THE ANNIVERSARY OF MY MOM'S DEATH.

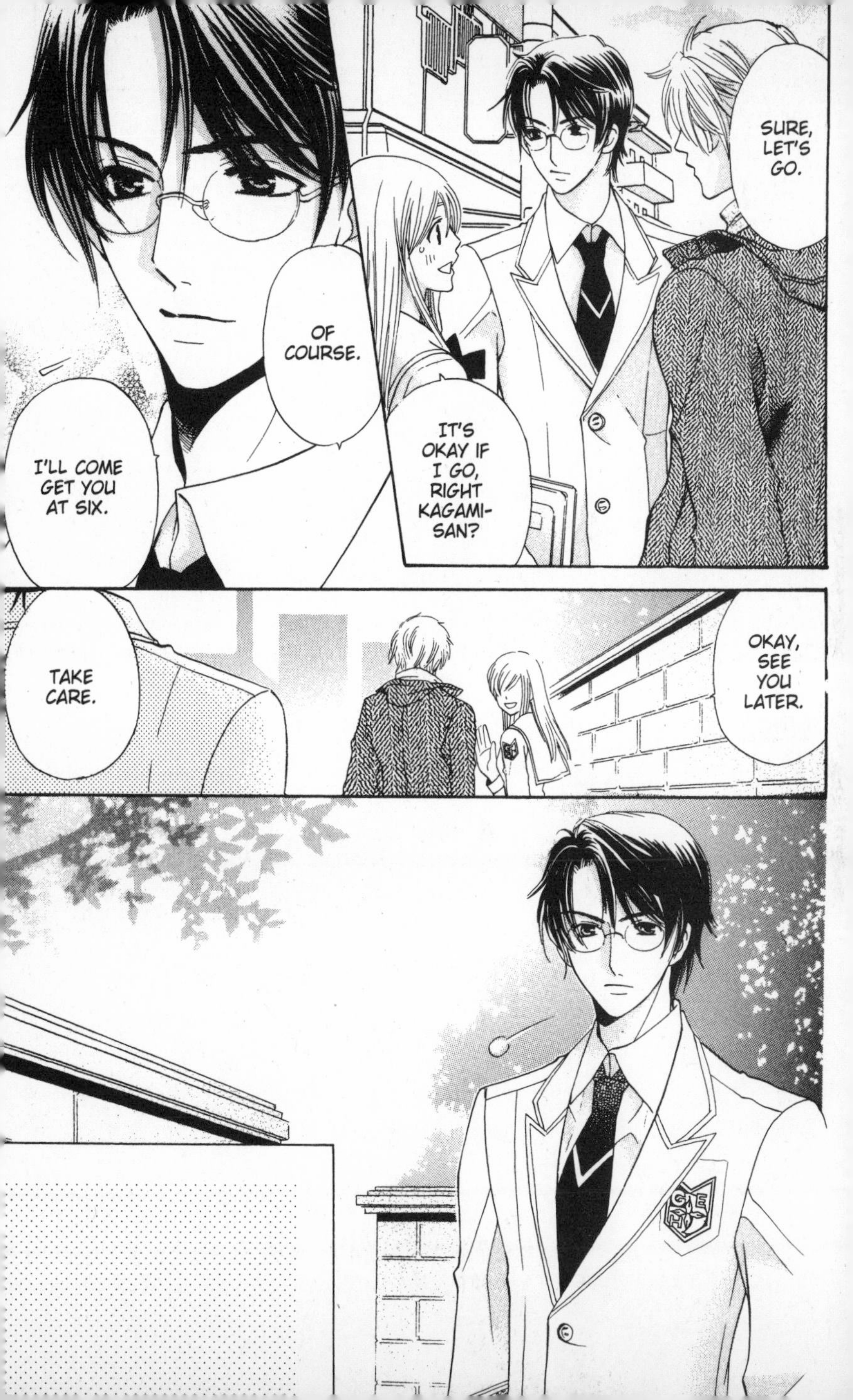
SURE, LET'S GO.
IT'S OKAY IF I GO, RIGHT KAGAMI-SAN?
OF COURSE.
I'LL COME GET YOU AT SIX.
OKAY, SEE YOU LATER.
TAKE CARE.

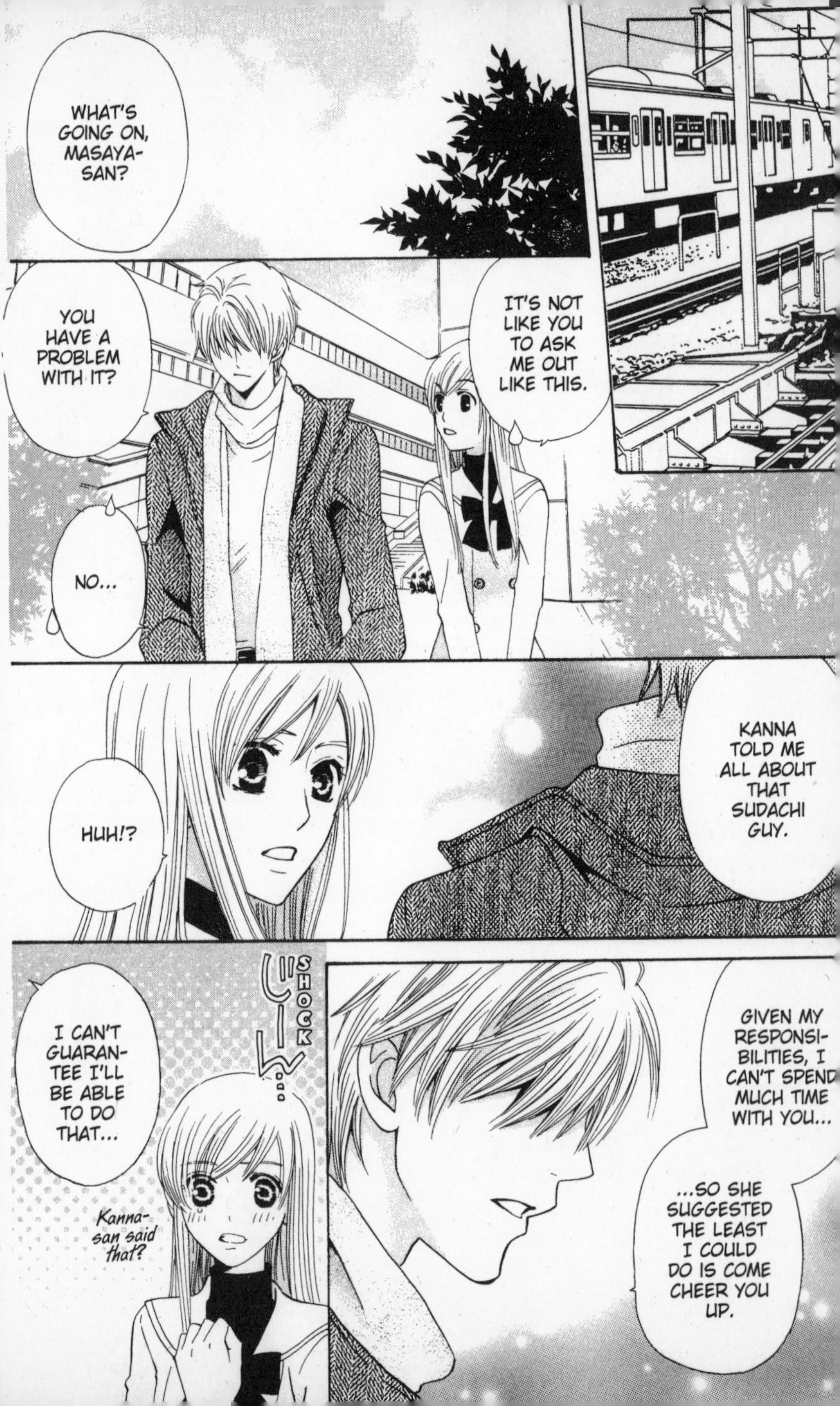
WHAT'S GOING ON, MASAYA-SAN?
IT'S NOT LIKE YOU TO ASK ME OUT LIKE THIS.
YOU HAVE A PROBLEM WITH IT?
NO...
KANNA TOLD ME ALL ABOUT THAT SUDACHI GUY.
HUH!?
GIVEN MY RESPONSIBILITIES, I CAN'T SPEND MUCH TIME WITH YOU...
...SO SHE SUGGESTED THE LEAST I COULD DO IS COME CHEER YOU UP.
SHOCK
Kanna-san said that?
I CAN'T GUARANTEE I'LL BE ABLE TO DO THAT...

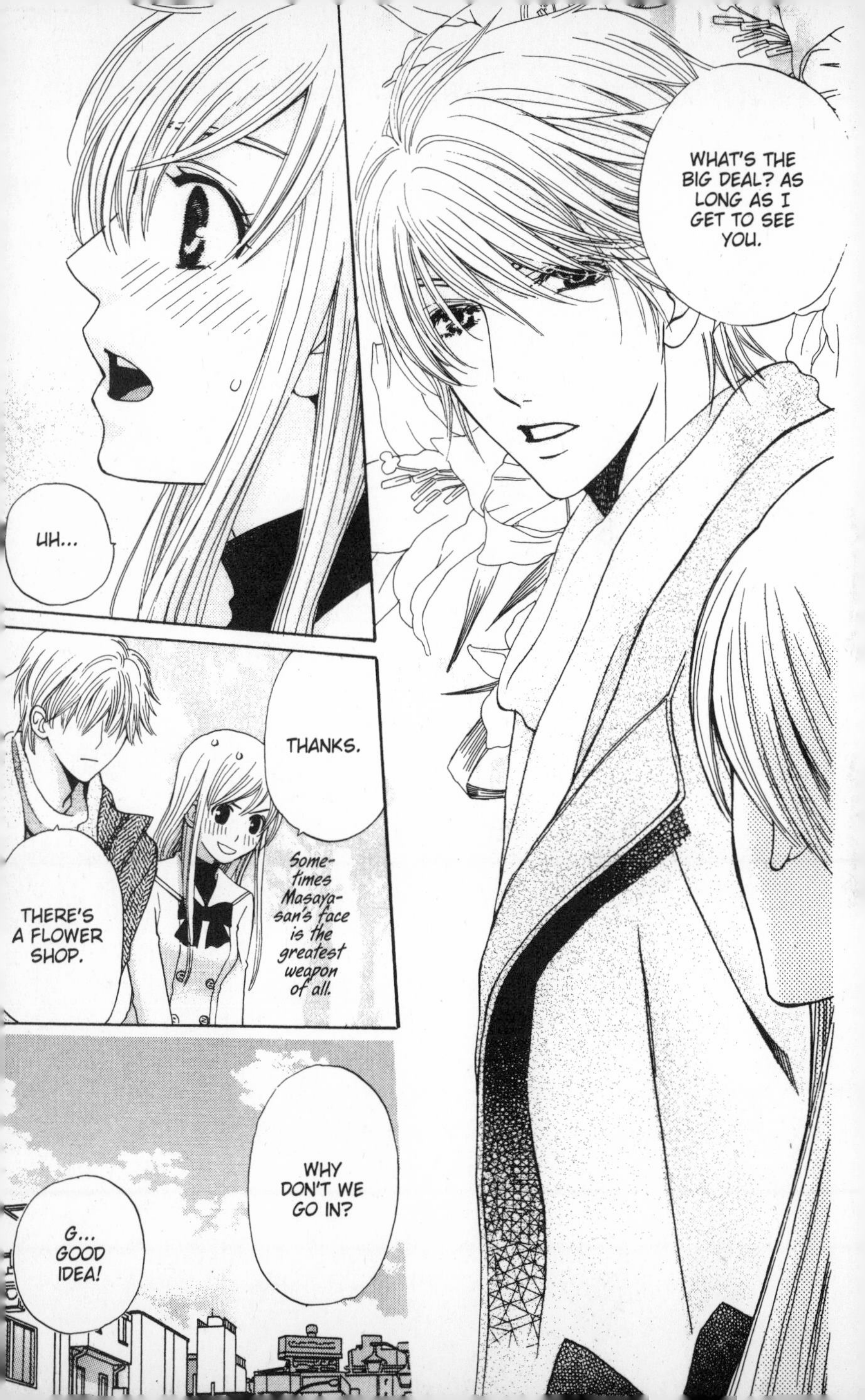
WHAT'S THE BIG DEAL? AS LONG AS I GET TO SEE YOU.
UH...
THANKS.
Sometimes Masaya-san's face is the greatest weapon of all.
THERE'S A FLOWER SHOP.
WHY DON'T WE GO IN?
G... GOOD IDEA!

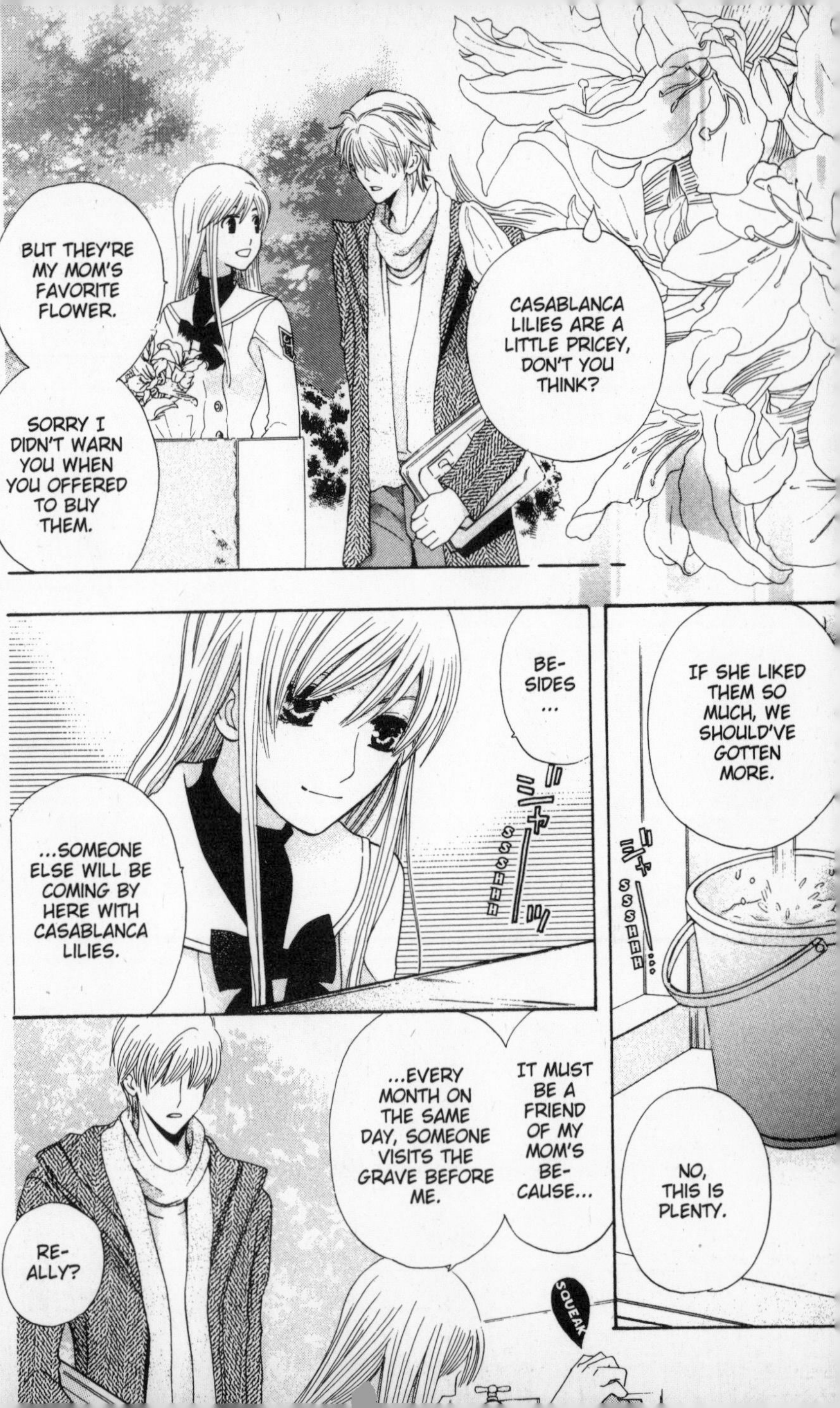
CASABLANCA LILIES ARE A LITTLE PRICEY, DON'T YOU THINK?
BUT THEY'RE MY MOM'S FAVORITE FLOWER.
SORRY I DIDN'T WARN YOU WHEN YOU OFFERED TO BUY THEM.
IF SHE LIKED THEM SO MUCH, WE SHOULD'VE GOTTEN MORE.
SSSHHH...
BE-SIDES...
SSSHHH
...SOMEONE ELSE WILL BE COMING BY HERE WITH CASABLANCA LILIES.
NO, THIS IS PLENTY.
IT MUST BE A FRIEND OF MY MOM'S BE-CAUSE...
...EVERY MONTH ON THE SAME DAY, SOMEONE VISITS THE GRAVE BEFORE ME.
RE-ALLY?
SQUEAK

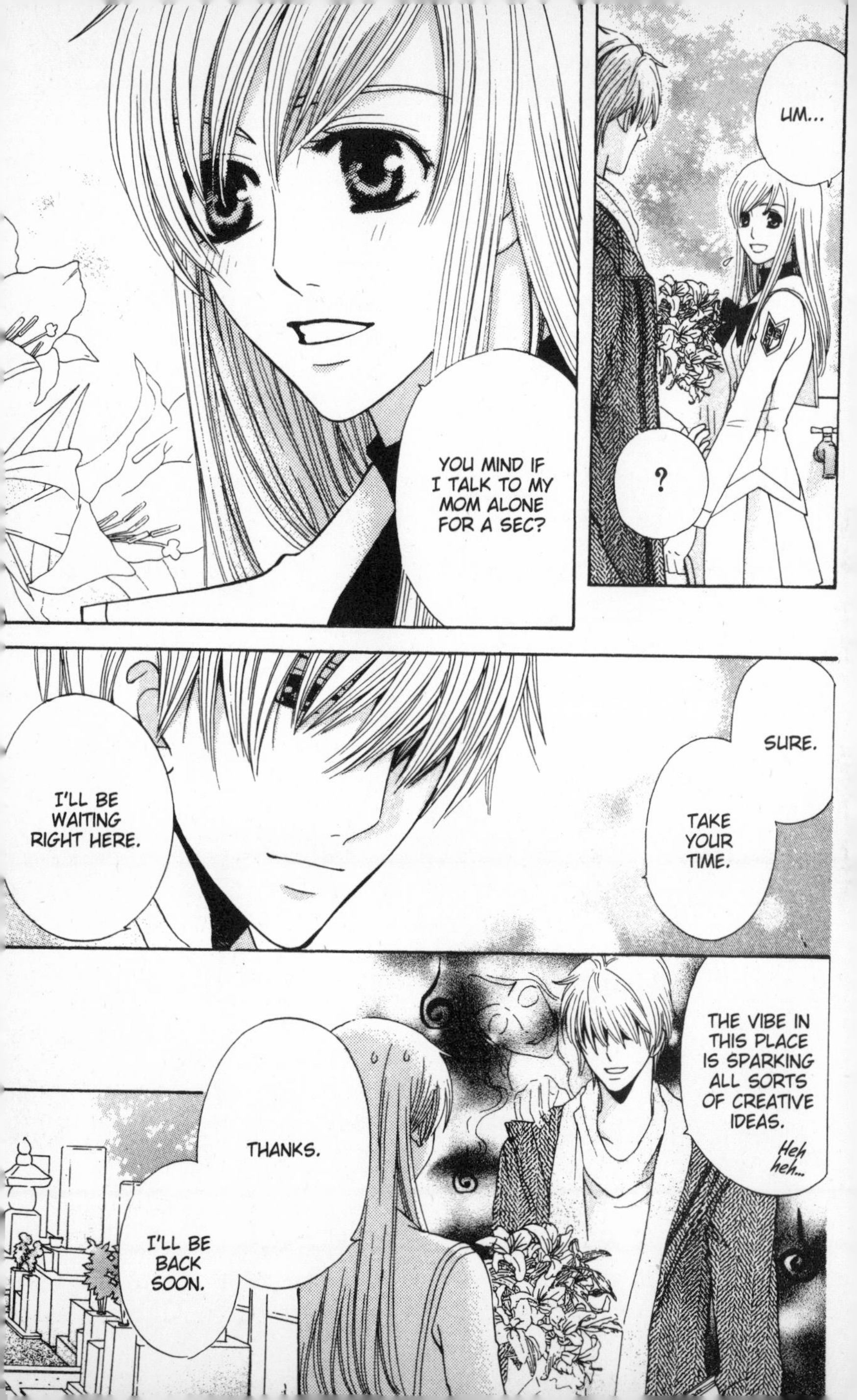
UM...
?
YOU MIND IF I TALK TO MY MOM ALONE FOR A SEC?
SURE.
TAKE YOUR TIME.
I'LL BE WAITING RIGHT HERE.
THE VIBE IN THIS PLACE IS SPARKING ALL SORTS OF CREATIVE IDEAS.
Heh heh...
THANKS.
I'LL BE BACK SOON.

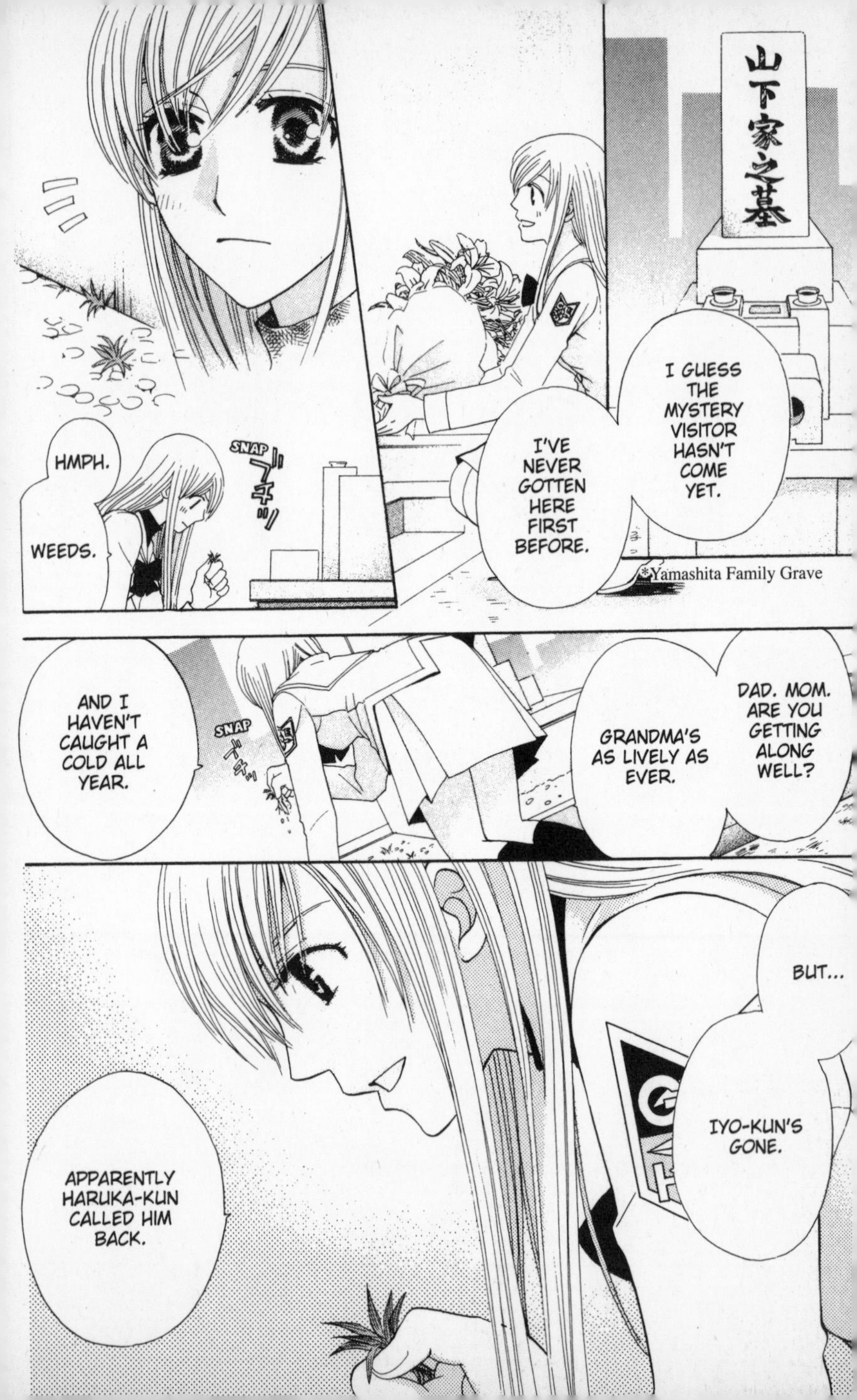
山下家之墓
I GUESS THE MYSTERY VISITOR HASN'T COME YET.
I'VE NEVER GOTTEN HERE FIRST BEFORE.
*Yamashita Family Grave
SNAP
HMPH.
WEEDS.
DAD. MOM. ARE YOU GETTING ALONG WELL?
GRANDMA'S AS LIVELY AS EVER.
SNAP
AND I HAVEN'T CAUGHT A COLD ALL YEAR.
BUT...
IYO-KUN'S GONE.
APPARENTLY HARUKA-KUN CALLED HIM BACK.

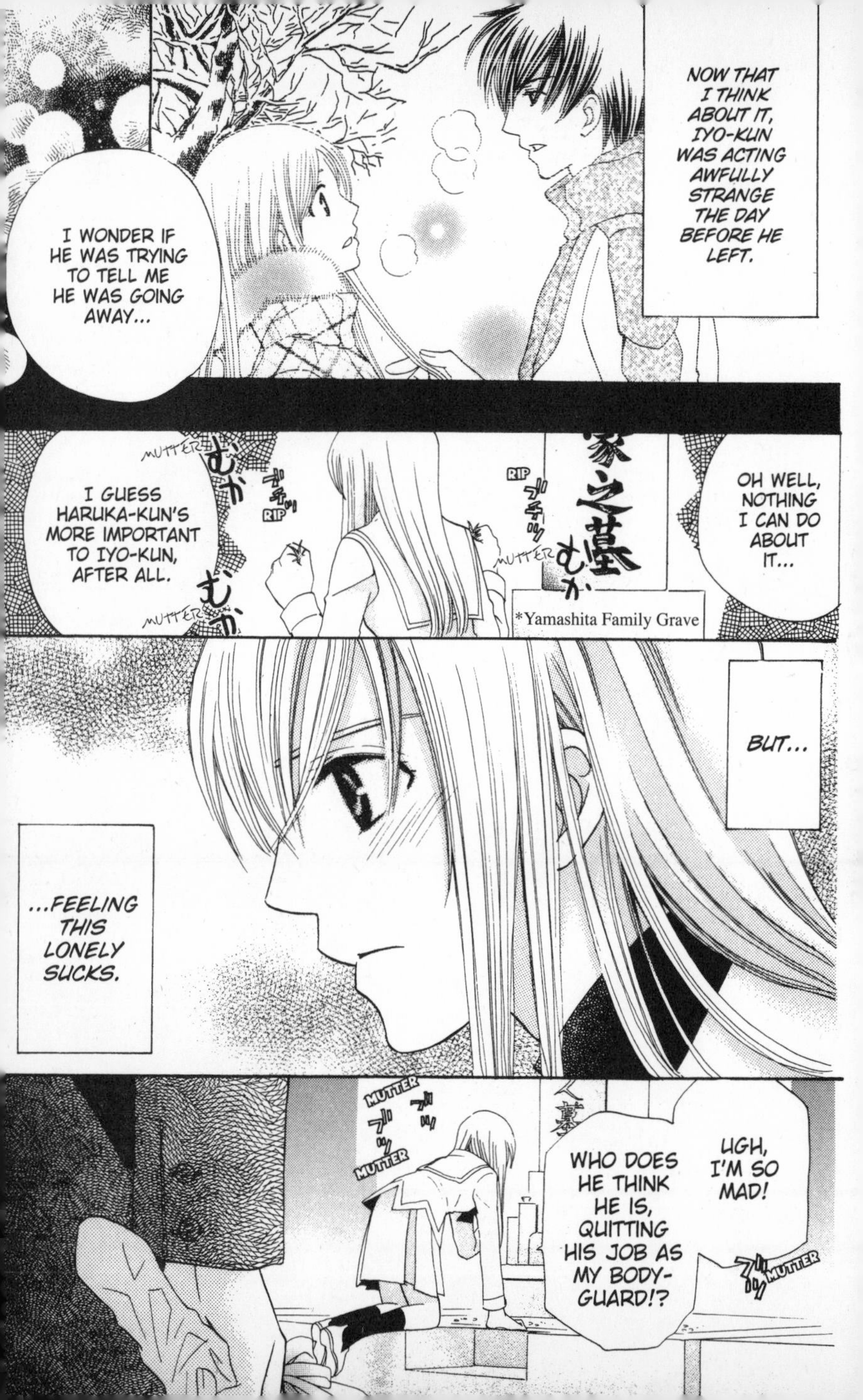
NOW THAT I THINK ABOUT IT, IYO-KUN WAS ACTING AWFULLY STRANGE THE DAY BEFORE HE LEFT.
I WONDER IF HE WAS TRYING TO TELL ME HE WAS GOING AWAY...
OH WELL, NOTHING I CAN DO ABOUT IT...
RIP
MUTTER
*Yamashita Family Grave
RIP
MUTTER
I GUESS HARUKA-KUN'S MORE IMPORTANT TO IYO-KUN, AFTER ALL.
MUTTER
BUT...
...FEELING THIS LONELY SUCKS.
MUTTER
UGH, I'M SO MAD!
WHO DOES HE THINK HE IS, QUITTING HIS JOB AS MY BODY-GUARD!?
MUTTER
MUTTER

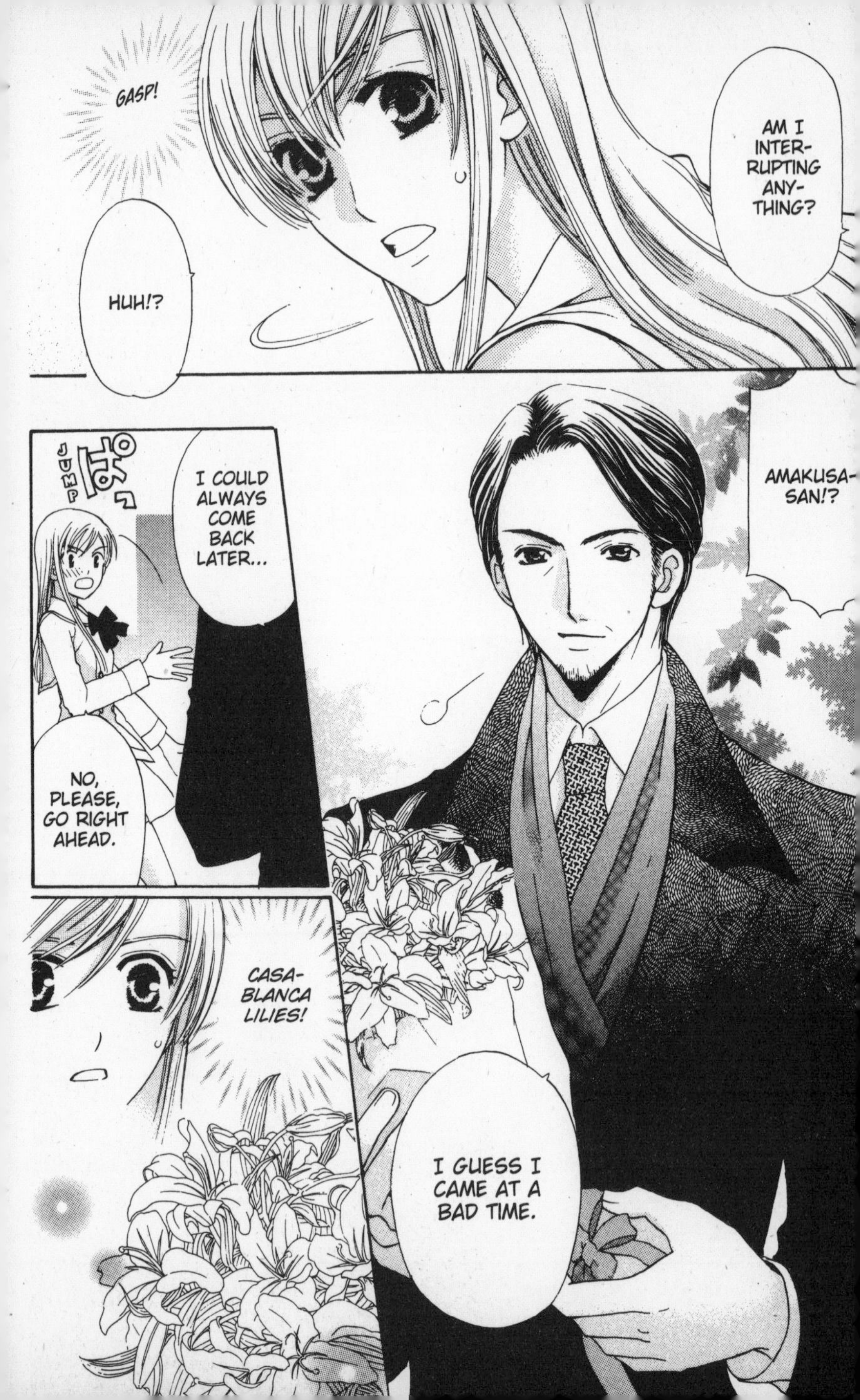
AM I INTER-RUPTING ANY-THING?
GASP!
HUH!?
AMAKUSA-SAN!?
JUMP
I COULD ALWAYS COME BACK LATER...
NO, PLEASE, GO RIGHT AHEAD.
I GUESS I CAME AT A BAD TIME.
CASA-BLANCA LILIES!

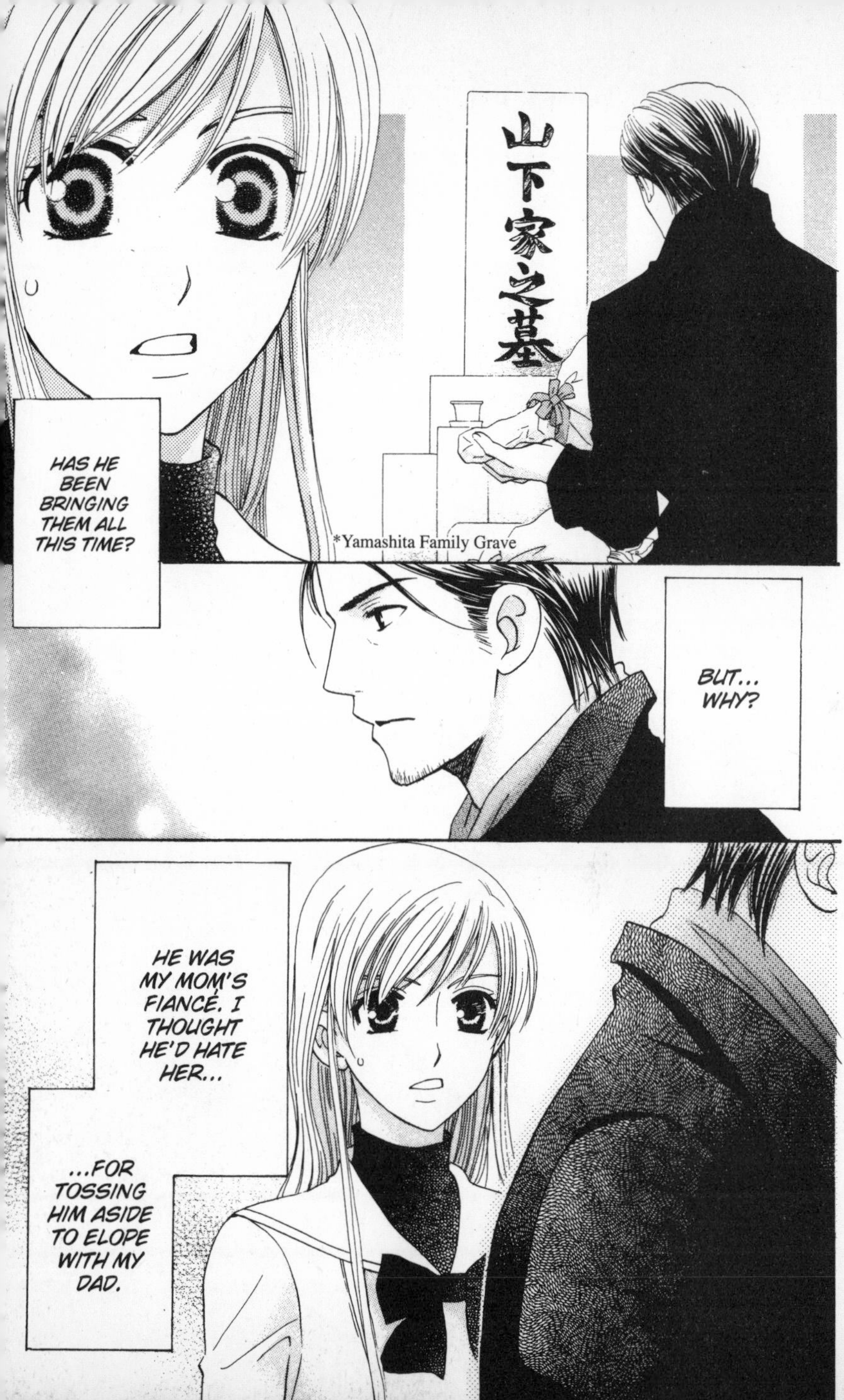
山下家之墓
*Yamashita Family Grave
HAS HE BEEN BRINGING THEM ALL THIS TIME?
BUT... WHY?
HE WAS MY MOM'S FIANCÉ. I THOUGHT HE'D HATE HER...
...FOR TOSSING HIM ASIDE TO ELOPE WITH MY DAD.

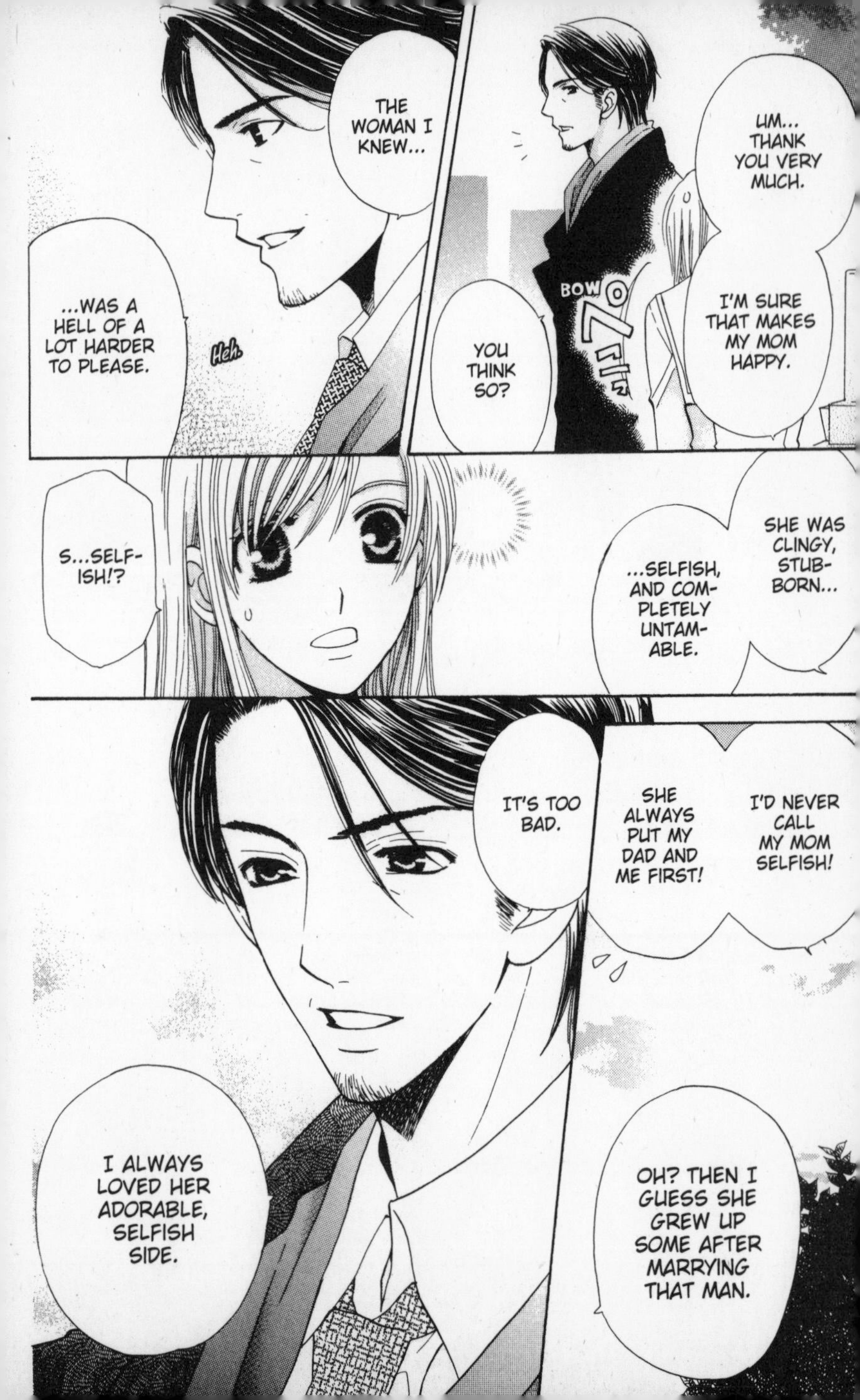
UM... THANK YOU VERY MUCH.
I'M SURE THAT MAKES MY MOM HAPPY.
BOW
YOU THINK SO?
THE WOMAN I KNEW...
...WAS A HELL OF A LOT HARDER TO PLEASE.
Heh.
SHE WAS CLINGY, STUBBORN...
...SELFISH, AND COMPLETELY UNTAMABLE.
S...SELFISH!?
I'D NEVER CALL MY MOM SELFISH!
SHE ALWAYS PUT MY DAD AND ME FIRST!
IT'S TOO BAD.
OH? THEN I GUESS SHE GREW UP SOME AFTER MARRYING THAT MAN.
I ALWAYS LOVED HER ADORABLE, SELFISH SIDE.

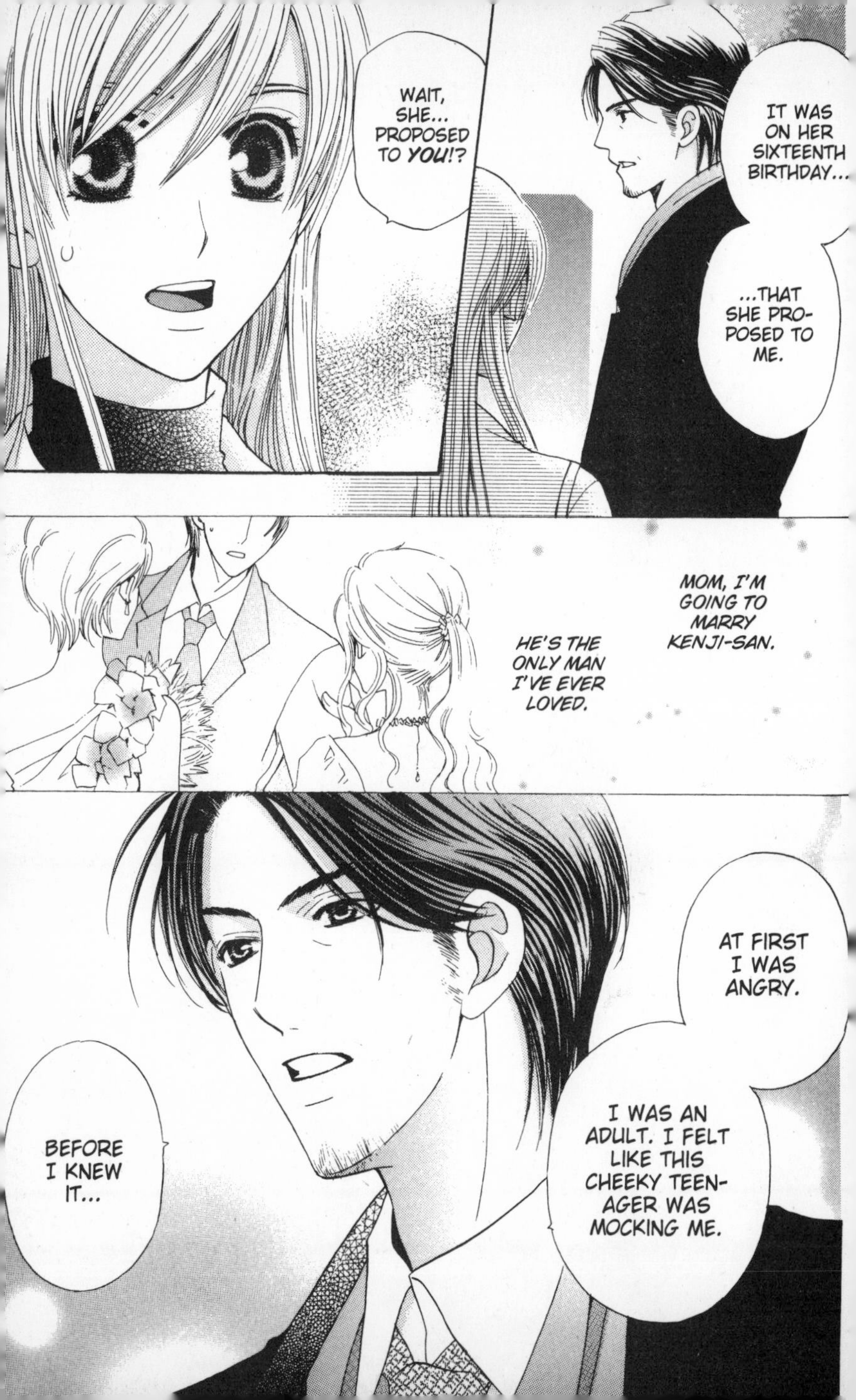
IT WAS ON HER SIXTEENTH BIRTHDAY...
...THAT SHE PROPOSED TO ME.
WAIT, SHE... PROPOSED TO *YOU*!?
MOM, I'M GOING TO MARRY KENJI-SAN.
HE'S THE ONLY MAN I'VE EVER LOVED.
AT FIRST I WAS ANGRY.
I WAS AN ADULT. I FELT LIKE THIS CHEEKY TEENAGER WAS MOCKING ME.
BEFORE I KNEW IT...

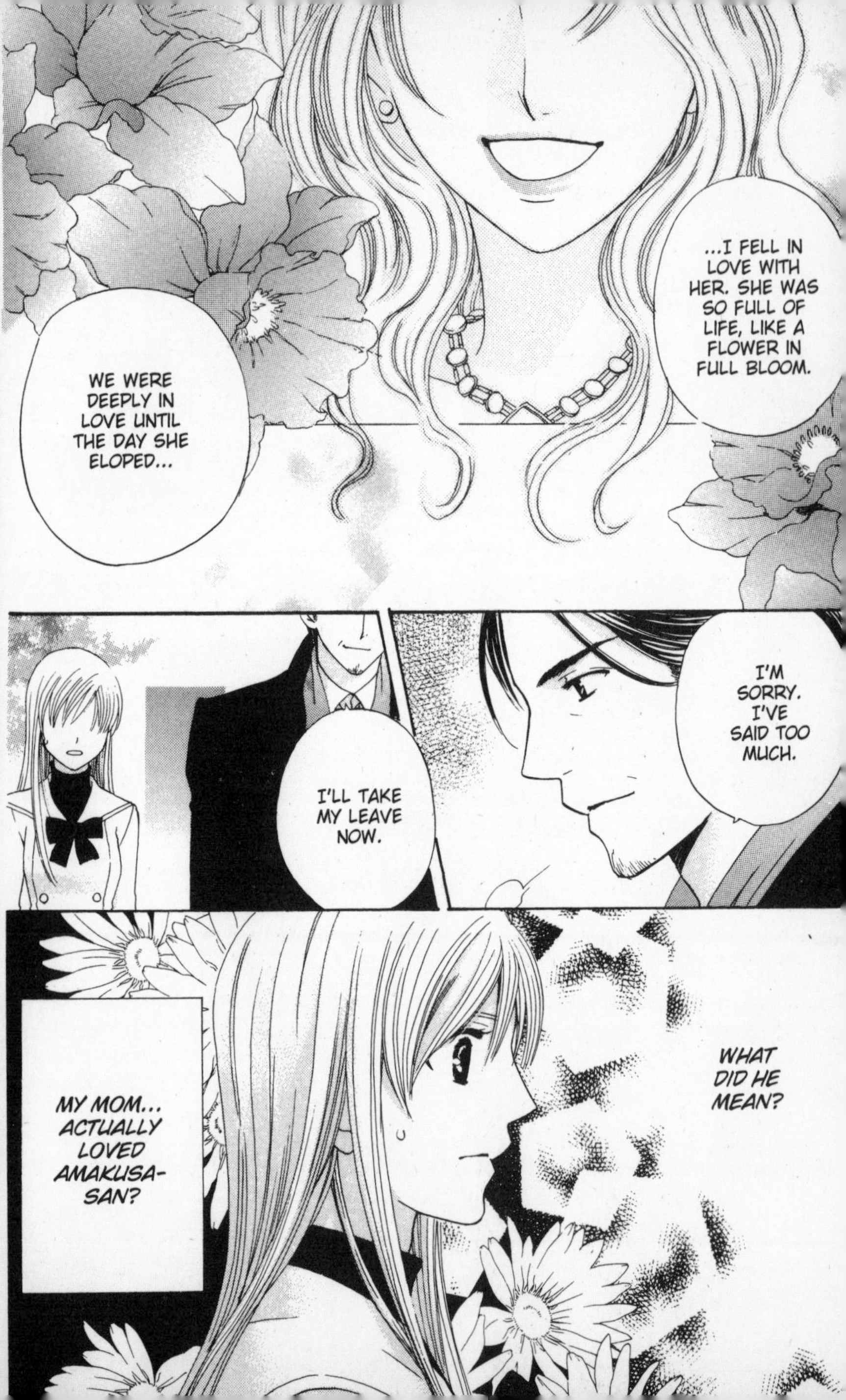
...I FELL IN LOVE WITH HER. SHE WAS SO FULL OF LIFE, LIKE A FLOWER IN FULL BLOOM.
WE WERE DEEPLY IN LOVE UNTIL THE DAY SHE ELOPED...
I'M SORRY. I'VE SAID TOO MUCH.
I'LL TAKE MY LEAVE NOW.
WHAT DID HE MEAN?
MY MOM... ACTUALLY LOVED AMAKUSA-SAN?

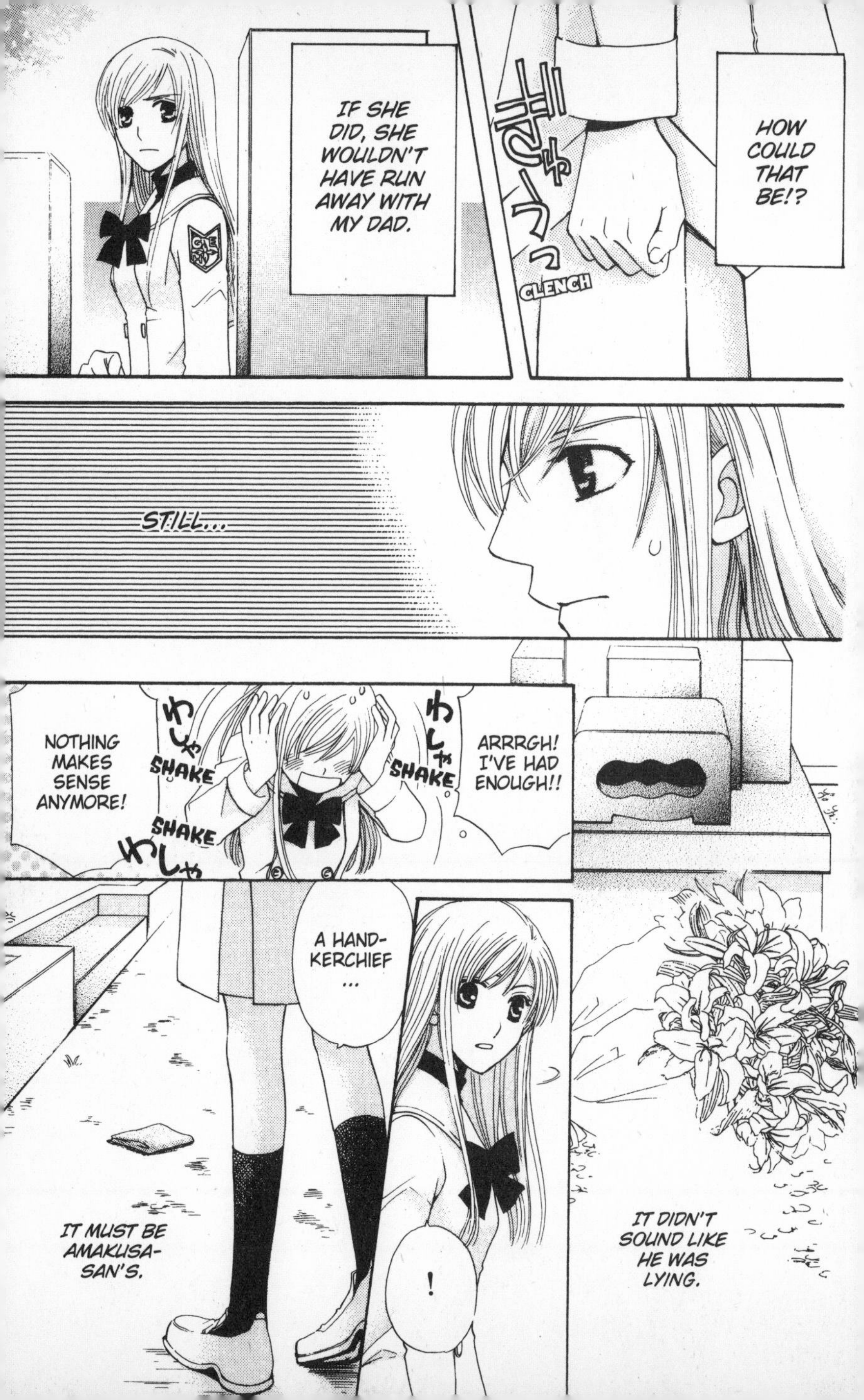
HOW COULD THAT BE!?
CLENCH
IF SHE DID, SHE WOULDN'T HAVE RUN AWAY WITH MY DAD.
STILL...
ARRRGH! I'VE HAD ENOUGH!!
SHAKE
SHAKE
SHAKE
NOTHING MAKES SENSE ANYMORE!
IT DIDN'T SOUND LIKE HE WAS LYING.
A HAND-KERCHIEF ...
!
IT MUST BE AMAKUSA-SAN'S.

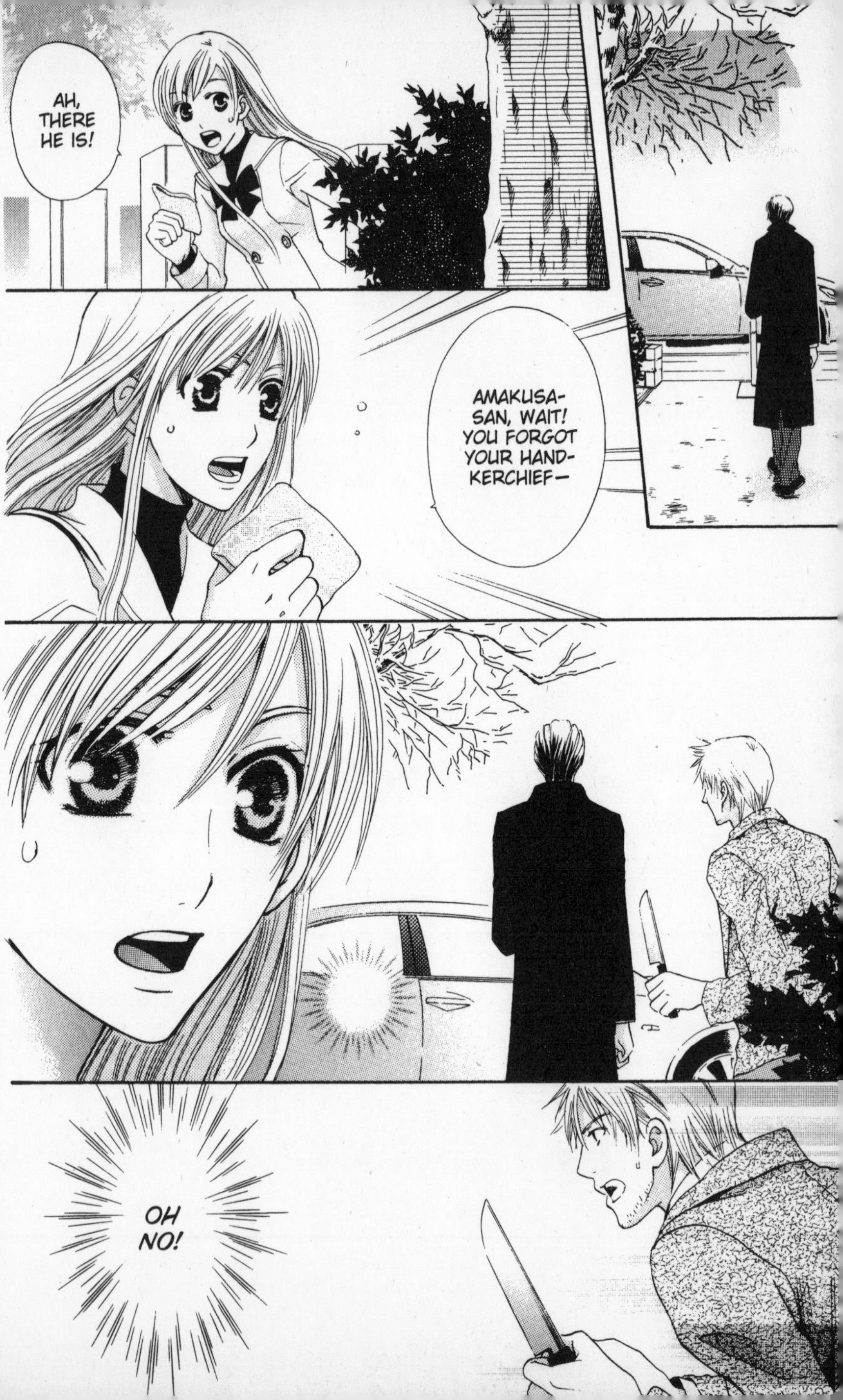
AH, THERE HE IS!
AMAKUSA-SAN, WAIT! YOU FORGOT YOUR HAND-KERCHIEF—
OH NO!

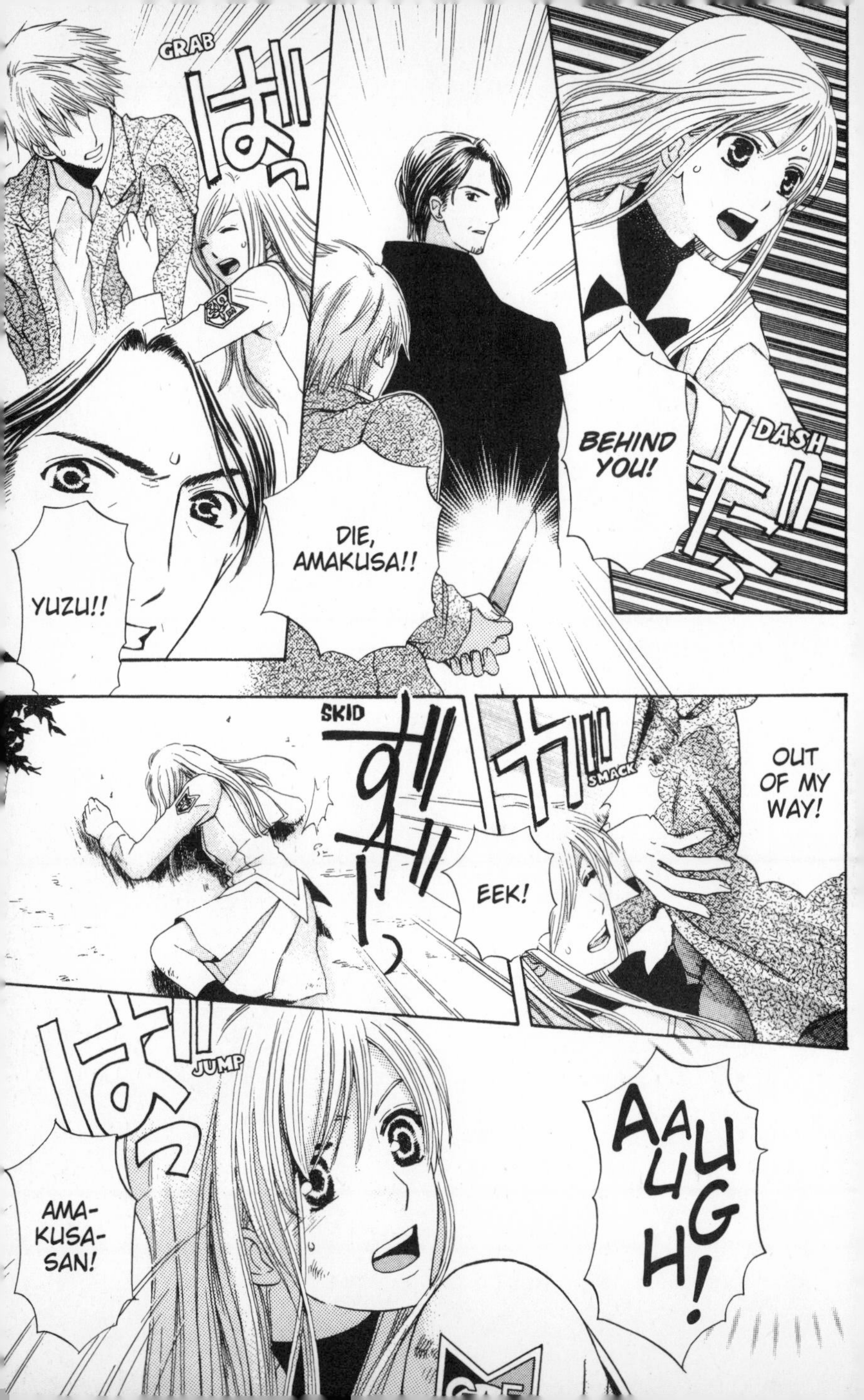
BEHIND YOU!
DASH
DIE, AMAKUSA!!
GRAB
YUZU!!
OUT OF MY WAY!
SMACK
EEK!
SKID
AAUUGH!
JUMP
AMA-KUSA-SAN!

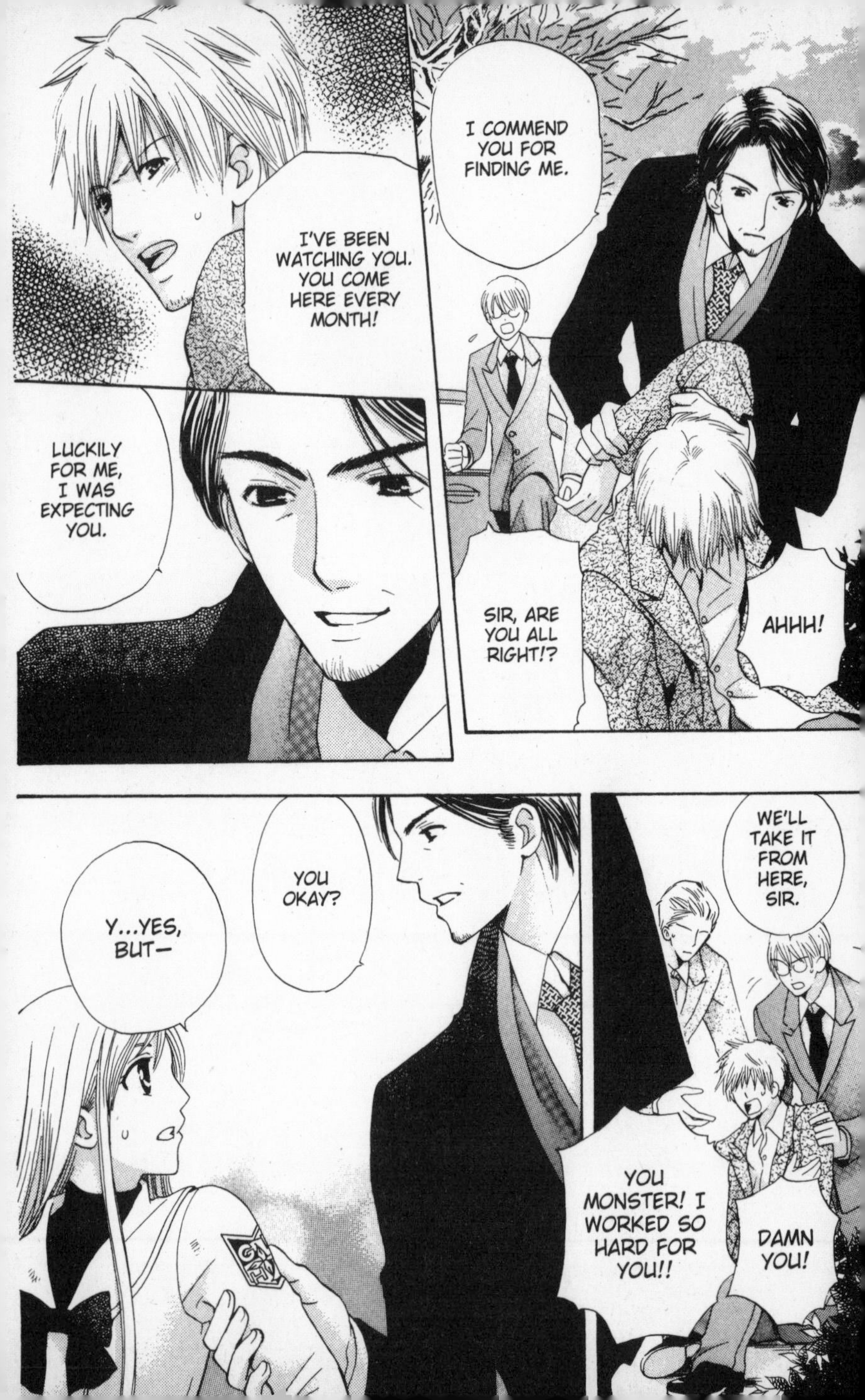
I COMMEND YOU FOR FINDING ME.
I'VE BEEN WATCHING YOU. YOU COME HERE EVERY MONTH!
LUCKILY FOR ME, I WAS EXPECTING YOU.
AHHH!
SIR, ARE YOU ALL RIGHT!?
WE'LL TAKE IT FROM HERE, SIR.
DAMN YOU!
YOU MONSTER! I WORKED SO HARD FOR YOU!!
YOU OKAY?
Y...YES, BUT—

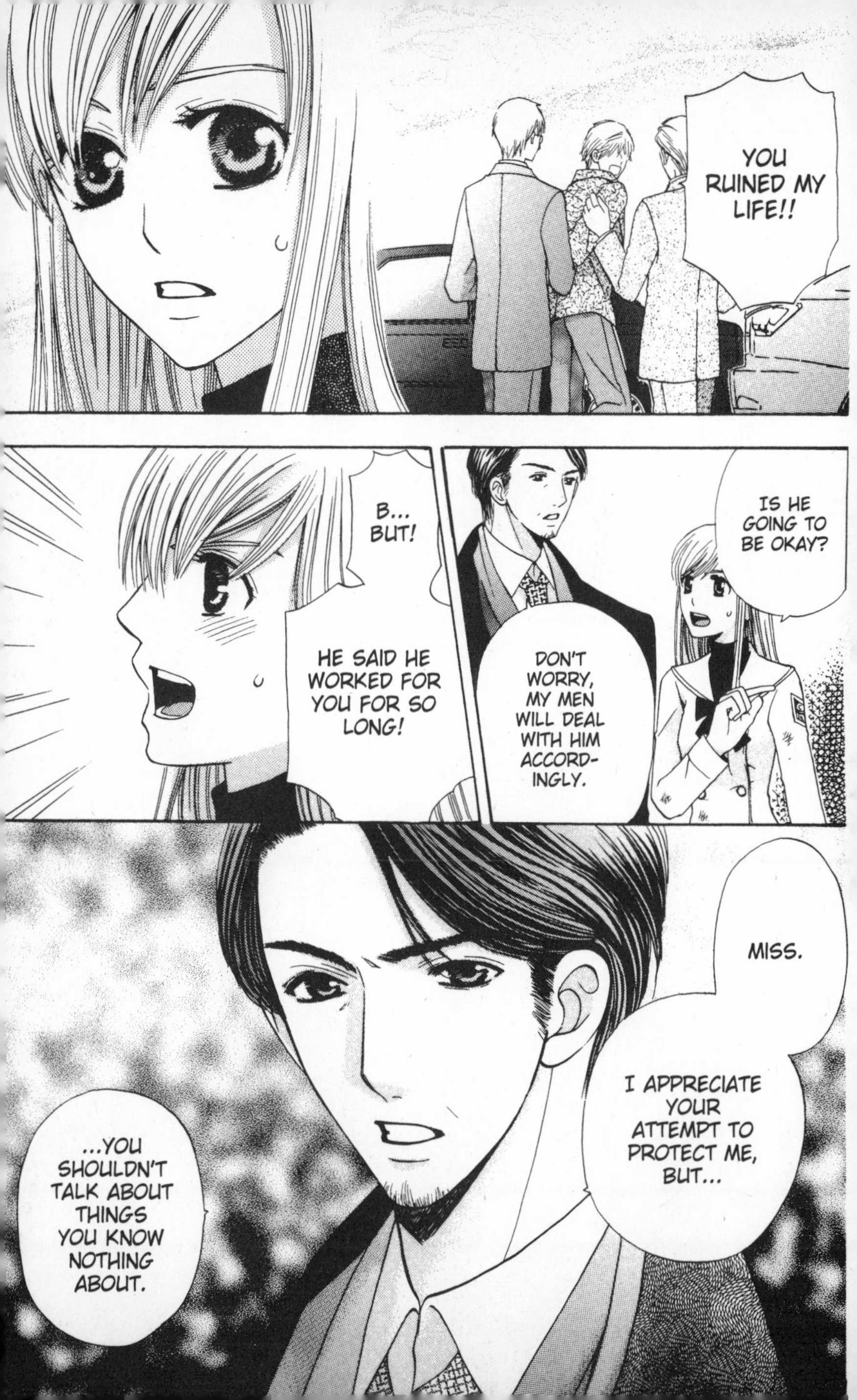
YOU RUINED MY LIFE!!
IS HE GOING TO BE OKAY?
DON'T WORRY, MY MEN WILL DEAL WITH HIM ACCORD-INGLY.
B... BUT!
HE SAID HE WORKED FOR YOU FOR SO LONG!
MISS.
I APPRECIATE YOUR ATTEMPT TO PROTECT ME, BUT...
...YOU SHOULDN'T TALK ABOUT THINGS YOU KNOW NOTHING ABOUT.

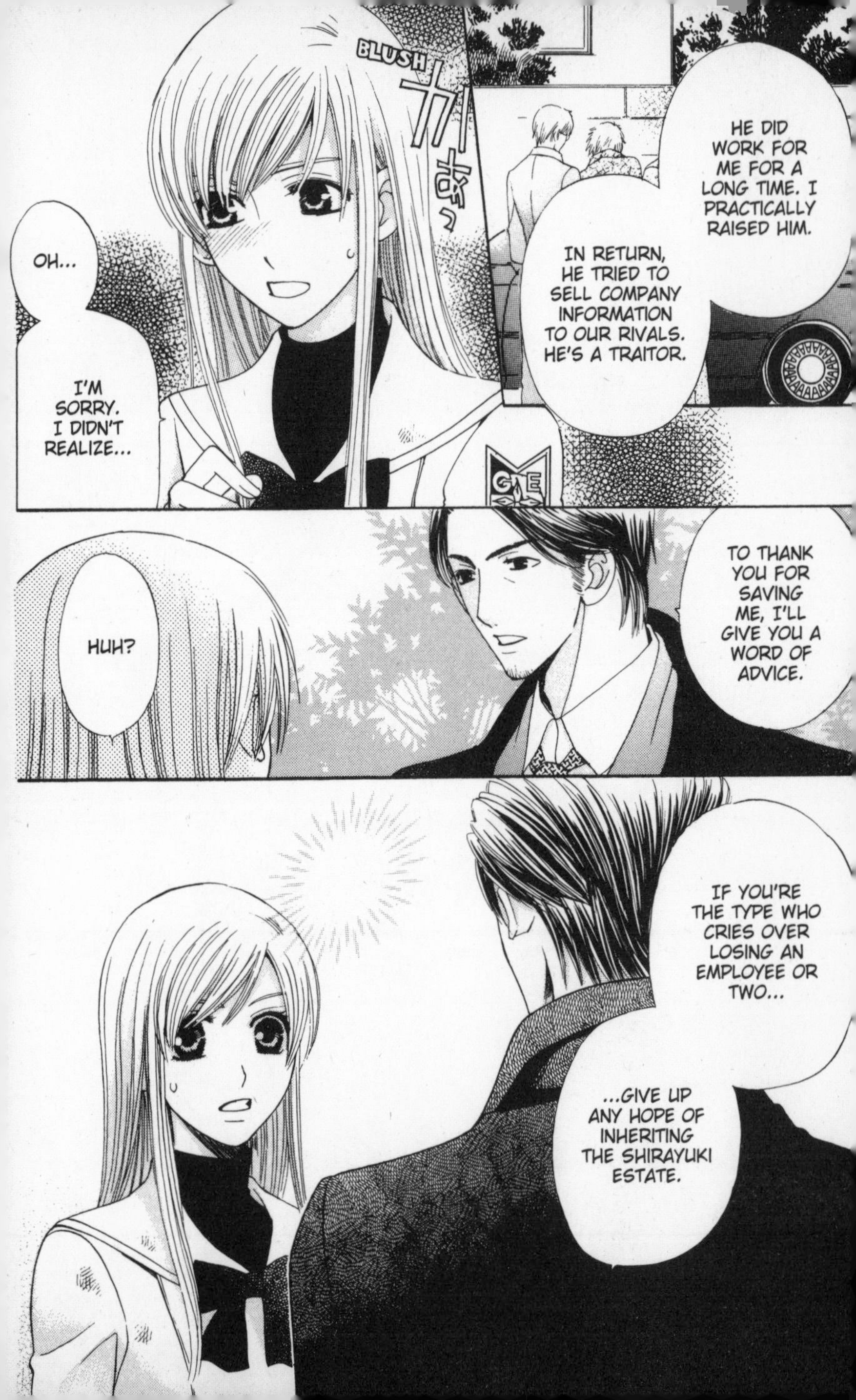
HE DID WORK FOR ME FOR A LONG TIME. I PRACTICALLY RAISED HIM.
IN RETURN, HE TRIED TO SELL COMPANY INFORMATION TO OUR RIVALS. HE'S A TRAITOR.
BLUSH
OH...
I'M SORRY. I DIDN'T REALIZE...
TO THANK YOU FOR SAVING ME, I'LL GIVE YOU A WORD OF ADVICE.
HUH?
IF YOU'RE THE TYPE WHO CRIES OVER LOSING AN EMPLOYEE OR TWO...
...GIVE UP ANY HOPE OF INHERITING THE SHIRAYUKI ESTATE.

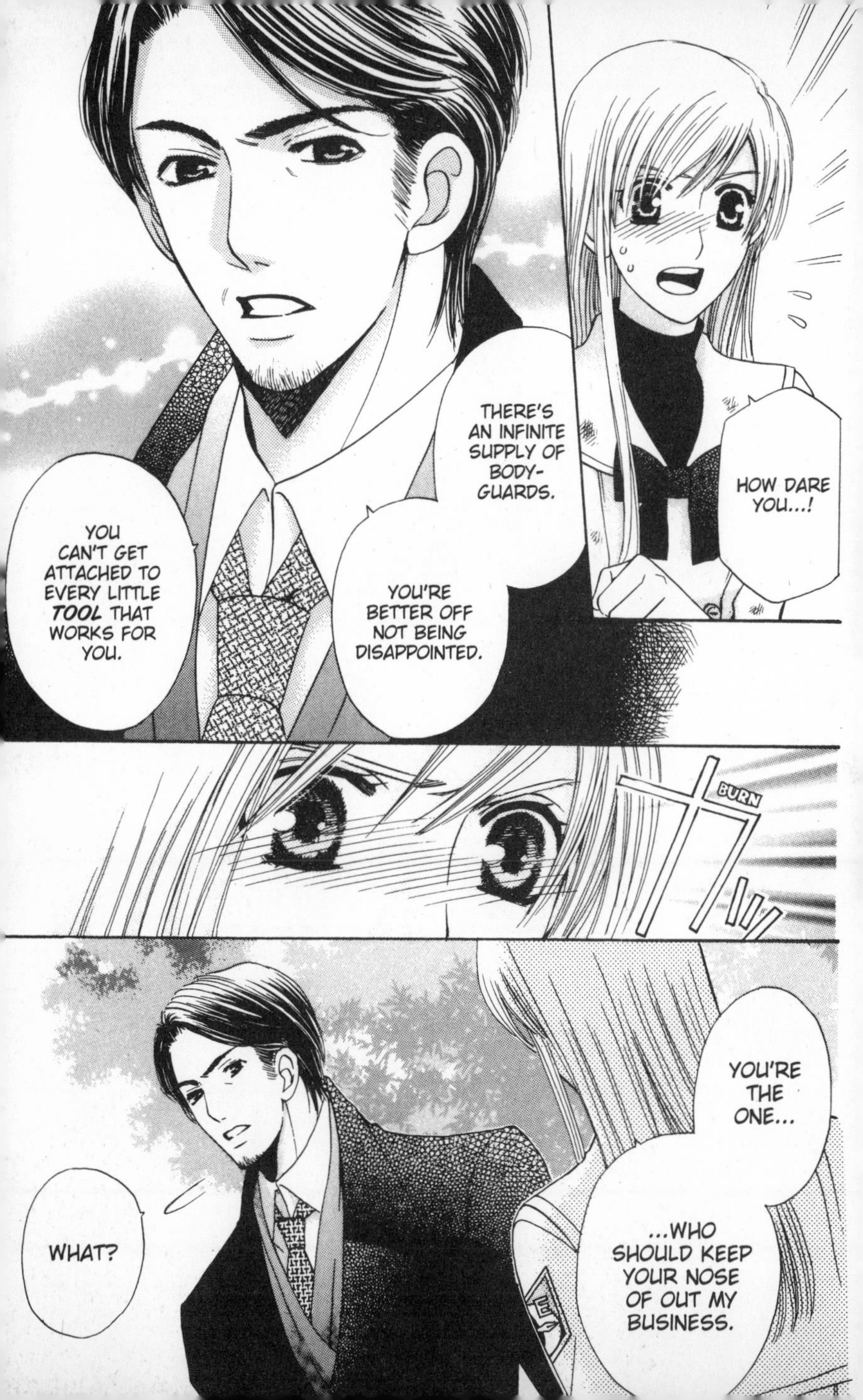
HOW DARE YOU...!
THERE'S AN INFINITE SUPPLY OF BODY-GUARDS.
YOU'RE BETTER OFF NOT BEING DISAPPOINTED.
YOU CAN'T GET ATTACHED TO EVERY LITTLE *TOOL* THAT WORKS FOR YOU.
BURN
YOU'RE THE ONE...
...WHO SHOULD KEEP YOUR NOSE OF OUT MY BUSINESS.
WHAT?

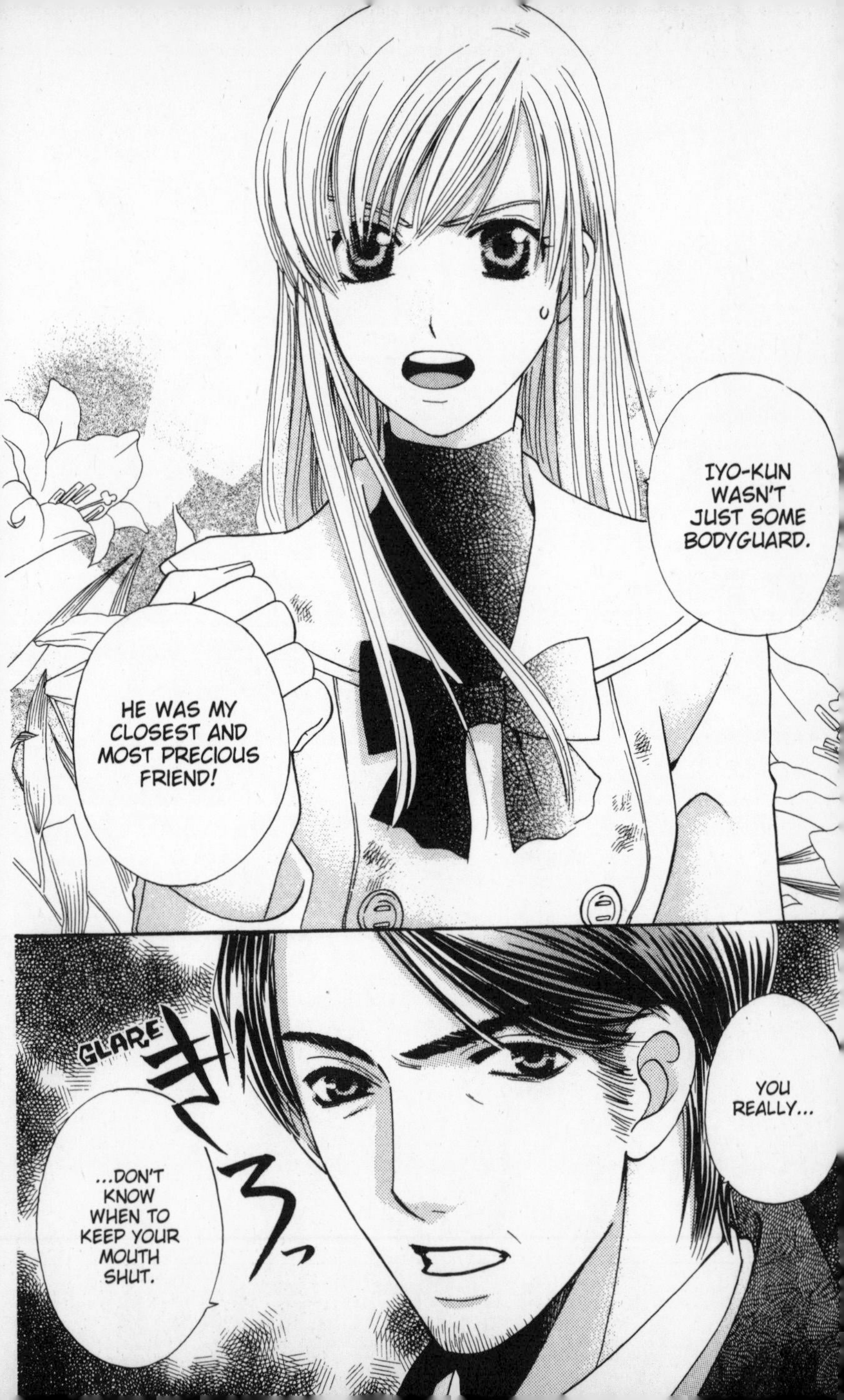
IYO-KUN WASN'T JUST SOME BODYGUARD.
HE WAS MY CLOSEST AND MOST PRECIOUS FRIEND!
GLARE
YOU REALLY...
...DON'T KNOW WHEN TO KEEP YOUR MOUTH SHUT.

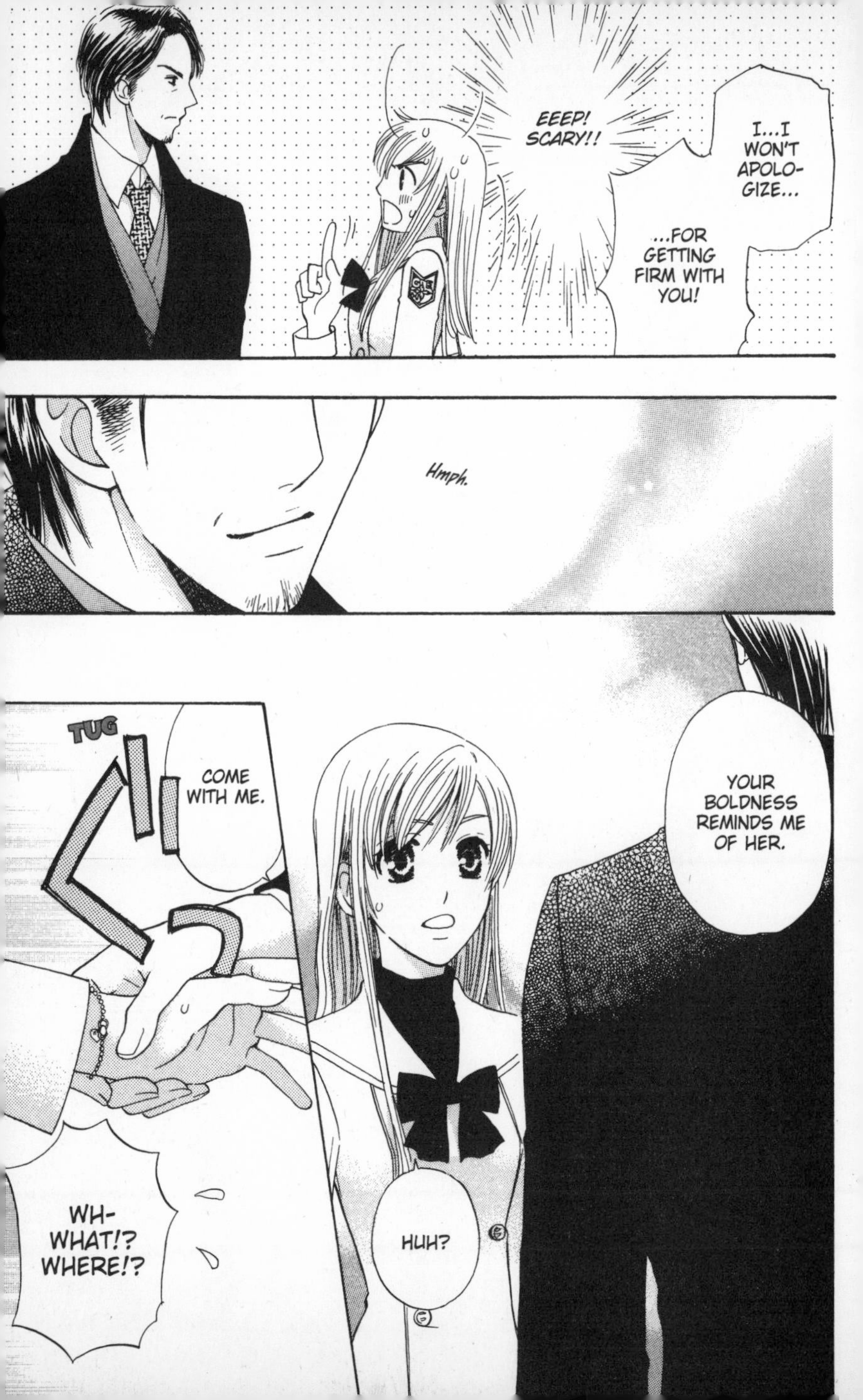
I...I WON'T APOLOGIZE...
...FOR GETTING FIRM WITH YOU!
EEEP! SCARY!!
Hmph.
YOUR BOLDNESS REMINDS ME OF HER.
HUH?
COME WITH ME.
TUG
WH-WHAT!? WHERE!?

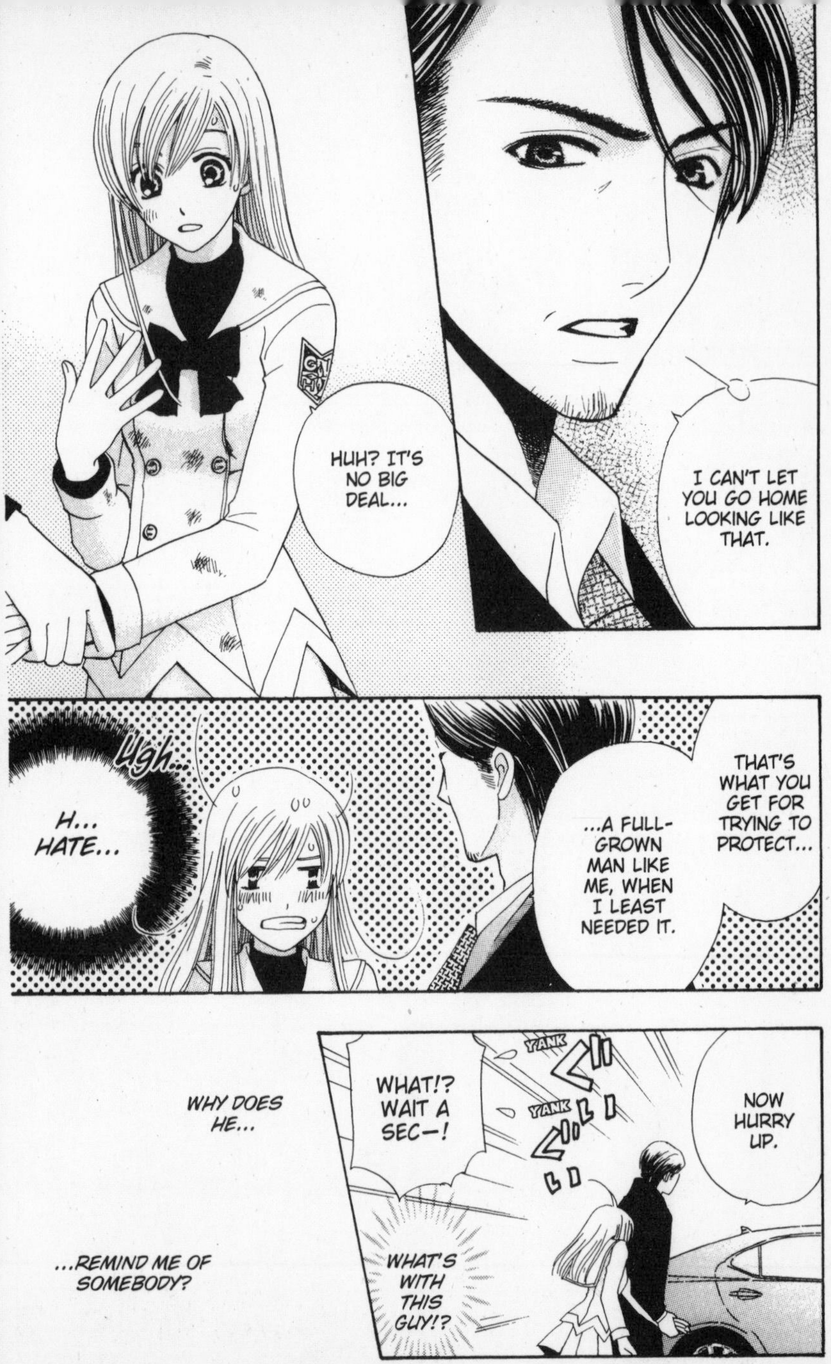
I CAN'T LET YOU GO HOME LOOKING LIKE THAT.
HUH? IT'S NO BIG DEAL...
THAT'S WHAT YOU GET FOR TRYING TO PROTECT...
...A FULL-GROWN MAN LIKE ME, WHEN I LEAST NEEDED IT.
Ugh...
H... HATE...
NOW HURRY UP.
YANK
YANK
WHAT!? WAIT A SEC—!
WHAT'S WITH THIS GUY!?
WHY DOES HE...
...REMIND ME OF SOMEBODY?

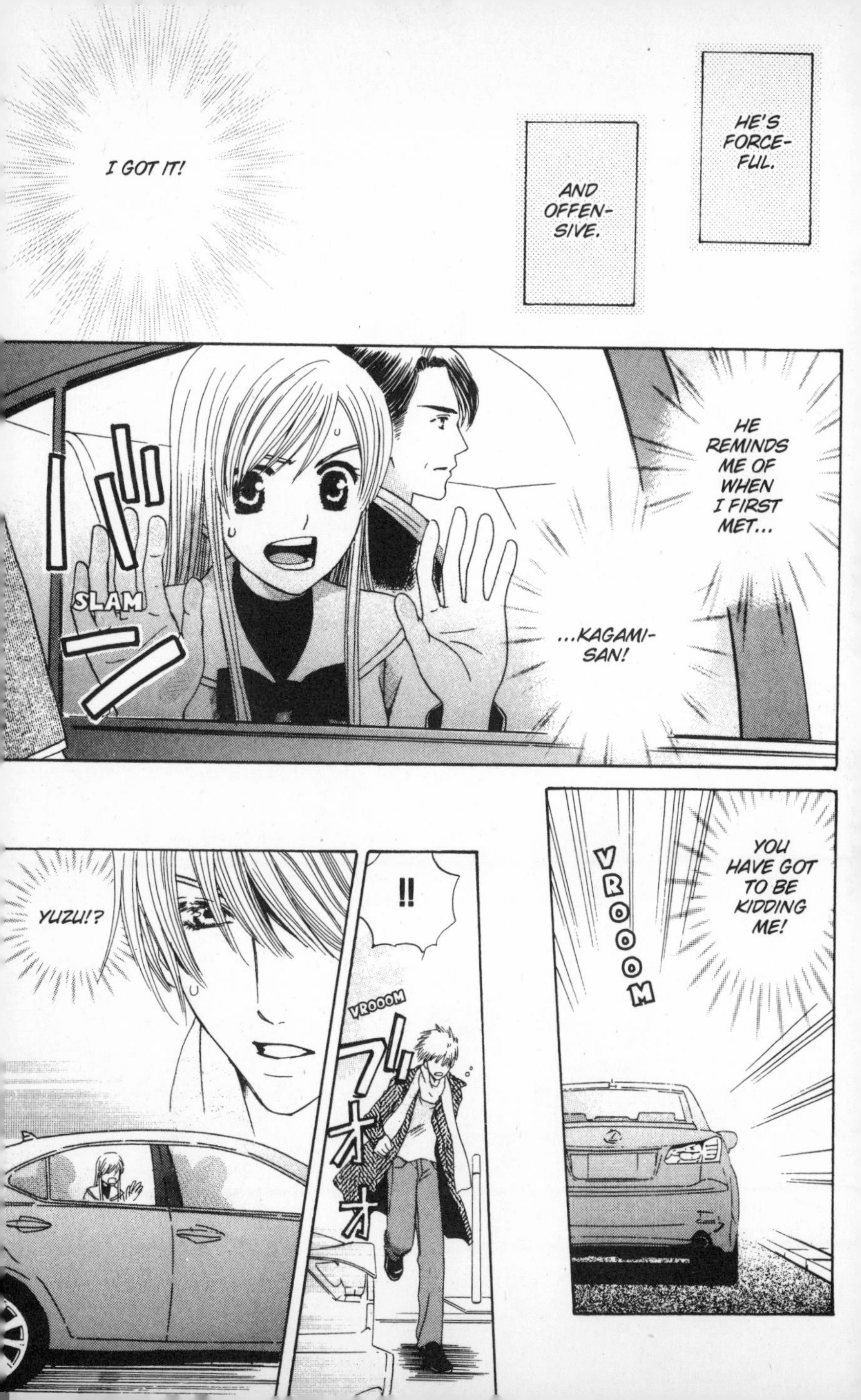

HE'S FORCE-FUL.
AND OFFEN-SIVE.
I GOT IT!
HE REMINDS ME OF WHEN I FIRST MET...
...KAGAMI-SAN!
SLAM
YOU HAVE GOT TO BE KIDDING ME!
VROOOOM
!!
VROOOM
YUZU!?

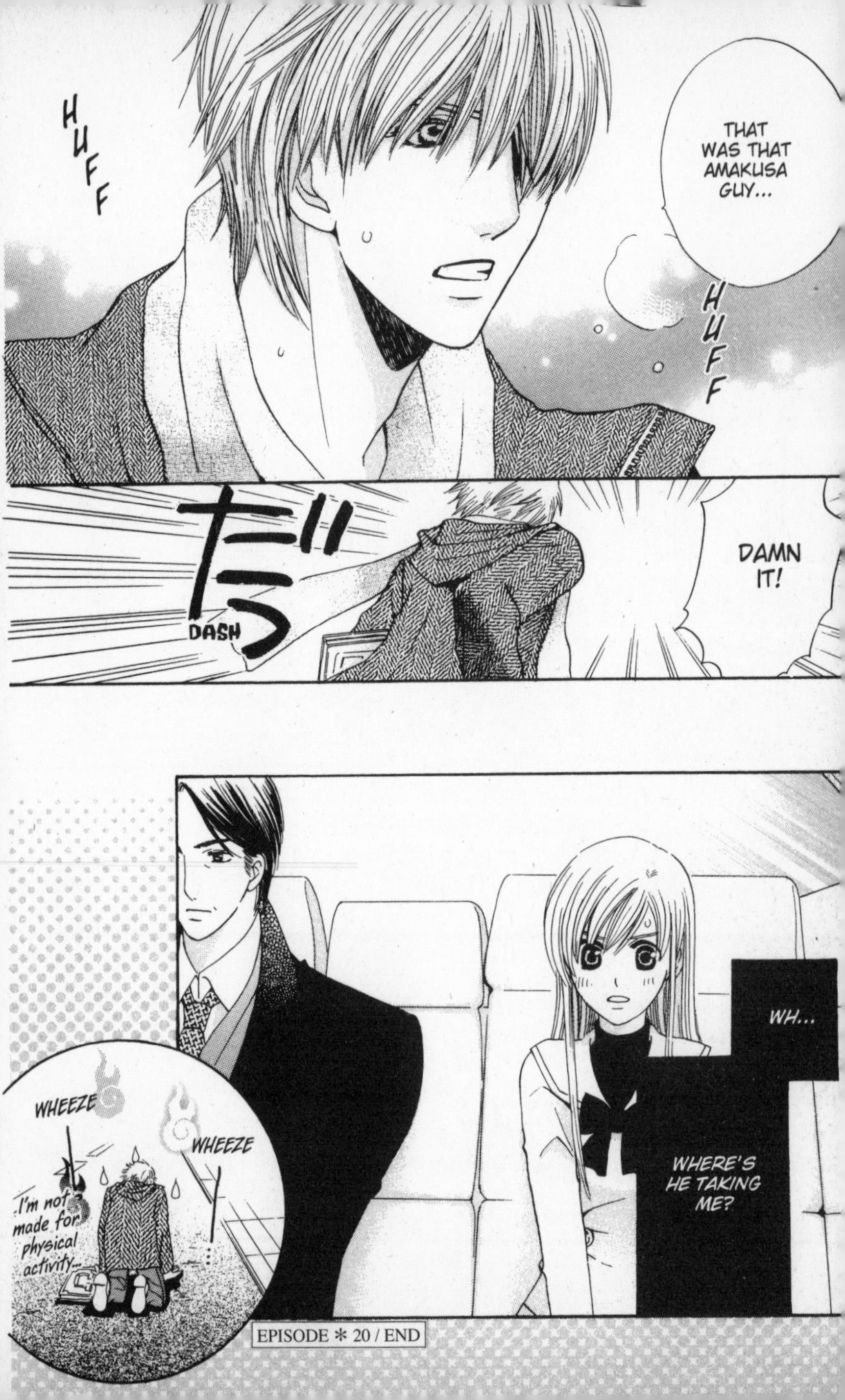
THAT WAS THAT AMAKUSA GUY...
HUFF HUFF
HUFF HUFF
DAMN IT!
だーっ
DASH
WH...
WHERE'S HE TAKING ME?
WHEEZE
WHEEZE
I'm not made for physical activity...
EPISODE ＊ 20 / END

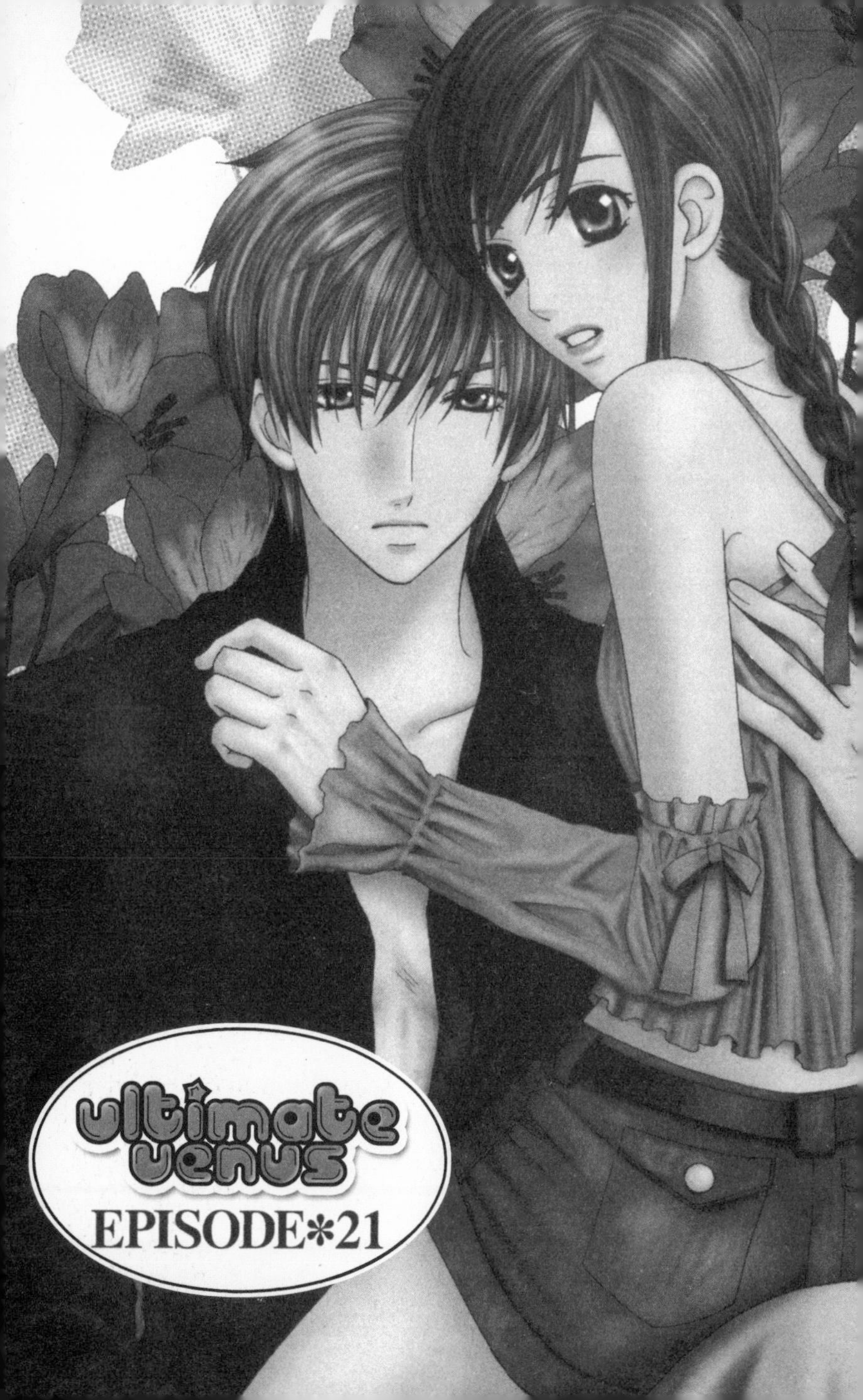
ultimate venus
EPISODE*21

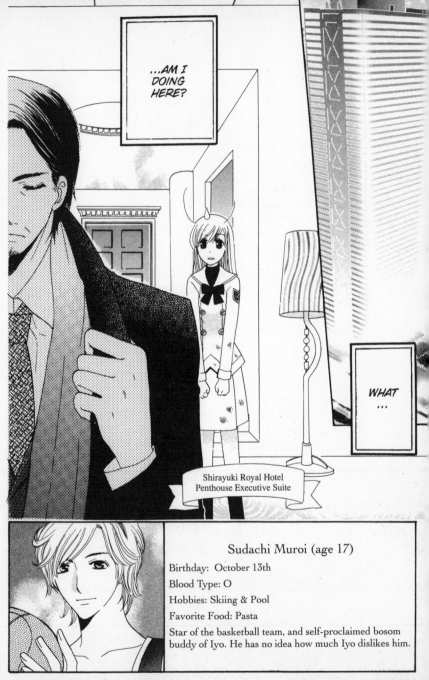

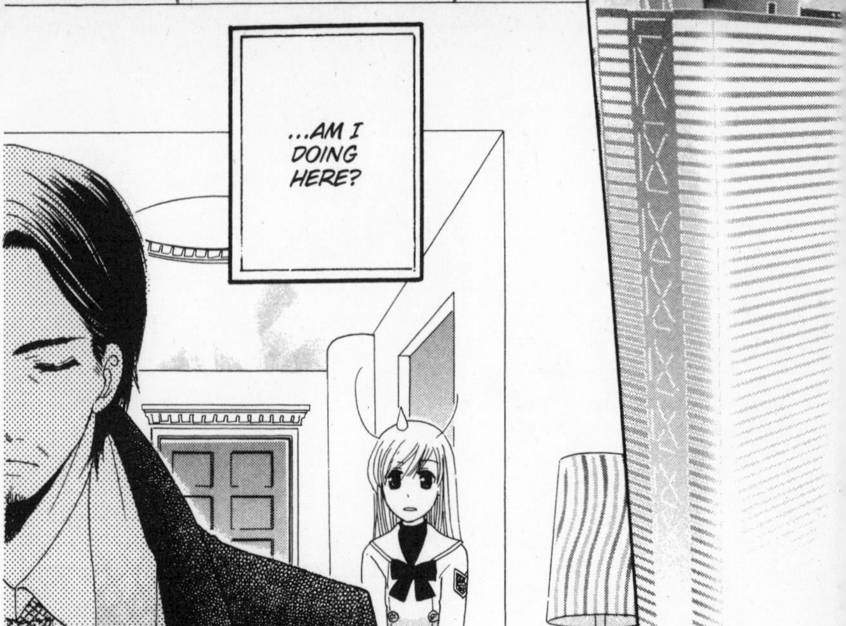
WHAT ...
...AM I DOING HERE?
Shirayuki Royal Hotel Penthouse Executive Suite

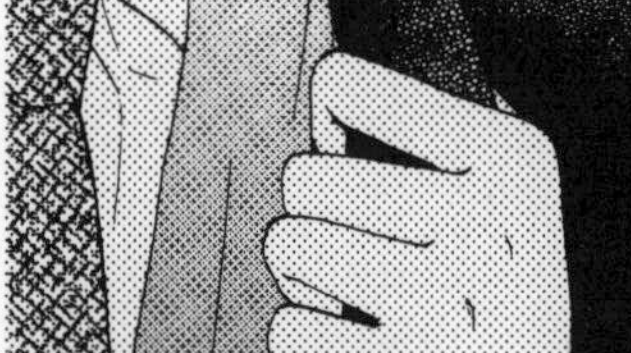

Sudachi Muroi (age 17)

Birthday: October 13th

Blood Type: O

Hobbies: Skiing & Pool

Favorite Food: Pasta

Star of the basketball team, and self-proclaimed bosom buddy of Iyo. He has no idea how much Iyo dislikes him.

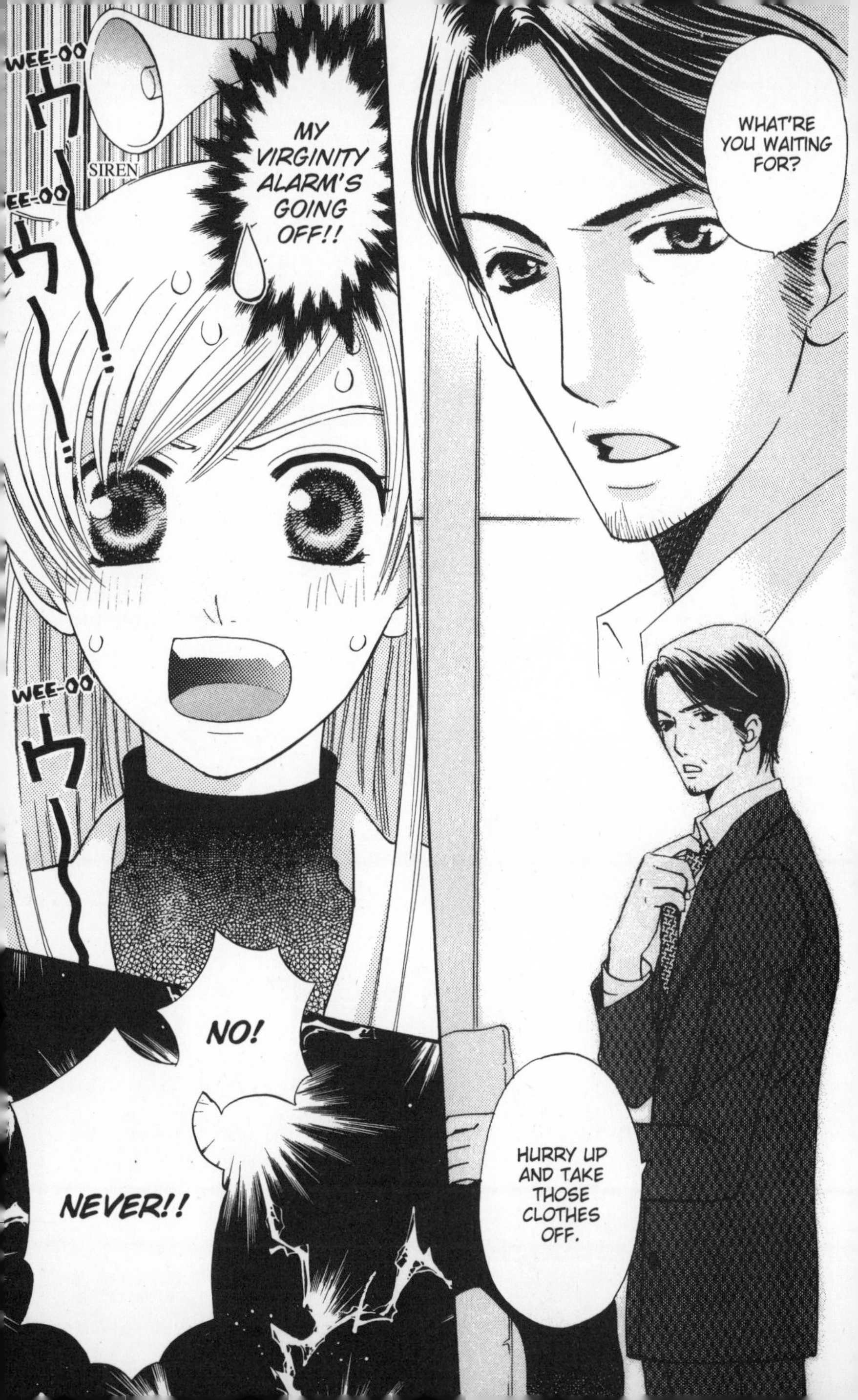
WHAT'RE YOU WAITING FOR?
MY VIRGINITY ALARM'S GOING OFF!!
SIREN
WEE-OO
EE-OO
WEE-OO
HURRY UP AND TAKE THOSE CLOTHES OFF.
NO!
NEVER!!

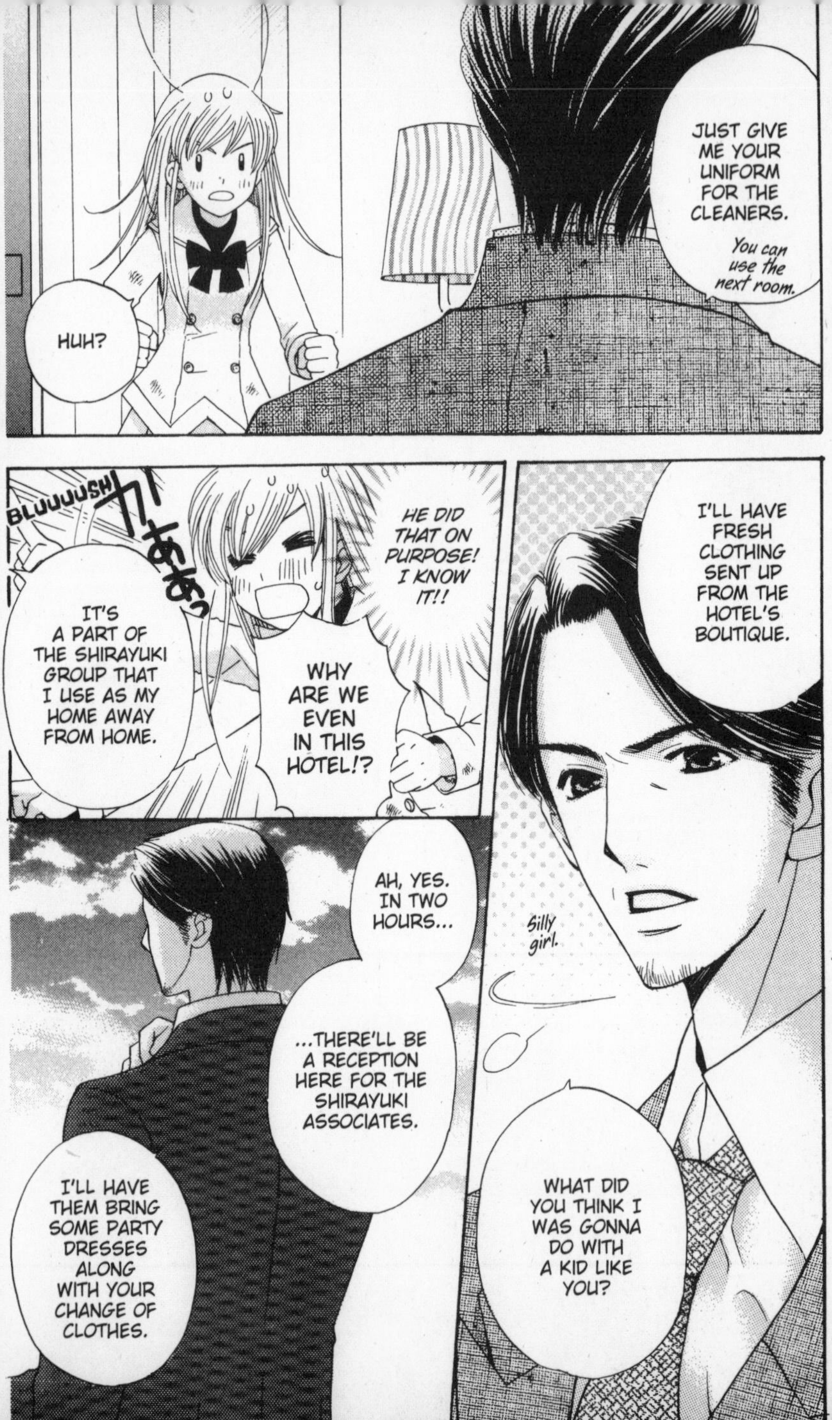

JUST GIVE ME YOUR UNIFORM FOR THE CLEANERS.
You can use the next room.
HUH?
I'LL HAVE FRESH CLOTHING SENT UP FROM THE HOTEL'S BOUTIQUE.
Silly girl.
WHAT DID YOU THINK I WAS GONNA DO WITH A KID LIKE YOU?
HE DID THAT ON PURPOSE! I KNOW IT!!
BLUUUUSH
カあぁっ
WHY ARE WE EVEN IN THIS HOTEL!?
IT'S A PART OF THE SHIRAYUKI GROUP THAT I USE AS MY HOME AWAY FROM HOME.
AH, YES. IN TWO HOURS...
...THERE'LL BE A RECEPTION HERE FOR THE SHIRAYUKI ASSOCIATES.
I'LL HAVE THEM BRING SOME PARTY DRESSES ALONG WITH YOUR CHANGE OF CLOTHES.

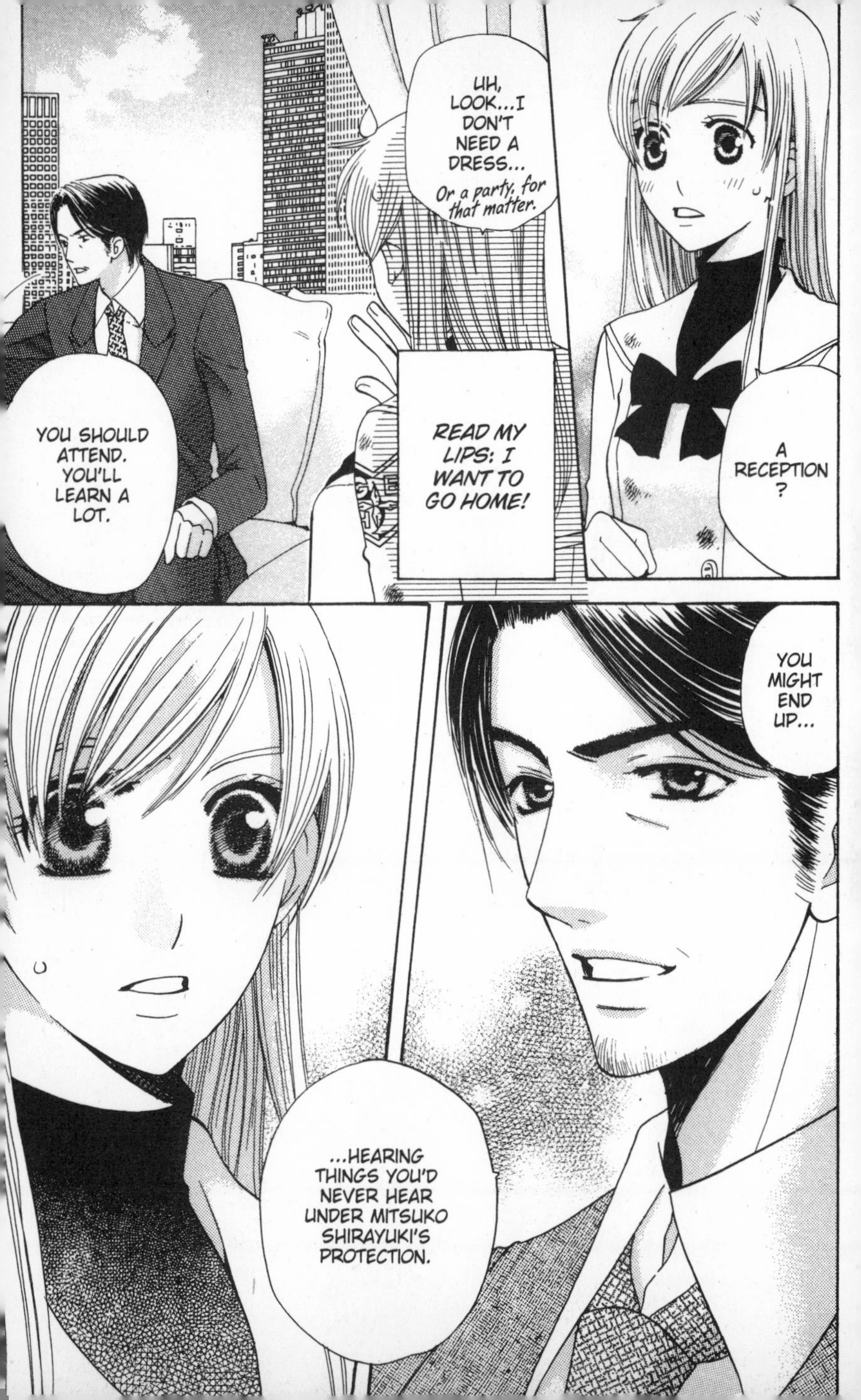
A RECEPTION?
UH, LOOK...I DON'T NEED A DRESS...
Or a party, for that matter.
READ MY LIPS: I WANT TO GO HOME!
YOU SHOULD ATTEND. YOU'LL LEARN A LOT.
YOU MIGHT END UP...
...HEARING THINGS YOU'D NEVER HEAR UNDER MITSUKO SHIRAYUKI'S PROTECTION.

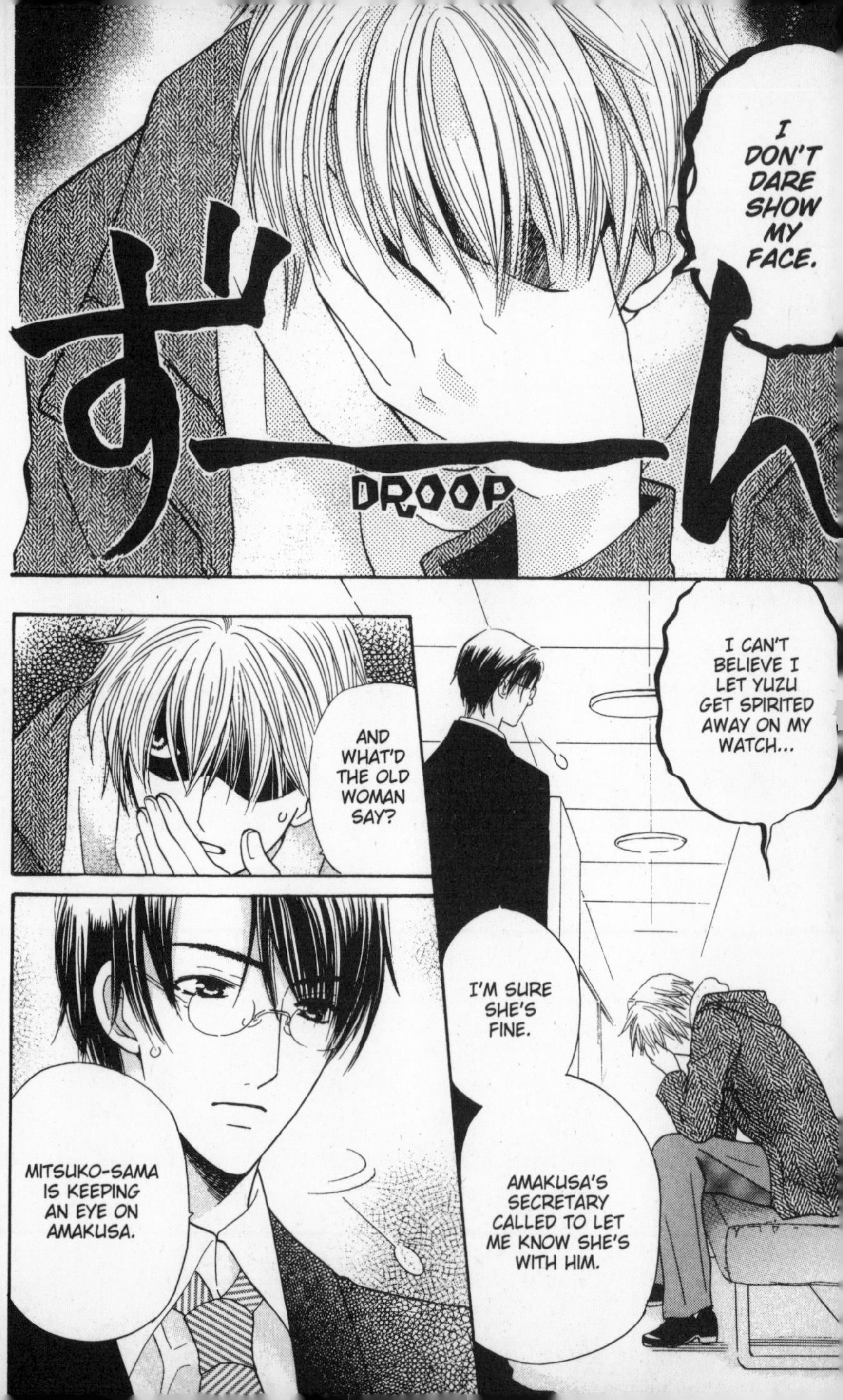
I DON'T DARE SHOW MY FACE.
ずーん
DROOP
I CAN'T BELIEVE I LET YUZU GET SPIRITED AWAY ON MY WATCH...
AND WHAT'D THE OLD WOMAN SAY?
I'M SURE SHE'S FINE.
AMAKUSA'S SECRETARY CALLED TO LET ME KNOW SHE'S WITH HIM.
MITSUKO-SAMA IS KEEPING AN EYE ON AMAKUSA.

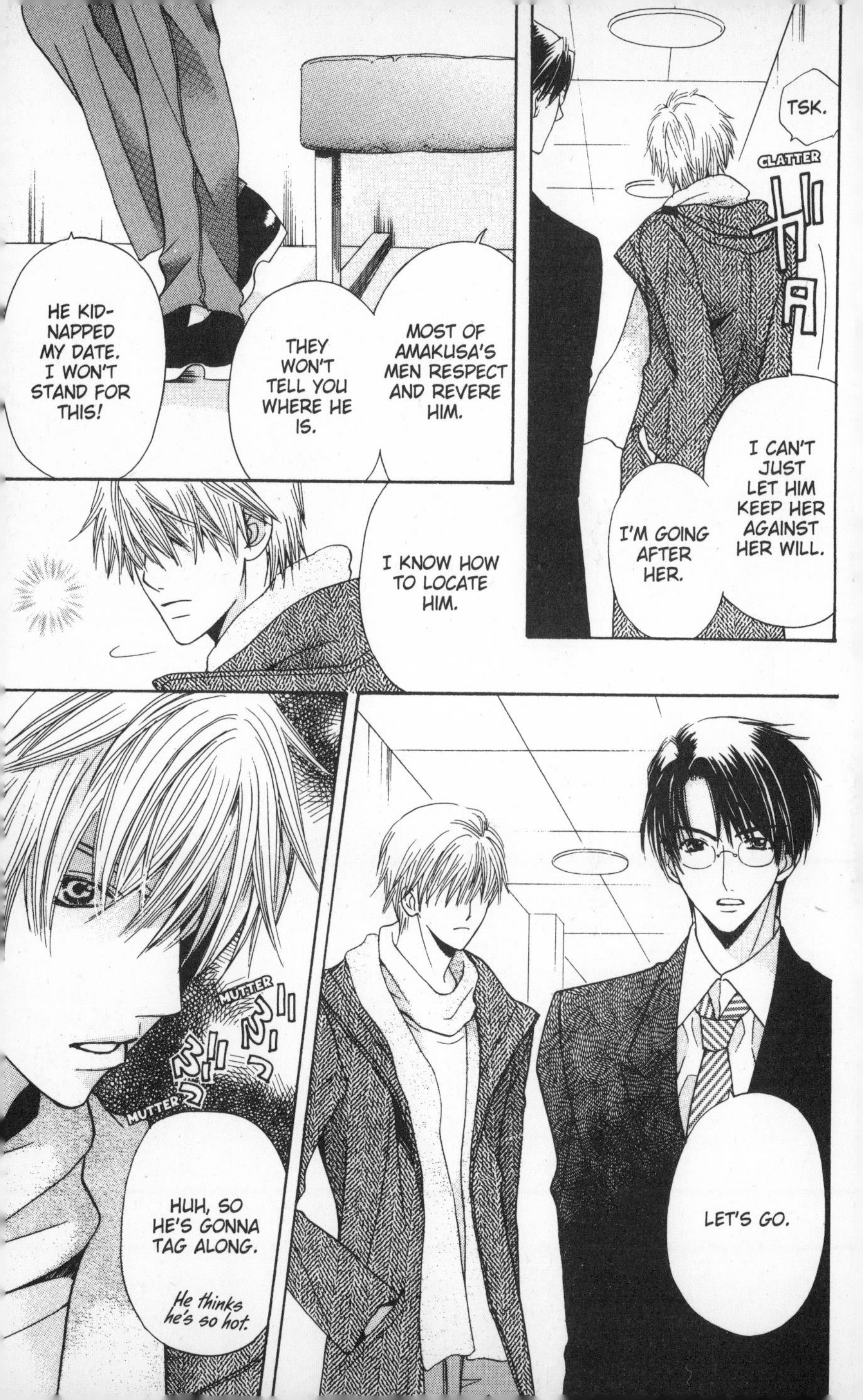
TSK.
CLATTER
I CAN'T JUST LET HIM KEEP HER AGAINST HER WILL.
I'M GOING AFTER HER.
MOST OF AMAKUSA'S MEN RESPECT AND REVERE HIM.
THEY WON'T TELL YOU WHERE HE IS.
HE KID-NAPPED MY DATE. I WON'T STAND FOR THIS!
I KNOW HOW TO LOCATE HIM.
LET'S GO.
MUTTER
MUTTER
HUH, SO HE'S GONNA TAG ALONG.
He thinks he's so hot.

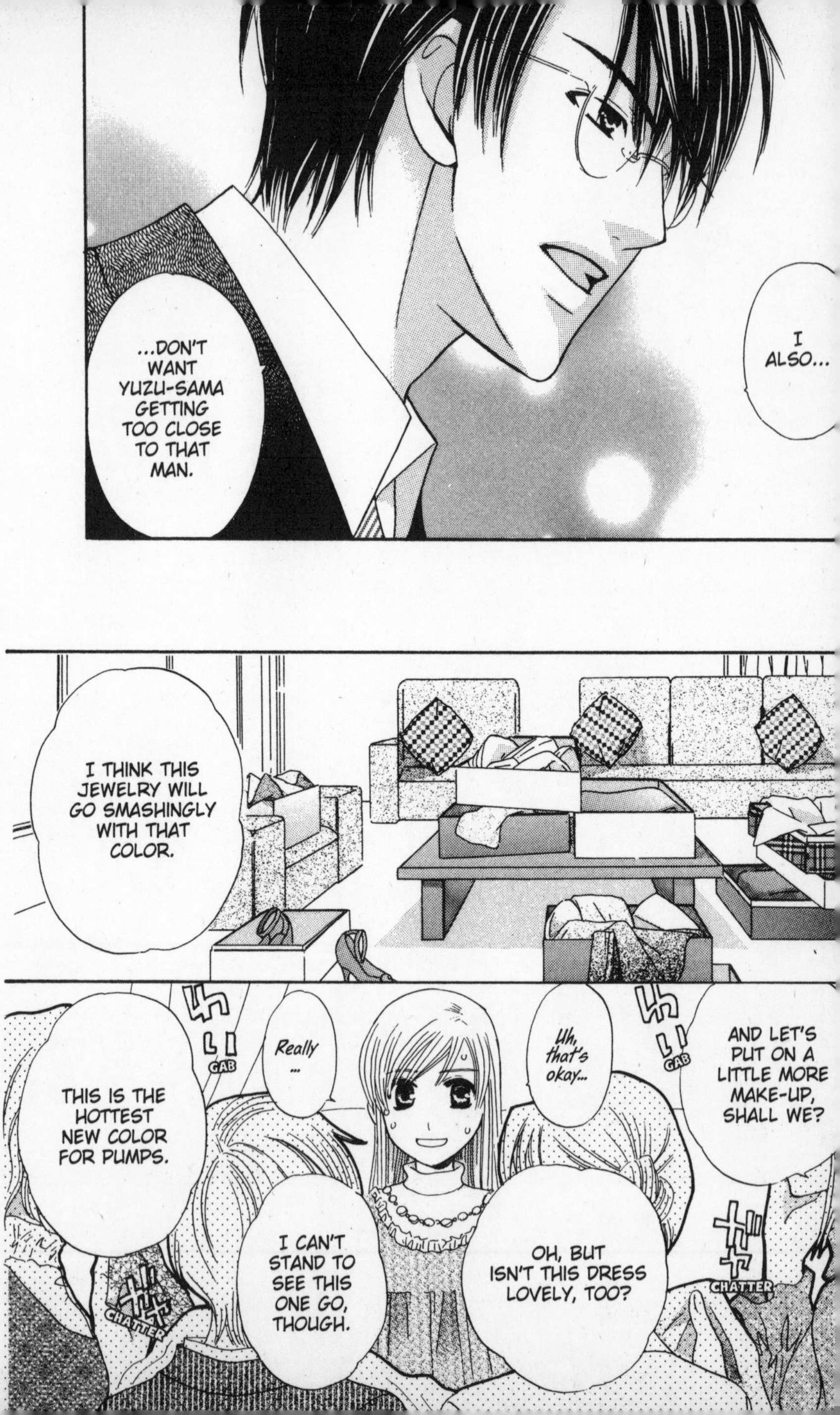
I ALSO...
...DON'T WANT YUZU-SAMA GETTING TOO CLOSE TO THAT MAN.
I THINK THIS JEWELRY WILL GO SMASHINGLY WITH THAT COLOR.
AND LET'S PUT ON A LITTLE MORE MAKE-UP, SHALL WE?
GAB
Uh, that's okay...
Really ...
GAB
THIS IS THE HOTTEST NEW COLOR FOR PUMPS.
CHATTER
OH, BUT ISN'T THIS DRESS LOVELY, TOO?
I CAN'T STAND TO SEE THIS ONE GO, THOUGH.
CHATTER

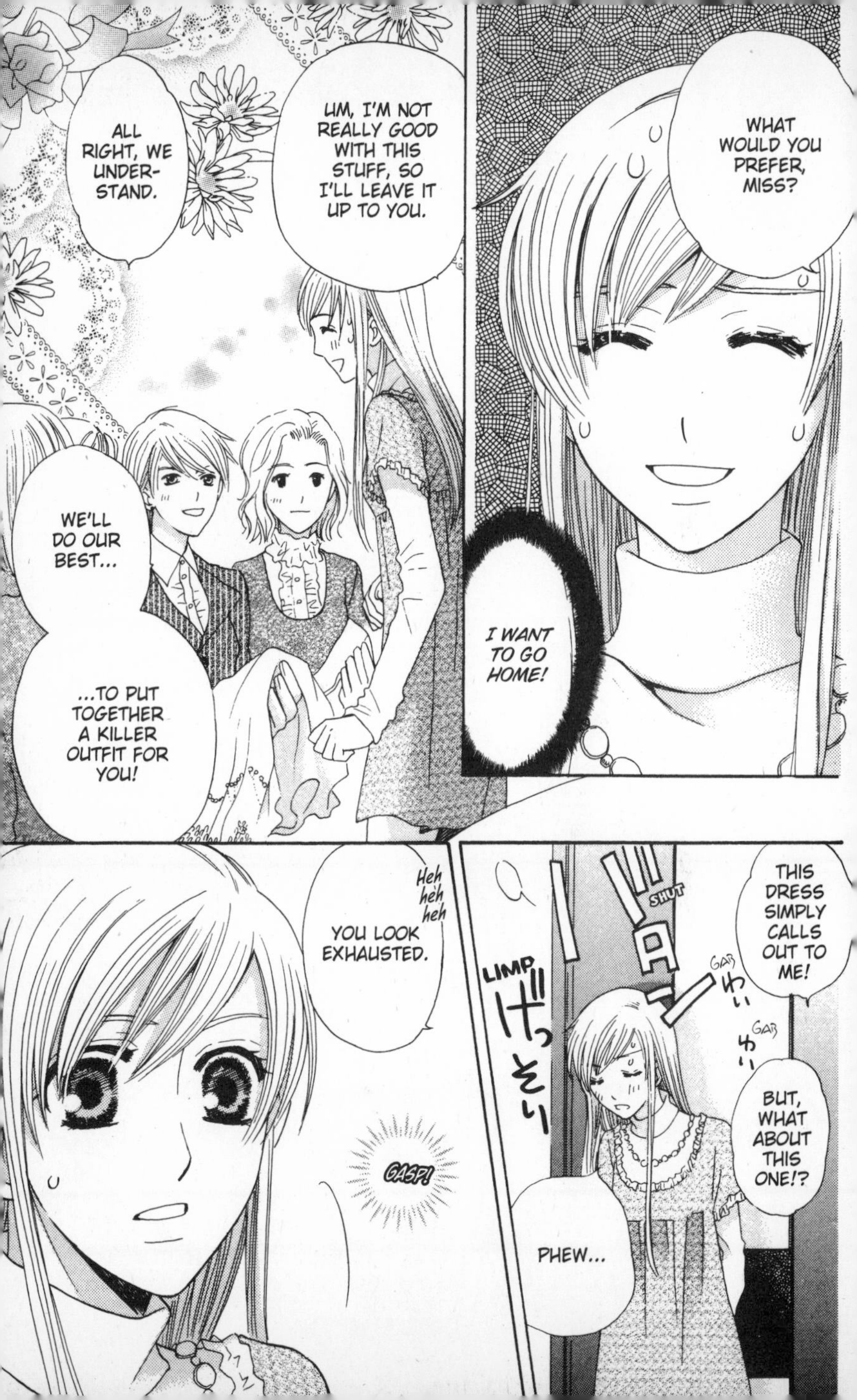
WHAT WOULD YOU PREFER, MISS?
I WANT TO GO HOME!
UM, I'M NOT REALLY GOOD WITH THIS STUFF, SO I'LL LEAVE IT UP TO YOU.
ALL RIGHT, WE UNDERSTAND.
WE'LL DO OUR BEST...
...TO PUT TOGETHER A KILLER OUTFIT FOR YOU!
SHUT
THIS DRESS SIMPLY CALLS OUT TO ME!
GAB
わい
GAB
わい
BUT, WHAT ABOUT THIS ONE!?
LIMP
げっそり
PHEW...
Heh heh heh
YOU LOOK EXHAUSTED.
GASP!

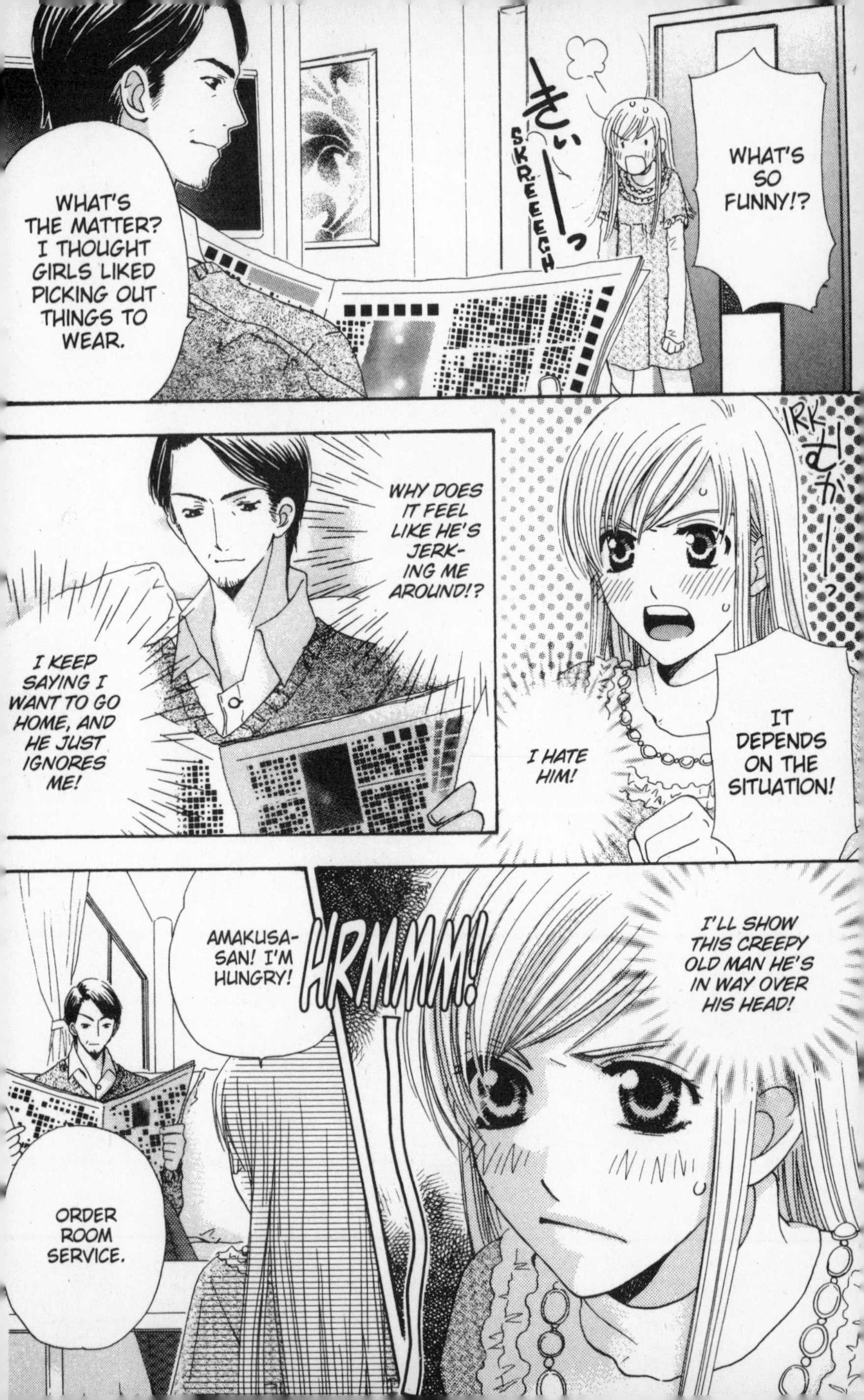
WHAT'S SO FUNNY!?
きぃーっ
SKREEEECH
WHAT'S THE MATTER? I THOUGHT GIRLS LIKED PICKING OUT THINGS TO WEAR.
IRK
IT DEPENDS ON THE SITUATION!
I HATE HIM!
WHY DOES IT FEEL LIKE HE'S JERK-ING ME AROUND!?
I KEEP SAYING I WANT TO GO HOME, AND HE JUST IGNORES ME!
I'LL SHOW THIS CREEPY OLD MAN HE'S IN WAY OVER HIS HEAD!
HRMMM!
AMAKUSA-SAN! I'M HUNGRY!
ORDER ROOM SERVICE.

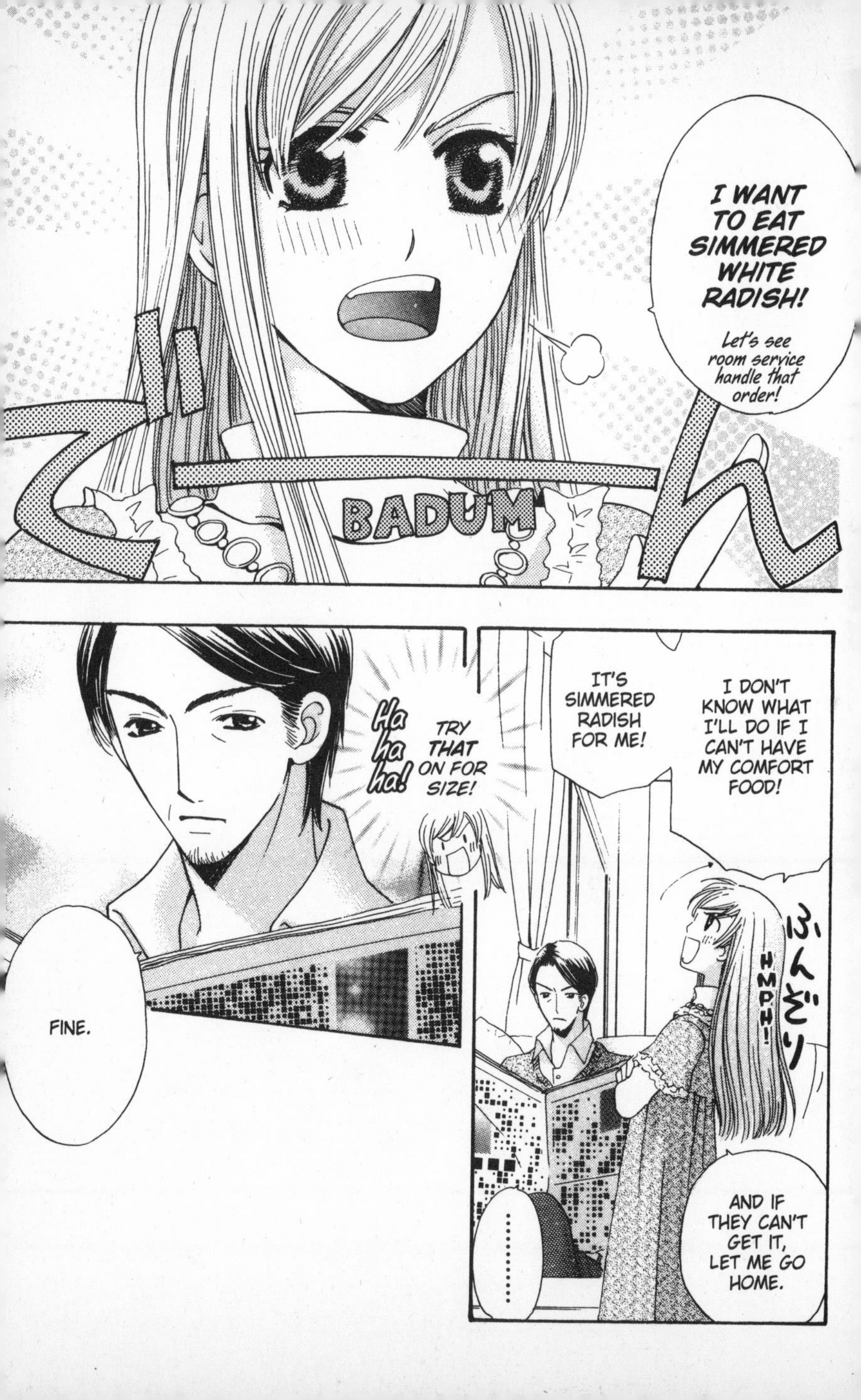
I WANT TO EAT SIMMERED WHITE RADISH!
Let's see room service handle that order!
BADUM
I DON'T KNOW WHAT I'LL DO IF I CAN'T HAVE MY COMFORT FOOD!
IT'S SIMMERED RADISH FOR ME!
TRY THAT ON FOR SIZE!
Ha ha ha!
HMPH!
AND IF THEY CAN'T GET IT, LET ME GO HOME.
......
FINE.

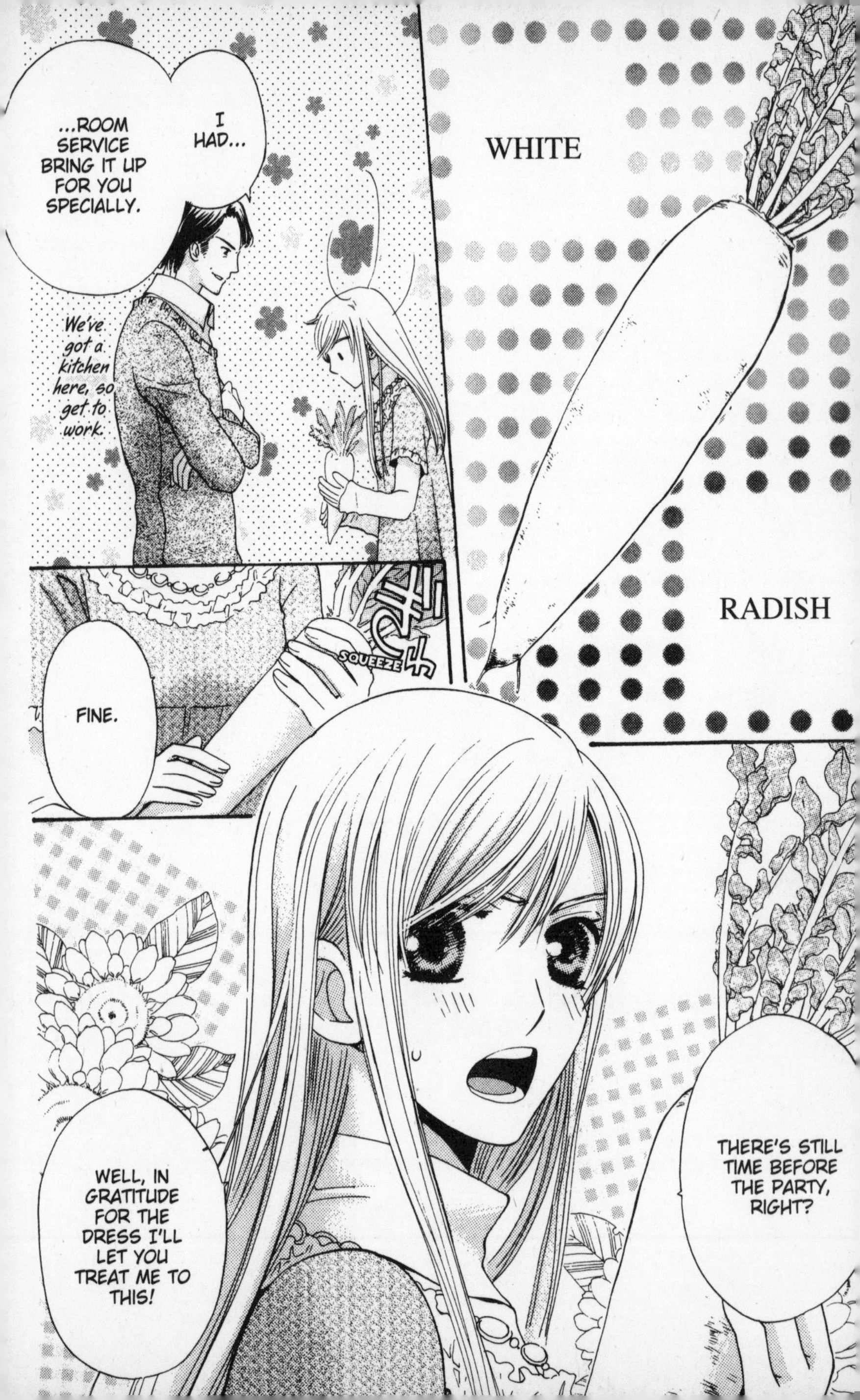
WHITE
RADISH
I HAD...
...ROOM SERVICE BRING IT UP FOR YOU SPECIALLY.
We've got a kitchen here, so get to work.
SQUEEZE
FINE.
THERE'S STILL TIME BEFORE THE PARTY, RIGHT?
WELL, IN GRATITUDE FOR THE DRESS I'LL LET YOU TREAT ME TO THIS!

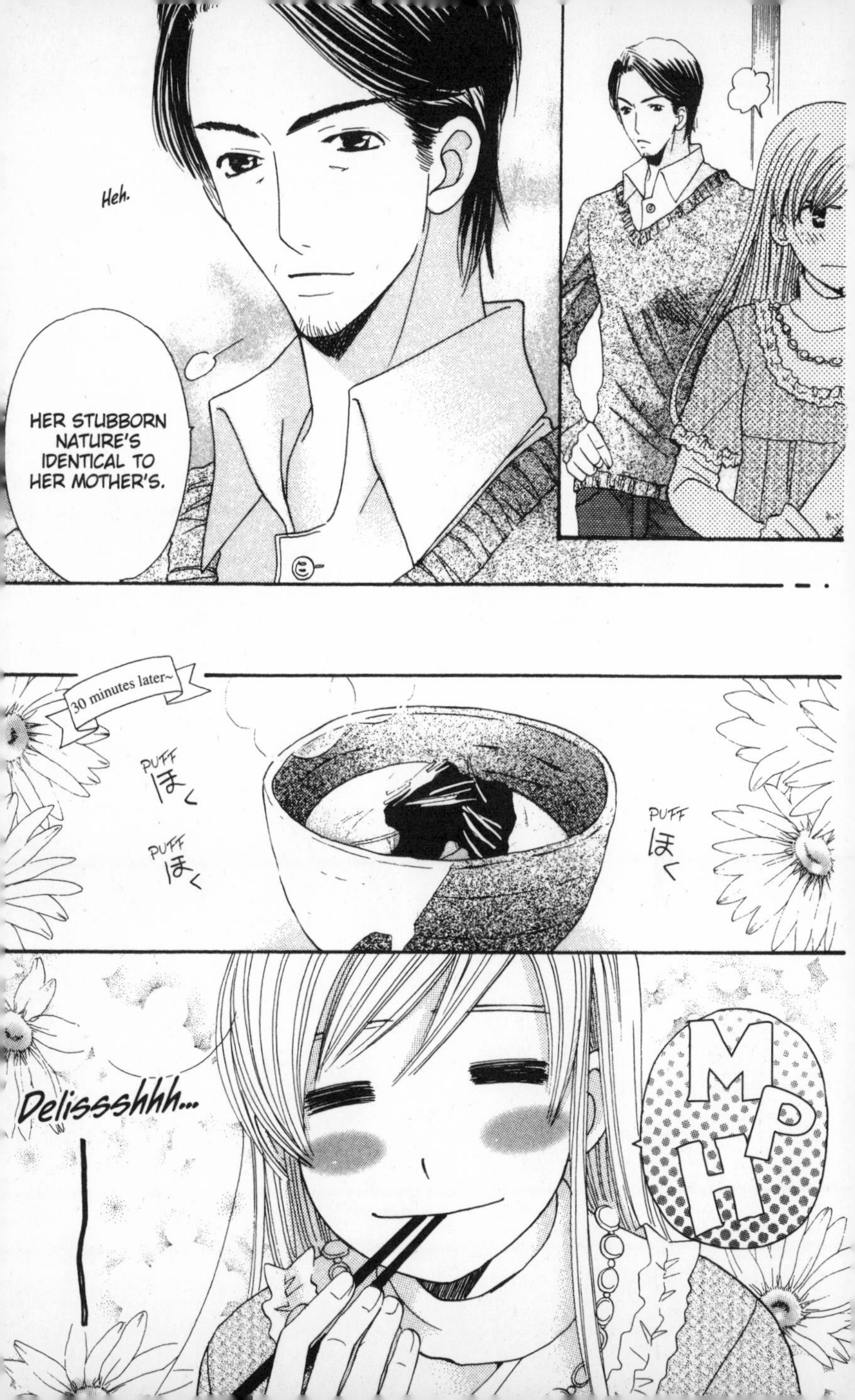

Heh.
HER STUBBORN NATURE'S IDENTICAL TO HER MOTHER'S.
30 minutes later~
PUFF ほく
PUFF ほく
PUFF ほく
MMPH
Delissshhh...

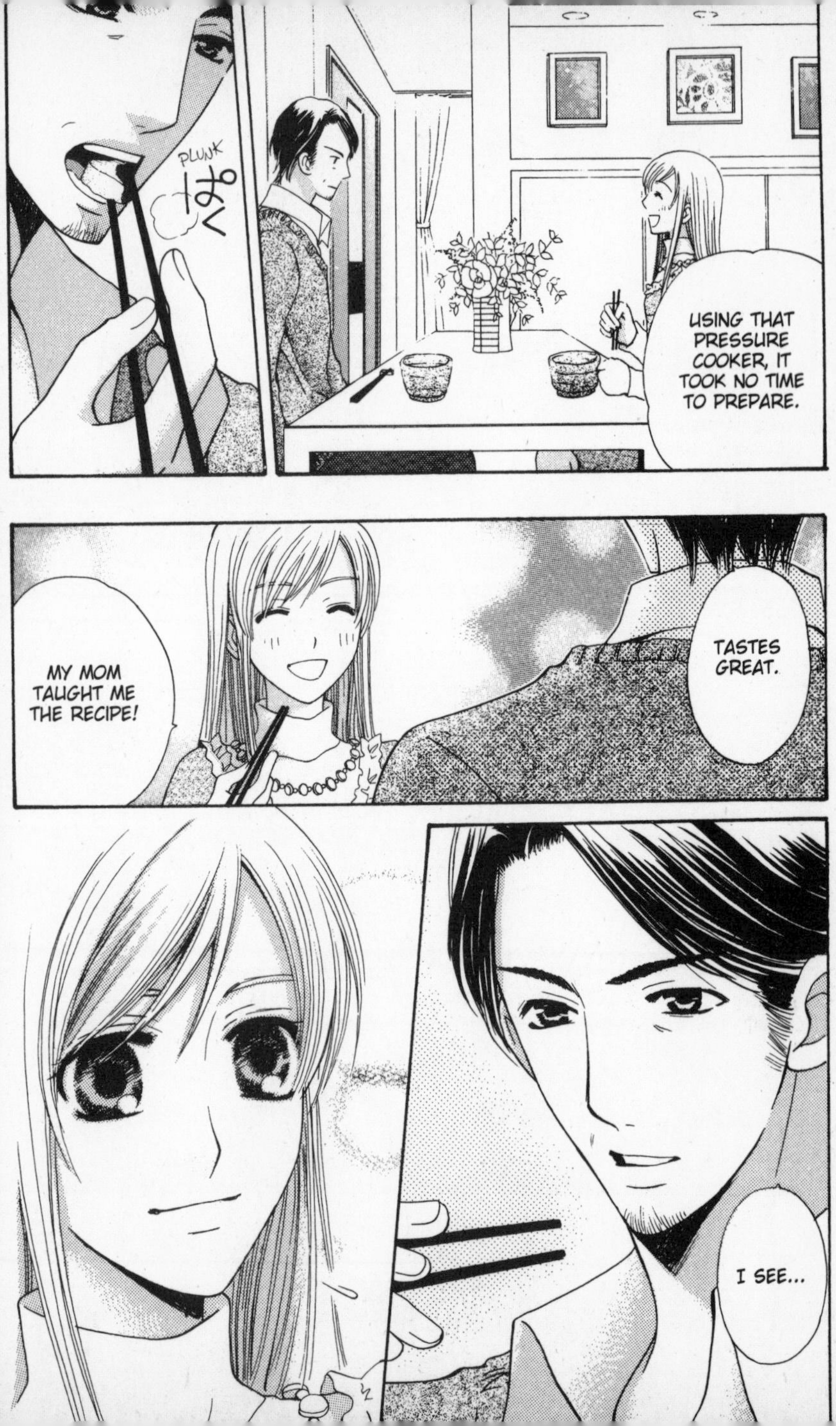
USING THAT PRESSURE COOKER, IT TOOK NO TIME TO PREPARE.
PLUNK
ぱく
TASTES GREAT.
MY MOM TAUGHT ME THE RECIPE!
I SEE...

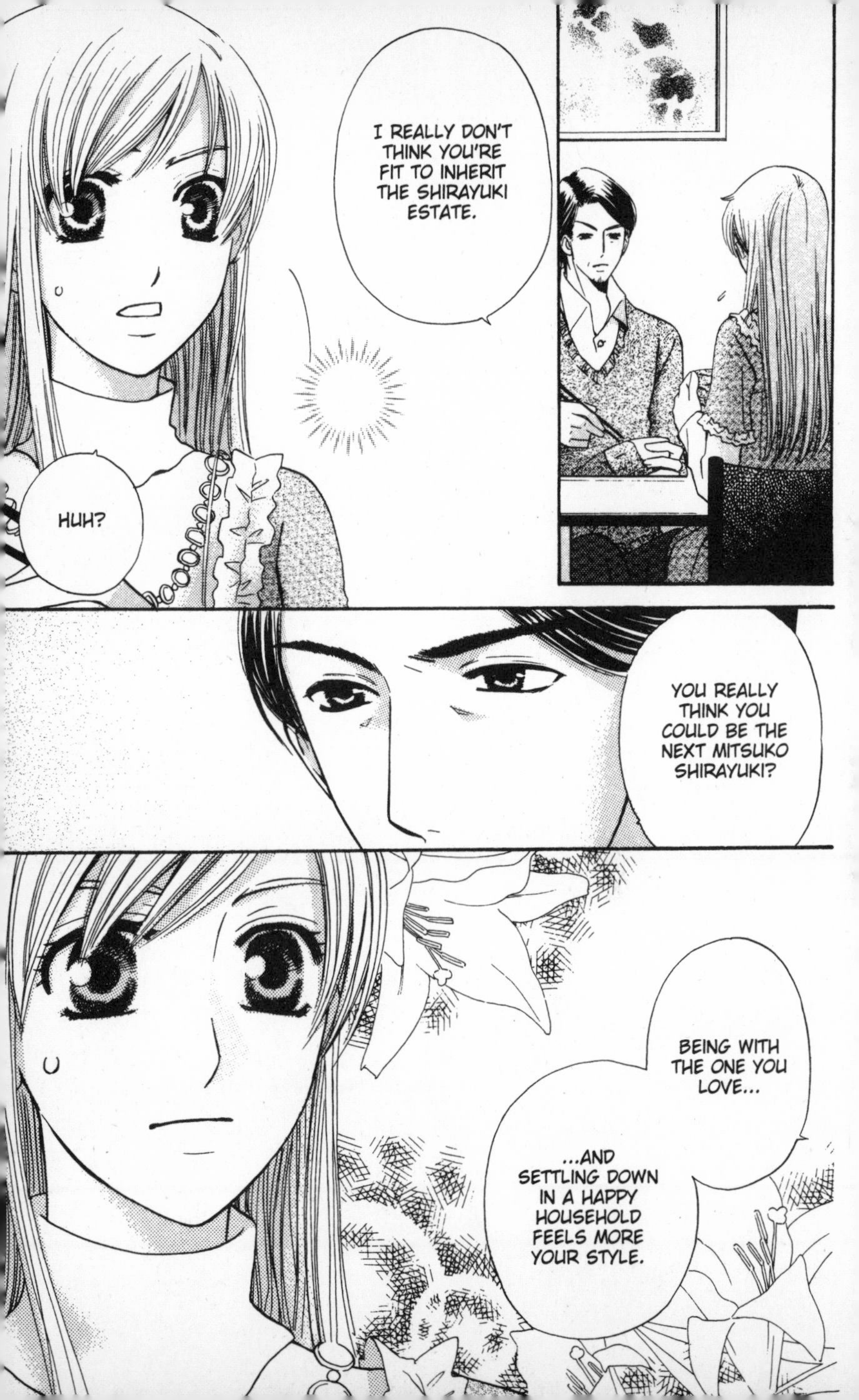
I REALLY DON'T THINK YOU'RE FIT TO INHERIT THE SHIRAYUKI ESTATE.
HUH?
YOU REALLY THINK YOU COULD BE THE NEXT MITSUKO SHIRAYUKI?
BEING WITH THE ONE YOU LOVE...
...AND SETTLING DOWN IN A HAPPY HOUSEHOLD FEELS MORE YOUR STYLE.

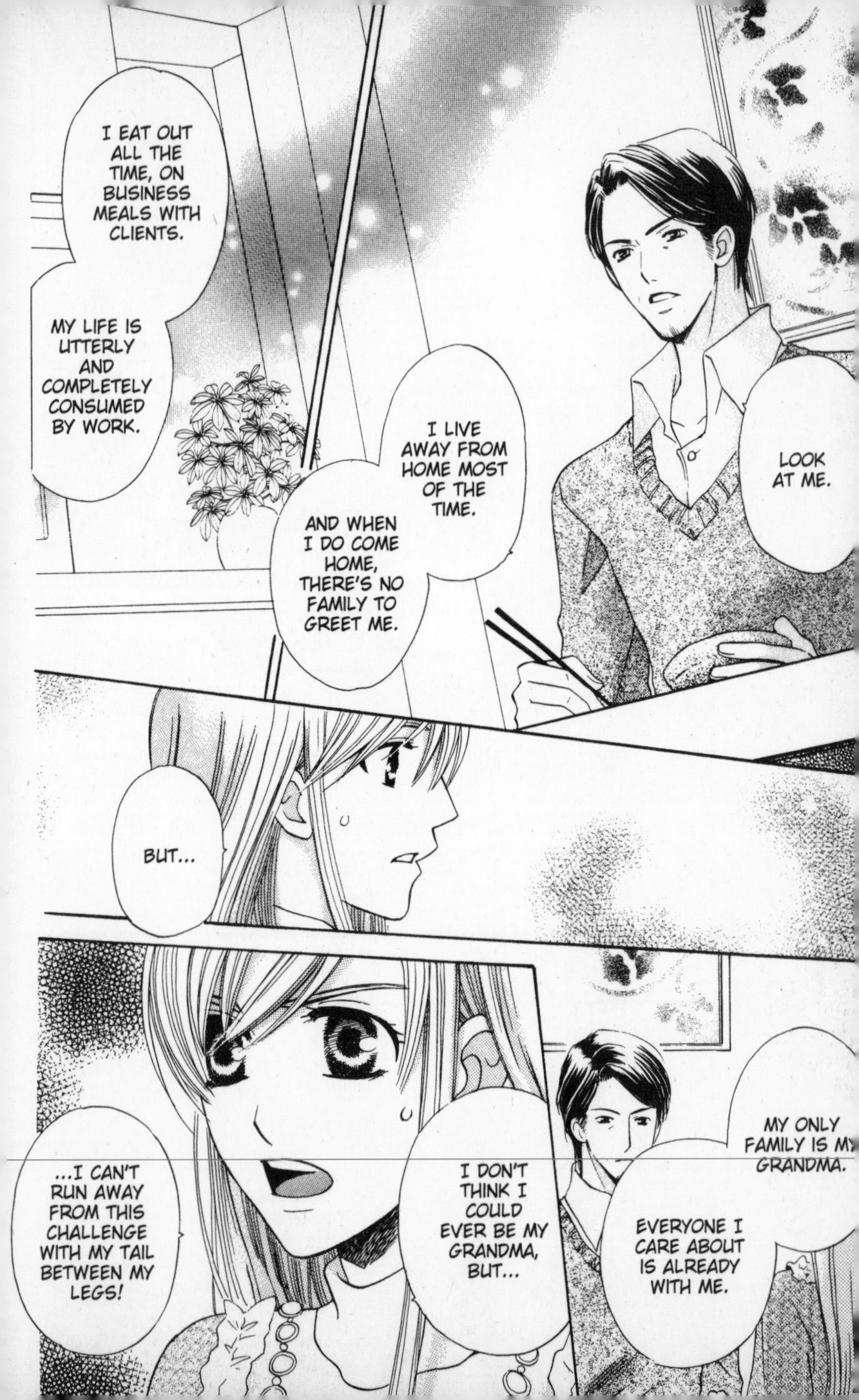
LOOK AT ME.
I LIVE AWAY FROM HOME MOST OF THE TIME.
AND WHEN I DO COME HOME, THERE'S NO FAMILY TO GREET ME.
I EAT OUT ALL THE TIME, ON BUSINESS MEALS WITH CLIENTS.
MY LIFE IS UTTERLY AND COMPLETELY CONSUMED BY WORK.
BUT...
MY ONLY FAMILY IS MY GRANDMA.
EVERYONE I CARE ABOUT IS ALREADY WITH ME.
I DON'T THINK I COULD EVER BE MY GRANDMA, BUT...
...I CAN'T RUN AWAY FROM THIS CHALLENGE WITH MY TAIL BETWEEN MY LEGS!

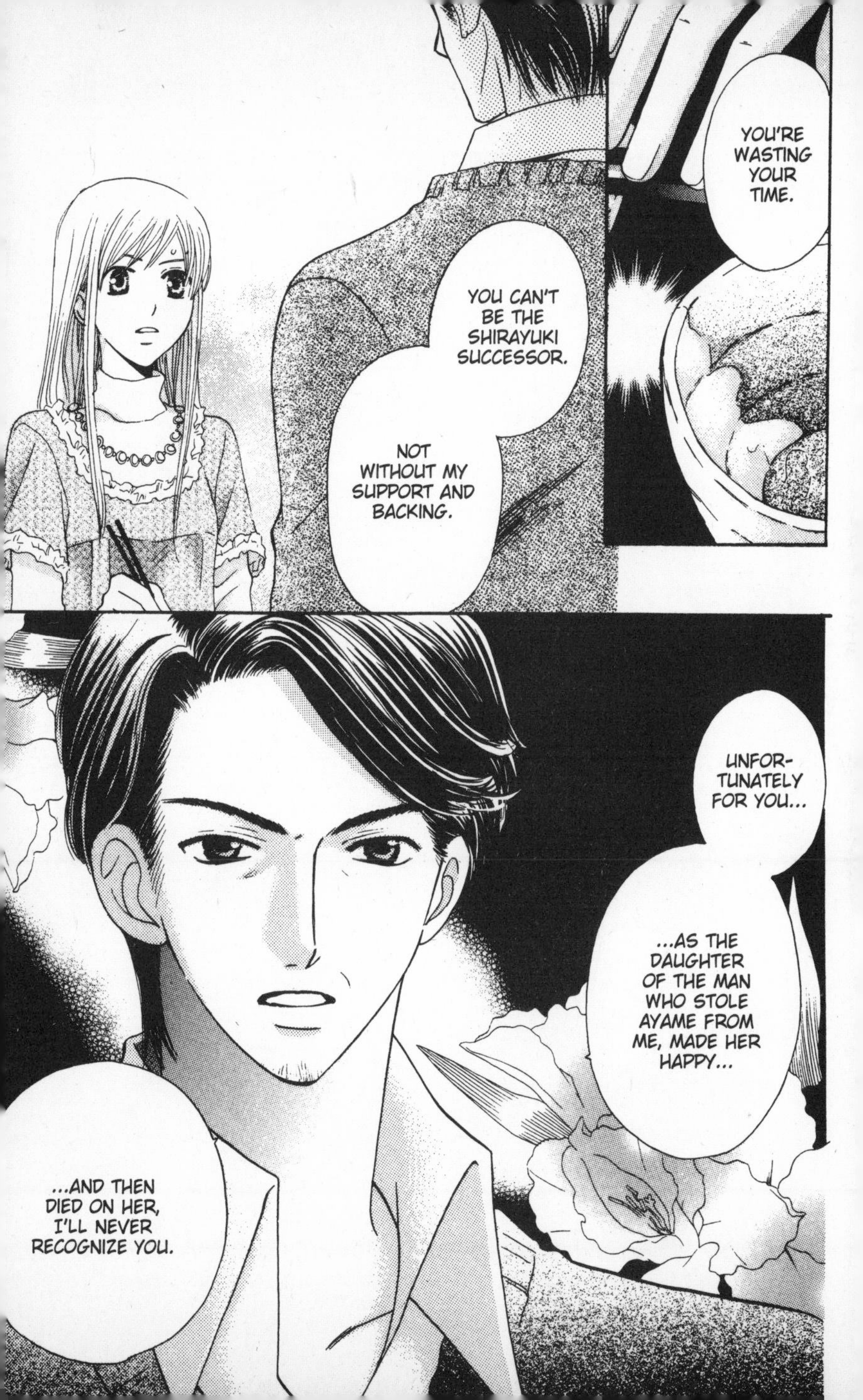
YOU'RE WASTING YOUR TIME.
YOU CAN'T BE THE SHIRAYUKI SUCCESSOR.
NOT WITHOUT MY SUPPORT AND BACKING.
UNFOR-TUNATELY FOR YOU...
...AS THE DAUGHTER OF THE MAN WHO STOLE AYAME FROM ME, MADE HER HAPPY...
...AND THEN DIED ON HER, I'LL NEVER RECOGNIZE YOU.

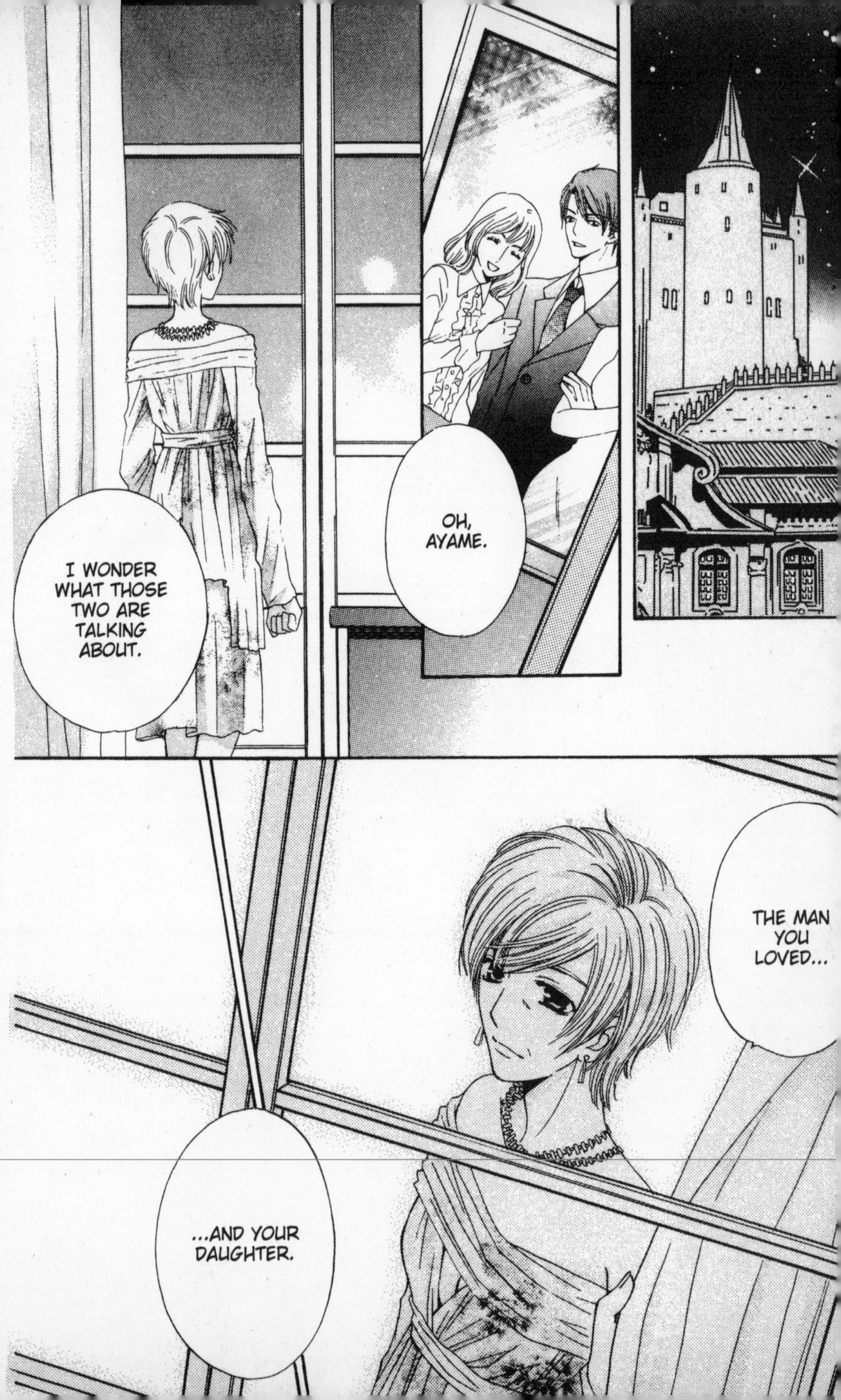
OH, AYAME.
I WONDER WHAT THOSE TWO ARE TALKING ABOUT.
THE MAN YOU LOVED...
...AND YOUR DAUGHTER.

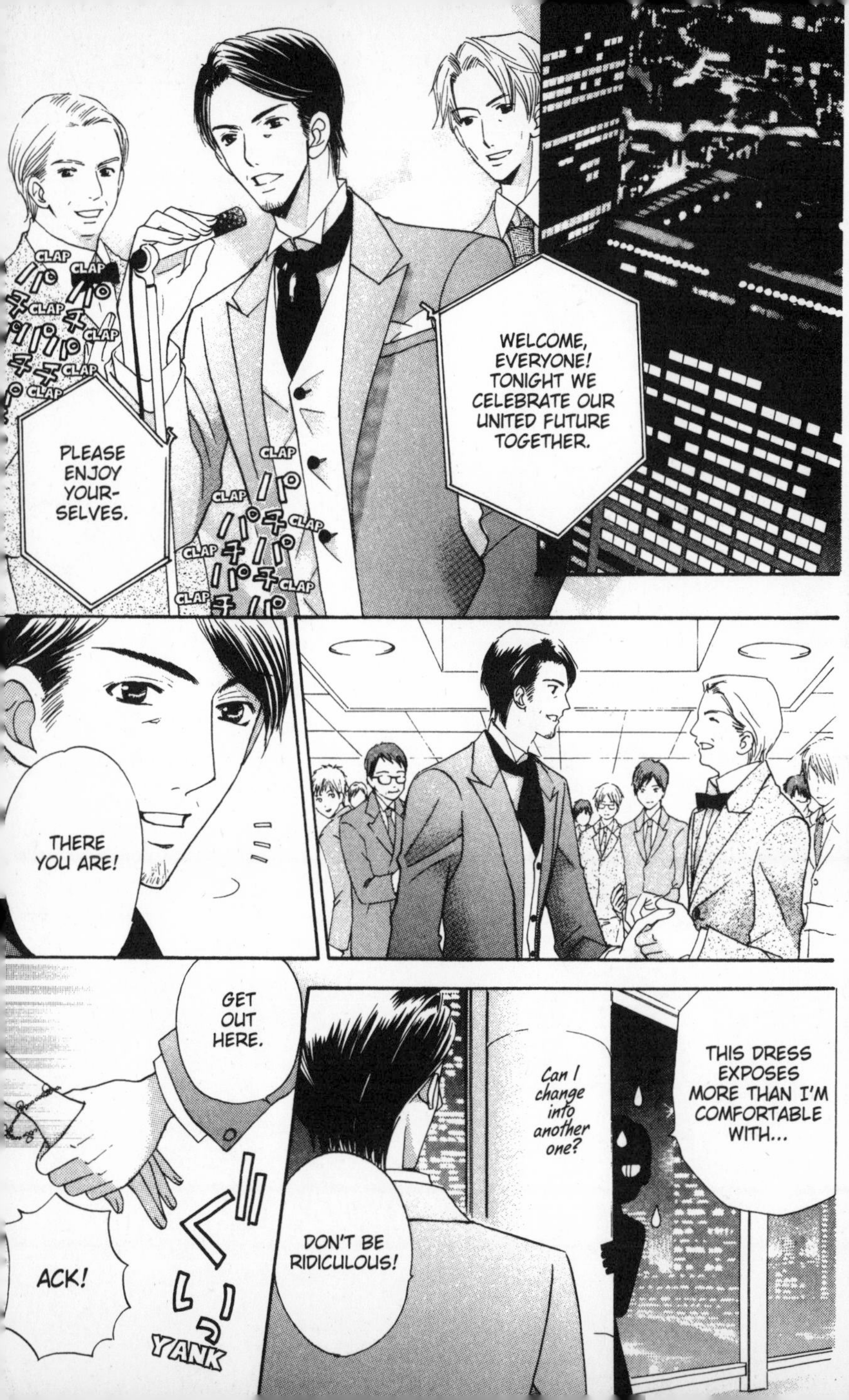
WELCOME, EVERYONE! TONIGHT WE CELEBRATE OUR UNITED FUTURE TOGETHER.
CLAP CLAP CLAP CLAP CLAP CLAP
パチパチパチパチ
PLEASE ENJOY YOUR-SELVES.
CLAP CLAP CLAP CLAP CLAP CLAP
パチパチパチパチ
THERE YOU ARE!
THIS DRESS EXPOSES MORE THAN I'M COMFORTABLE WITH...
Can I change into another one?
DON'T BE RIDICULOUS!
GET OUT HERE.
ACK!
YANK

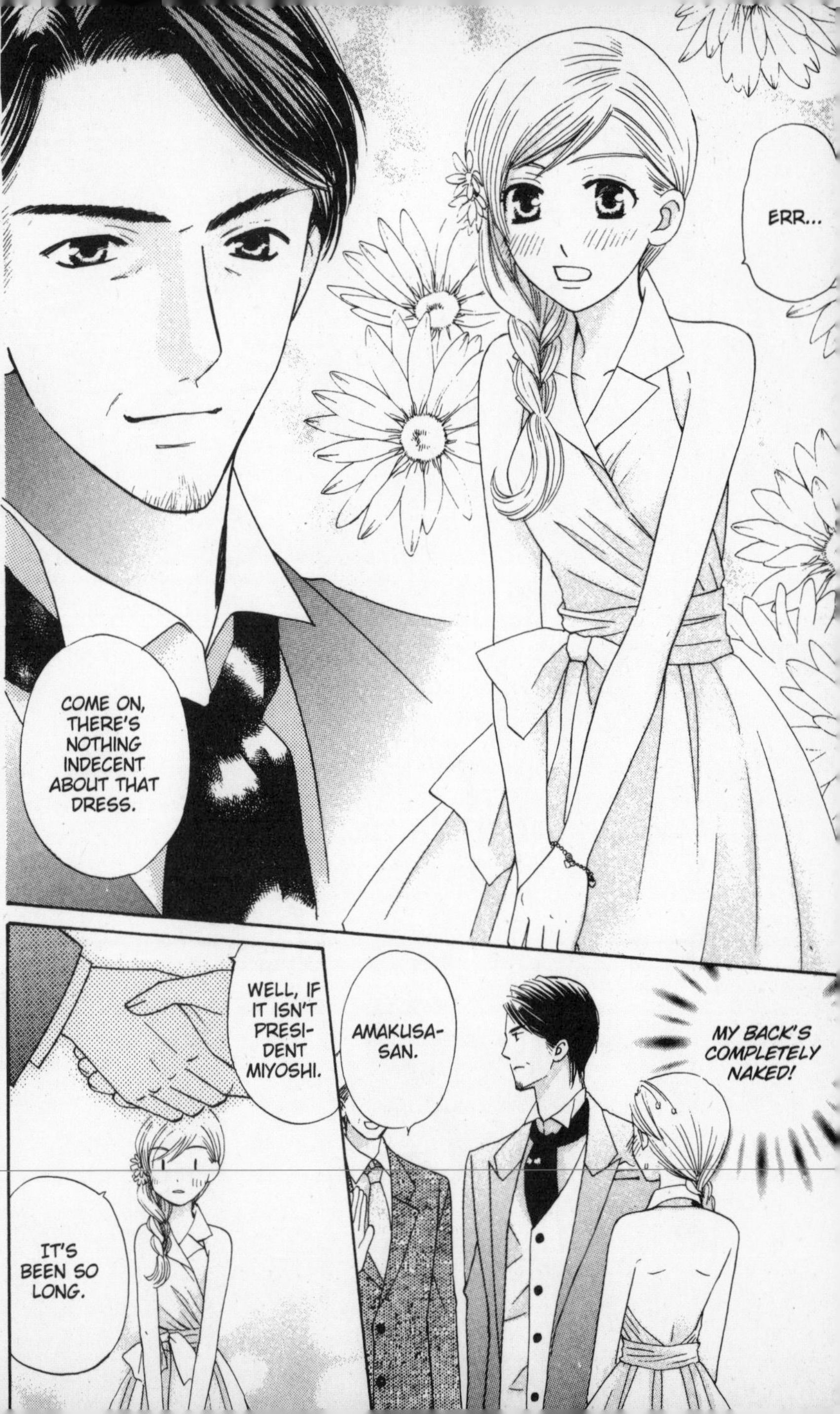
ERR...
COME ON, THERE'S NOTHING INDECENT ABOUT THAT DRESS.
MY BACK'S COMPLETELY NAKED!
AMAKUSA-SAN.
WELL, IF IT ISN'T PRESI-DENT MIYOSHI.
IT'S BEEN SO LONG.

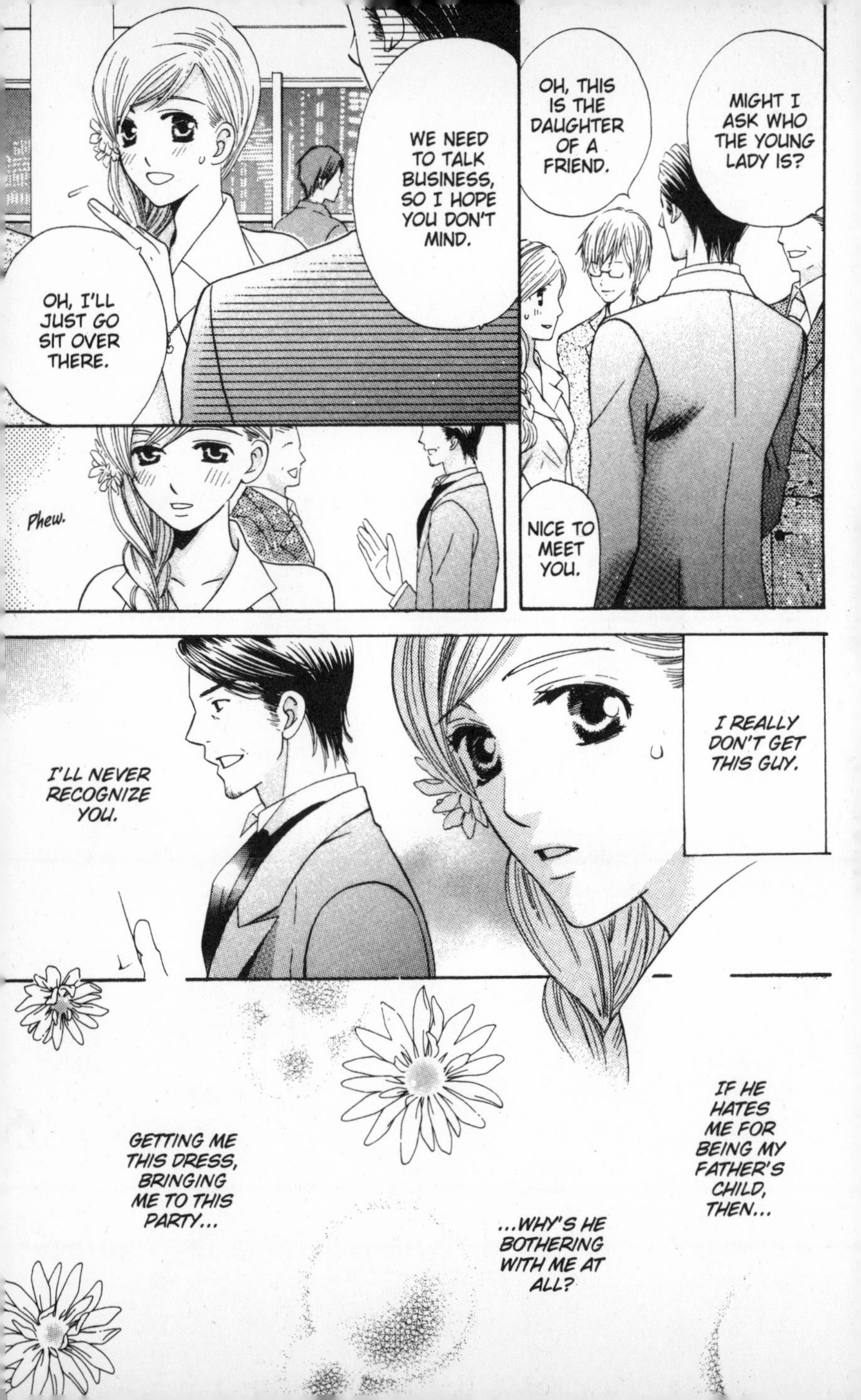
MIGHT I ASK WHO THE YOUNG LADY IS?
OH, THIS IS THE DAUGHTER OF A FRIEND.
NICE TO MEET YOU.
WE NEED TO TALK BUSINESS, SO I HOPE YOU DON'T MIND.
OH, I'LL JUST GO SIT OVER THERE.
Phew.
I REALLY DON'T GET THIS GUY.
I'LL NEVER RECOGNIZE YOU.
IF HE HATES ME FOR BEING MY FATHER'S CHILD, THEN...
GETTING ME THIS DRESS, BRINGING ME TO THIS PARTY...
...WHY'S HE BOTHERING WITH ME AT ALL?

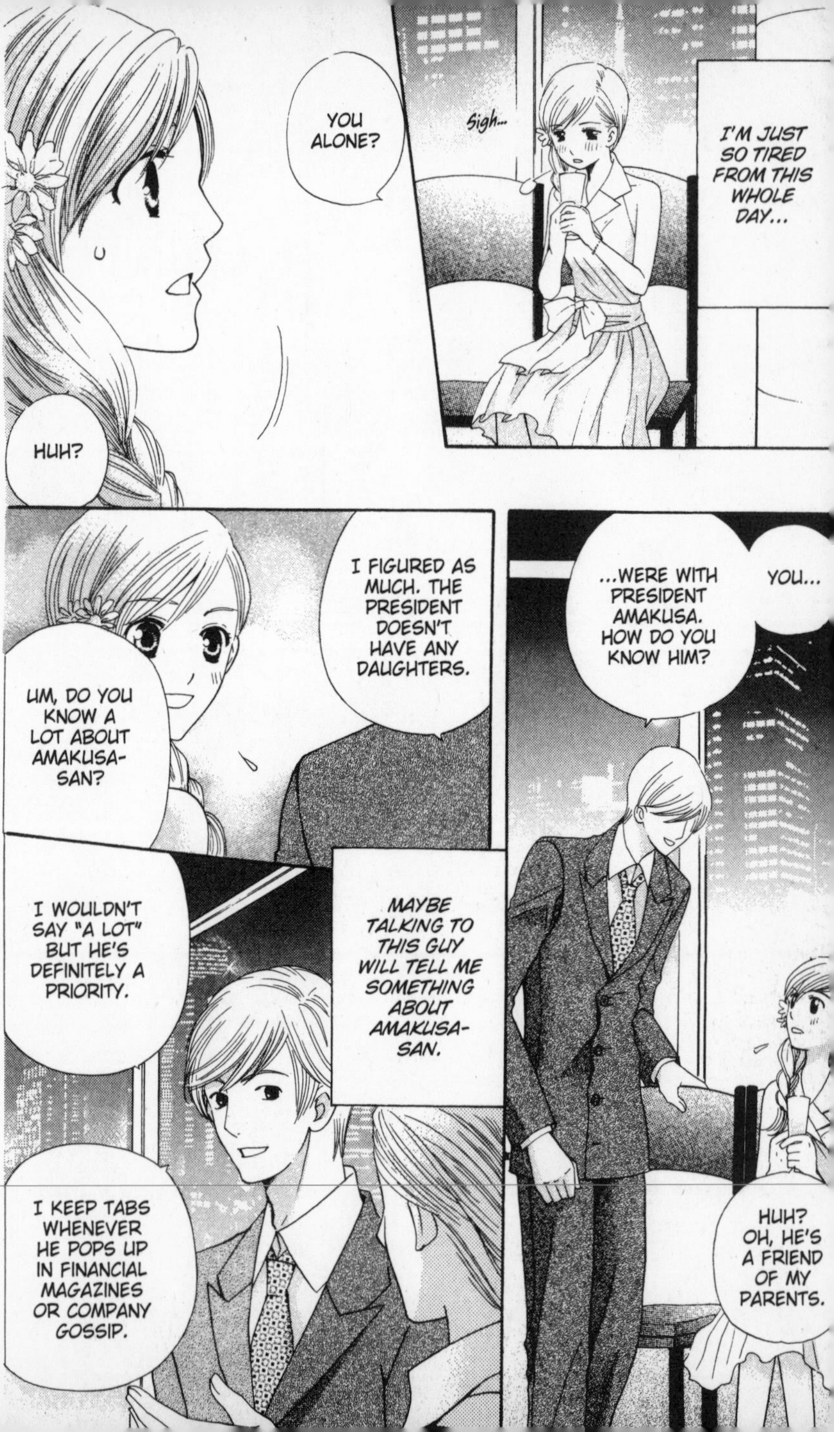
I'M JUST SO TIRED FROM THIS WHOLE DAY...
Sigh...
YOU ALONE?
HUH?
YOU...
...WERE WITH PRESIDENT AMAKUSA. HOW DO YOU KNOW HIM?
HUH? OH, HE'S A FRIEND OF MY PARENTS.
I FIGURED AS MUCH. THE PRESIDENT DOESN'T HAVE ANY DAUGHTERS.
UM, DO YOU KNOW A LOT ABOUT AMAKUSA-SAN?
MAYBE TALKING TO THIS GUY WILL TELL ME SOMETHING ABOUT AMAKUSA-SAN.
I WOULDN'T SAY "A LOT" BUT HE'S DEFINITELY A PRIORITY.
I KEEP TABS WHENEVER HE POPS UP IN FINANCIAL MAGAZINES OR COMPANY GOSSIP.

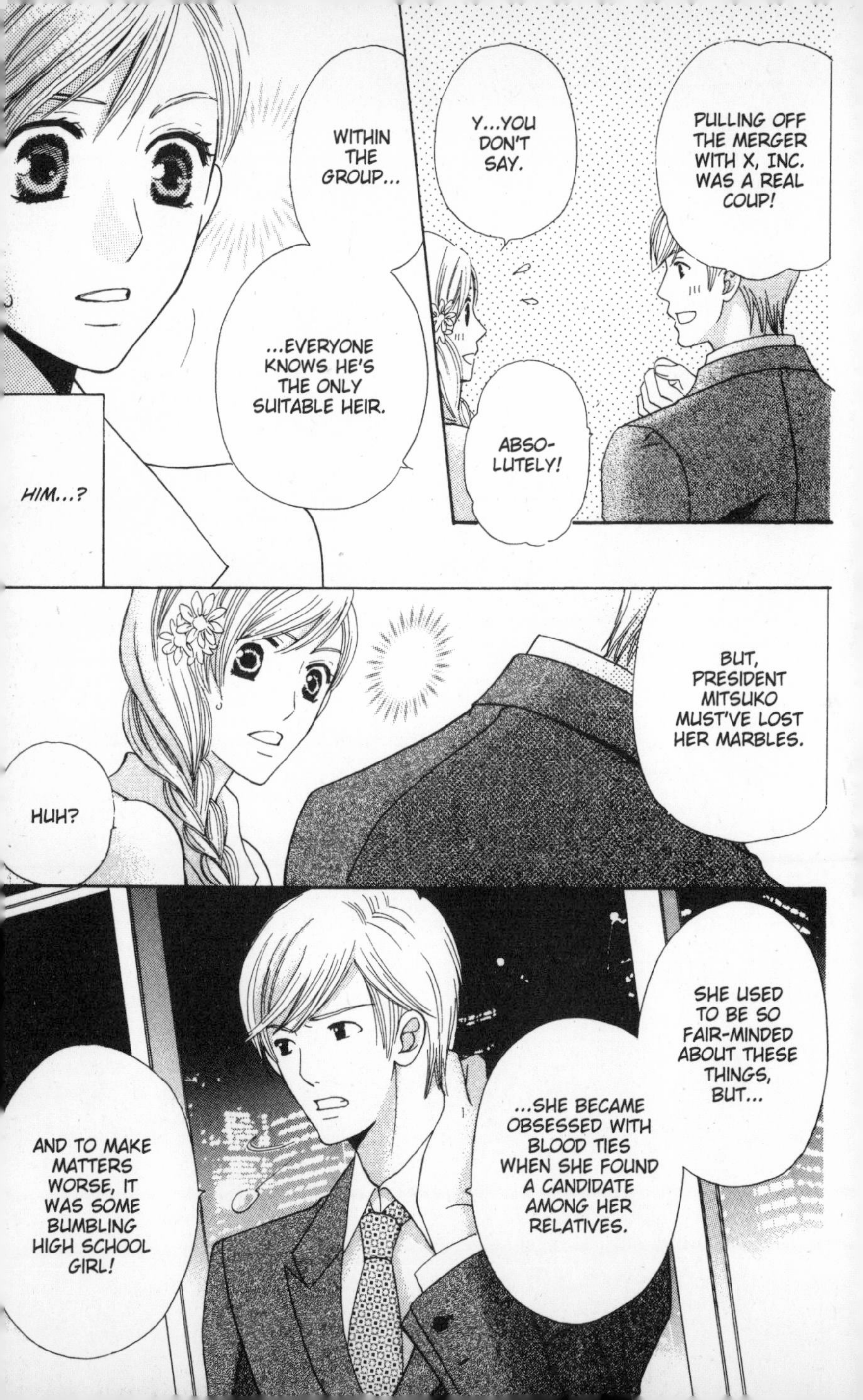
PULLING OFF THE MERGER WITH X, INC. WAS A REAL COUP!
Y...YOU DON'T SAY.
ABSO-LUTELY!
WITHIN THE GROUP...
...EVERYONE KNOWS HE'S THE ONLY SUITABLE HEIR.
HIM...?
BUT, PRESIDENT MITSUKO MUST'VE LOST HER MARBLES.
HUH?
SHE USED TO BE SO FAIR-MINDED ABOUT THESE THINGS, BUT...
...SHE BECAME OBSESSED WITH BLOOD TIES WHEN SHE FOUND A CANDIDATE AMONG HER RELATIVES.
AND TO MAKE MATTERS WORSE, IT WAS SOME BUMBLING HIGH SCHOOL GIRL!

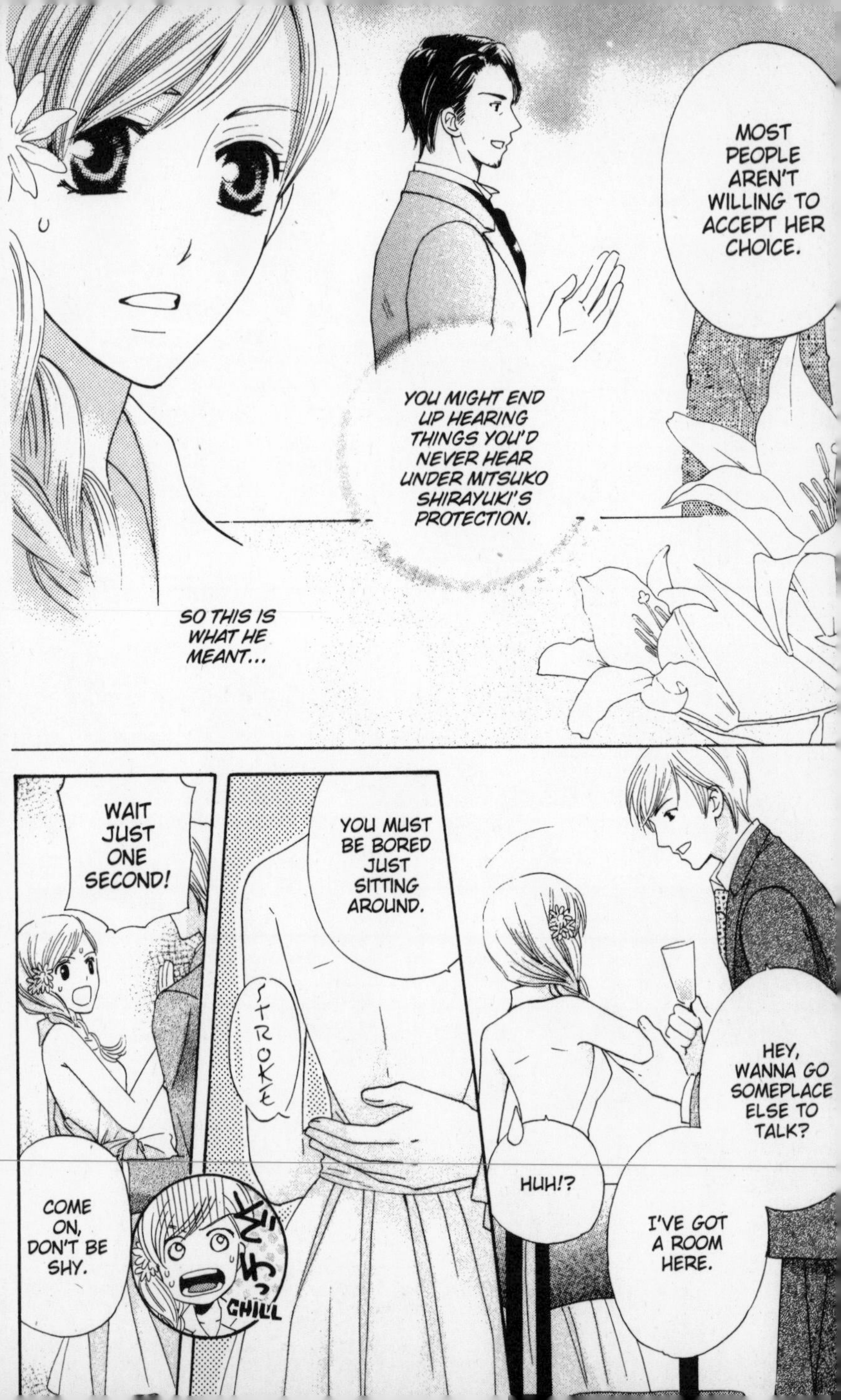
MOST PEOPLE AREN'T WILLING TO ACCEPT HER CHOICE.
YOU MIGHT END UP HEARING THINGS YOU'D NEVER HEAR UNDER MITSUKO SHIRAYUKI'S PROTECTION.
SO THIS IS WHAT HE MEANT...
HEY, WANNA GO SOMEPLACE ELSE TO TALK?
YOU MUST BE BORED JUST SITTING AROUND.
STROKE
WAIT JUST ONE SECOND!
I'VE GOT A ROOM HERE.
HUH!?
COME ON, DON'T BE SHY.
CHILL

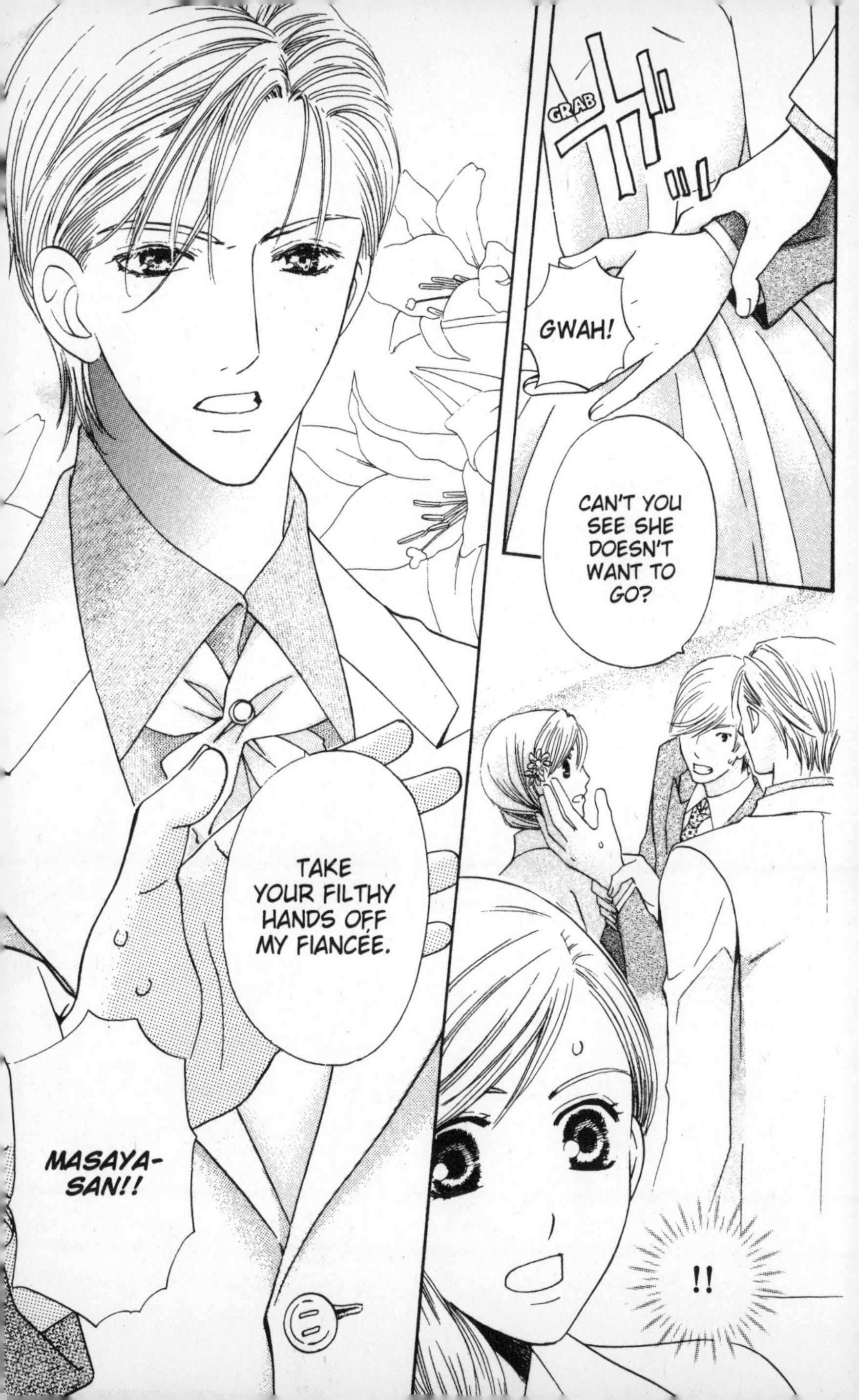
GRAB
GWAH!
CAN'T YOU SEE SHE DOESN'T WANT TO GO?
TAKE YOUR FILTHY HANDS OFF MY FIANCÉE.
!!
MASAYA-SAN!!

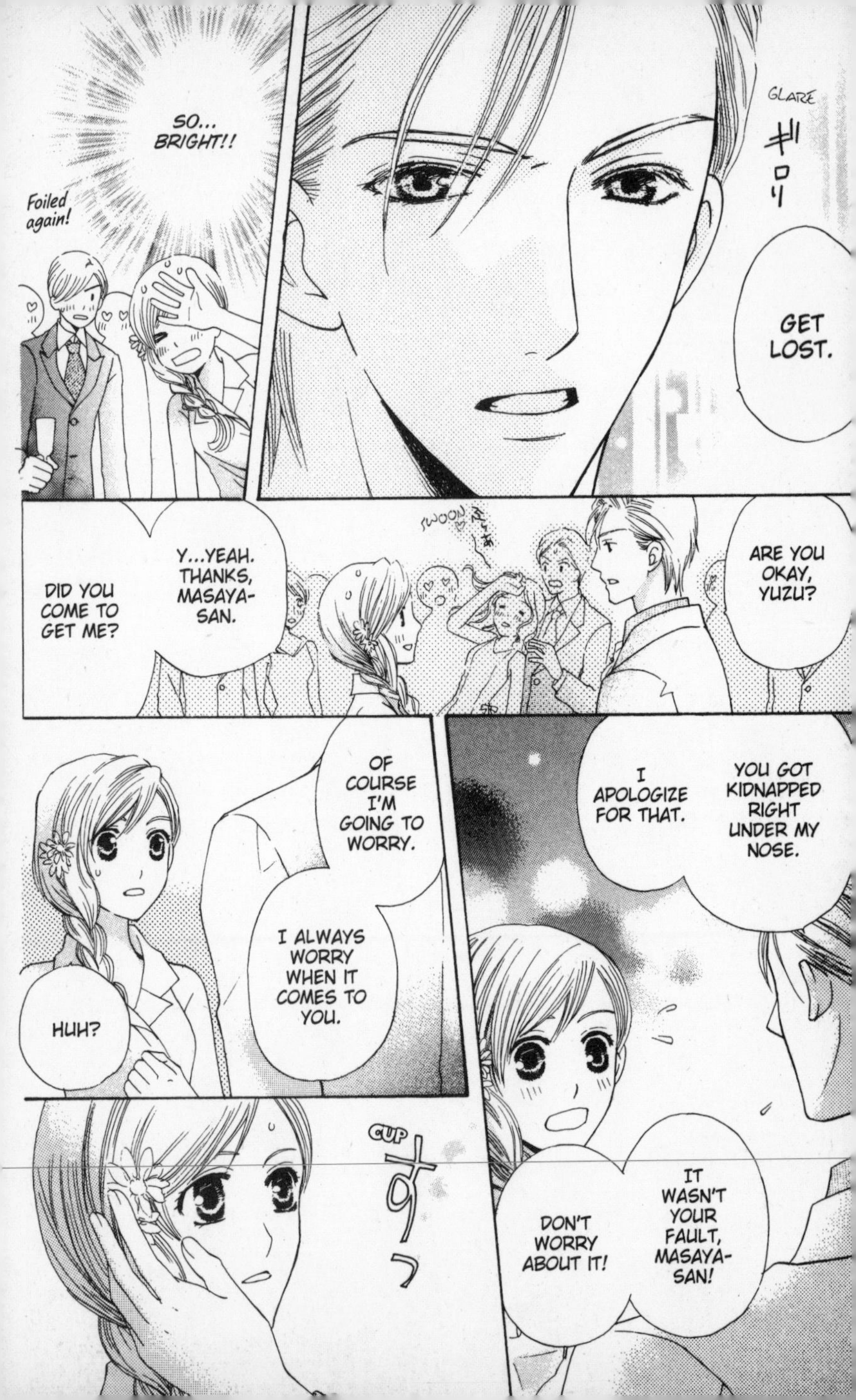
GLARE
ギロリ
GET LOST.
SO... BRIGHT!!
Foiled again!
ARE YOU OKAY, YUZU?
SWOON
Y...YEAH. THANKS, MASAYA-SAN.
DID YOU COME TO GET ME?
YOU GOT KIDNAPPED RIGHT UNDER MY NOSE.
I APOLOGIZE FOR THAT.
IT WASN'T YOUR FAULT, MASAYA-SAN!
DON'T WORRY ABOUT IT!
OF COURSE I'M GOING TO WORRY.
I ALWAYS WORRY WHEN IT COMES TO YOU.
HUH?
CUP
すっ

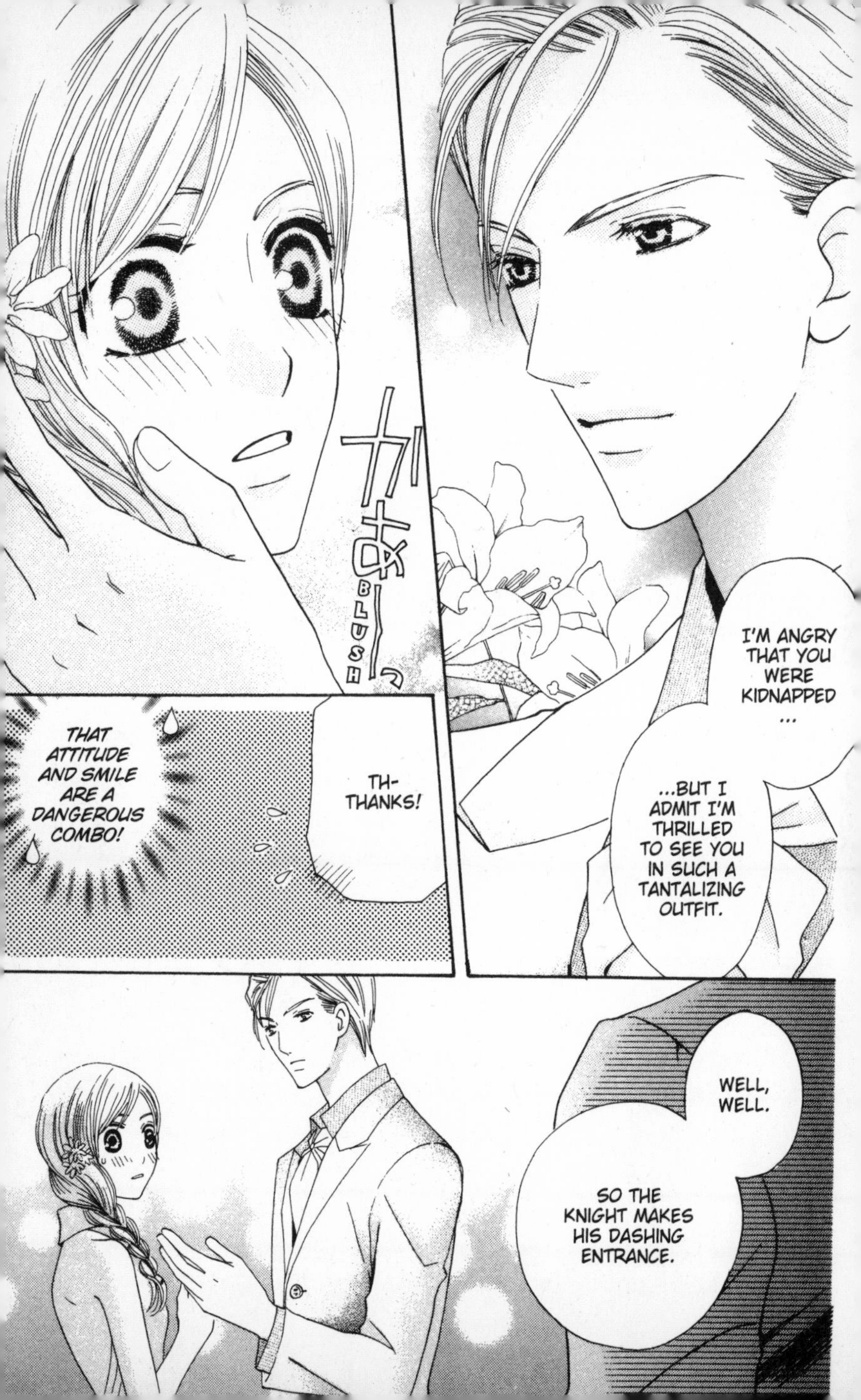
I'M ANGRY THAT YOU WERE KIDNAPPED ...
...BUT I ADMIT I'M THRILLED TO SEE YOU IN SUCH A TANTALIZING OUTFIT.
BLUSH
TH-THANKS!
THAT ATTITUDE AND SMILE ARE A DANGEROUS COMBO!
WELL, WELL.
SO THE KNIGHT MAKES HIS DASHING ENTRANCE.

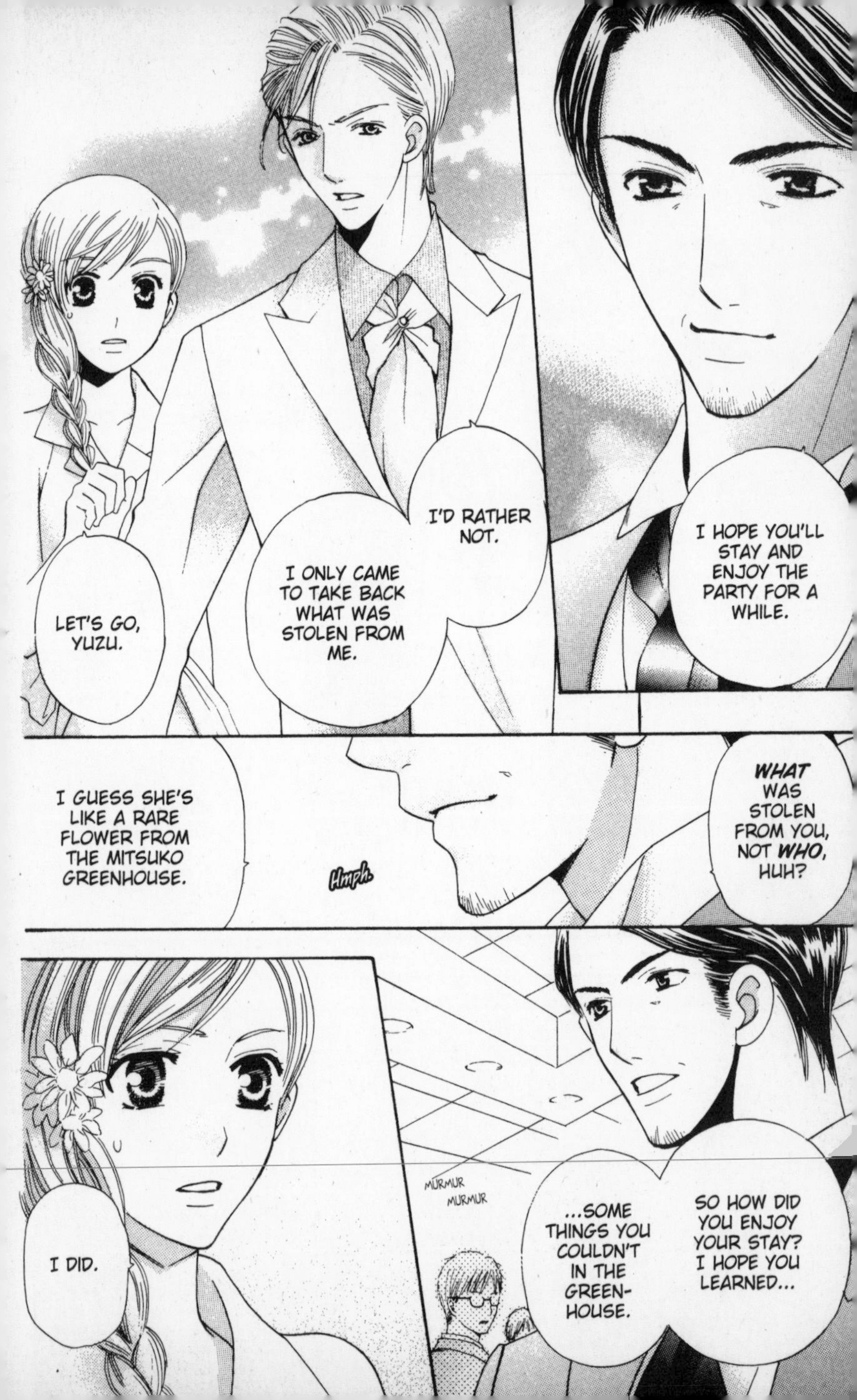
I HOPE YOU'LL STAY AND ENJOY THE PARTY FOR A WHILE.
I'D RATHER NOT.
I ONLY CAME TO TAKE BACK WHAT WAS STOLEN FROM ME.
LET'S GO, YUZU.
WHAT WAS STOLEN FROM YOU, NOT *WHO*, HUH?
Hmph.
I GUESS SHE'S LIKE A RARE FLOWER FROM THE MITSUKO GREENHOUSE.
SO HOW DID YOU ENJOY YOUR STAY? I HOPE YOU LEARNED...
...SOME THINGS YOU COULDN'T IN THE GREEN-HOUSE.
MURMUR MURMUR
I DID.

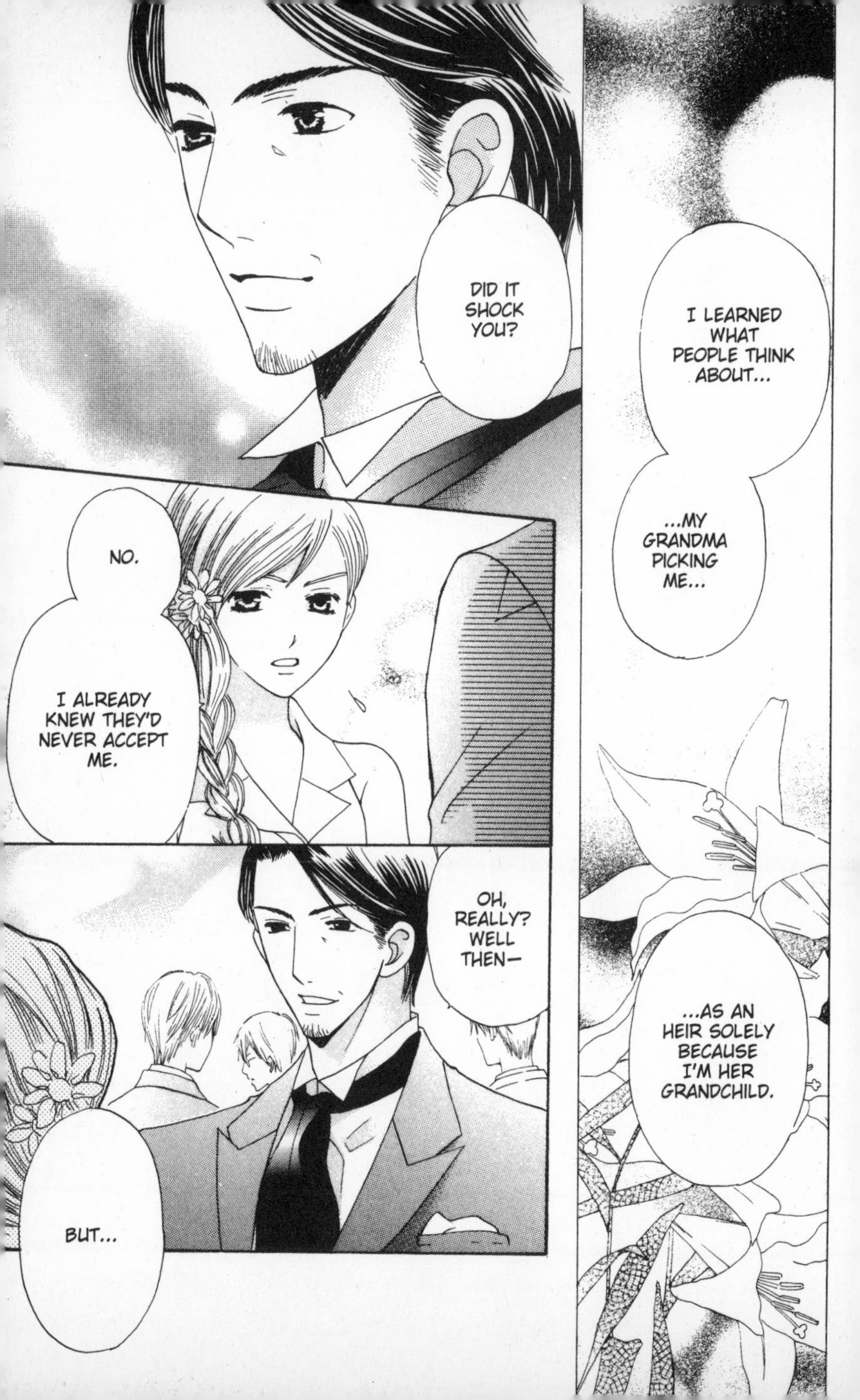
I LEARNED WHAT PEOPLE THINK ABOUT...
...MY GRANDMA PICKING ME...
...AS AN HEIR SOLELY BECAUSE I'M HER GRANDCHILD.
DID IT SHOCK YOU?
NO.
I ALREADY KNEW THEY'D NEVER ACCEPT ME.
OH, REALLY? WELL THEN—
BUT...

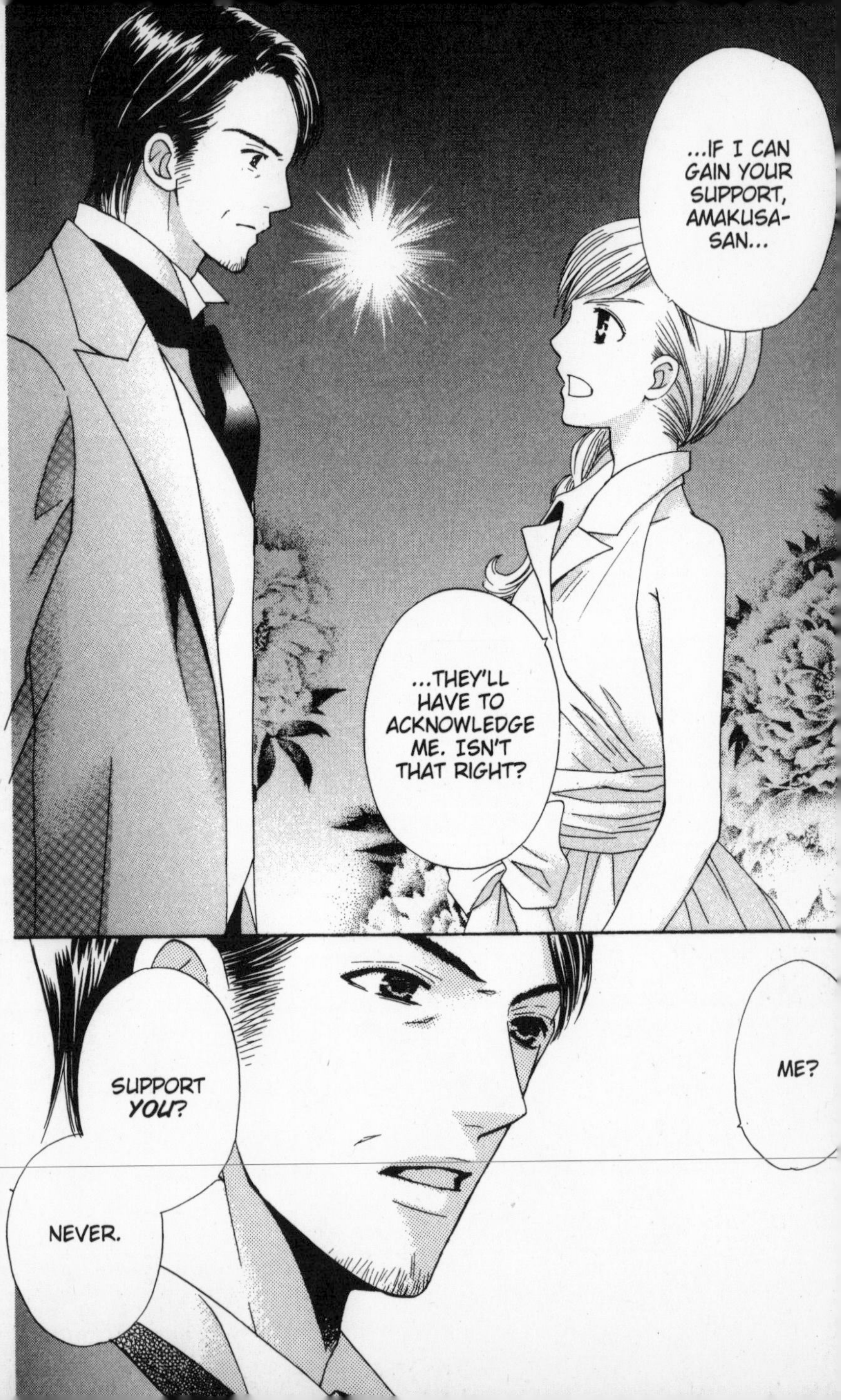
...IF I CAN GAIN YOUR SUPPORT, AMAKUSA-SAN...
...THEY'LL HAVE TO ACKNOWLEDGE ME. ISN'T THAT RIGHT?
ME?
SUPPORT *YOU*?
NEVER.

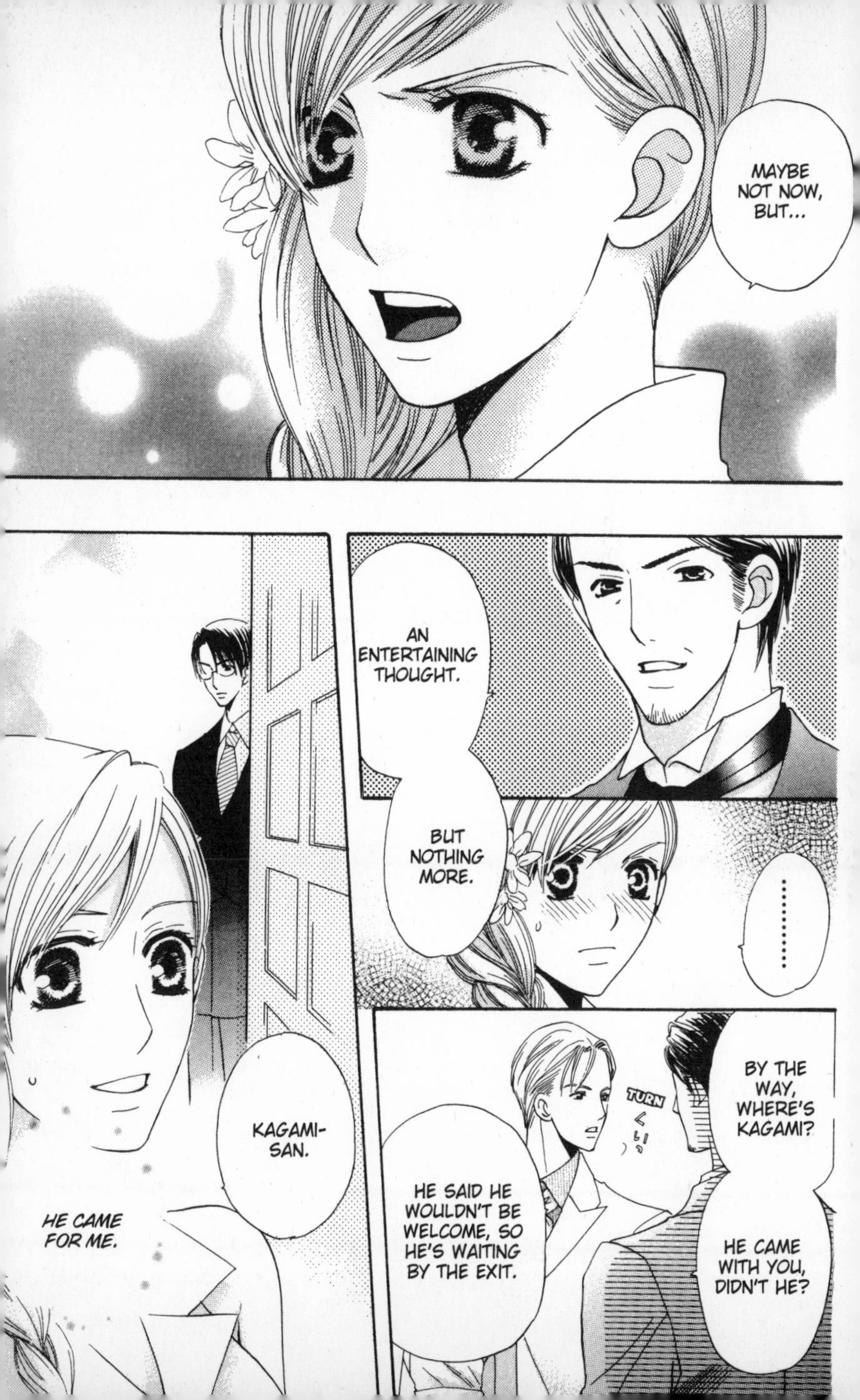
MAYBE NOT NOW, BUT...
AN ENTERTAINING THOUGHT.
BUT NOTHING MORE.
......
BY THE WAY, WHERE'S KAGAMI?
HE CAME WITH YOU, DIDN'T HE?
TURN
HE SAID HE WOULDN'T BE WELCOME, SO HE'S WAITING BY THE EXIT.
KAGAMI-SAN.
HE CAME FOR ME.

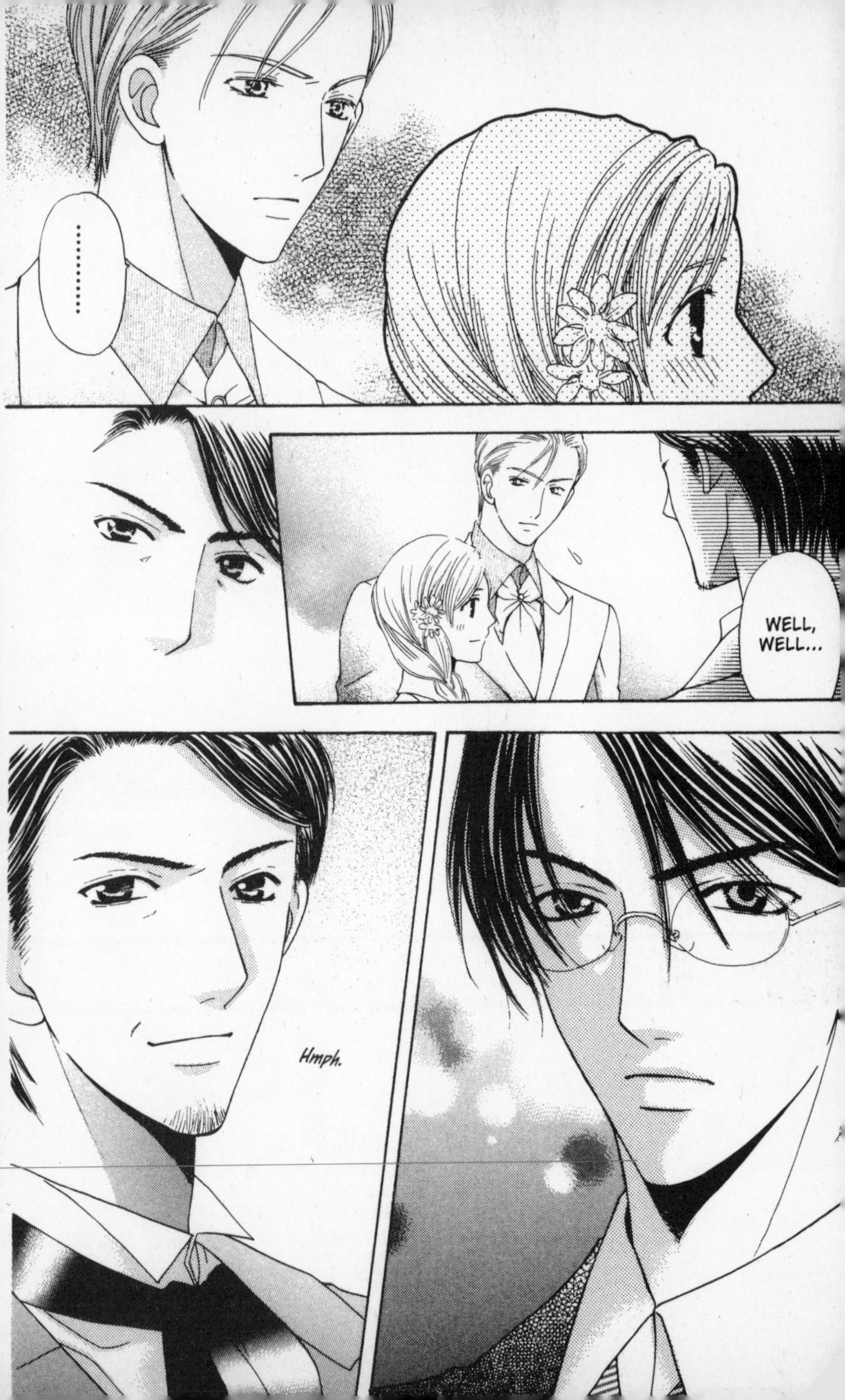
......
WELL, WELL...
Hmph.

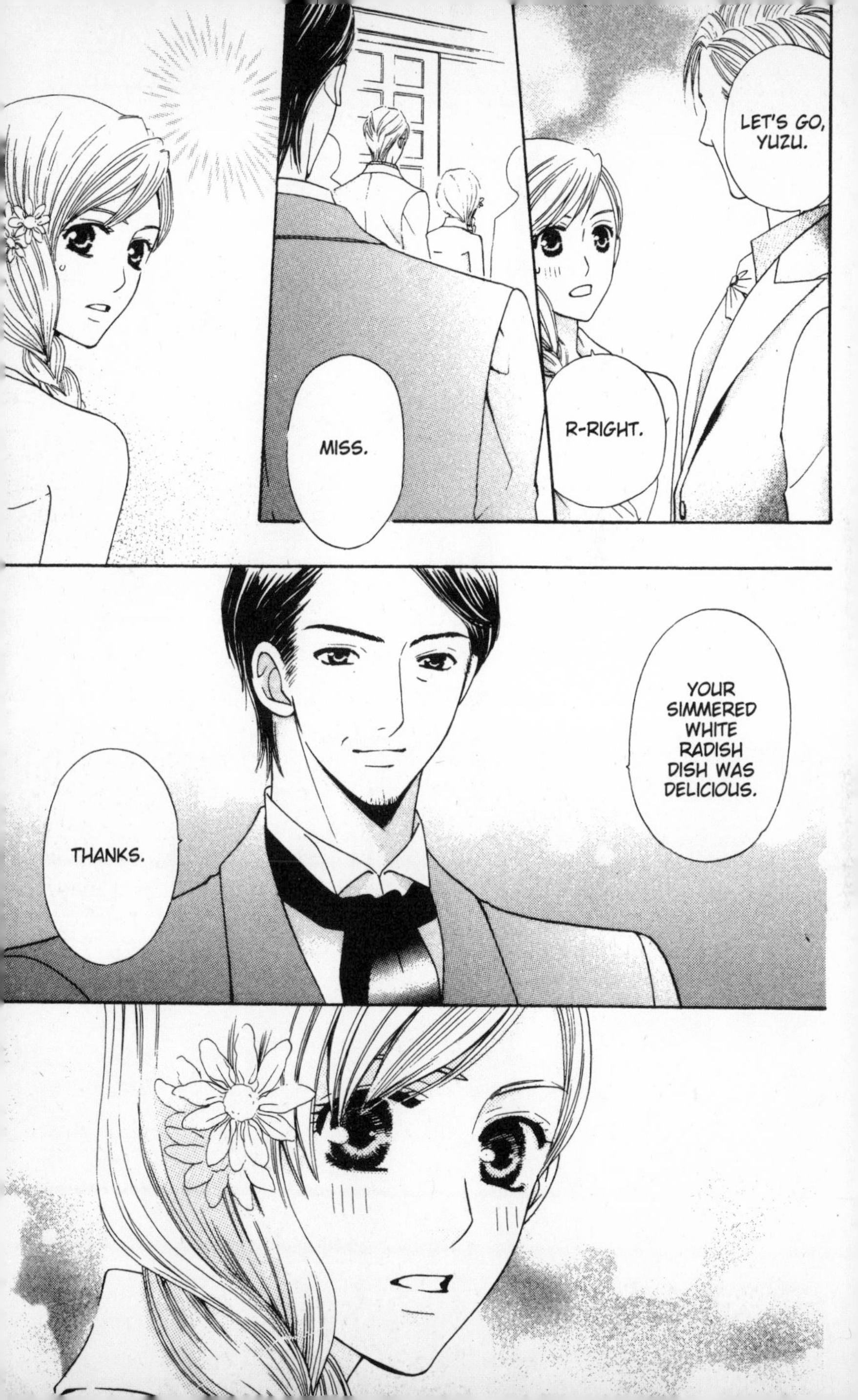
LET'S GO, YUZU.
R-RIGHT.
MISS.
YOUR SIMMERED WHITE RADISH DISH WAS DELICIOUS.
THANKS.

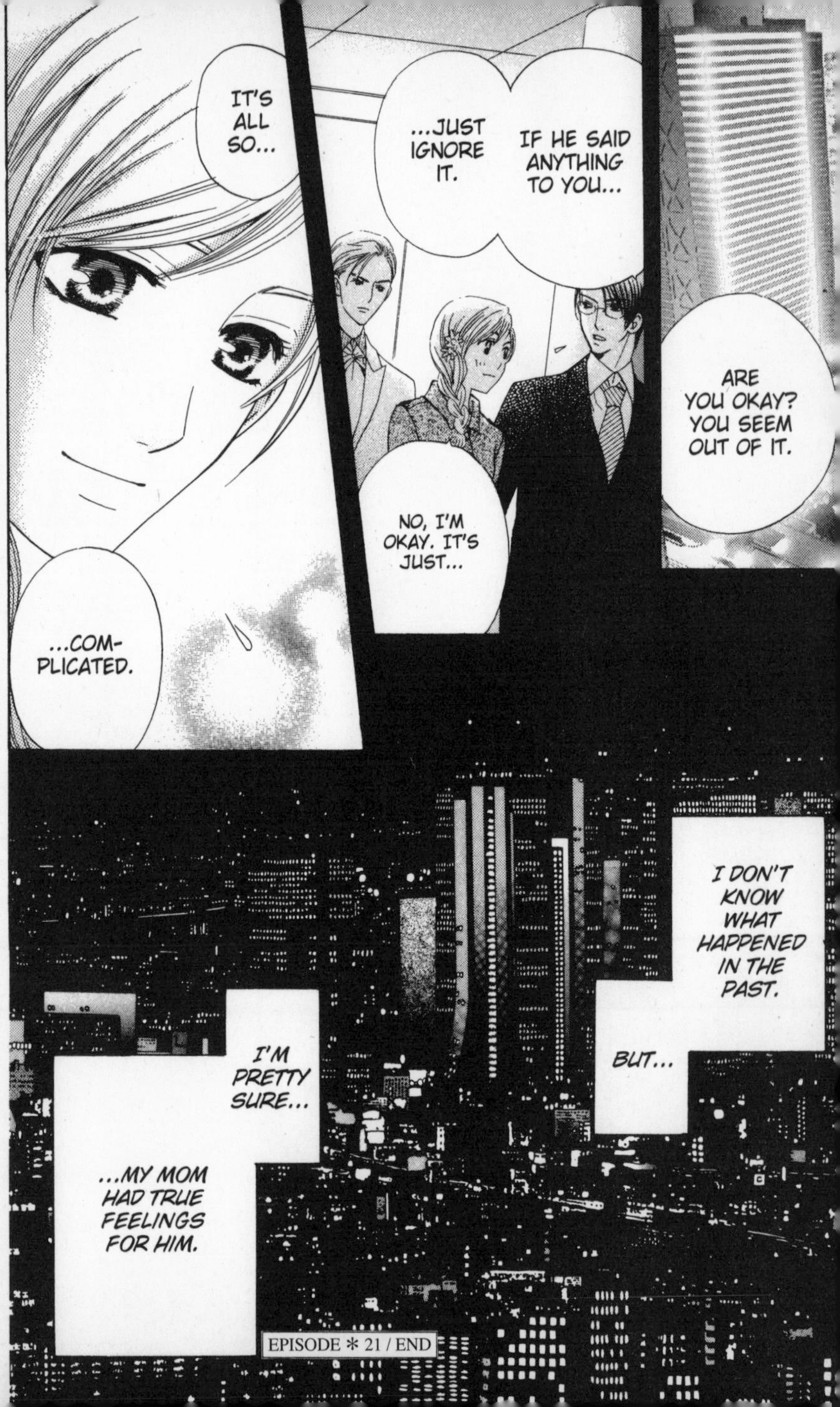
ARE YOU OKAY? YOU SEEM OUT OF IT.
NO, I'M OKAY. IT'S JUST...
IF HE SAID ANYTHING TO YOU...
...JUST IGNORE IT.
IT'S ALL SO...
...COM-PLICATED.
I DON'T KNOW WHAT HAPPENED IN THE PAST.
BUT...
I'M PRETTY SURE...
...MY MOM HAD TRUE FEELINGS FOR HIM.
EPISODE * 21 / END

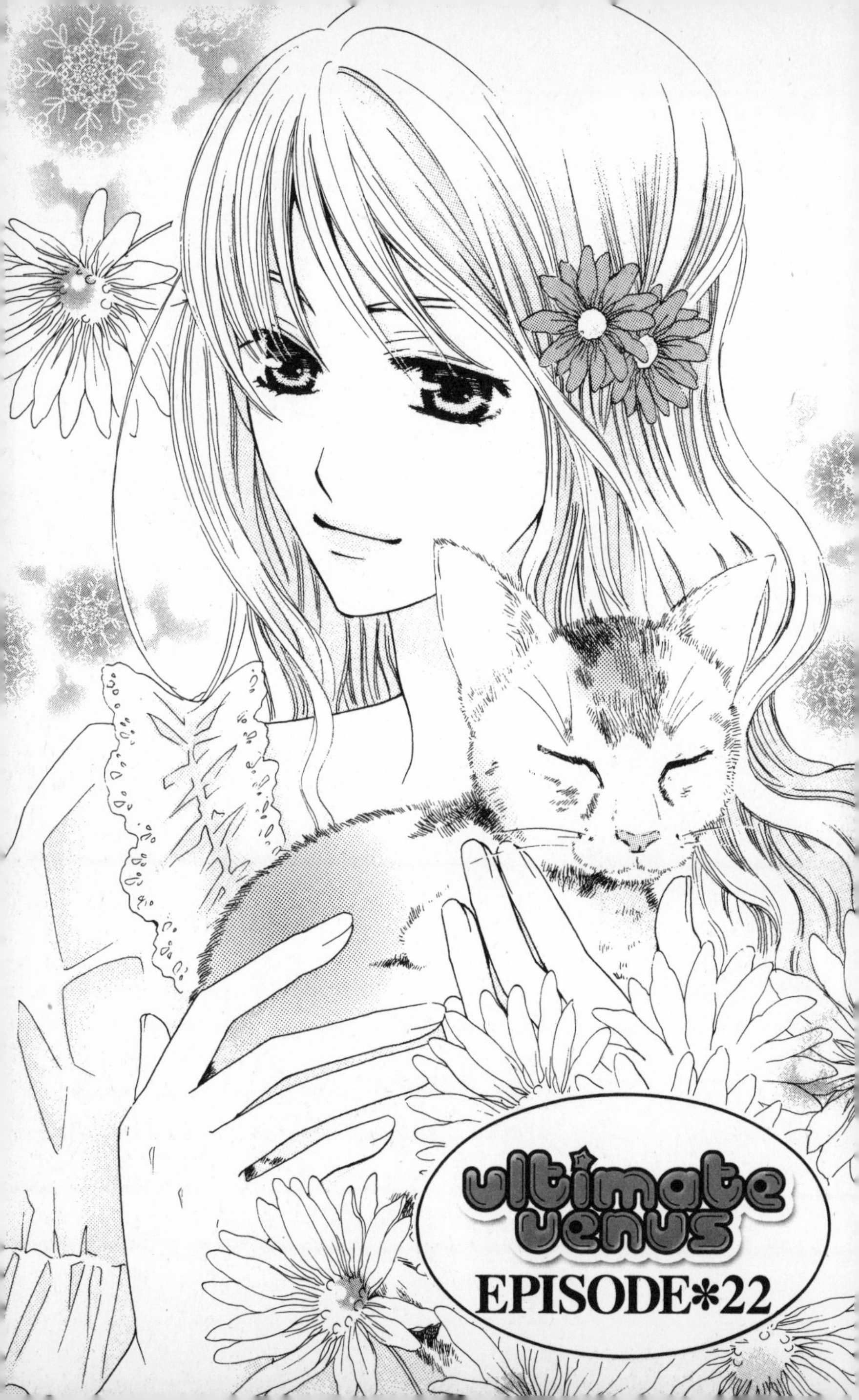
ultimate venus
EPISODE*22

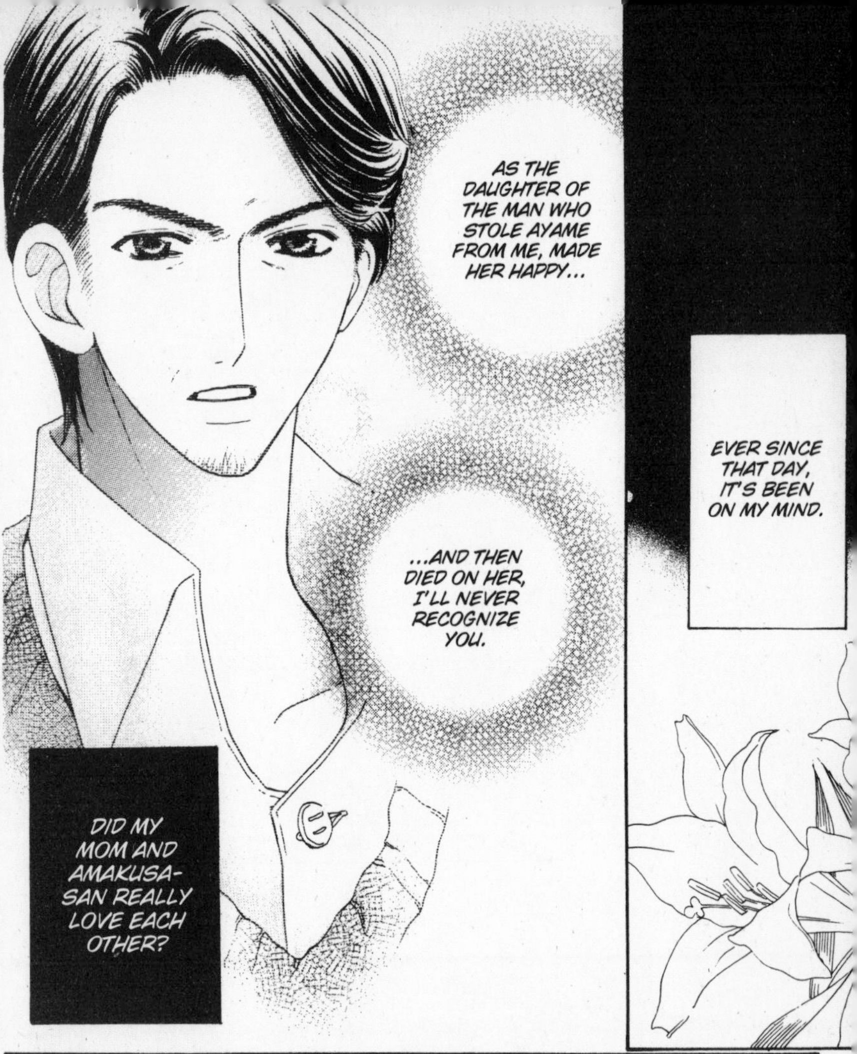
EVER SINCE THAT DAY, IT'S BEEN ON MY MIND.
AS THE DAUGHTER OF THE MAN WHO STOLE AYAME FROM ME, MADE HER HAPPY...
...AND THEN DIED ON HER, I'LL NEVER RECOGNIZE YOU.
DID MY MOM AND AMAKUSA-SAN REALLY LOVE EACH OTHER?

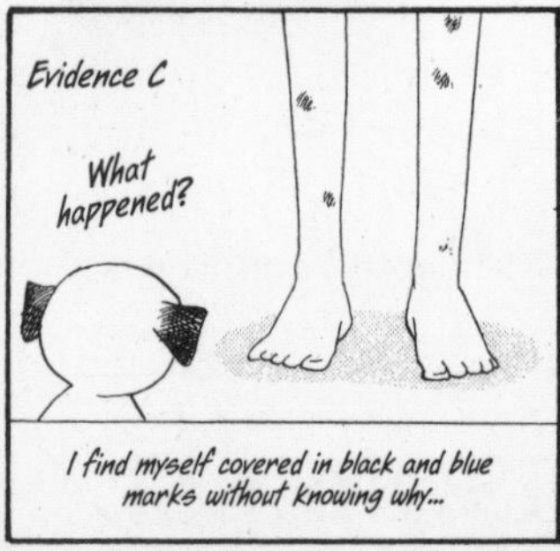
Evidence C
What happened?
I find myself covered in black and blue marks without knowing why...

FREE TALK. ③

It's been tough confessing all these embarrassing facts about myself, but in doing so I think I've learned to face my shortcomings. I've resolved to double my efforts at beating my exercise shortage!!

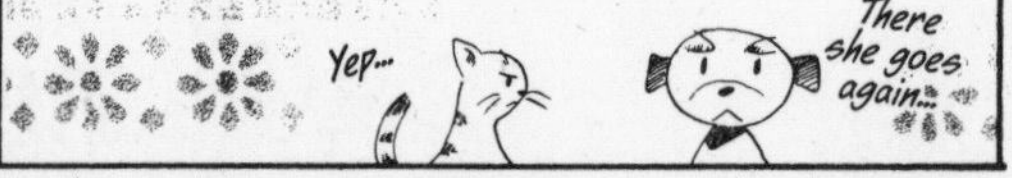
Yep...
There she goes again...

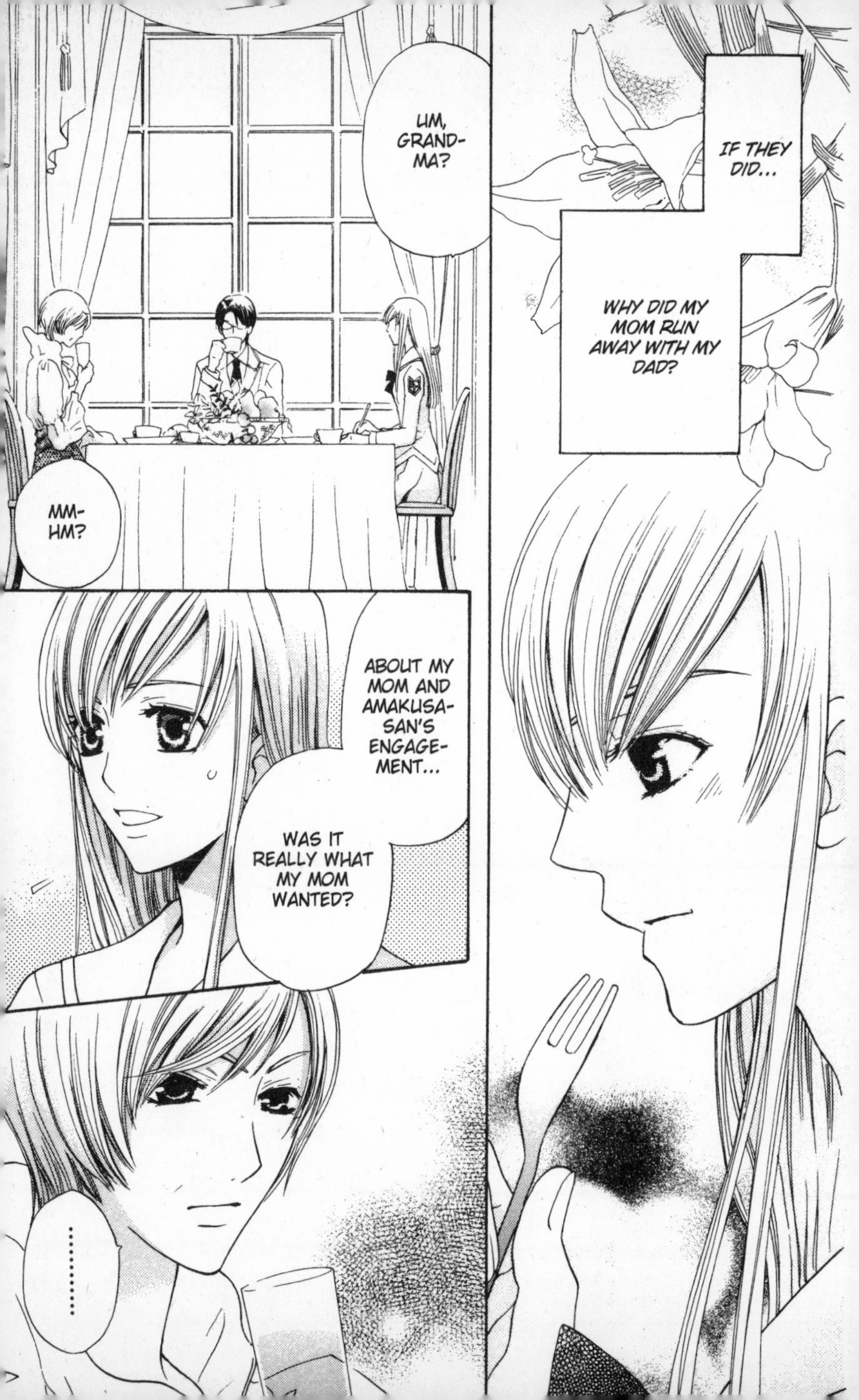
UM, GRANDMA?
MM-HM?
ABOUT MY MOM AND AMAKUSA-SAN'S ENGAGEMENT...
WAS IT REALLY WHAT MY MOM WANTED?
....
IF THEY DID...
WHY DID MY MOM RUN AWAY WITH MY DAD?

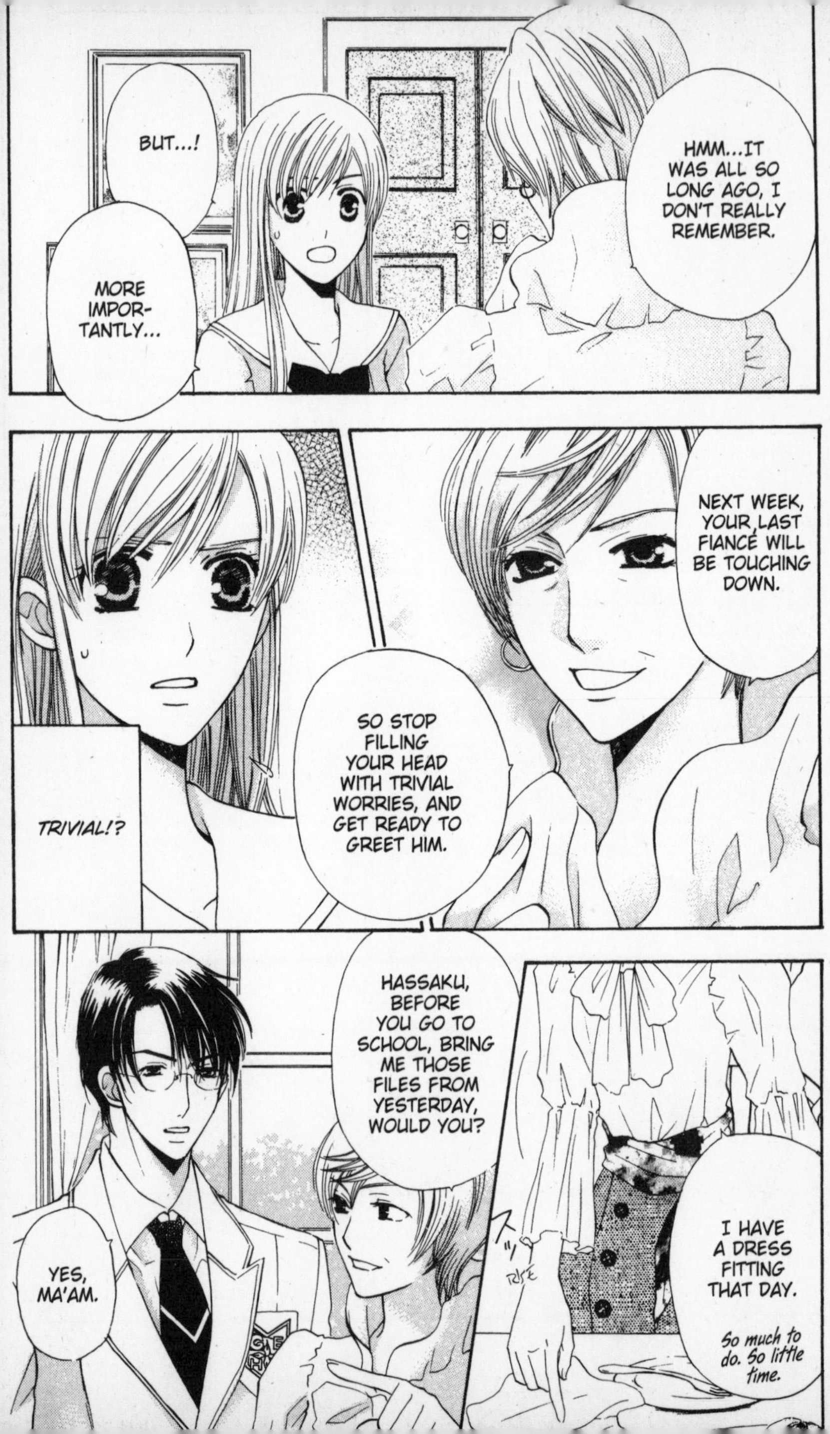
HMM...IT WAS ALL SO LONG AGO, I DON'T REALLY REMEMBER.
BUT...!
MORE IMPORTANTLY...
NEXT WEEK, YOUR LAST FIANCÉ WILL BE TOUCHING DOWN.
SO STOP FILLING YOUR HEAD WITH TRIVIAL WORRIES, AND GET READY TO GREET HIM.
TRIVIAL!?
RISE
I HAVE A DRESS FITTING THAT DAY.
So much to do. So little time.
HASSAKU, BEFORE YOU GO TO SCHOOL, BRING ME THOSE FILES FROM YESTERDAY, WOULD YOU?
YES, MA'AM.

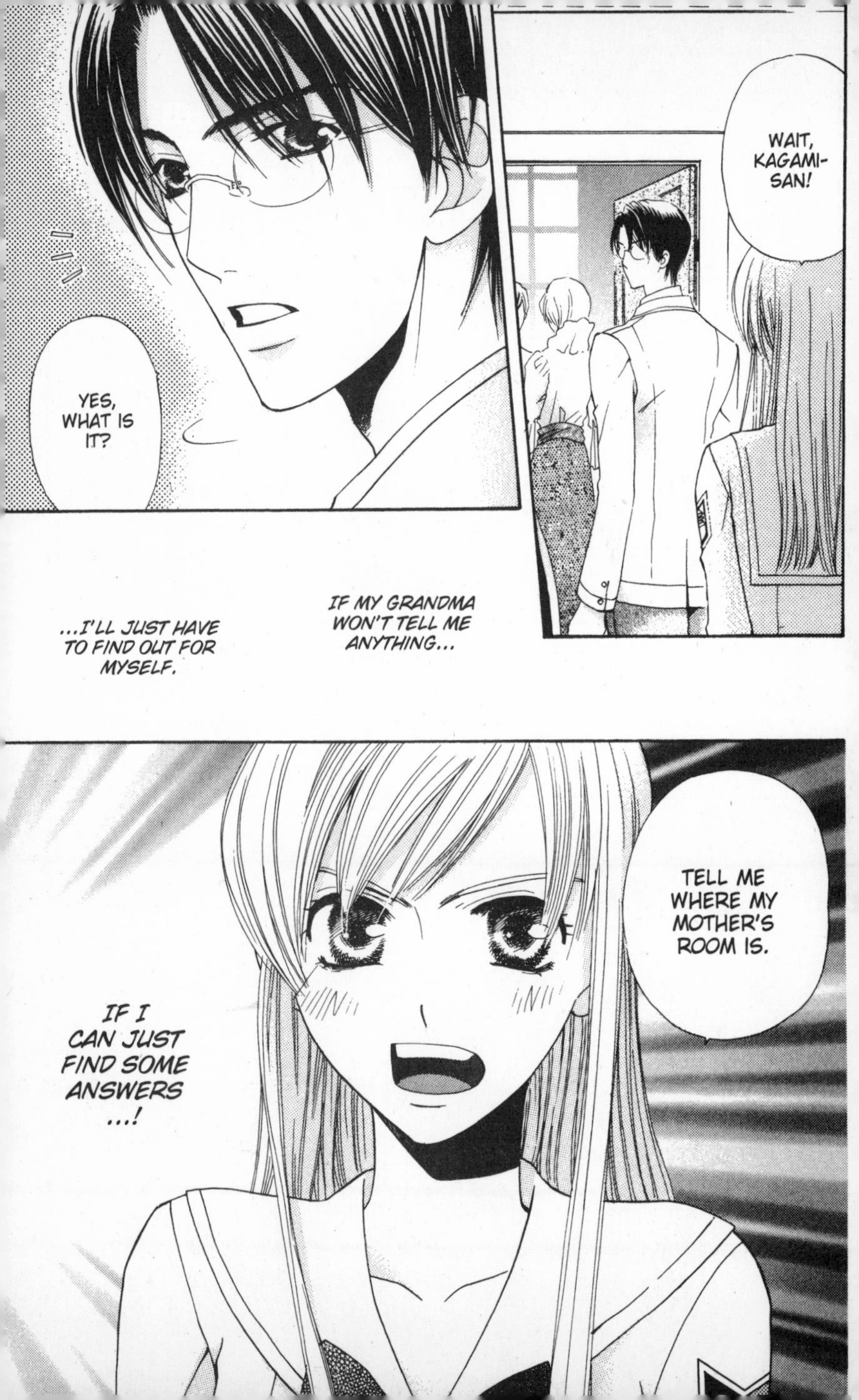
WAIT, KAGAMI-SAN!
YES, WHAT IS IT?
IF MY GRANDMA WON'T TELL ME ANYTHING...
...I'LL JUST HAVE TO FIND OUT FOR MYSELF.
TELL ME WHERE MY MOTHER'S ROOM IS.
IF I CAN JUST FIND SOME ANSWERS ...!

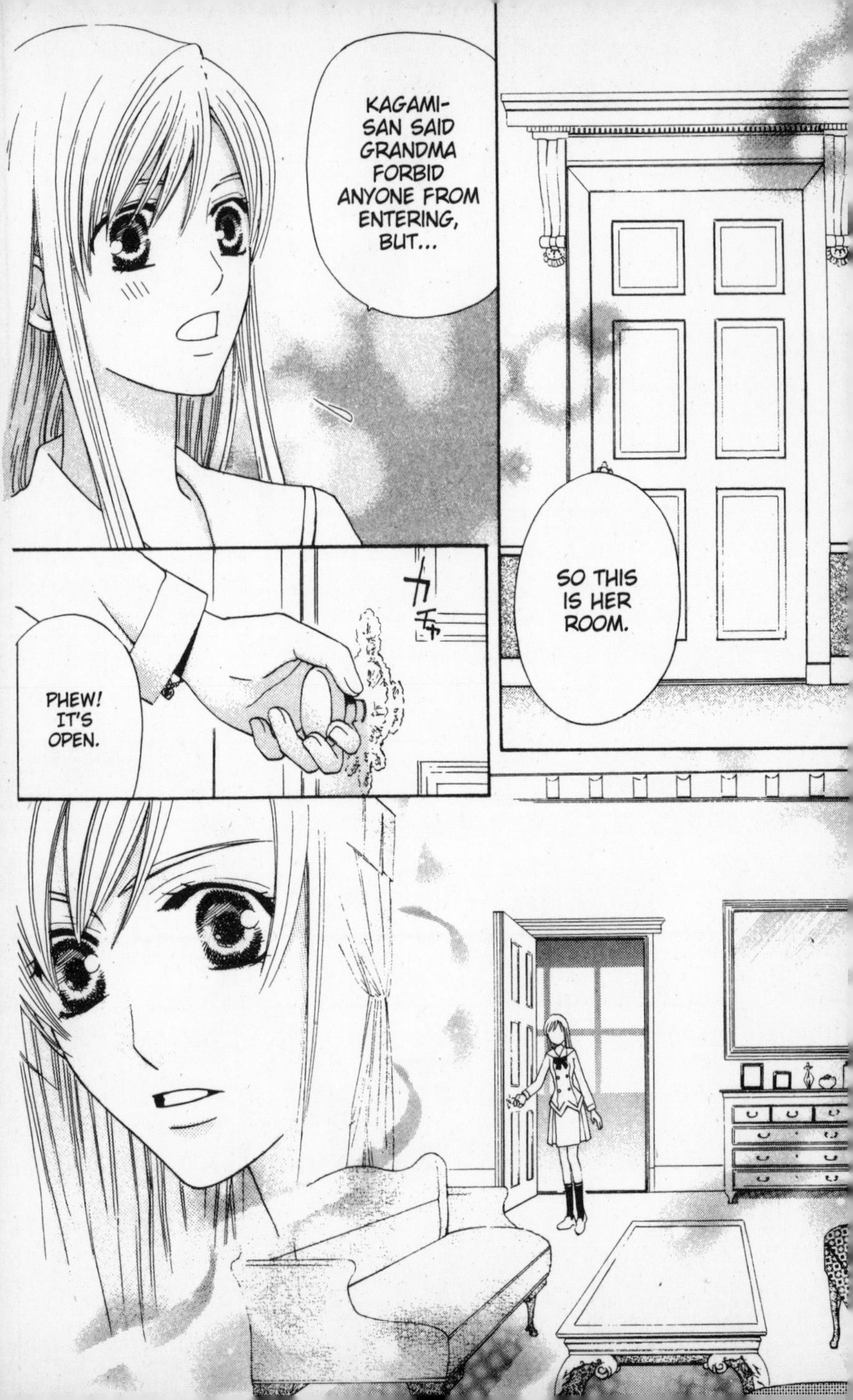
SO THIS IS HER ROOM.
KAGAMI-SAN SAID GRANDMA FORBID ANYONE FROM ENTERING, BUT...
カチャ
PHEW! IT'S OPEN.

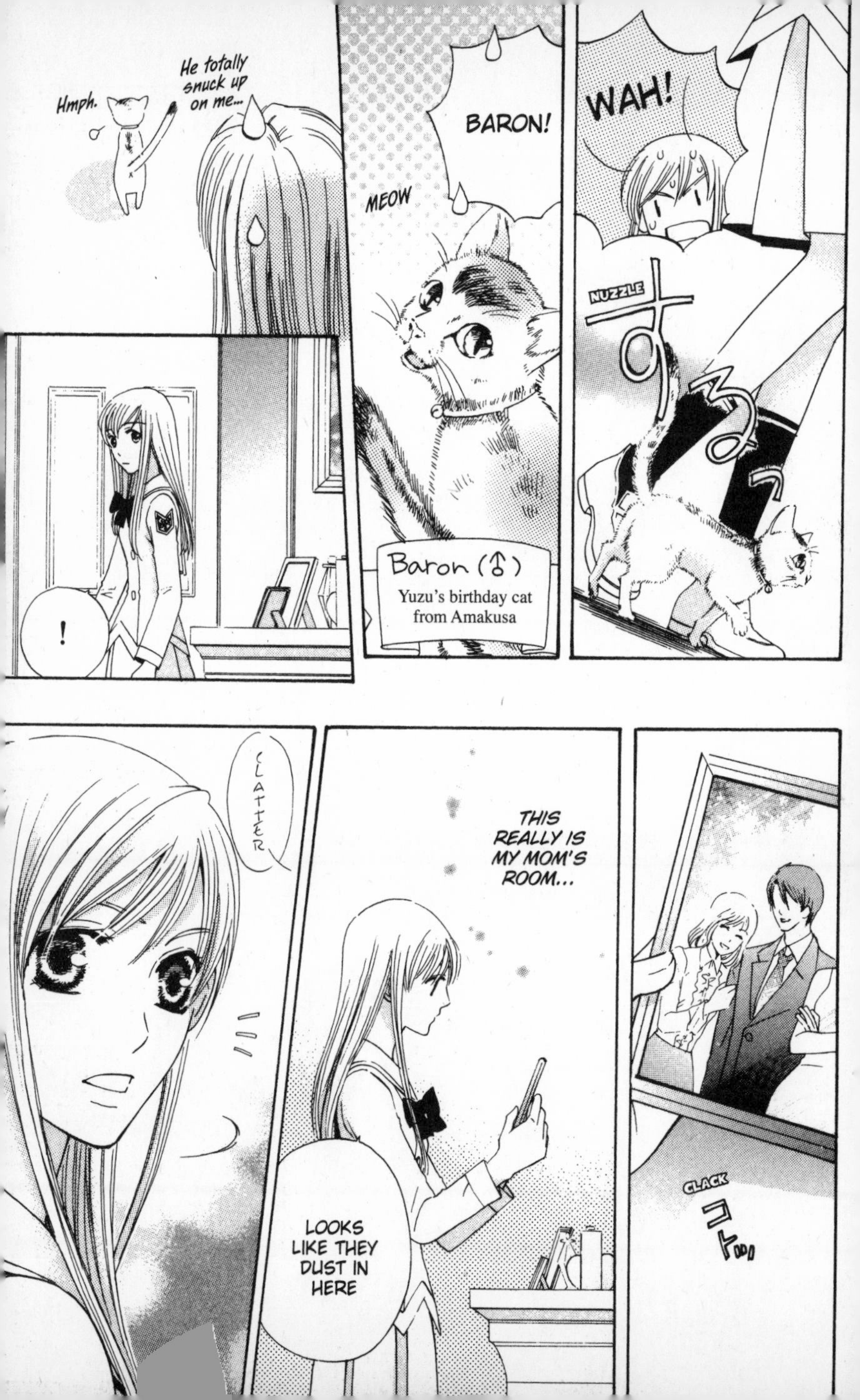
WAH!
NUZZLE
BARON!
MEOW
Baron (♂)
Yuzu's birthday cat from Amakusa
He totally snuck up on me...
Hmph.
!
CLACK
THIS REALLY IS MY MOM'S ROOM...
LOOKS LIKE THEY DUST IN HERE
CLATTER

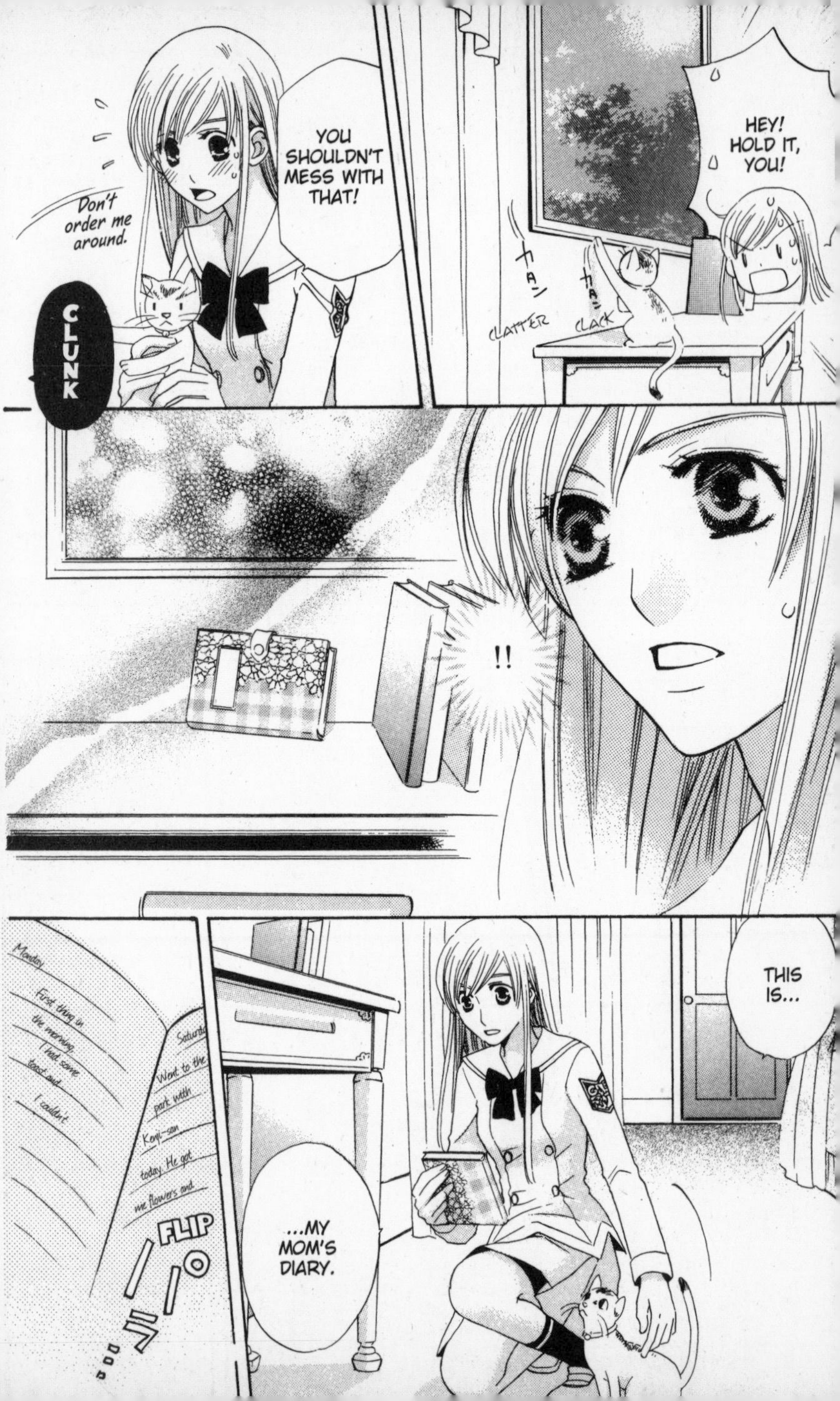
HEY! HOLD IT, YOU!
CLATTER
CLACK
YOU SHOULDN'T MESS WITH THAT!
Don't order me around.
CLUNK
!!
THIS IS...
...MY MOM'S DIARY.
FLIP
Monday
First thing in the morning, I had some toast and I couldn't
Saturday
Went to the park with Kenji-san today. He got me flowers and

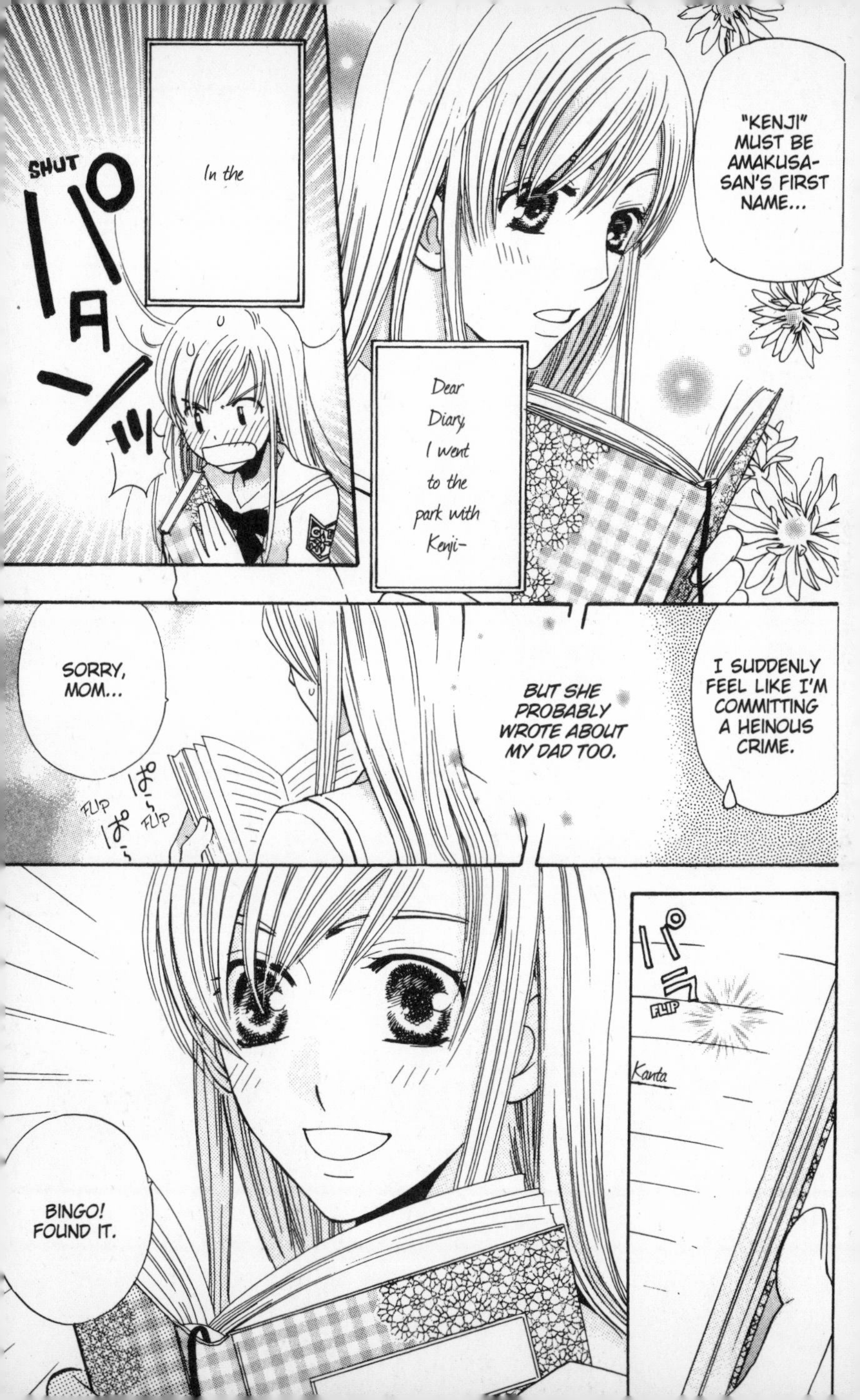
"KENJI" MUST BE AMAKUSA-SAN'S FIRST NAME...
Dear Diary, I went to the park with Kenji-
In the
SHUT
I SUDDENLY FEEL LIKE I'M COMMITTING A HEINOUS CRIME.
BUT SHE PROBABLY WROTE ABOUT MY DAD TOO.
SORRY, MOM...
FLIP FLIP
FLIP
Kanta
BINGO! FOUND IT.

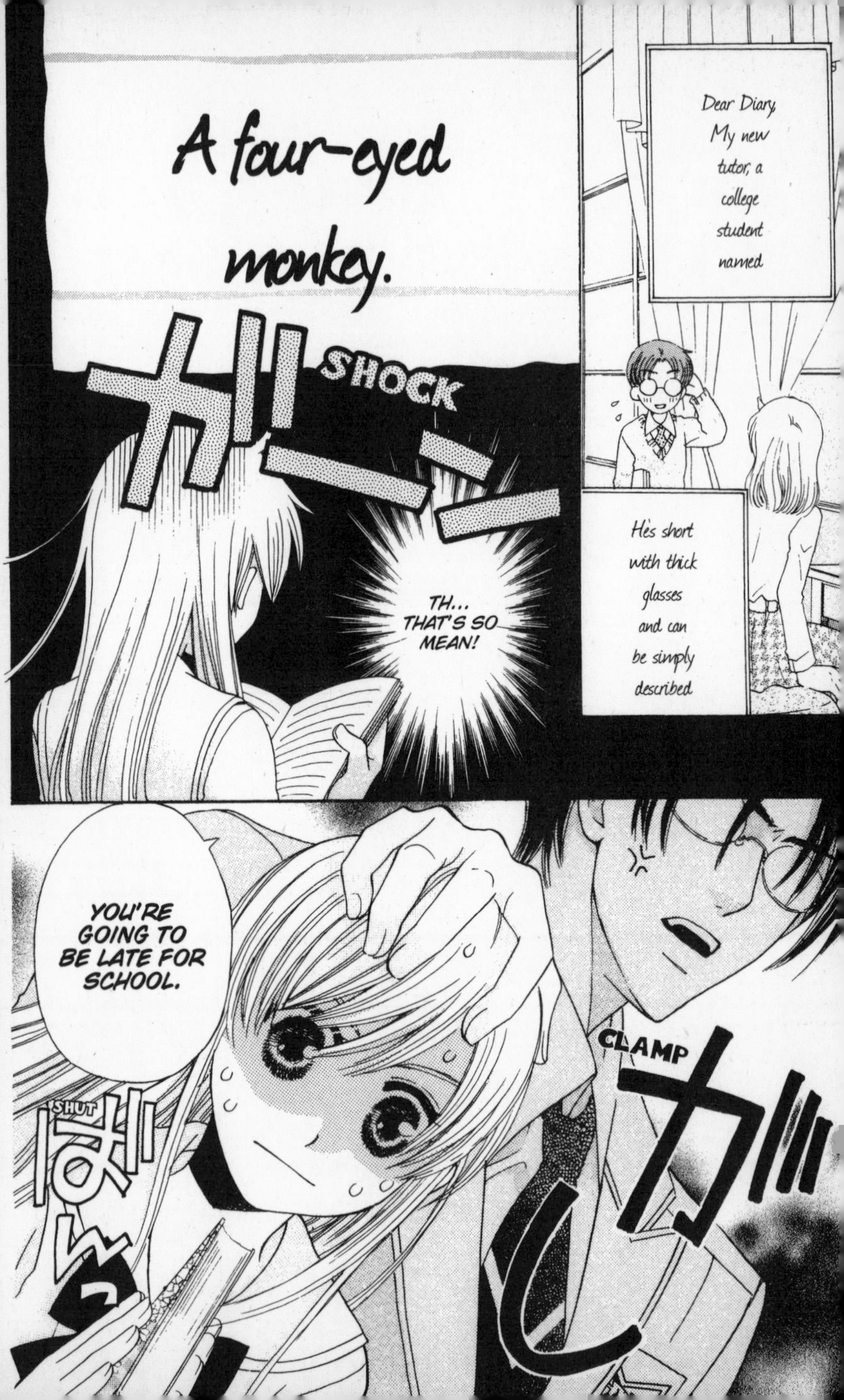
Dear Diary, My new tutor, a college student named
He's short with thick glasses and can be simply described
A four-eyed monkey.
SHOCK
TH... THAT'S SO MEAN!
YOU'RE GOING TO BE LATE FOR SCHOOL.
CLAMP
SHUT

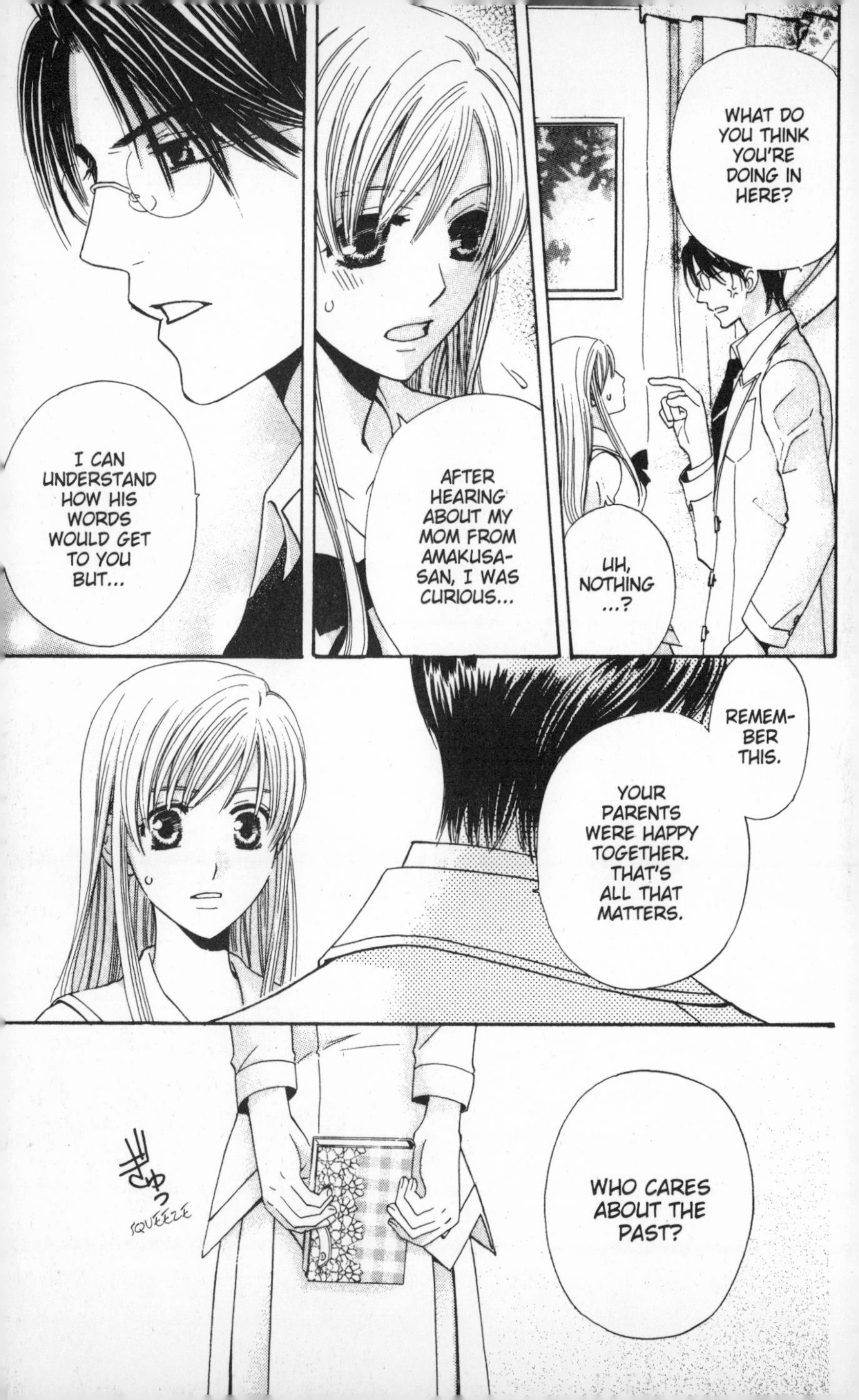
WHAT DO YOU THINK YOU'RE DOING IN HERE?
UH, NOTHING ...?
AFTER HEARING ABOUT MY MOM FROM AMAKUSA-SAN, I WAS CURIOUS...
I CAN UNDERSTAND HOW HIS WORDS WOULD GET TO YOU BUT...
REMEMBER THIS.
YOUR PARENTS WERE HAPPY TOGETHER. THAT'S ALL THAT MATTERS.
ぎゅっ
SQUEEZE
WHO CARES ABOUT THE PAST?

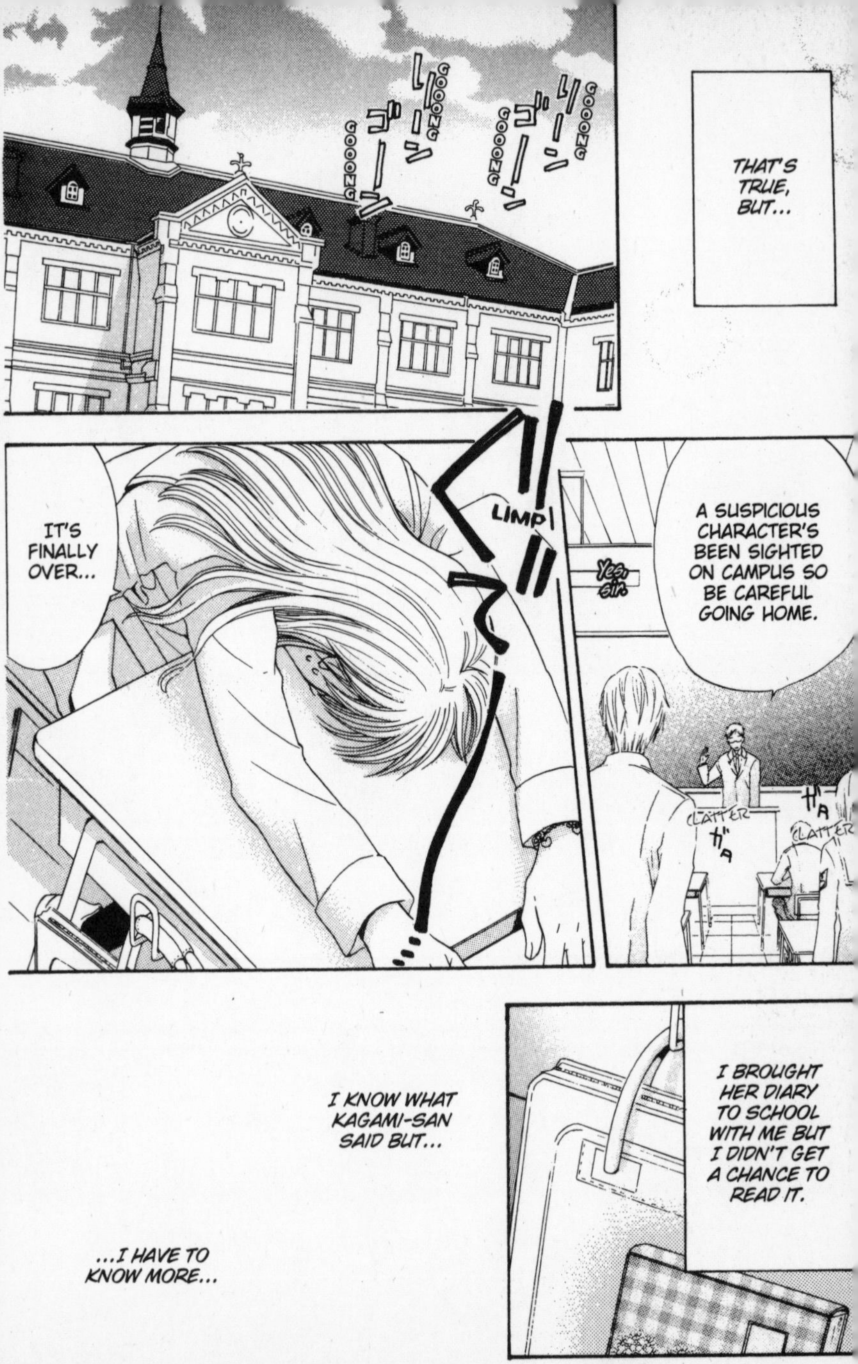
THAT'S TRUE, BUT...
GOOOONG
GOOOONG
GOOOONG
GOOOONG
A SUSPICIOUS CHARACTER'S BEEN SIGHTED ON CAMPUS SO BE CAREFUL GOING HOME.
Yes, sir.
CLATTER
CLATTER
LIMP
IT'S FINALLY OVER...
I BROUGHT HER DIARY TO SCHOOL WITH ME BUT I DIDN'T GET A CHANCE TO READ IT.
I KNOW WHAT KAGAMI-SAN SAID BUT...
...I HAVE TO KNOW MORE...

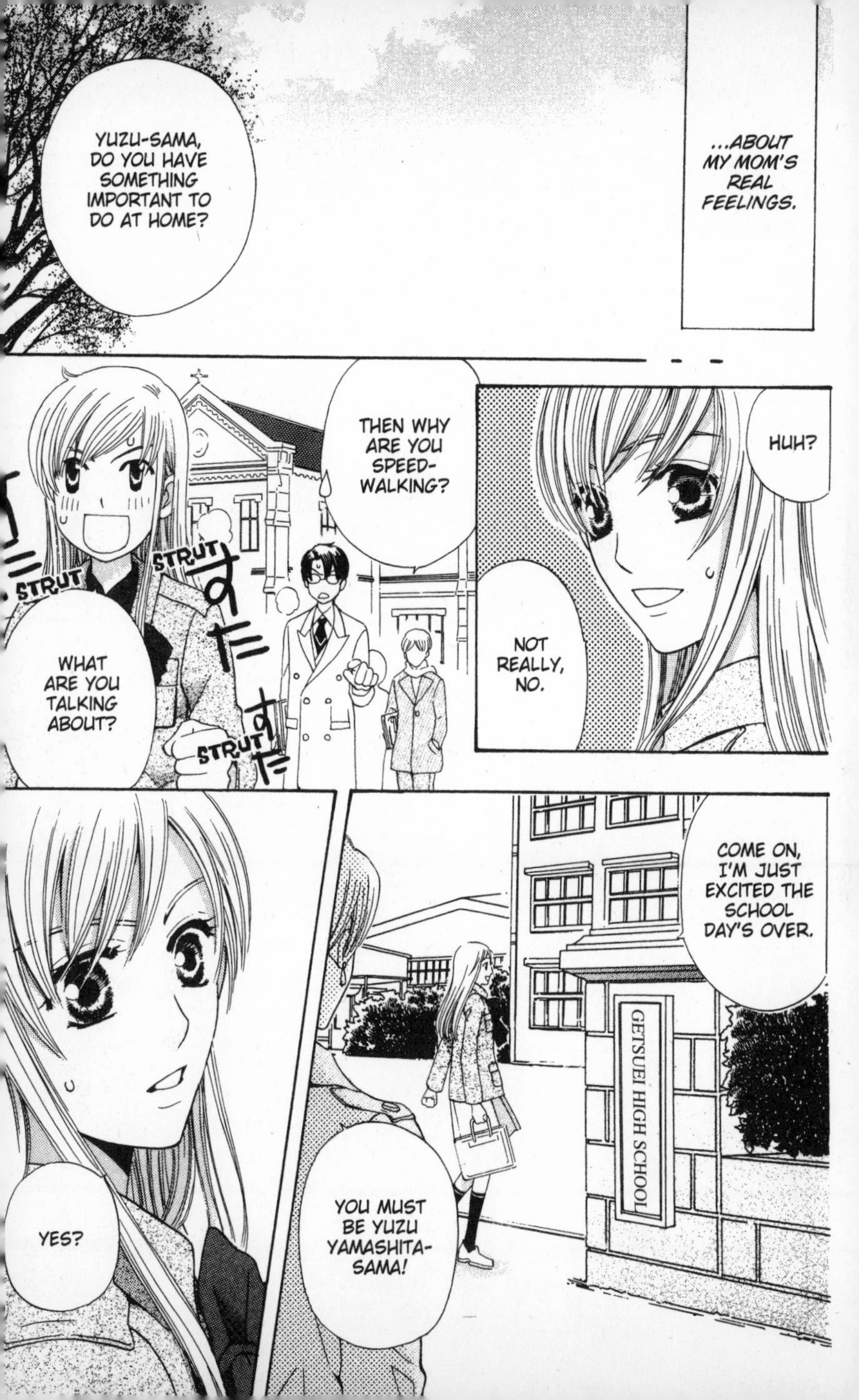
...ABOUT MY MOM'S REAL FEELINGS.
YUZU-SAMA, DO YOU HAVE SOMETHING IMPORTANT TO DO AT HOME?
HUH?
NOT REALLY, NO.
THEN WHY ARE YOU SPEED-WALKING?
STRUT
STRUT
STRUT
WHAT ARE YOU TALKING ABOUT?
COME ON, I'M JUST EXCITED THE SCHOOL DAY'S OVER.
GETSUEI HIGH SCHOOL
YOU MUST BE YUZU YAMASHITA-SAMA!
YES?

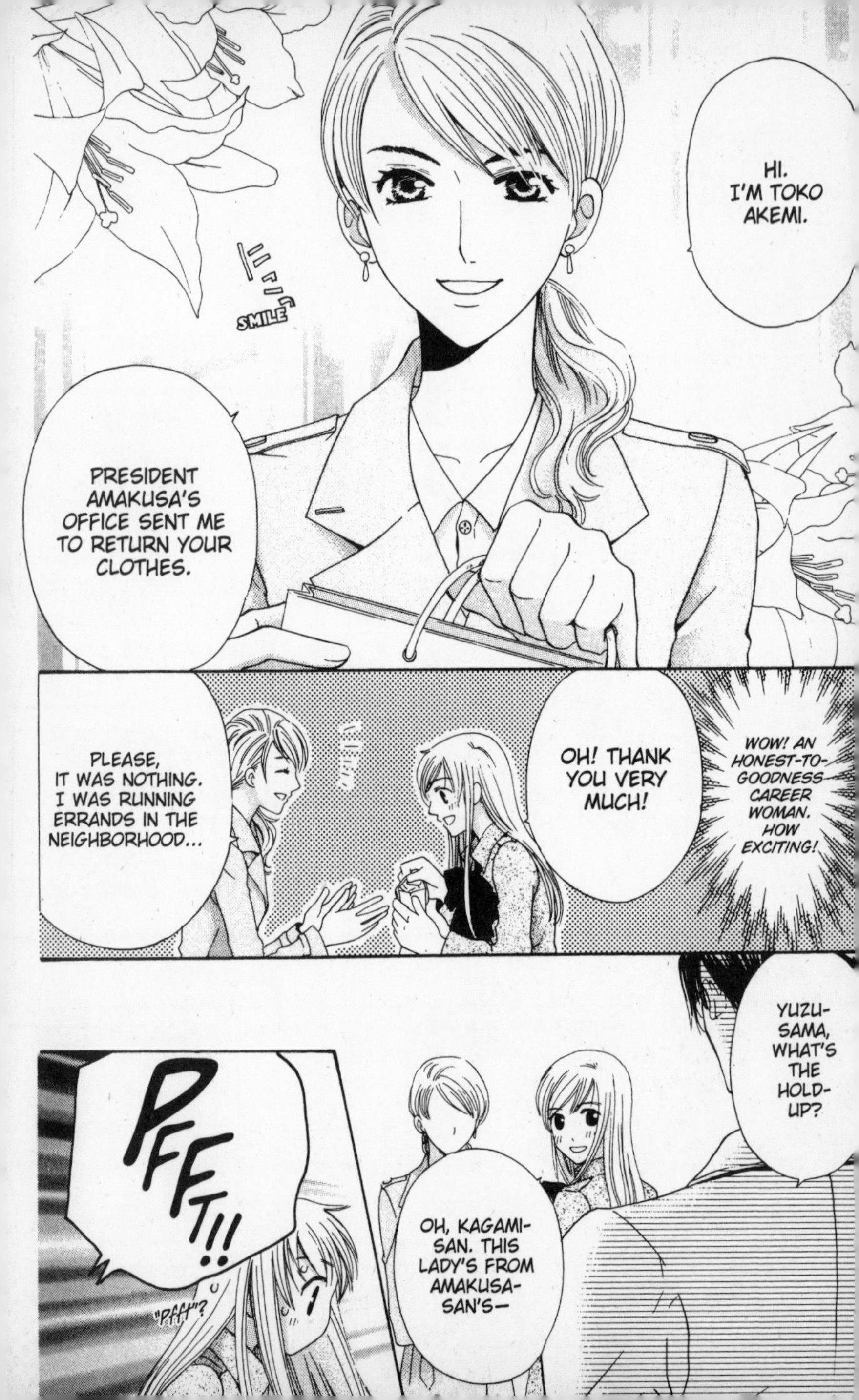
HI. I'M TOKO AKEMI.
SMILE
PRESIDENT AMAKUSA'S OFFICE SENT ME TO RETURN YOUR CLOTHES.
WOW! AN HONEST-TO-GOODNESS CAREER WOMAN. HOW EXCITING!
OH! THANK YOU VERY MUCH!
PLEASE, IT WAS NOTHING. I WAS RUNNING ERRANDS IN THE NEIGHBORHOOD...
YUZU-SAMA, WHAT'S THE HOLD-UP?
OH, KAGAMI-SAN. THIS LADY'S FROM AMAKUSA-SAN'S—
PFFT!!
"PFFT"?

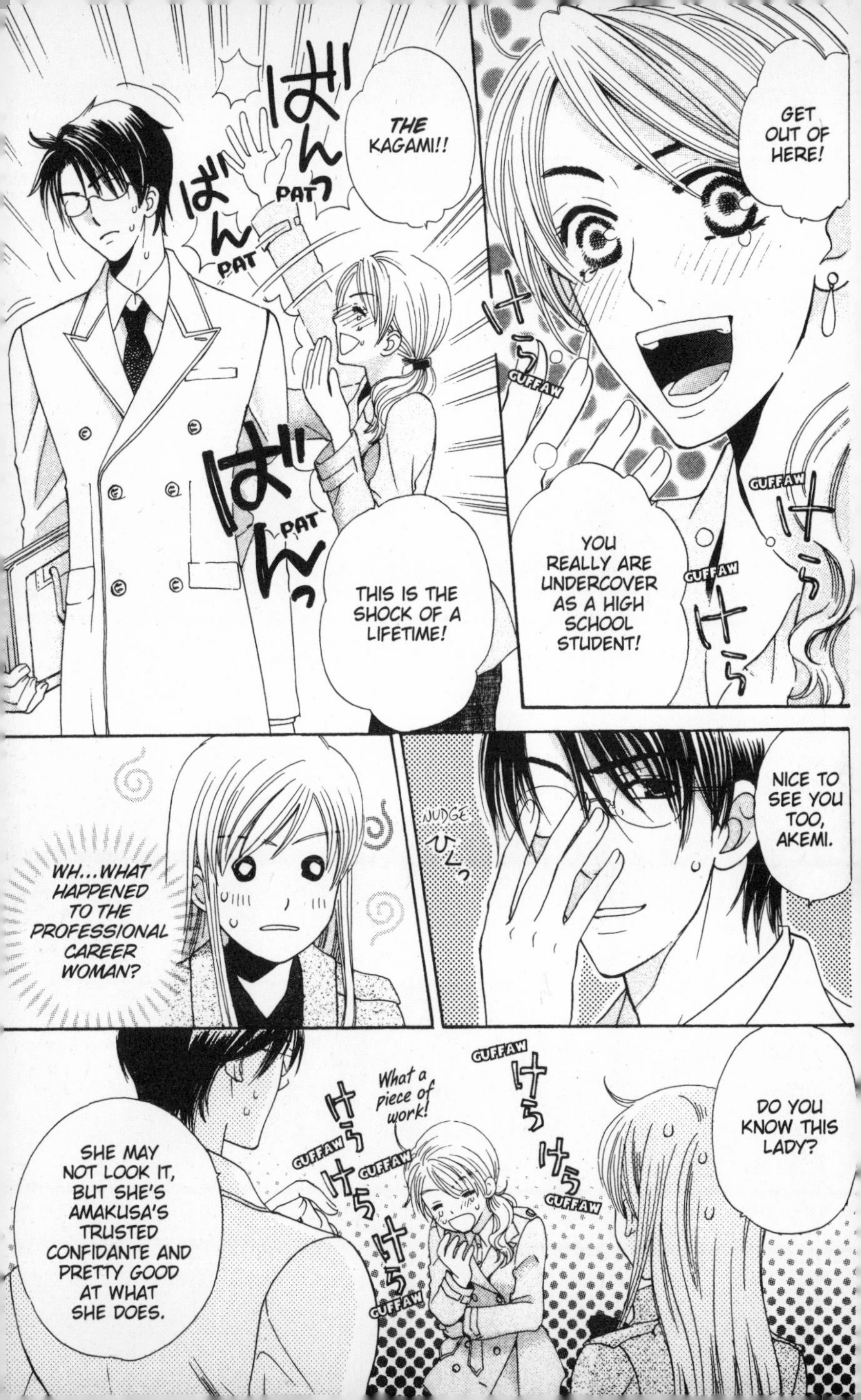
GET OUT OF HERE!
けら
GUFFAW
YOU REALLY ARE UNDERCOVER AS A HIGH SCHOOL STUDENT!
GUFFAW
けら
GUFFAW
けら
ばんっ
PAT
THE KAGAMI!!
ばん
PAT
ばんっ
PAT
THIS IS THE SHOCK OF A LIFETIME!
NICE TO SEE YOU TOO, AKEMI.
NUDGE
ひくっ
WH...WHAT HAPPENED TO THE PROFESSIONAL CAREER WOMAN?
DO YOU KNOW THIS LADY?
GUFFAW
けら
けら
GUFFAW
What a piece of work!
けら
GUFFAW
けら
GUFFAW
けら
GUFFAW
SHE MAY NOT LOOK IT, BUT SHE'S AMAKUSA'S TRUSTED CONFIDANTE AND PRETTY GOOD AT WHAT SHE DOES.

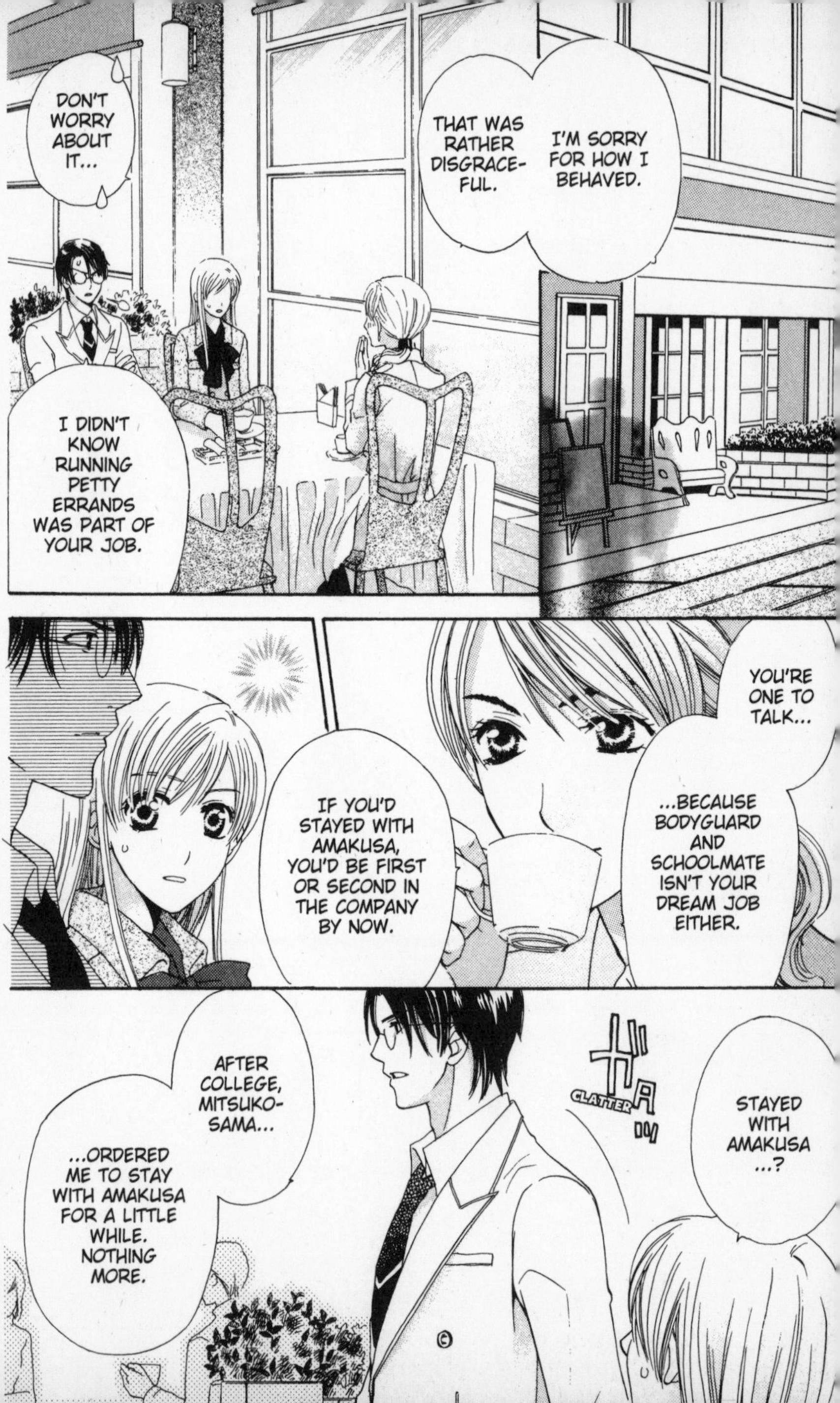
I'M SORRY FOR HOW I BEHAVED.
THAT WAS RATHER DISGRACE-FUL.
DON'T WORRY ABOUT IT...
I DIDN'T KNOW RUNNING PETTY ERRANDS WAS PART OF YOUR JOB.
YOU'RE ONE TO TALK...
...BECAUSE BODYGUARD AND SCHOOLMATE ISN'T YOUR DREAM JOB EITHER.
IF YOU'D STAYED WITH AMAKUSA, YOU'D BE FIRST OR SECOND IN THE COMPANY BY NOW.
CLATTER
STAYED WITH AMAKUSA ...?
AFTER COLLEGE, MITSUKO-SAMA...
...ORDERED ME TO STAY WITH AMAKUSA FOR A LITTLE WHILE. NOTHING MORE.

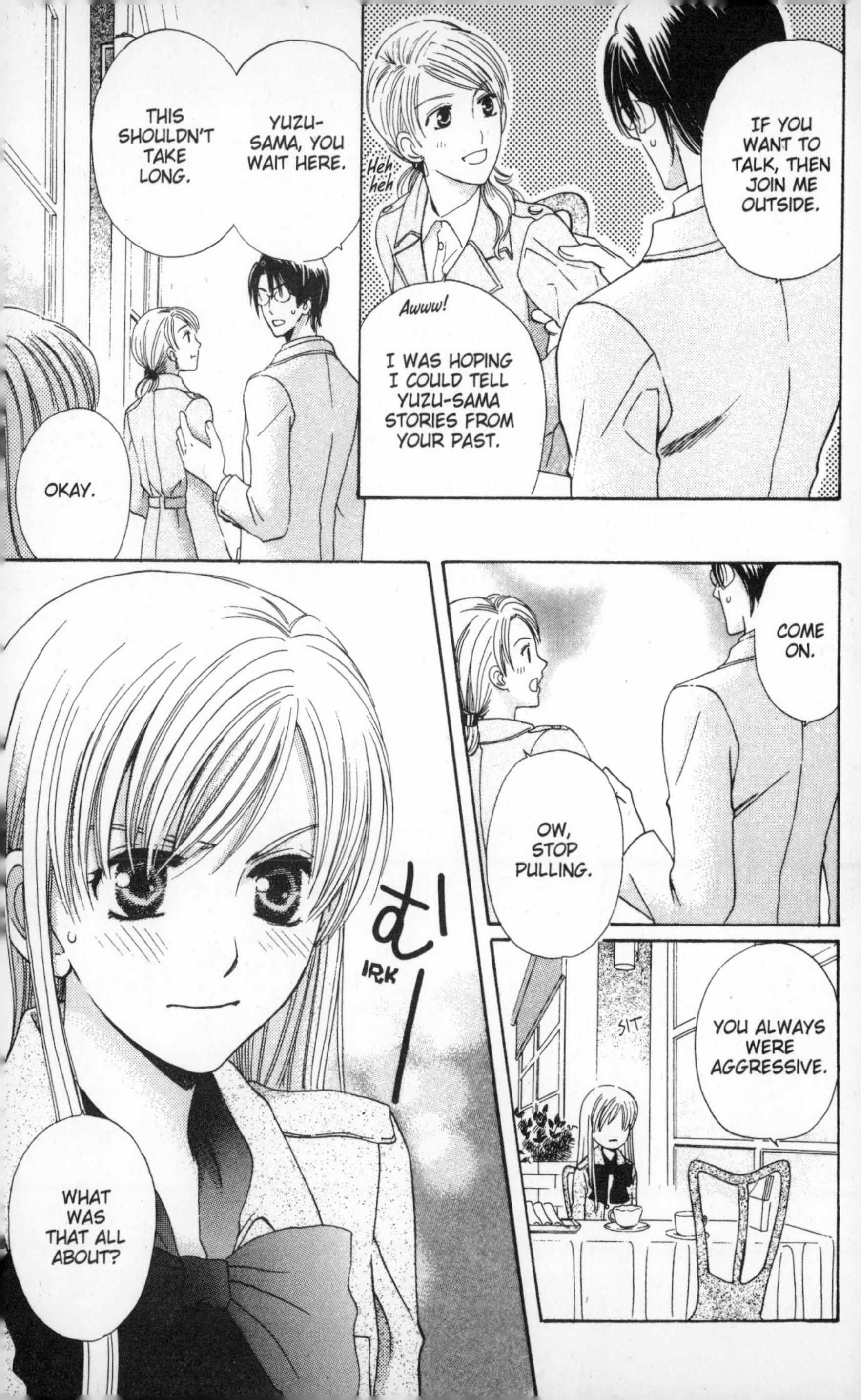
IF YOU WANT TO TALK, THEN JOIN ME OUTSIDE.
Heh heh
Awww!
I WAS HOPING I COULD TELL YUZU-SAMA STORIES FROM YOUR PAST.
YUZU-SAMA, YOU WAIT HERE.
THIS SHOULDN'T TAKE LONG.
OKAY.
COME ON.
OW, STOP PULLING.
SIT
YOU ALWAYS WERE AGGRESSIVE.
IRK
WHAT WAS THAT ALL ABOUT?

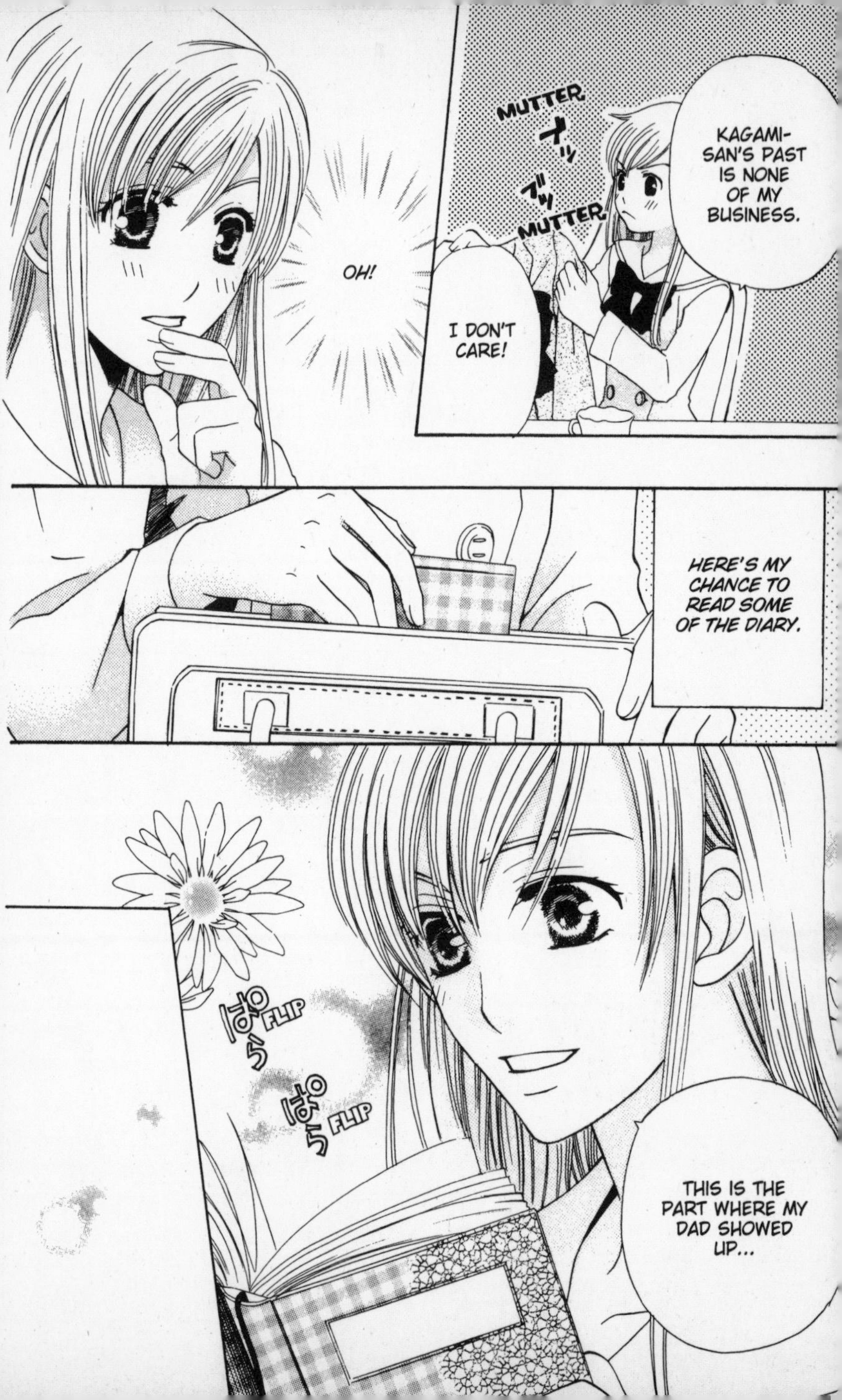
MUTTER
MUTTER
KAGAMI-SAN'S PAST IS NONE OF MY BUSINESS.
I DON'T CARE!
OH!
HERE'S MY CHANCE TO READ SOME OF THE DIARY.
ぱら FLIP
ぱら FLIP
THIS IS THE PART WHERE MY DAD SHOWED UP...

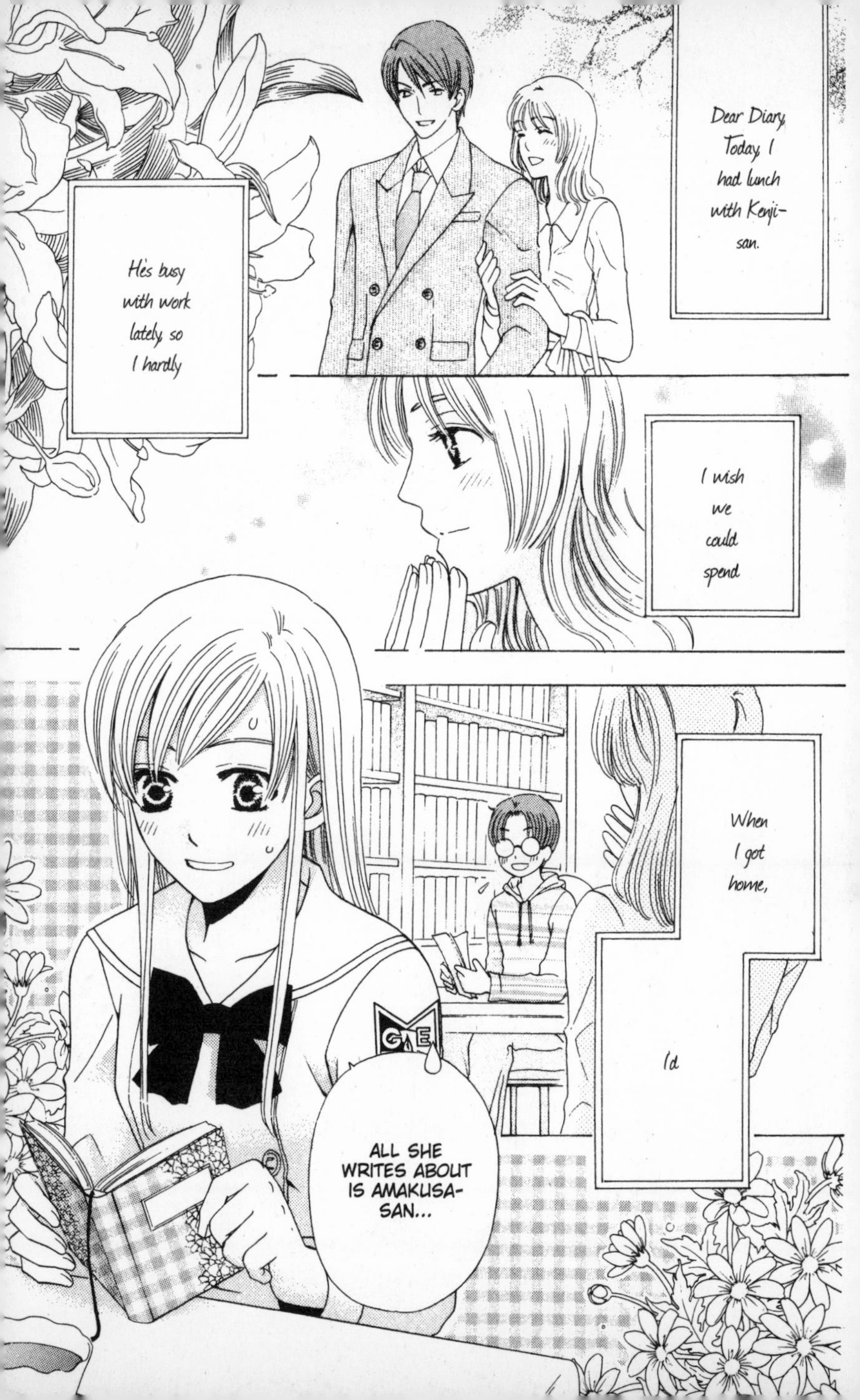
Dear Diary, Today, I had lunch with Kenji-san.
He's busy with work lately, so I hardly
I wish we could spend
When I got home,
I'd
ALL SHE WRITES ABOUT IS AMAKUSA-SAN...

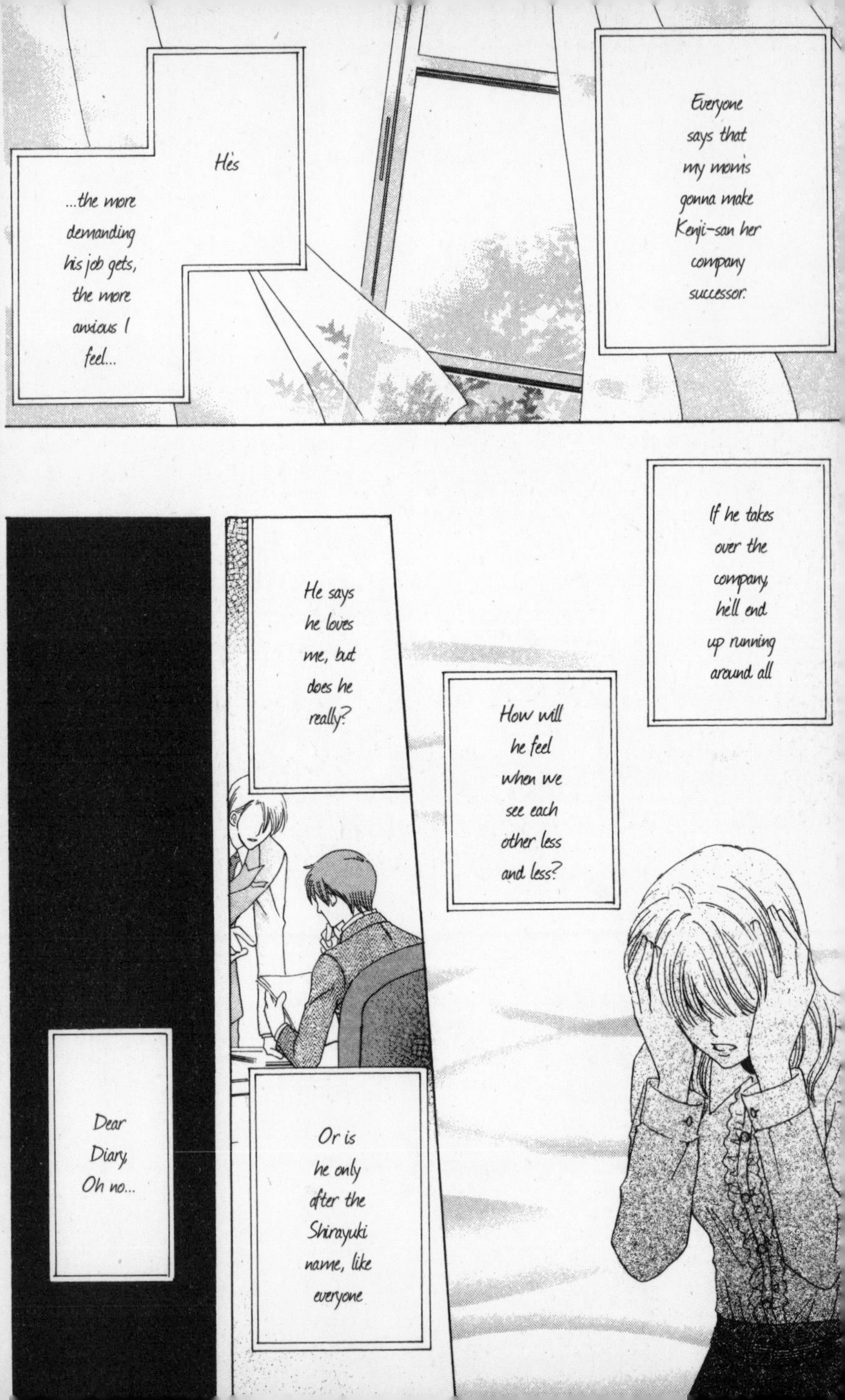
Everyone says that my mom's gonna make Kenji-san her company successor.
He's
...the more demanding his job gets, the more anxious I feel...
If he takes over the company, he'll end up running around all
How will he feel when we see each other less and less?
He says he loves me, but does he really?
Or is he only after the Shirayuki name, like everyone
Dear Diary, Oh no...

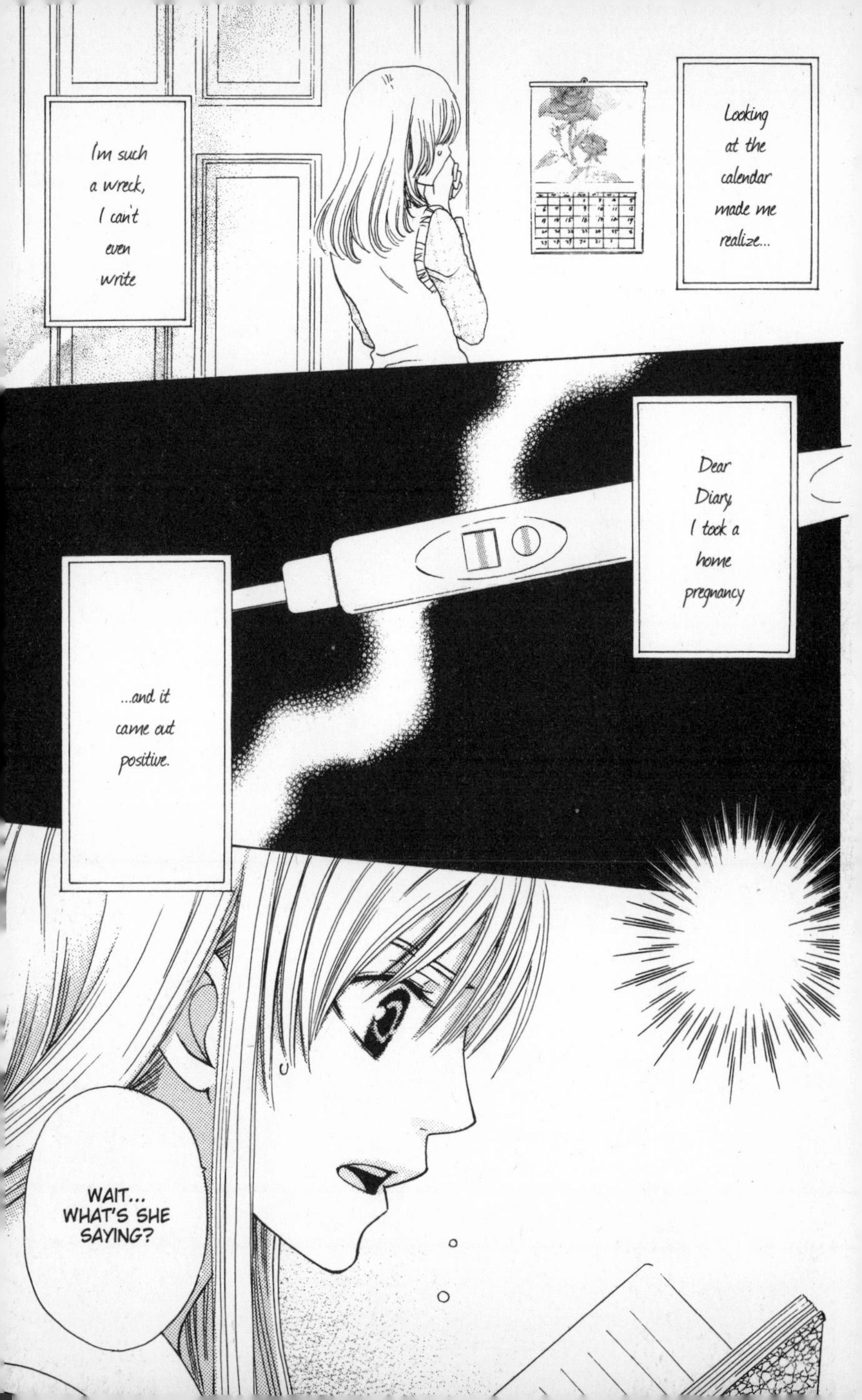
Looking at the calendar made me realize...
I'm such a wreck, I can't even write
Dear Diary, I took a home pregnancy
...and it came out positive.
WAIT... WHAT'S SHE SAYING?

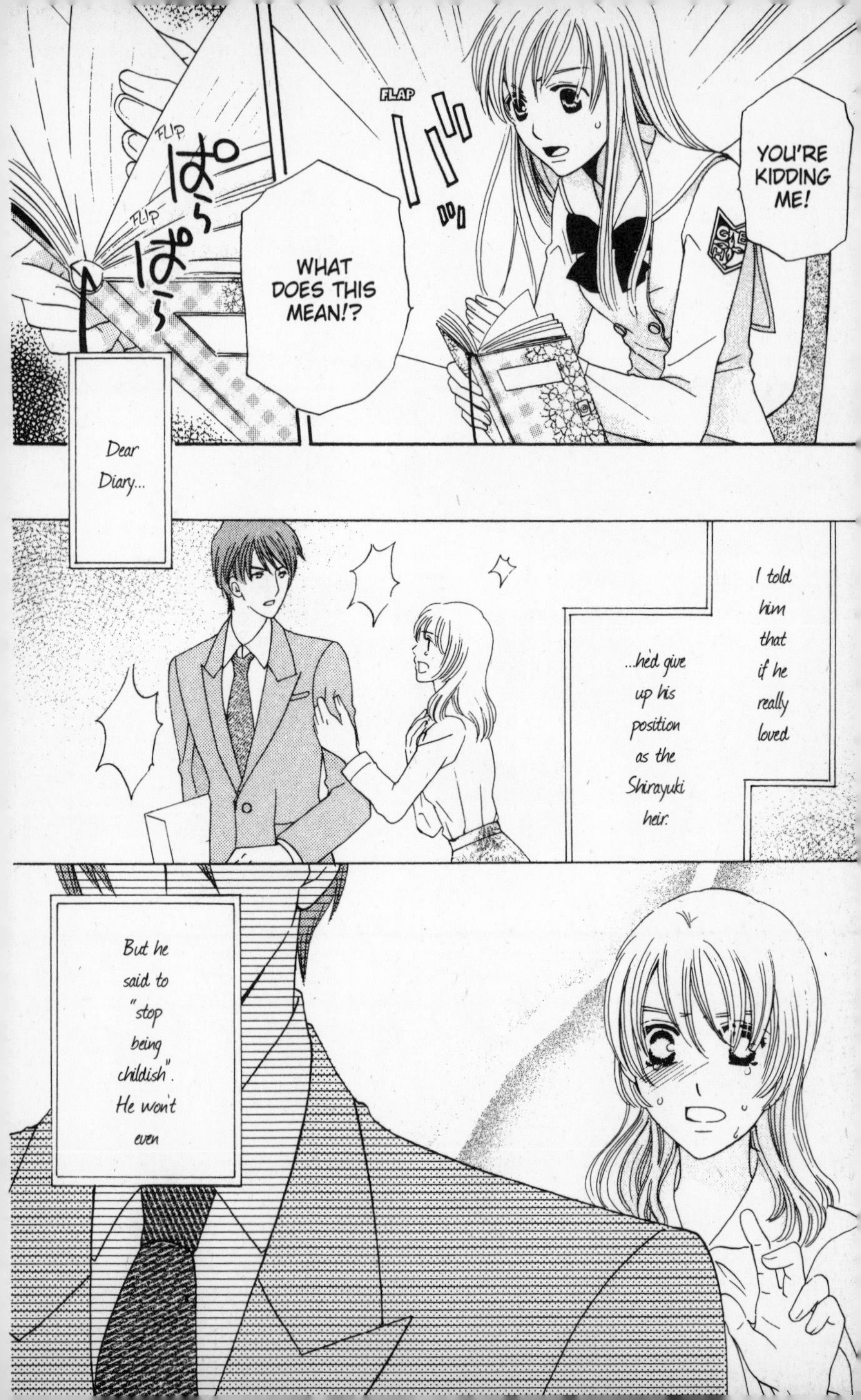
YOU'RE KIDDING ME!
FLAP
WHAT DOES THIS MEAN!?
FLIP
FLIP
ぱらぱら
Dear Diary...
I told him that if he really loved
...he'd give up his position as the Shirayuki heir.
But he said to "stop being childish". He won't even

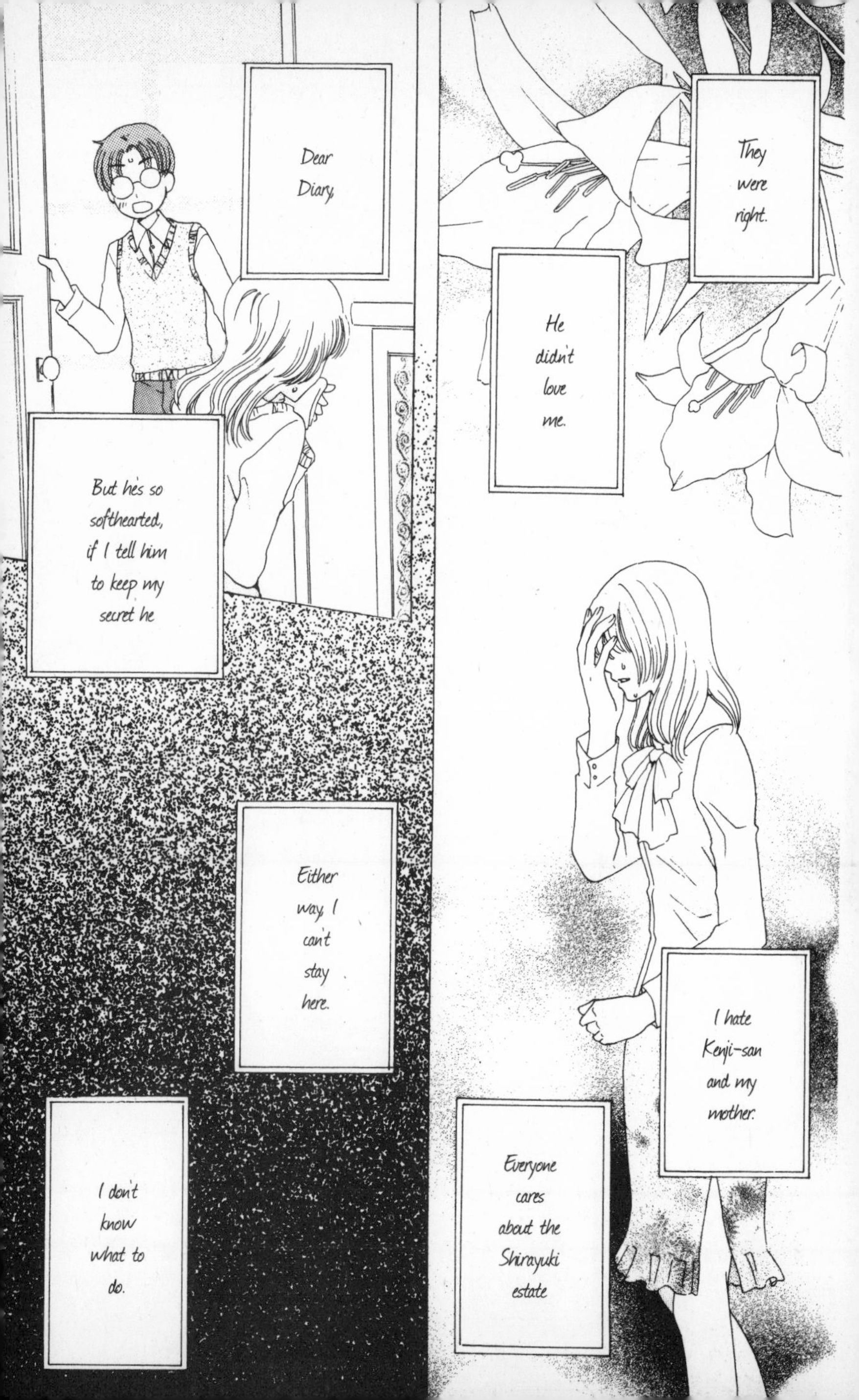
They were right.
He didn't love me.
I hate Kenji-san and my mother.
Everyone cares about the Shirayuki estate
Dear Diary,
But he's so softhearted, if I tell him to keep my secret he
Either way, I can't stay here.
I don't know what to do.

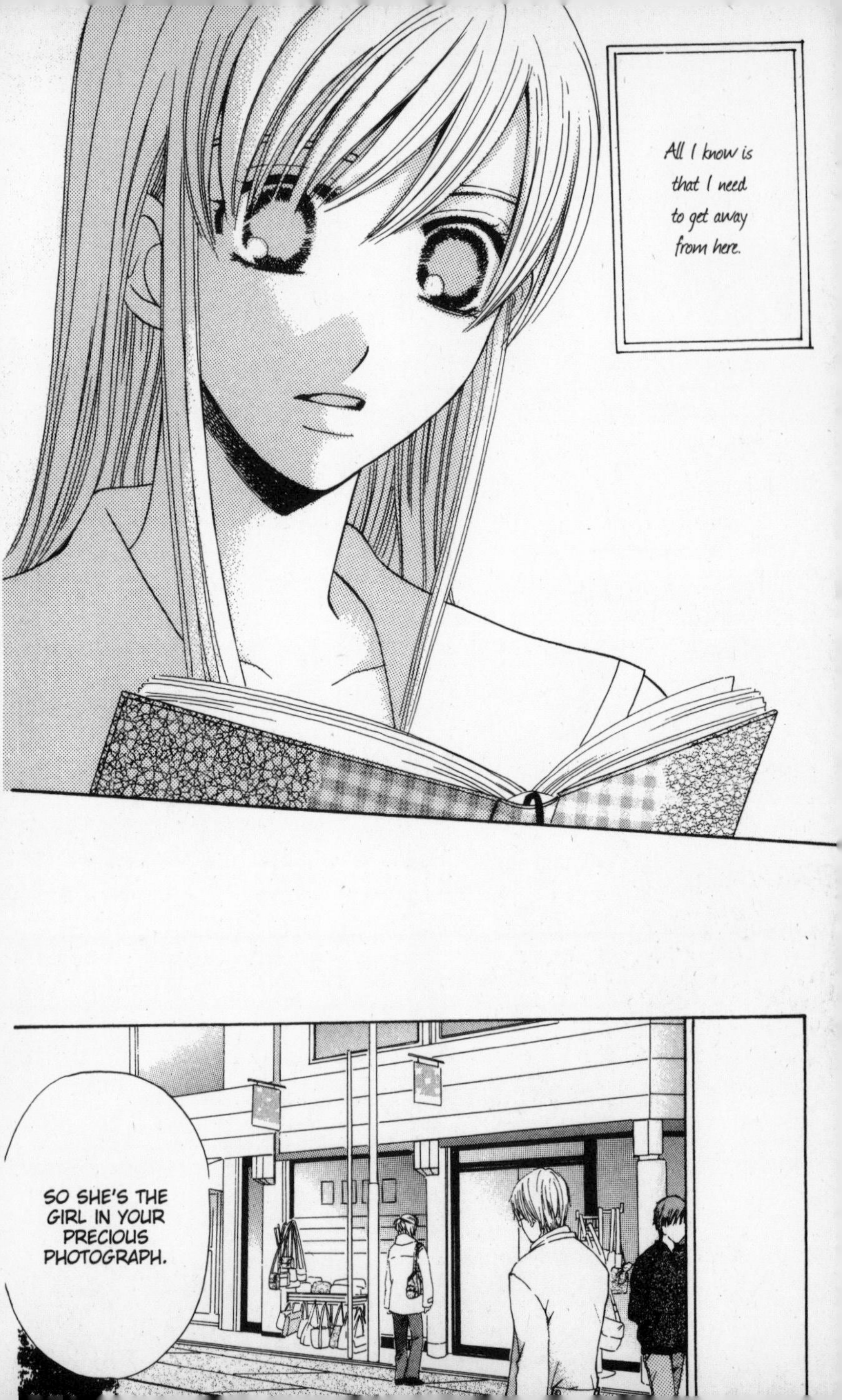
All I know is that I need to get away from here.
SO SHE'S THE GIRL IN YOUR PRECIOUS PHOTOGRAPH.

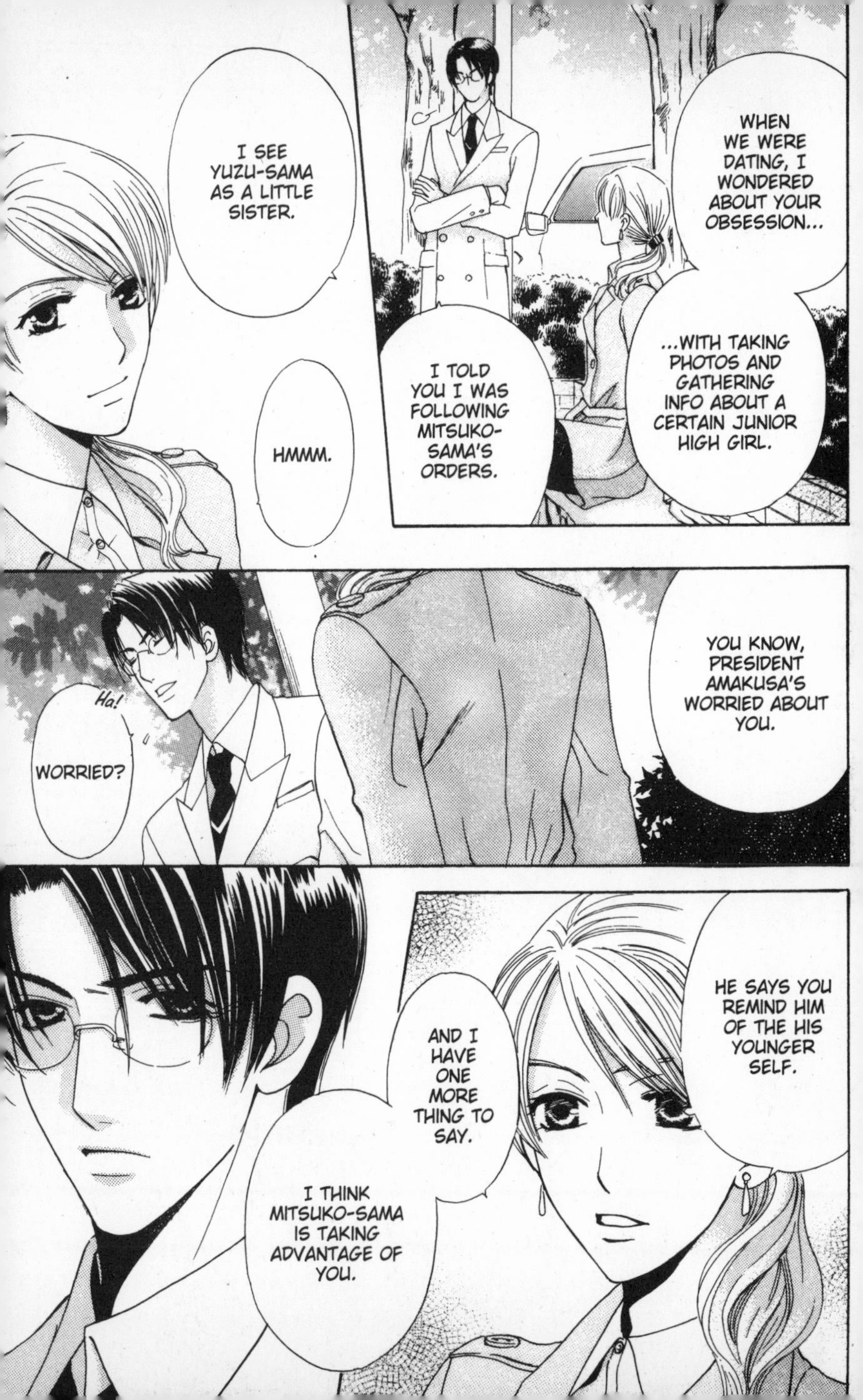
WHEN WE WERE DATING, I WONDERED ABOUT YOUR OBSESSION...
...WITH TAKING PHOTOS AND GATHERING INFO ABOUT A CERTAIN JUNIOR HIGH GIRL.
I TOLD YOU I WAS FOLLOWING MITSUKO-SAMA'S ORDERS.
I SEE YUZU-SAMA AS A LITTLE SISTER.
HMMM.
YOU KNOW, PRESIDENT AMAKUSA'S WORRIED ABOUT YOU.
Ha!
WORRIED?
HE SAYS YOU REMIND HIM OF THE HIS YOUNGER SELF.
AND I HAVE ONE MORE THING TO SAY.
I THINK MITSUKO-SAMA IS TAKING ADVANTAGE OF YOU.

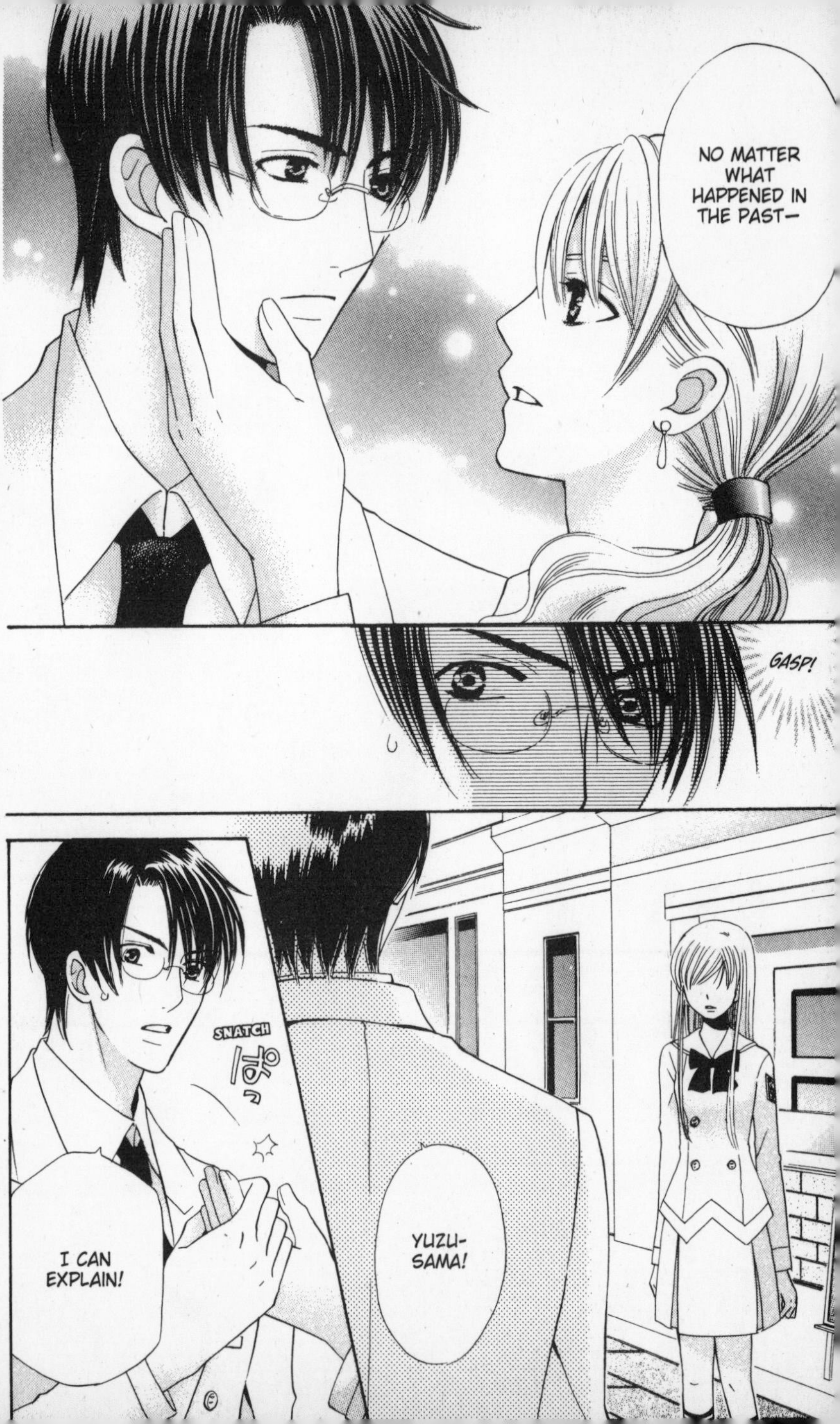
NO MATTER WHAT HAPPENED IN THE PAST—
GASP!
YUZU-SAMA!
SNATCH
ぱっ
I CAN EXPLAIN!

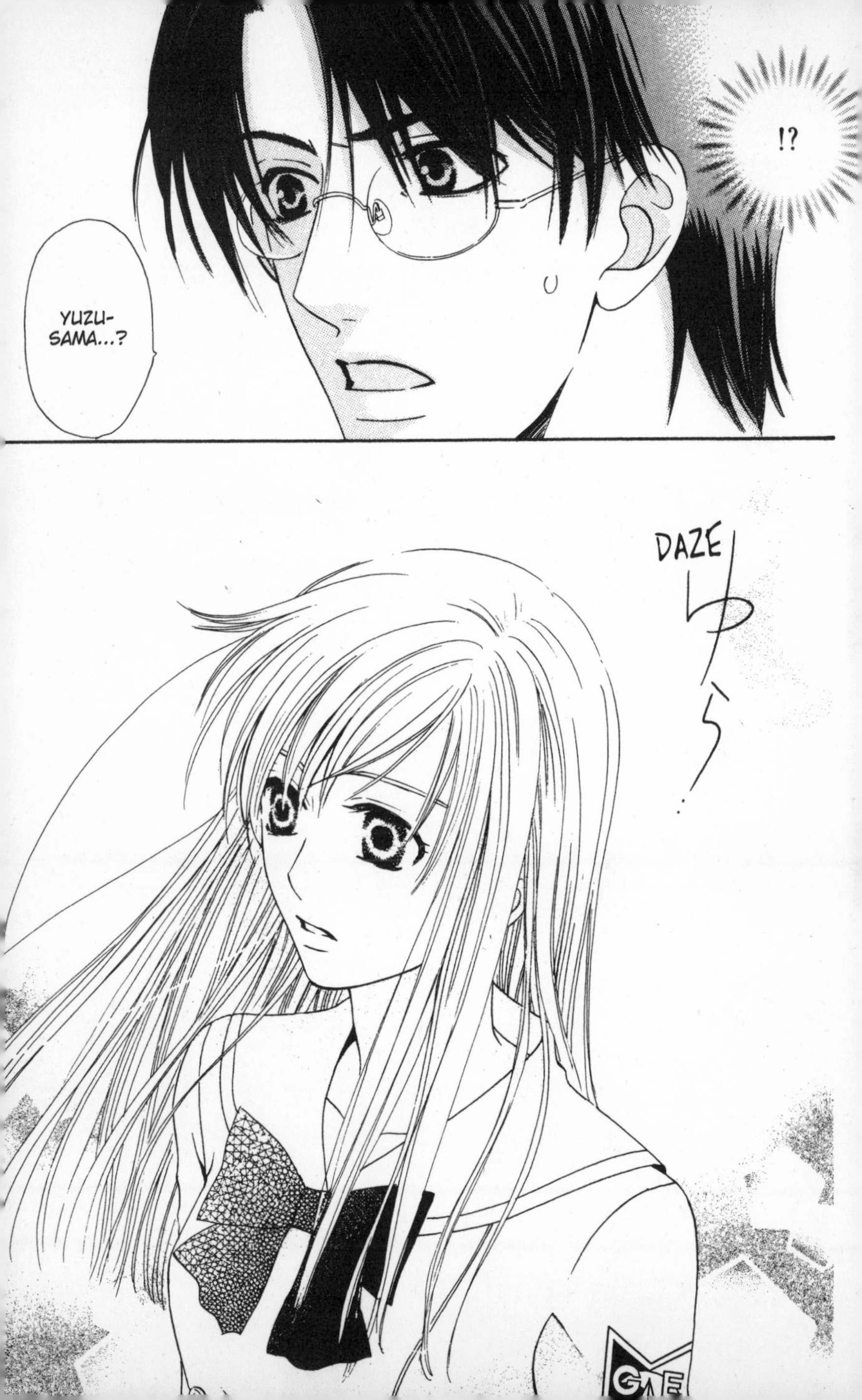
!?
YUZU-SAMA...?
DAZE
ゆら…

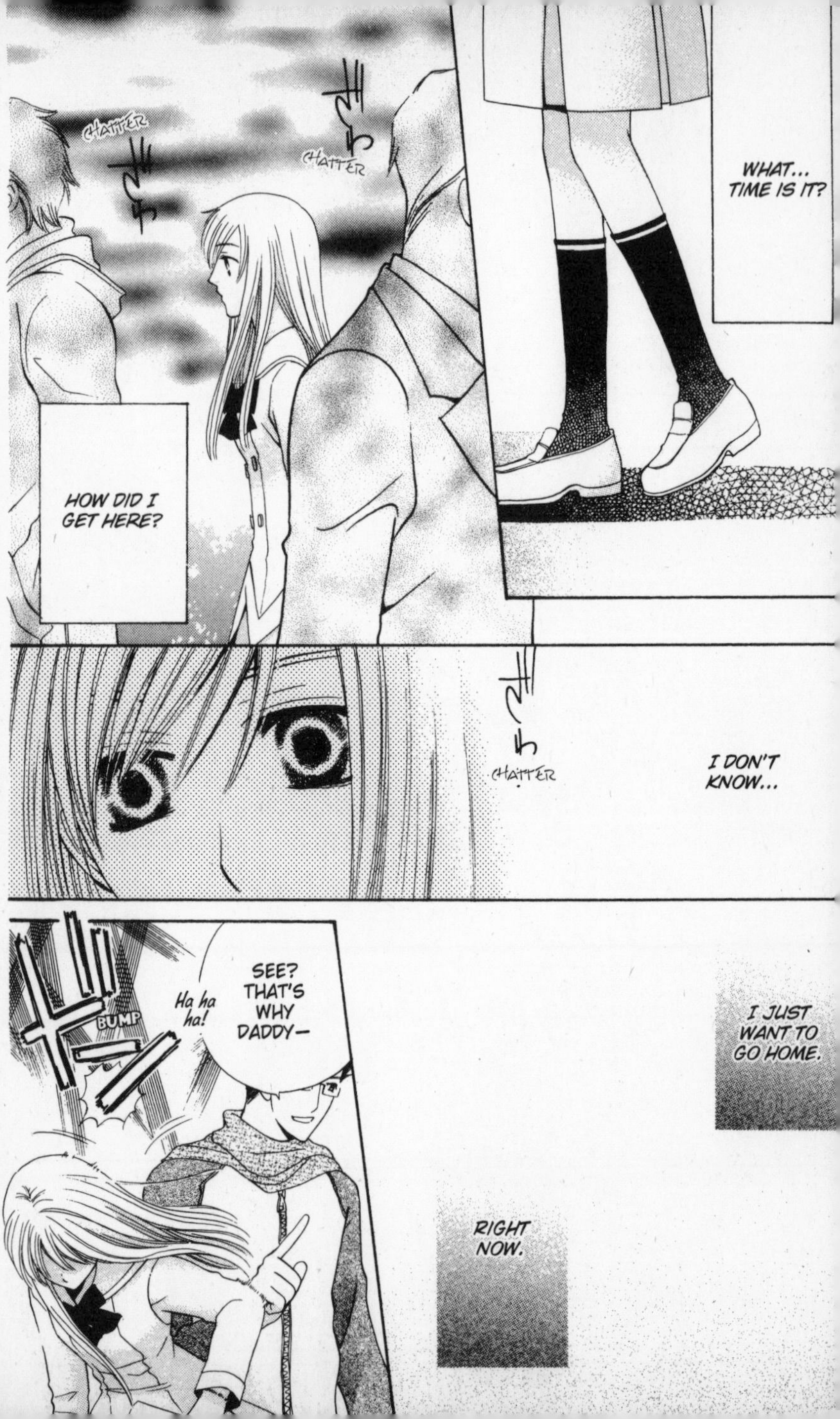
WHAT... TIME IS IT?
CHATTER
CHATTER
HOW DID I GET HERE?
I DON'T KNOW...
CHATTER
I JUST WANT TO GO HOME.
RIGHT NOW.
SEE? THAT'S WHY DADDY—
Ha ha ha!
BUMP

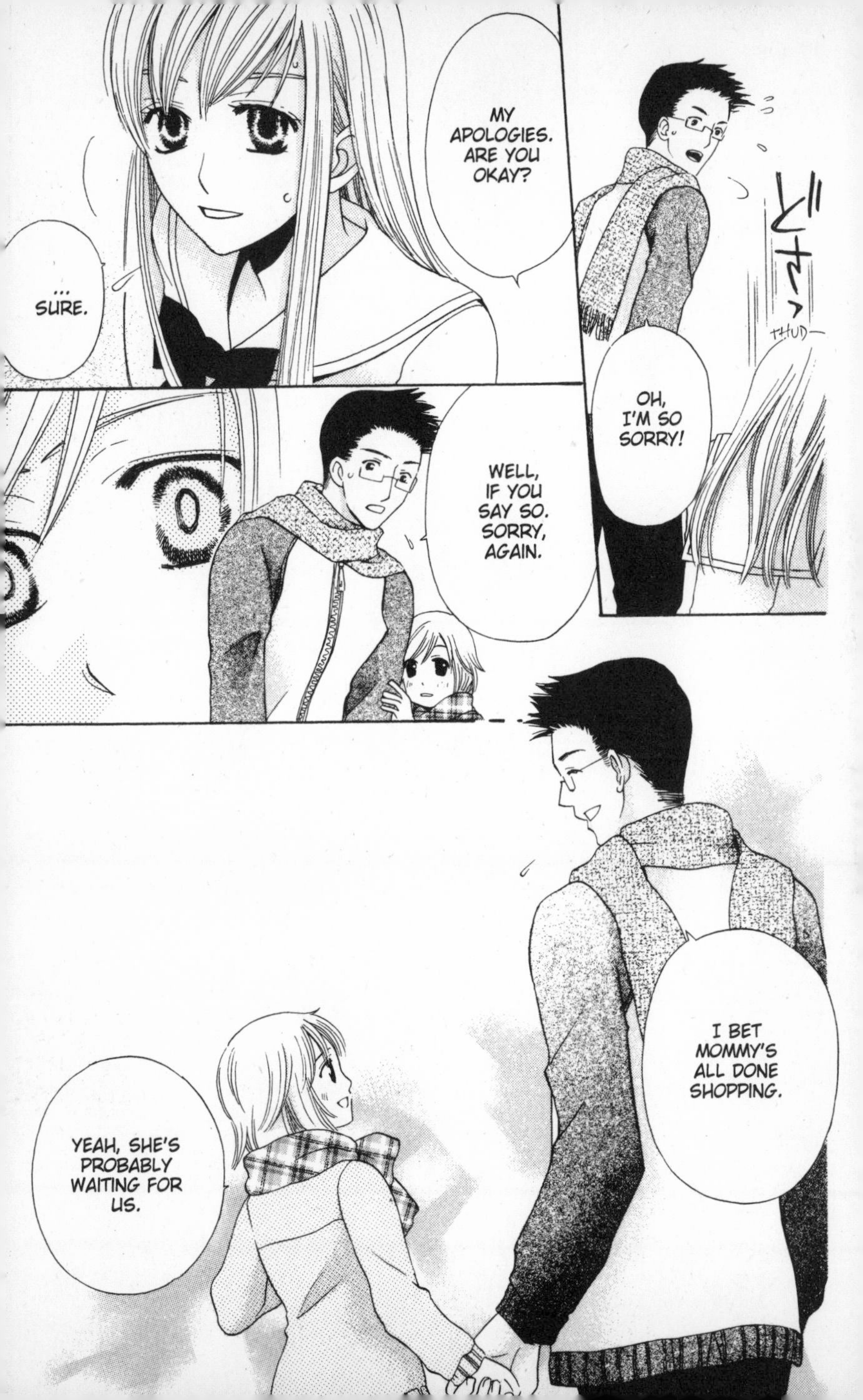
THUD
OH, I'M SO SORRY!
MY APOLOGIES. ARE YOU OKAY?
... SURE.
WELL, IF YOU SAY SO. SORRY, AGAIN.
I BET MOMMY'S ALL DONE SHOPPING.
YEAH, SHE'S PROBABLY WAITING FOR US.

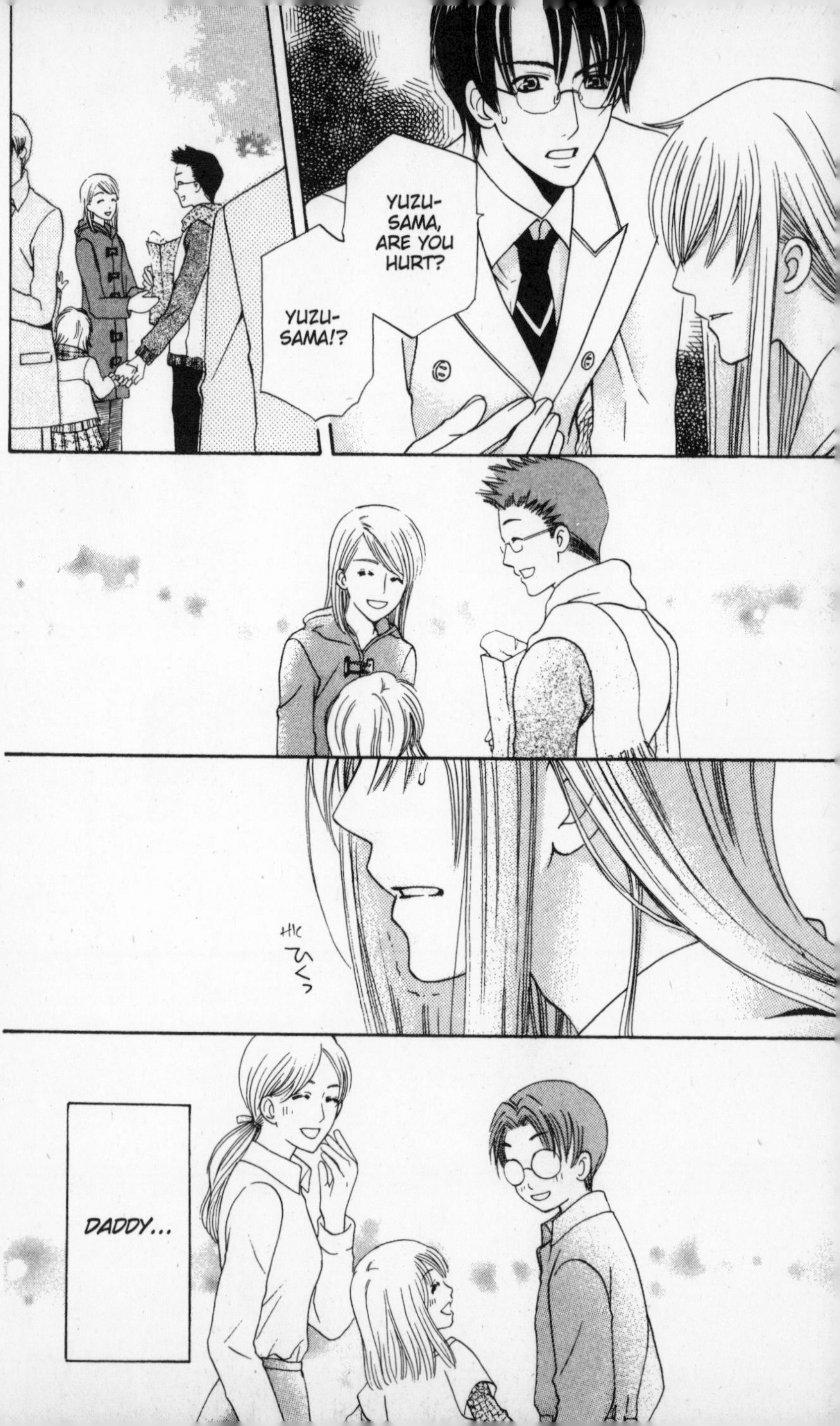
YUZU-SAMA, ARE YOU HURT?
YUZU-SAMA!?
HIC
DADDY...

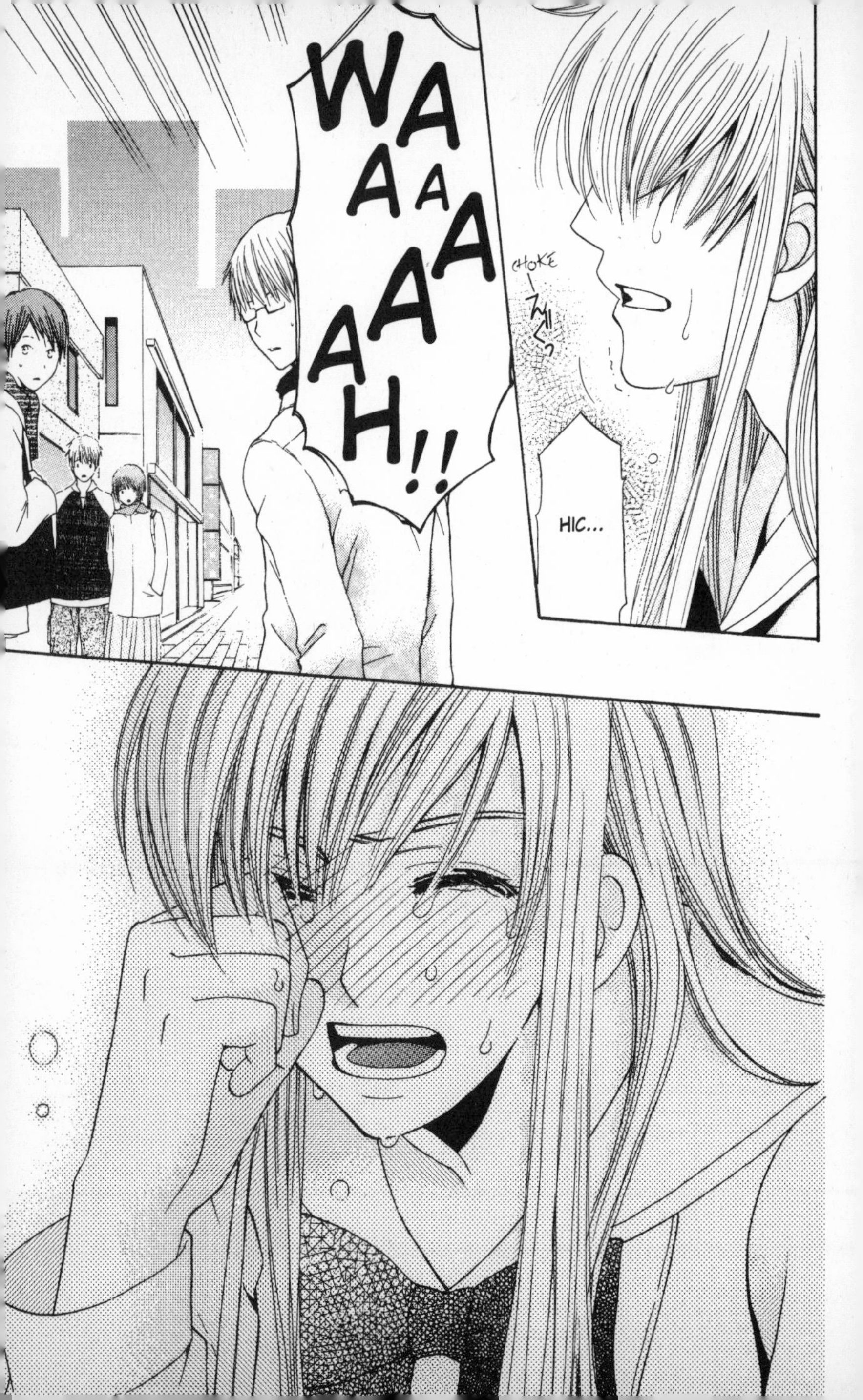
CHOKE
HIC...
WAAAAAAH!!

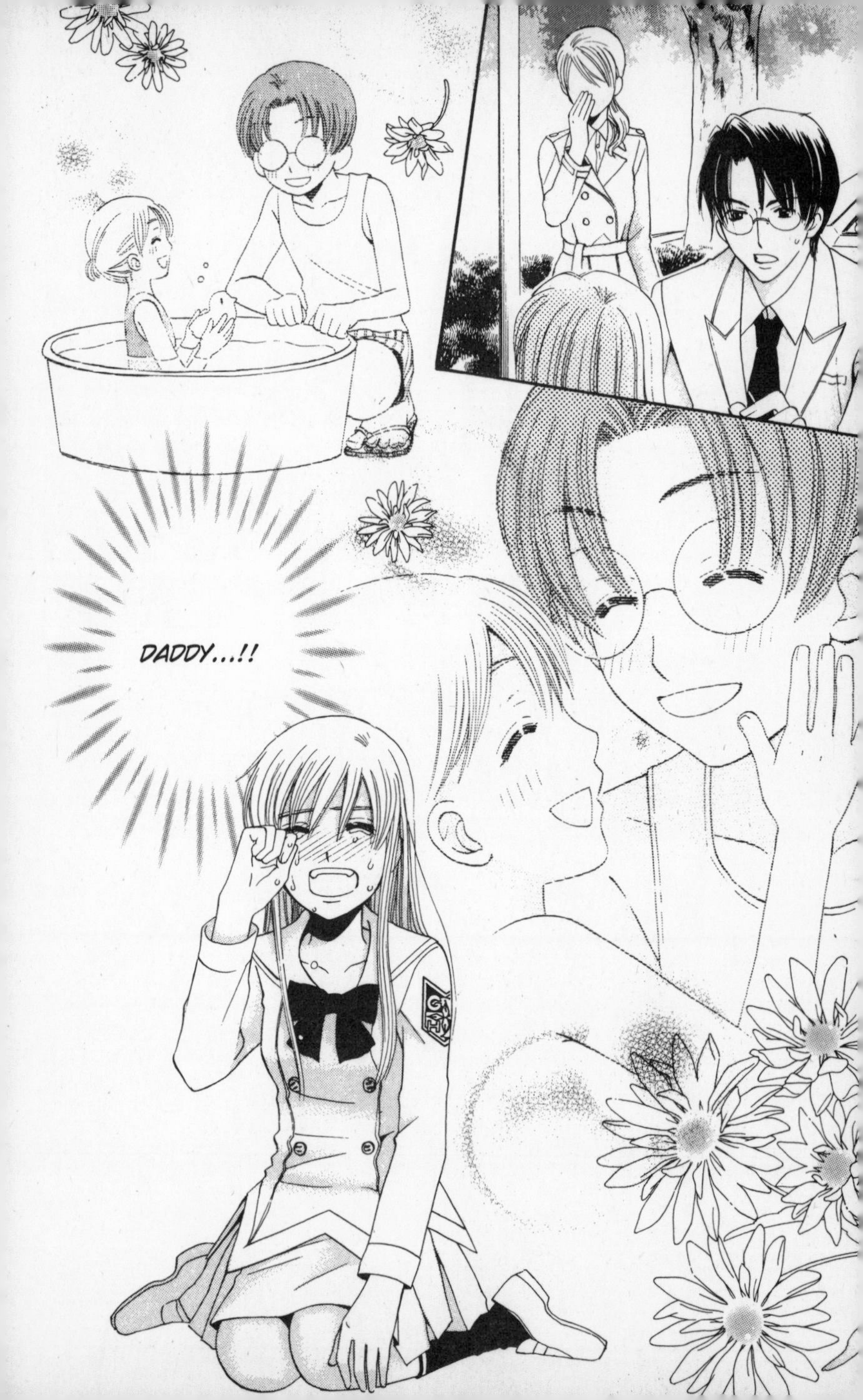
DADDY...!!

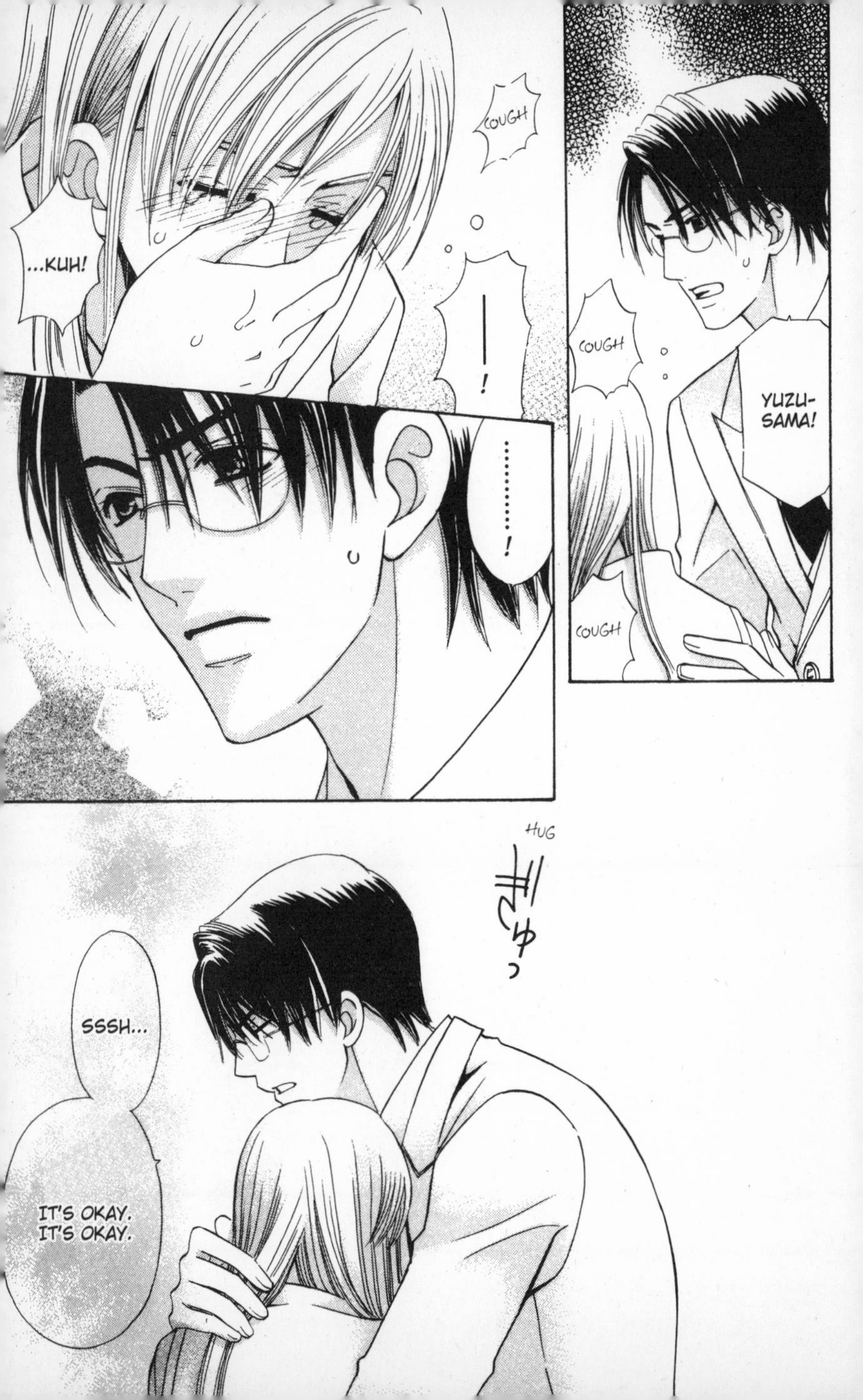
YUZU-SAMA!
COUGH
COUGH
COUGH
—!
...KUH!
......!
HUG
SSSH...
IT'S OKAY.
IT'S OKAY.

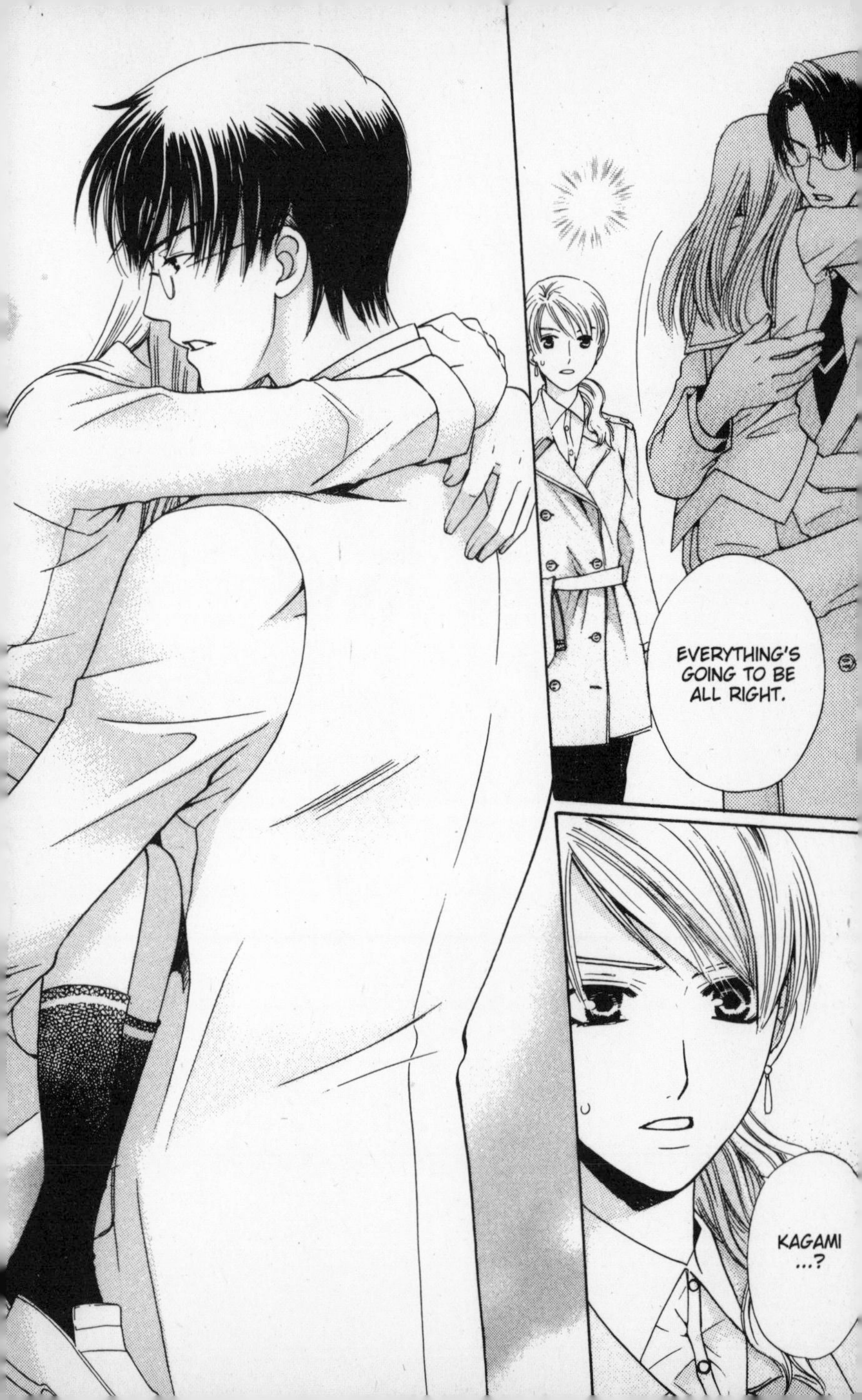
EVERYTHING'S GOING TO BE ALL RIGHT.
KAGAMI ...?

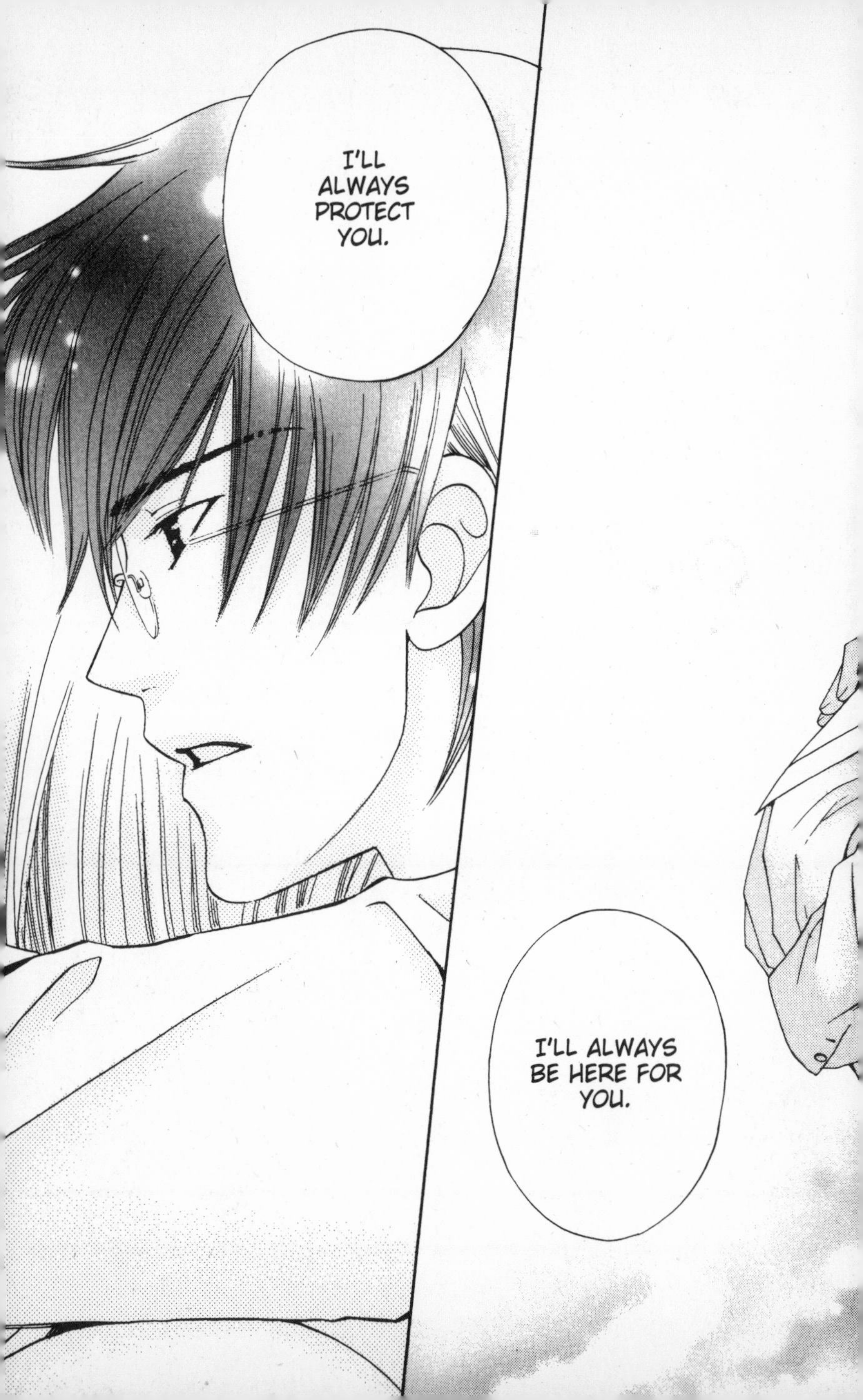
I'LL ALWAYS PROTECT YOU.
I'LL ALWAYS BE HERE FOR YOU.

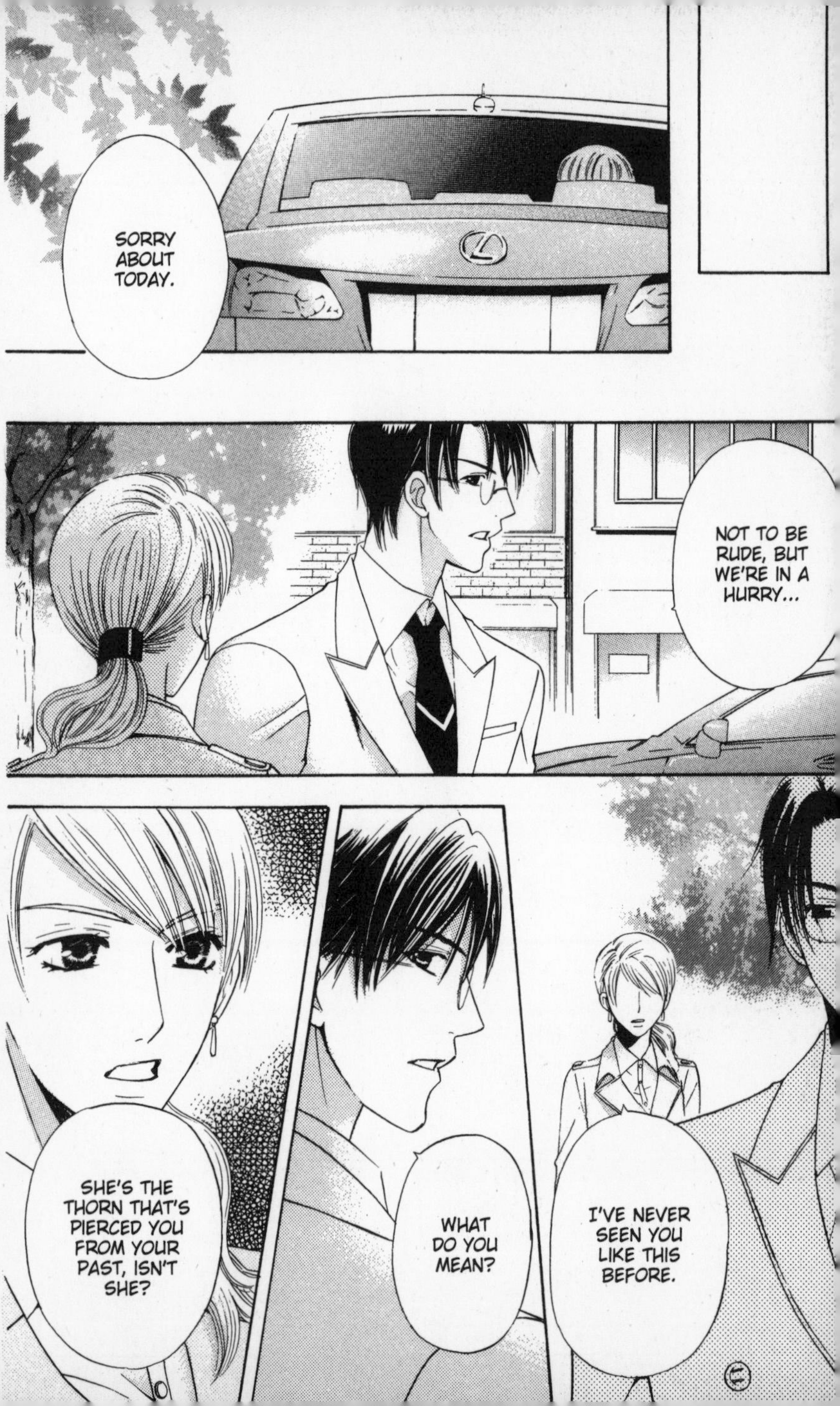
SORRY ABOUT TODAY.
NOT TO BE RUDE, BUT WE'RE IN A HURRY...
I'VE NEVER SEEN YOU LIKE THIS BEFORE.
WHAT DO YOU MEAN?
SHE'S THE THORN THAT'S PIERCED YOU FROM YOUR PAST, ISN'T SHE?

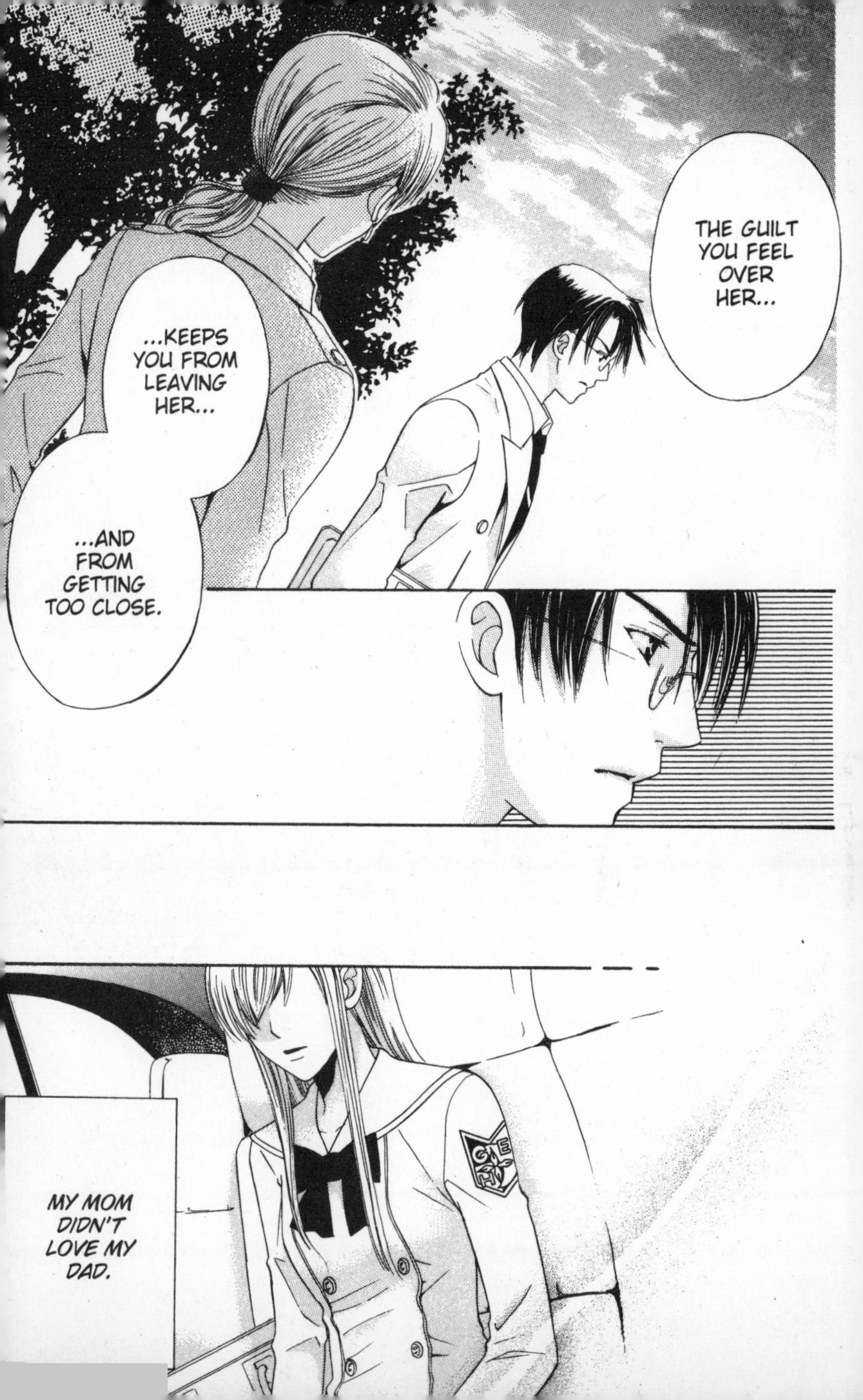
THE GUILT YOU FEEL OVER HER...
...KEEPS YOU FROM LEAVING HER...
...AND FROM GETTING TOO CLOSE.
MY MOM DIDN'T LOVE MY DAD.

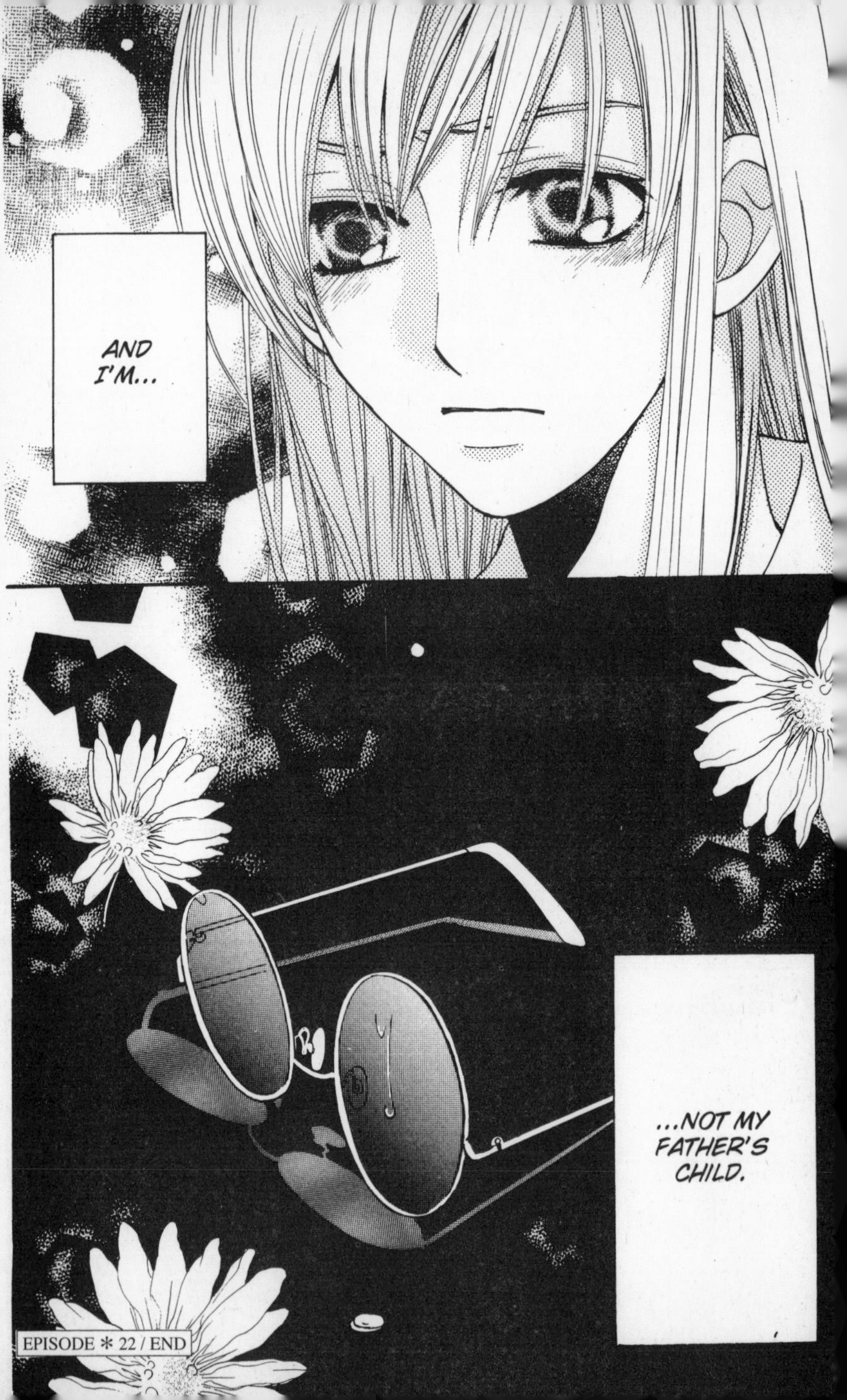
AND I'M...
...NOT MY FATHER'S CHILD.
EPISODE ✻ 22 / END

AFTERWORD + SPECIAL THANKS

Thank you very much, everyone who read this. To my editor Kishima-san, and my assistants

Hariguchi-san and Fujiyama-san: thank you!

Please look upon me kindly in the future!

May 16, 2008

Takako Shigematsu

I'm awaiting your letters~

Takako Shigematsu

C/O Go! Comi

28047 Dorothy Drive, Suite 200

Agoura Hills, CA 91301

in RPG

Level 26 Samurai

Level 1 Hack Hunter

Level 47 Monk/White Magic User

ULTIMATE VENUS VOLUME 5 / END

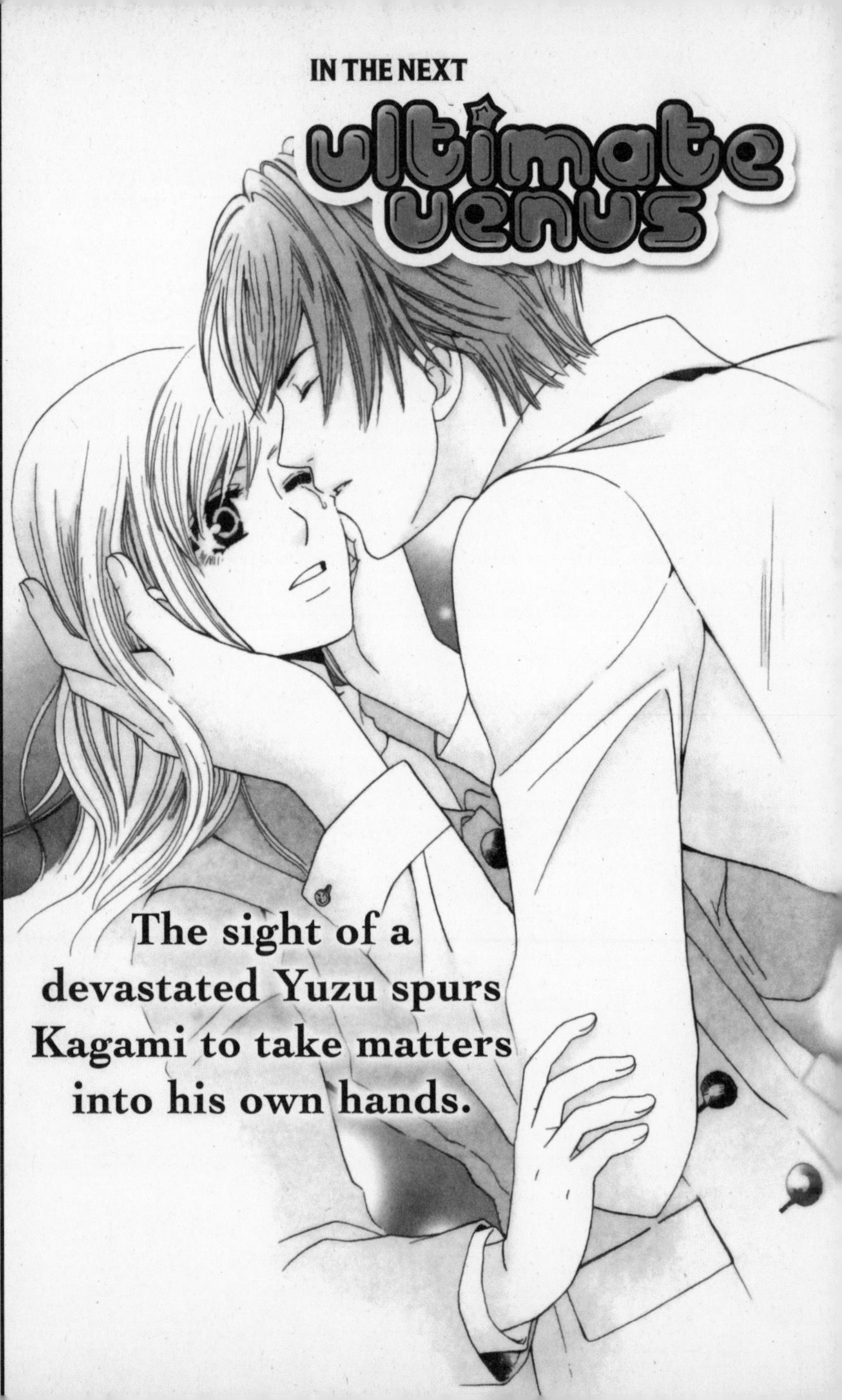
IN THE NEXT
ultimate venus
The sight of a devastated Yuzu spurs Kagami to take matters into his own hands.

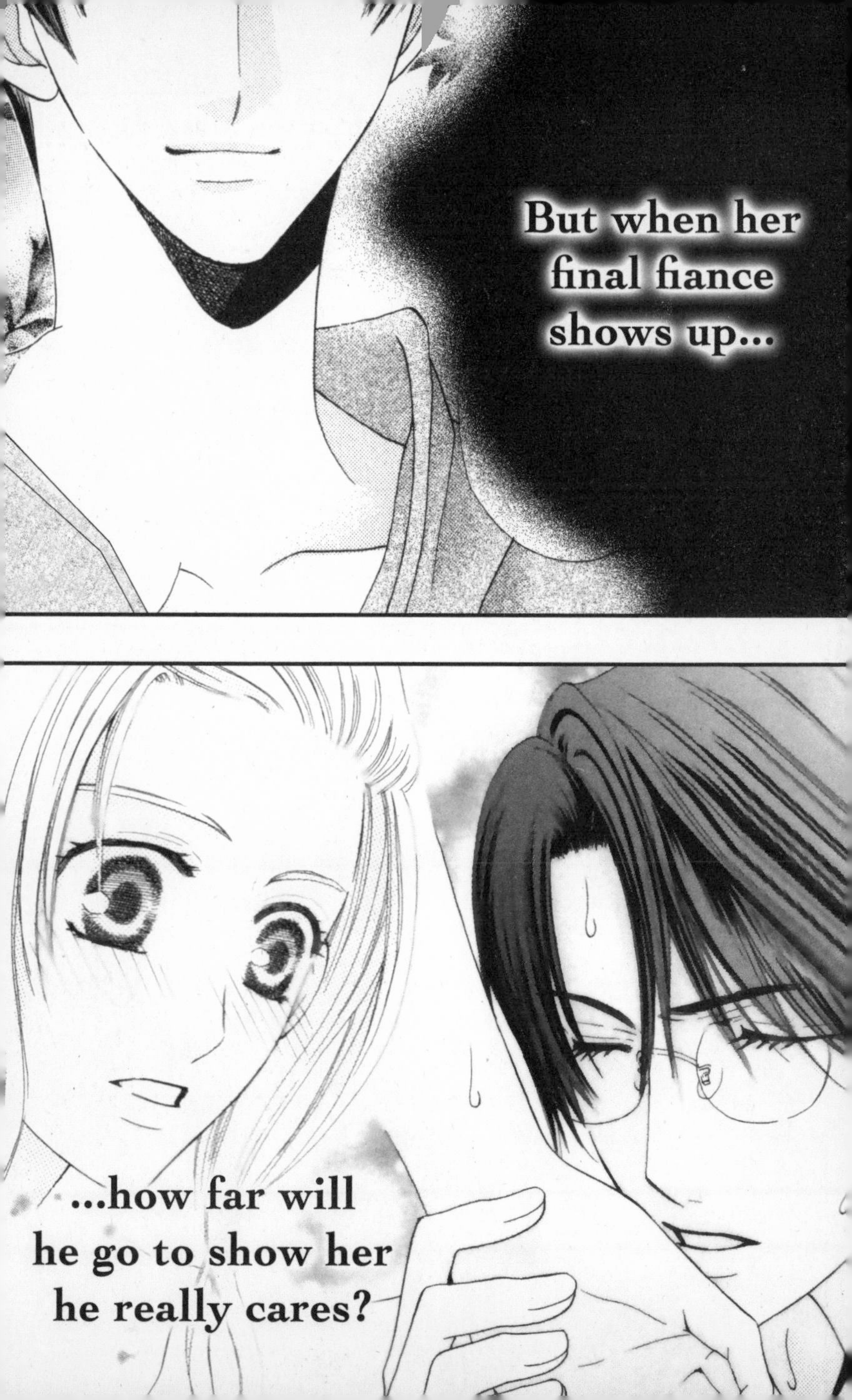
But when her final fiance shows up...
...how far will he go to show her he really cares?

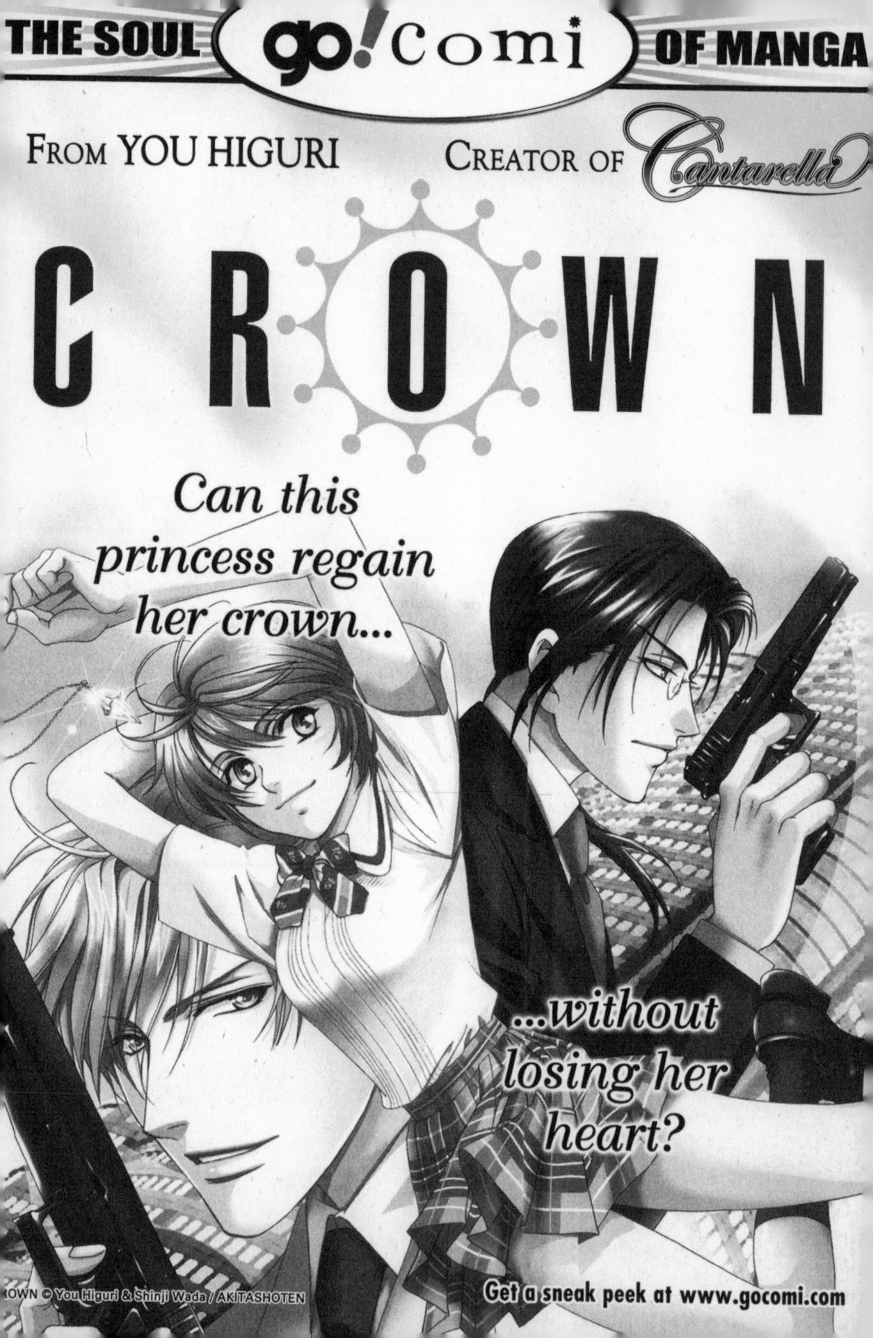
THE SOUL go!comi OF MANGA
FROM YOU HIGURI CREATOR OF Cantarella
CROWN
Can this princess regain her crown...
...without losing her heart?
CROWN © You Higuri & Shinji Wada / AKITASHOTEN
Get a sneak peek at www.gocomi.com

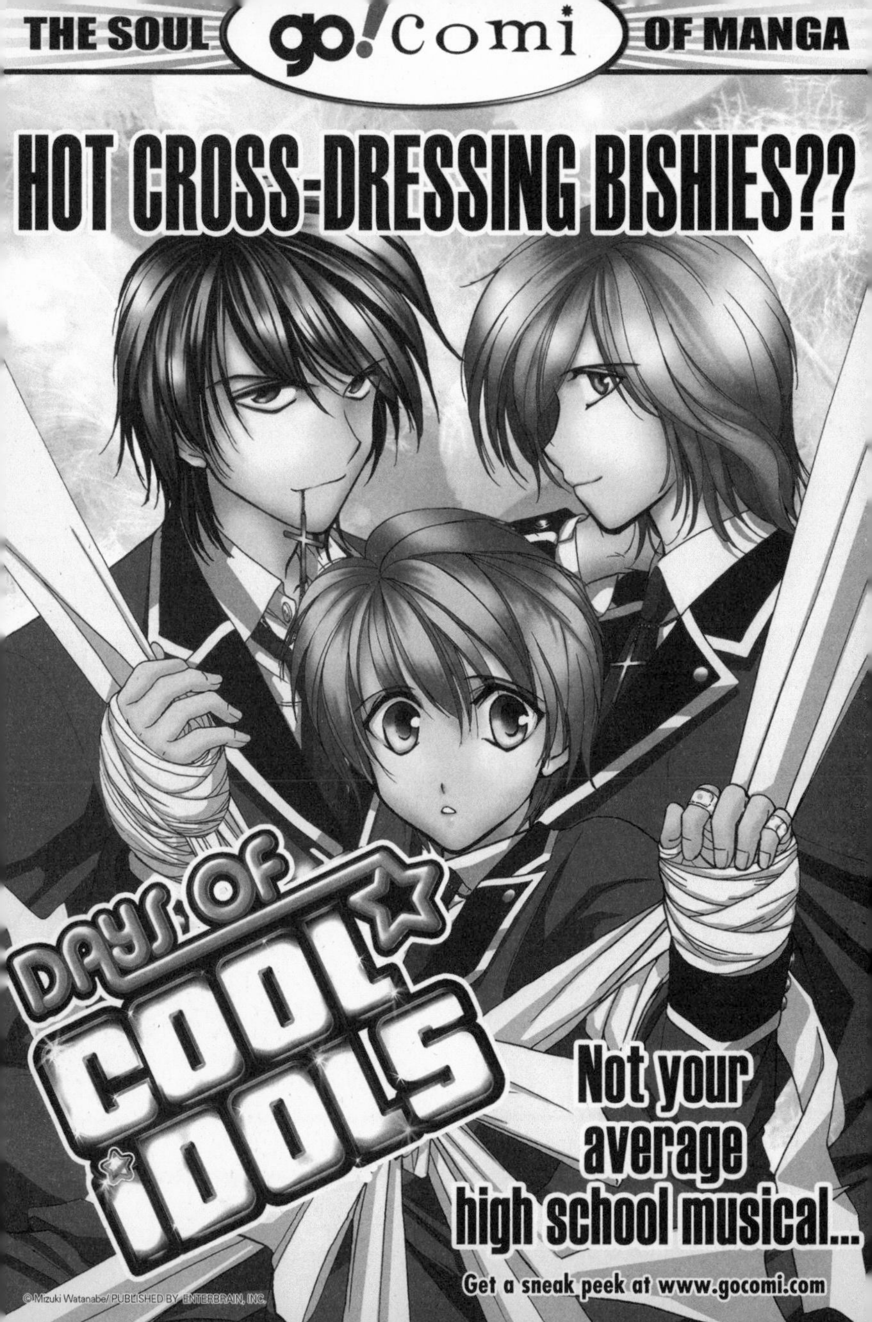
THE SOUL go!comi OF MANGA
HOT CROSS-DRESSING BISHIES??
DAYS OF COOL IDOLS
Not your average high school musical...
Get a sneak peek at www.gocomi.com
© Mizuki Watanabe/ PUBLISHED BY ENTERBRAIN, INC.

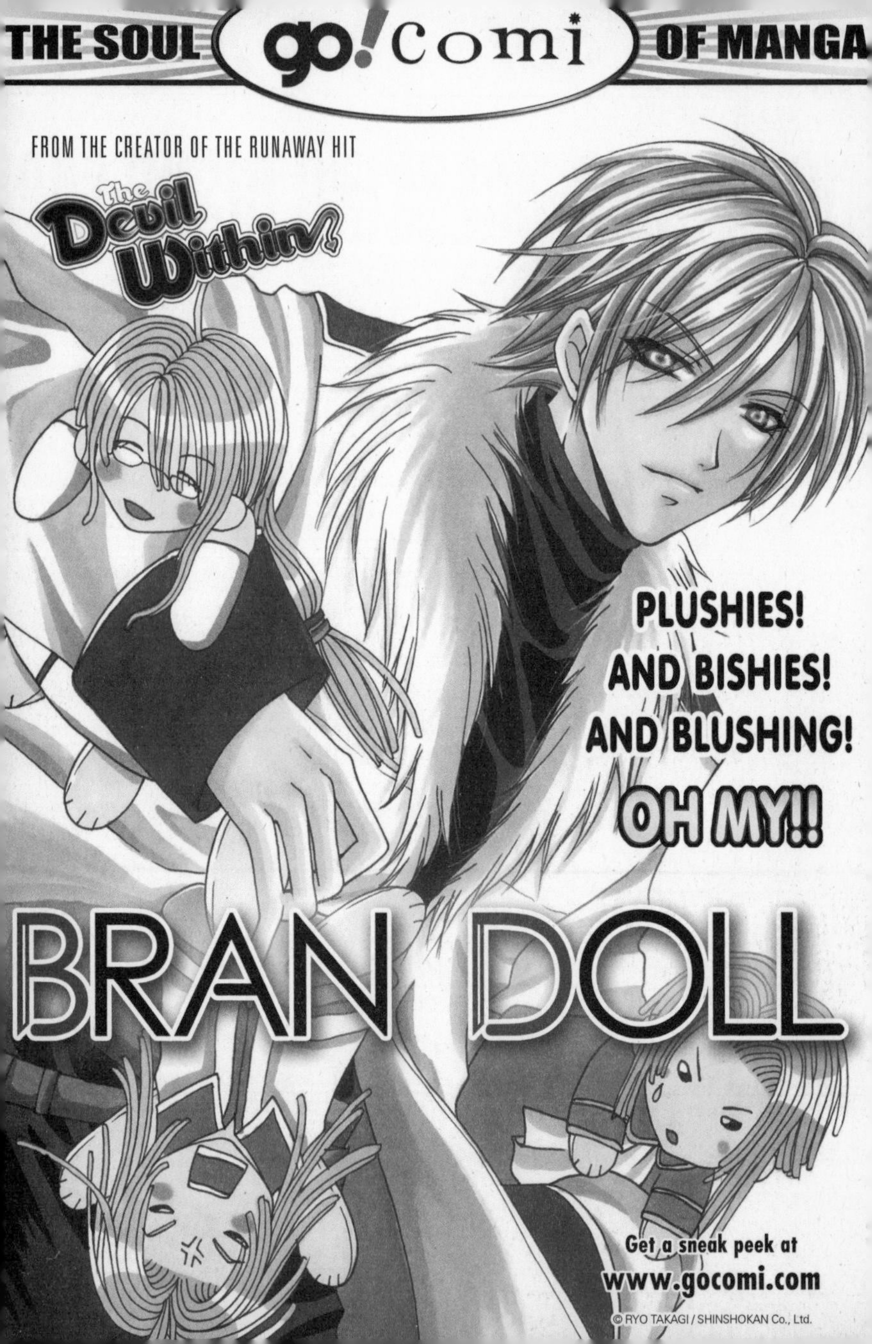
THE SOUL go!comi OF MANGA
FROM THE CREATOR OF THE RUNAWAY HIT
The Devil Within!
PLUSHIES!
AND BISHIES!
AND BLUSHING!
OH MY!!
BRAN DOLL
Get a sneak peek at
www.gocomi.com
© RYO TAKAGI / SHINSHOKAN Co., Ltd.

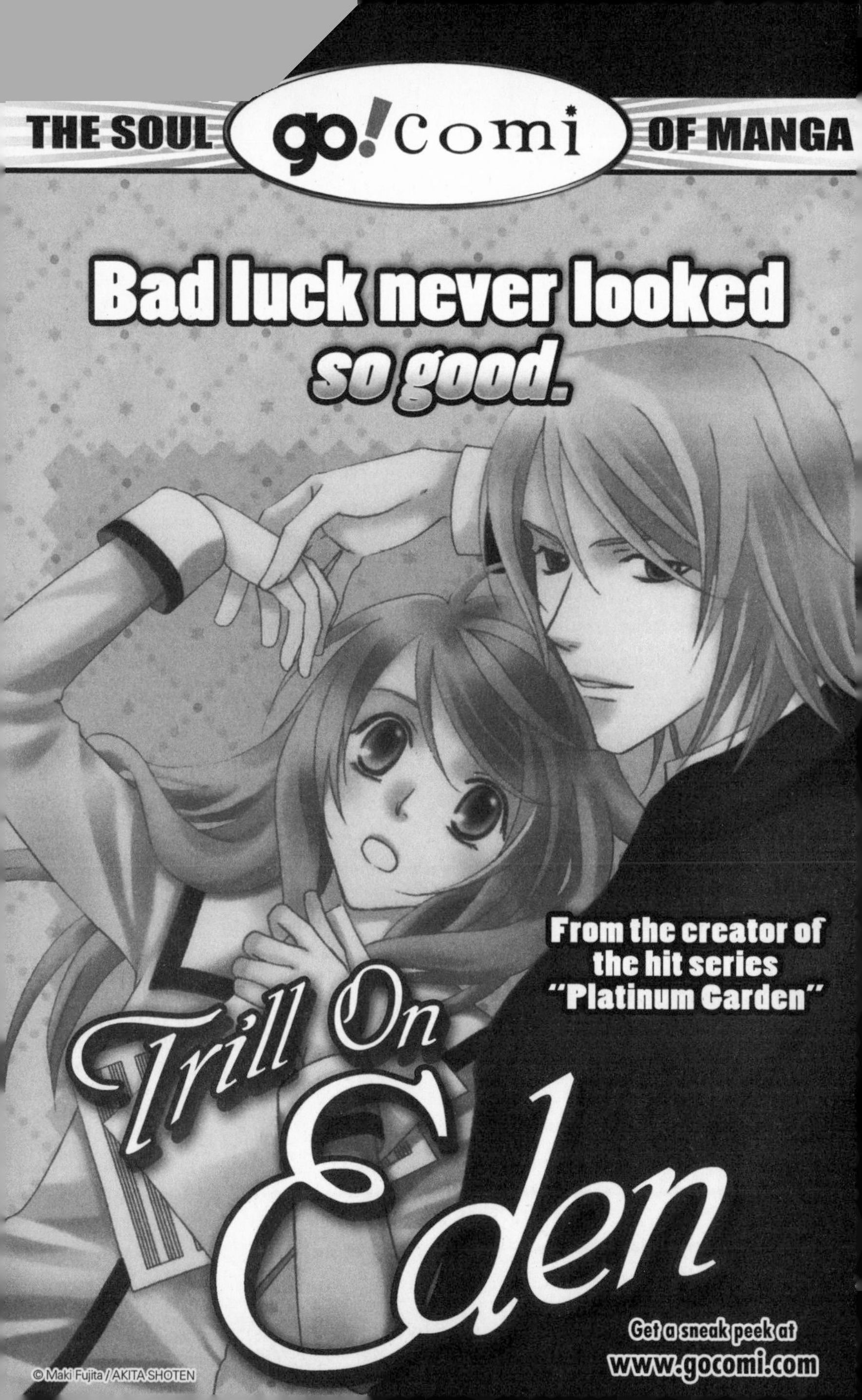
THE SOUL go!comi OF MANGA
Bad luck never looked
so good.
From the creator of
the hit series
"Platinum Garden"
Trill On
Eden
Get a sneak peek at
www.gocomi.com
© Maki Fujita / AKITA SHOTEN

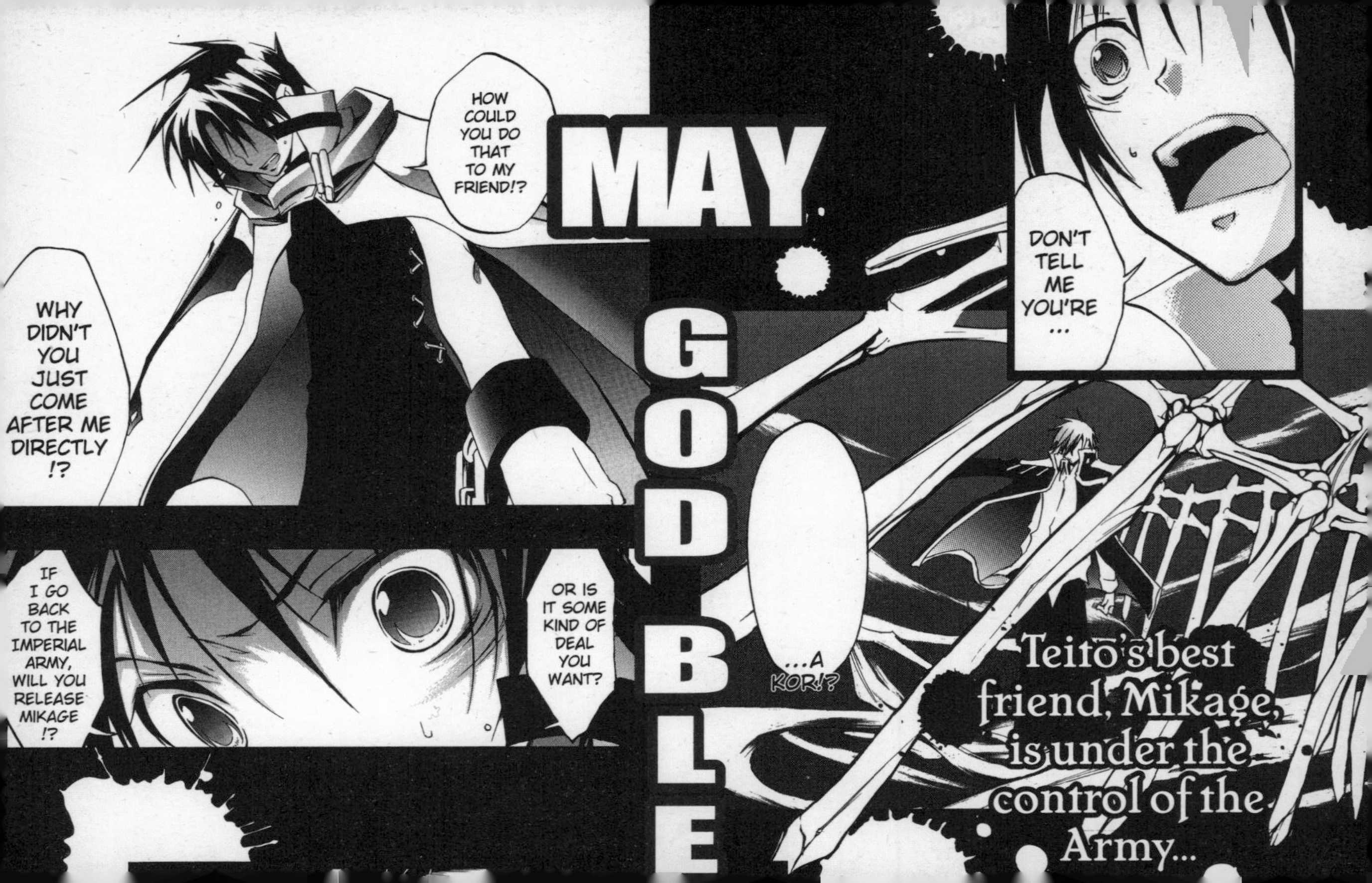
DON'T TELL ME YOU'RE ...
...A KOR!?
MAY GOD BLE
HOW COULD YOU DO THAT TO MY FRIEND!?
WHY DIDN'T YOU JUST COME AFTER ME DIRECTLY !?
OR IS IT SOME KIND OF DEAL YOU WANT?
IF I GO BACK TO THE IMPERIAL ARMY, WILL YOU RELEASE MIKAGE !?
Teito's best friend, Mikage, is under the control of the Army...

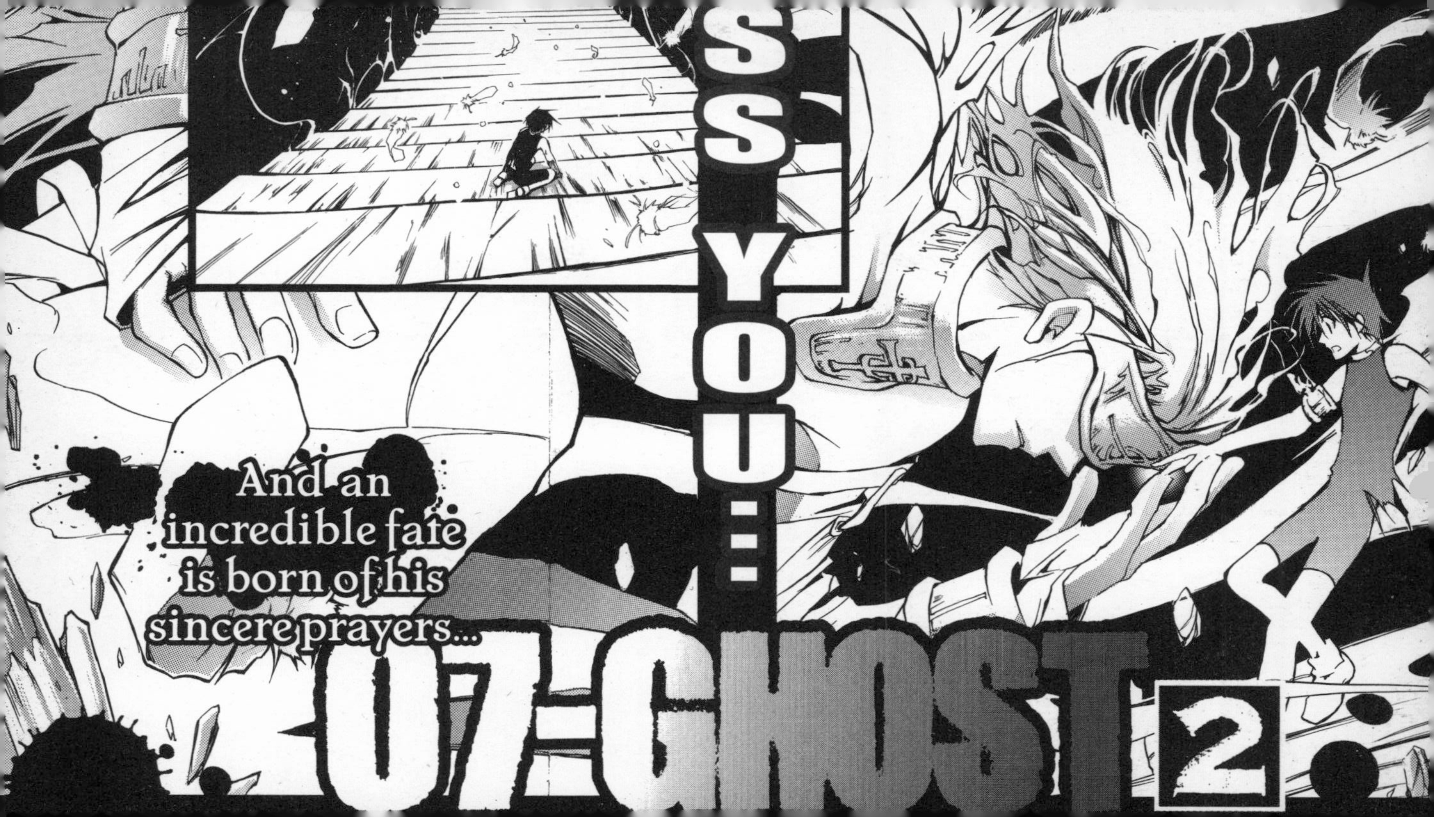
SSYOU...
And an incredible fate is born of his sincere prayers...
07-GHOST 2

Takako Shigematsu

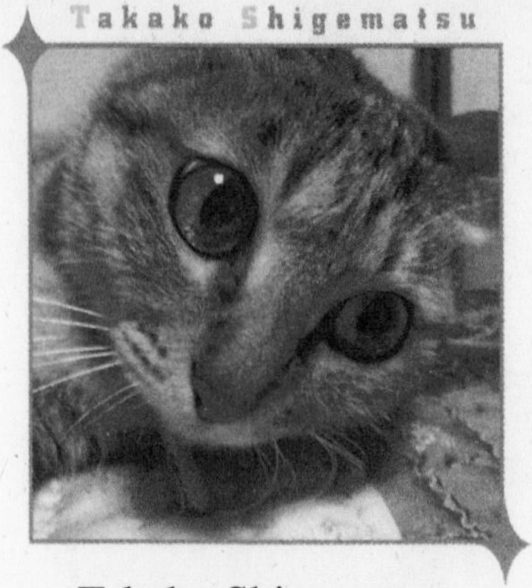

Takako Shigematsu

Day by day, it's
been getting hotter.
With summer here, just
looking at my furry feline
friends makes me sweat!
Just as my two kitties are
braving the heat, I'm also
doing my best to survive!
Wish me luck!!